Social Concerns

Social Concerns

Gwynn Nettler

Professor of Sociology
The University of Alberta, Canada

McGraw-Hill Book Company

New York   St. Louis   San Francisco   Auckland
Düsseldorf   Johannesburg   Kuala Lumpur   London
Mexico   Montreal   New Delhi   Panama   Paris
São Paulo   Singapore   Sydney   Tokyo   Toronto

To my wives, enemies, and loves,
who taught me

Social Concerns

Copyright © 1976 by McGraw-Hill, Inc. All rights reserved. Printed in the United States of America. No part of this publication may be reproduced, stored in a retrieval system, or transmitted, in any form or by any means, electronic, mechanical, photocopying, recording, or otherwise, without the prior written permission of the publisher.

1 2 3 4 5 6 7 8 9 0 D O D O 7 9 8 7 6 5

This book was set in Helvetica by Black Dot, Inc. The editors were Lyle Linder and Barry Benjamin; the production supervisor was Charles Hess.
R. R. Donnelley & Sons Company was printer and binder.

Library of Congress Cataloging in Publication Data

Nettler, Gwynn.
    Social concerns.

    Bibliography: p.
    Includes index.
    1. Sociology. 2. Social problems. I. Title.
HM251.N39 1976   362'.042   75-9712
ISBN 0-07-046295-X

Contents

Preface

"The intellect is a whore," believed Nicholas of Cusa, "for it can prostitute itself to anything." Nicholas was saying that thinking is the servant of desire. We believe what we wish, according to this, and our ideas justify our interests.

Nicholas had a point, but only one. We do take thought in order to get more of what we want and to justify our being the way we are. However, we also think in order to survive. We do not think only with our hopes, therefore, but also with our theories of how the world works. For survival's sake, we test these theories against experience so that we may behave rationally and not just willfully.

We think, too, for another reason that Nicholas neglected. We think because we can't help it. "We're made that way," as a popular song puts it. Curiosity is a built-in feature of mammalian physiology. It is not an accessory. This built-in feature makes thinking fun as well as work. We *play* with ideas as often as we *use* them. We think, then, to scratch an intellectual itch as well as to improve our efficiency or justify our hopes.

Everyone who ponders personal difficulties or public issues is caught in this tangle of reasons for thinking. There is a continuous struggle between believing *what we wish* and *what is true.* We agree, most of us, that what we want is not to be confused with how things are. "Ought" is not "is." However, we have been told that wishing and willing sometimes make things so. Unfortunately, we have not been shown when our desire for something—a better world, for example—is enough to make it come true.

Professionally thoughtful persons, those called intellectuals, have not resolved the tensions among the reasons for taking thought. We wish to be truthful—"scientific," even—but we also wish to be useful for goodness's sake. Unfortunately, it cannot be assumed that truth and goodness keep close company. Desire forever tugs at playful curiosity to become passionate and to find that "whatsoever things are true" will have a happy ending.

The resolution of this flickering conflict between believing *good* stories and *true* ones about human behavior requires this recognition: that, as *students,* you and I can tell the difference between a fact and a wish, but that, as *actors,* we confuse the two. In our studies, we can distinguish between a statement of *how things are* and a statement of *how we want them to be.* In our personal lives, however, fact and fantasy get confused. And in our social policies we seldom, if ever, distinguish between *what works* and *what we prefer.* When we become political, we believe that what we prefer *ought* to work.

This is one of the reasons why social policies are less than rational. It is one of the reasons, too, why social concerns are not puzzles to be solved with information but difficulties to be met with uncertain knowledge and an attitude that is neither hopeful nor desperate.

This is a theme of the discussion to follow. This theme does not view social issues as "symptoms of social pathology" or as "problems," which, like puzzles, have solutions if only we think hard enough. Nor does this work regard social concerns as necessarily being "deviations" in the sense of their being abnormalities, although, obviously, what concerns us deviates at some distance from how we wish things were.

Social concerns are the conditions and behaviors that are the object of people's hopes and fears. Our attention will be given to a sample of such concerns in their modern setting. Information will be brought to our consideration of these concerns. The interpretation of this information is given with an attitude that is historical rather than discontinuous, that is global rather than local, and that is skeptical of "final solutions."

Acknowledgment

Colleagues have read some of these pages and have counseled me about our concerns. They are not responsible for my continuing faults, but they should be thanked for their attempts to help me. My appreciation is due William Avison, Ronald Gillis, Vincent Jeffries, Wayne McVey, Norman Storer, and Carol Urquhart-Ross. I owe a debt also to Ronald Kissack, a kind and reasonable editor, who, until his death, struggled to keep me clear.

Gwynn Nettler

A Point of View

We have enduring concerns. These concerns vary in importance for particular persons, but they persist among all people.

Social settings change, and with them the ways in which individuals respond to their interests. Technologies differ and so do the attitudinal sites from which people interpret their worlds, but the objects of human concern have a universal quality.

We are concerned to stay alive and well and to feel good about it. We are interested in getting along with the people to whom we are connected—particularly parents, spouses, children, and friends—and in having these intimates, in turn, live well. We want to live in peace, but with enough adventure to keep life salty. We wish, also, to satisfy curiosity, to exercise mind and muscle, and to have the opportunity to rest and do nothing.

To study these social concerns is to engage in a difficult task, the task of using our heads so that we may get more of what we want at lower cost. This is the purpose of our attempting to think clearly. It is not a purpose, however, that is easily achieved, and our discussion of some universal issues will indicate how difficult it is to develop knowledge and how little can be guaranteed in the resolution of our concerns.

THE INTENTION

The intention of the chapters to follow is to define issues, to provide information about them, and to add interpretations that seem reasonable. The principal objective of these definitions and interpretations is to stimulate each student toward his own conclusions.

A sampling of social concerns will be described in their modern setting. The descriptions will attempt to keep clear the differences between our moral concerns, the facts of our lives, and the interpretations and recommendations made in response to both. Keeping what we *know* distinct from what we *want* reduces the arrogance that comes from believing that complex matters have simple answers. This distinction warns us, too, that knowing facts is not the same as having knowledge and that having faith is not enough to ensure right consequences.

The present intention is grounded in the belief that it is more important to acquire a framework for thinking about our lives than it is to acquire any particular set of facts about them. The facts are important, but they vary in their importance and they change. They change as rapidly as one cares to inquire—daily, for example. A thoughtful style of analysis need not be revised every year, however. It need not endure forever either, but a way of thinking may represent a style where collections of facts about specific issues are, like fashions, fleeting.

The intention, then, is to ask questions about our concerns; to ascertain which facts, if any, might help us answer these questions; and to offer interpretations of these facts that seem reasonable.

OTHER POINTS OF VIEW

Our discussion is in the tradition of textbooks that follow the first course in social science and that attempt to apply "the concepts, principles, and data" of introductory sociology to the resolution of social issues. The present study differs from such previous works in that its scope and its attitude are *international* rather than local, *historical* rather than discontinuous, and *critical* of many of those stories about human behavior that are called its explanation.

Our treatment recognizes that the generalized strivings to be studied become concerns as people become conscious of them. Consciousness, in this sense, is a function of a *distance between aspiration and actuality.* A person feels little concern about being well until he or she has suffered illness or its threat. One is not much concerned about peace until chaos or its image has been experienced. It follows, then, that social concerns tend to be directed toward perceived deficiencies or toward disparities between how things seem to be and how one feels they should be. Hence, earlier works have considered social concerns in the context of *disapproved* behaviors and conditions. These earlier textbooks have attempted to give order to the diversity of human concerns and thereby to explain them by locating their causes in different segments of social relations. Four major ways of thinking about disapproved social behaviors and conditions have been employed. They have regarded our miseries as symptoms of social pathology, or as results of social disorganization, or, more recently, as problems, or types of deviance.

There are, of course, many windows through which to view one's world. Every vista is partial, but some are more narrow than others. Each of the following four sociological views of human discontent provides an orientation with its own advantage and limitation. The principal disadvantage of these commonly used interpretations of our troubles is that they presume the location of the causes of what bothers us and the kind of remedy that will work. A brief description of these previously employed points of view justifies a fresh approach, one that attends to *what concerns people* rather than one that defines for individuals the proper nature of their concern.

Bad Behavior as Social Sickness

The idea that unwanted behaviors or conditions signify social pathology assumes that societies are like organisms whose healthy function is known and whose sickness can be treated. This metaphor encourages a way of thinking about social life that carries its own consequences. The consequences are contained in assumptions that may be misleading, such as the popular notions that (1) behaviors defined as undesirable are "symptoms," (2) "causes" underlie these symptoms, (3) these causes can be known, and (4) treating causes produces cures.

To call these beliefs assumptions is to question them. The questioning proceeds from a preferred test of the uses of thought: does thinking that way get you where you want to go? In more academic language, the question is, "What are the consequences for action of thinking with these assumptions rather than with others?"

A *sensible* consequence of considering undesirable behaviors to be symptoms of social pathology is that attention is called to the interrelation between circumstance and behavior, to the relation between *where* one is and *what* one does.

A *disadvantage* of thinking of societies as healthy or sick is that these adjectives are inexact. They moralize. As a result, people who use the idea of societal sickness are likely to confuse *approval* or *disapproval* of how things are with their *description,* and, furthermore, to confuse disapproval and description with knowledge of how to make matters better.

A second disadvantage of using the terminology of social pathology is that "symptom" becomes a dirty word when employed on the social scene. We do not call desirable actions symptoms, although they must be as frequently "caused" as undesirable behaviors. We use the word as a *transfer term.* Calling something a symptom transfers attention from the undesirable condition itself to something else that is allegedly its cause. In the social studies, defining symptoms and their victims *shifts the burden of blame* from the actor to his social setting. "Symptom" signifies bad acts that are not to be considered the fault of their actors but which are to be blamed upon their circumstances.

In translating this way of thinking into personal or social policy, it remains debatable which unwanted behaviors in ourselves or others are best treated through attention to the behaviors themselves—as with reward or punishment—and which through treatment of the alleged causes of the behaviors.

It is also questionable whether shifting the load of responsibility from the individual to society has the consequences we desire for ourselves and our communities. It is difficult, if not impossible, to regard oneself as a *victim* of circumstance and, at the same time, as *responsible* for his conduct. To regard oneself as nothing more than a product is to define oneself as less than a person.

It will be a theme of our study that calling some undesirable behaviors symptoms and attending to their dimly discerned causes can be, as they say, a "cop out," a way of postponing the surgery that needs to be done. This point applies to such diverse conflicts as those between parents and children, between feuding spouses, and between governments and their subverters.

Discontent as Social Disorganization

For a while sociologists thought it advantageous to look upon the matters of concern as the result of social disorganization. To do so is *to assume the cause of our miseries,* that is, to assume that they arise from something vaguely labeled the "disorganization" of our "society."[1] This assumption, in turn, leads to a train of correlative assumptions such as that (1) if a society were organized, our troubles would disappear, or that (2) people know how to create an organized society, or that (3) if people organized in some way to attack their miseries, a happy result would be assured.

This outline of assumptions indicates that locating the cause of our discontent in social disorganization and the cure in organization is to have in mind some model of social organization free of concern. To do this is to construct a utopia. While utopias are of interest as part of our study of humanity's thought about itself, our dictionaries remind us that utopia is literally *nowhere*. (From the Greek, *ou,* "not," and *topos,* "a place".)

The risk of thinking about the human condition with some utopia in mind is, again, the hazard of confusing possibility with probability and dream with reality. This confusion motivates the dreamer to impose his will upon us, for "our own good," of course. Thus, the very organization that would relieve us of our misery produces an element of our concern. In short, the "disorganization" schema disallows the possibility that the causes it chooses may not be the efficient ones and that the cures it proposes may generate conflict and some of the very concern from which people would like to be relieved.

This criticism does not foreclose the possibility that *some* kinds of social concerns may be found more frequently in disorderly societies than in those groupings where "everyone knows his place." However, rather than assume a

---

[1]"Society" and "disorganization" are placed in quotation marks to indicate the vagueness of these terms. The words are used because they refer to *something,* we think, and because they have a resonance; but looking for their meanings in dictionaries, even in sociological dictionaries (Fairchild, 1944; Hoult, 1969; Mitchell, 1968), is not reassuring. Such an exercise leads one to agree with the Spanish philosopher Ortega (1946, p. 24), who told us that "the very name, 'society,' as denoting groups of men who live together, is equivocal and utopian."

causal connection between a model of organized society and freedom from care, our study is directed toward matters of general concern without prejudging their association with disorganization, however that might be defined.

Social Concerns as Social Problems

A third attitude that has characterized sociological attention to human discontent has defined undesirable social relations as "social problems." A major disadvantage of this definition is that, if one studies social concerns as though they were problems, the history of that word evokes the presumption that there are solutions. Note a standard definition of "problem":

> *problem,* n.1 a question proposed for solution or consideration. 3. in mathematics, anything required to be done, or requiring the doing of something [*Webster's New World Dictionary,* 1955]

There are other connotations of the problematic, as, for example, that which is *difficult.* There is no objection to regarding social concerns as full of difficulties, but the popular idea that these matters are social problems that call for solutions and have them is both modern and presumptuous. Another tribe would regard such thinking as superstitious (Evans-Pritchard, 1965).

A wiser interpretation of social concerns regards some of them as reducible to problems and thus made manageable, as, for example, the easing of urban traffic congestion through technology. However, the persistent civilized concerns with living peacefully and happily, with reducing misery and brutality, *involve difficulties for which there is no solution in the sense of there being a correct course of action likely to produce known and wanted results at a known and acceptable price.*

Weldon (1953, p. 76) makes the distinction clearly:

> [Problems do have solutions, but] . . . difficulties are quite another matter. We do not solve them . . . we surmount them, avoid them, reduce them or ignore them. There may be all sorts of ways of dealing with them and getting out of them, but there is no demonstrably correct way . . . The vicar may advise his parishioners as to their matrimonial difficulties, but he cannot do their difficulties for them as he can do their crossword puzzles.

The Moral Limits of Rationality The defect in thinking about our hopes and fears as though they were problems can be emphasized in another way. To speak of human anxieties and aspirations as if they were problems to be solved implies that we can be rational about our troubles. It suggests that the trouble comes from our not knowing something—from a lack of information, from a lack of communication of that information, and from someone's lack of understanding of that information. The idea of a problem contains the idea of a solution, which usually means finding the formula.

A different attitude is suggested here. One of the themes of our study will be that *we are less than rational about our social concerns because we are moral about them.*

In the chapters to follow we shall see repeatedly that we do not seek just any solution to a social dilemma, however efficient that policy might be. We seek, instead, good ways out. That is, we seek ways of reducing our concerns that will not offend our values. We cannot, then, accept just any efficient means toward our ends. Our morals are intertwined with our desires, and our concerns therefore involve difficulties in living for which *practical* answers may not be *acceptable* answers.

Undesirable Behavior as Deviance

Recent textbooks have presented unwanted social conditions and behaviors as "deviations" from some standard of conduct. The immediate question is, "Whose norms shall define normality?" Just as one man's problem may be another's way of life, so one student's sense of deviance may be another's expectation. The "problems" and "deviance" schemata stand accused of an unjustified selectivity.

The bias concealed in the concept of deviance can be exposed by tabulating the kinds of persons and situations studied under this title. A reading of the tables of contents of textbooks in deviance shows that "deviance" is *not* defined in terms of abnormal behaviors or conditions—that is, those that are *rare*—but rather as involving behaviors and conditions that are *disapproved* by someone. Thus the works on deviance do not discuss those differences from the ordinary that are considered *good,* such as being rich and beautiful, creative and intelligent, or radiantly happy and socially sensitive. Furthermore, the notion of deviance has been stretched to include many behaviors that are *common,* or at least not rare, and that from someone else's moral elevation may even be approved—behaviors such as stealing, warring, divorcing, committing suicide, taking drugs, or being a prostitute, a drunk, or a deceiver.

The trouble with studying deviance is that there is no rationale for selecting one set of behaviors rather than another as deviant. Such a rationale would require that one specify, and justify, the standard against which behaviors or situations are considered deviant.

THE SEARCH FOR UNIVERSAL STANDARDS

The charge that disapproval represents "standards of judgment"—and that standards of judgment are themselves time-bound and, perhaps, prejudiced— could be avoided if there were universal norms. Some philosophers, therefore, have attempted to promote supraclass and supranational standards that would allow them to define "problems and deviations" universally and absolutely. Two approaches have been used in the attempted discovery of universal norms. One procedure is to invent and impose the norm. The other is to observe how people vote their standards.

The Invention of Universal Standards

One way of finding a universal standard by which to define problematic conditions is to *invent* a norm, *justify* it with argument, and then seek to *impose* it through persuasion or force. Two examples of such constructed universals are the appeals to needs and to justice.

Human Needs as a Standard   One proposal for a universal norm would employ a "naturalistic ethic" based on "human needs" (Etzioni, 1968a). In this revival, "human nature" would provide the universal criterion for defining "problems and deviance." Unsatisfied needs would then define deviation from the normal.

At the survival level, we agree about human needs. When we get beyond the need to breathe and eat, however, we run into a hierarchy of needs where some wants, depending upon the theorist, seem more necessary than others. Thus, when this proposal is put to use, it tends to function as a camouflage for a particular system of values. For if it is "human nature" for people to continue to behave badly, as they do, the would-be universalist calls such needs "unreal" and "unauthentic" (Etzioni, 1968b, p. 11). By this token, our good deeds are "authentic, truly human," and our bad acts are false to our natures. In short, people are said to need, really, only those things that the standard-bearer approves. If, for example, people continue to act as if they needed rough entertainment, violence, and higher levels of material comfort, the employer of the "needs" framework defines away these interests as being somehow less than human.

Justice as a Standard   Another suggestion for an imposed, universal criterion of a problem is a sense of justice. Injustice in its many forms then becomes *the* deviation.

Justice, however, has many meanings (Kelsen, 1957), and what is deemed just varies, as do other elements of moral codes. We are back where we started: lacking a universal sense of justice, whose morality shall define the norm for a study of deviance?

Again, there are two conceivable ways to respond to this question. One method is to take a vote to see whether there is a near-universal idea of justice. The other procedure is to invent a conception of justice, to defend it on "intuitive" grounds, and then to impose it. Thus one of the most praised philosophic works of recent years has invented a "theory of justice" (Rawls, 1971). Rawls's definition of justice is defended *not* on the ground that most human beings agree with his sense of fairness but on the ground that people should agree or that they would agree *if* we could all be returned to some "original position" and be filled with the requisite knowledge.[2]

---

[2]Rawls's invention of an idea of justice is bound with many qualifications and rests upon unsupported assumptions about the kind of social arrangement people might prefer *if* human evolution were to start all over again from some primitive state of ignorance about our destiny. His thesis is, therefore, in the tradition of J. J. Rousseau and other proponents of the social contract (Nisbet, 1974). Rawls's two principles of justice are that

1. Each person is to have an equal right to the most extensive total system of equal basic liberties compatible with a similar system of liberty for all . . .
2. Social and economic inequalities are to be arranged so that they are both:
   (*a*)   to the greatest benefit of the least advantaged . . . and
   (*b*)   attached to offices and positions open to all under conditions of fair equality of opportunity [p. 302].

Insofar as present human desires and present human behaviors are *not* just as the philosopher defines "justice," taking people's votes on the matter becomes irrelevant. Rawls calls "the procedure of majority rule . . . subordinate" to *his* principles of justice (p. 356). This is to say that if majority wish does *not* accord with the invented sense of justice, it is to be put aside. Thus, also in this vein, Jean Jacques Rousseau urged (1754, p. 169), "Let us begin, then, by laying aside facts, for they do not affect the question."

Attempts to invent universal standards of right conduct are good philosophic exercise. But they do not answer the question, "Whose standard defines a problem, a deviation, a pathology?" And such exercise does stimulate the risk that philosopher-kings will seek to impose their morality upon others.

An Alternative View: Social Concerns

A more democratic way of finding a universal standard with which to define the disparity between how things are and how we want them to be is to let people vote. The closest approximation to a universal standard of judgment that does not involve its imposition by a particular believer is the *criterion of general concern.*

It is our thesis that, quite apart from local manifestations, ideological interpretations, and temporal remedies, there are behaviors and social conditions about which people have expressed their concern, now and historically. This volume is an introduction to a sample of these concerns in their modern setting.

An advantage of the present orientation is that it does not depend upon the author's judgment of what is a symptom, a deviation, or a need. It takes at face value people's common worries and hopes.

Furthermore, the present position does not assume that people agree about how to react to their concerns. Our point of view accepts the reality of conflict. It recognizes that human beings continue to dispute their ideals and the methods of achieving them. It acknowledges that one person's cause for gratitude is another's motive for reform and a third person's stimulus to rebellion. The present viewpoint admits that the interpretations of social concerns and the recommendations made in response to them differ not merely because we *know* different things but also because we *want* different things, or different shares of the same things that are in short supply.

This theme underwrites the chapters that follow. It describes human beings as at the same time affiliating and conflictive. It does not subscribe to the optimism that holds conflict to be "misunderstanding" and both to be soluble in information. The cheering assumption that a conflict of ideals will decrease with knowledge is not only unwarranted in the twentieth century but also devalues the other person's ideals.

A treatment of social concerns that would be fair can do no better than report these issues and the data about them along with their competing interpretations and recommendations. Social science has a distinctive contribution to make here insofar as it can combine techniques of societal accounting with a scholarly distance[3] from the fray that permits reasoned criticism.

This attitude toward the human predicament and the author's professional role as its student does not cleanse his descriptions of personal judgment. The judgment is there. From time to time, personal advice will be given and marked as such. The judgment seeks to be sound, but it is subject to error and correction.

IDENTIFYING SOCIAL CONCERNS

What concerns people can be known by asking them, as Cantril (1965) has done, or by listening to their conversations, as the ethnomethodologist would prefer (Garfinkel, 19670, or through a content analysis of the mass media, or from a coding of the demands for attention made upon a nation's civic representatives.

Such concerns have been reliably classified as dimensions of aspiration and anxiety. These varied indexes of worry and desire yield pictures of wide generality. Local conditions produce shifts in the importance assigned one area of concern over another and in the quality of attention, but the hopes and fears that people think about do not characterize a province. They characterize humanity.

Cantril puts it this way (1965, p. 35, emphasis added):

In the United States, *as in nearly all the countries studied,* the major hopes and aspirations are those involved in maintaining and improving a decent, healthy family life. A considerable number of Americans seem to aspire to a resolution of psychological problems such as those concerned with religion, emotional stability, and group acceptance. Only about half as many people are worried about having an inadequate standard of living as aspire to a decent or better standard of living. On the other hand, the fear of war is mentioned twice as frequently as is the hope for peace. It is clear from these results that the two major threats to the aspirations of Americans are health for oneself or family and war.

With variations in valence around the world and among segments of a society, these concerns are both general and perennial—concern for physical and psychic health for oneself and loved others; concern for a happy family; concern about one's standard of living and quality of work, and with education as a means of improving both; concern for peace, internally and international-ly; and concern for leisure and its use.

---

[3]"Scholarly distance" is unpopular today among those who prefer "being committed" to acquiring knowledge and who prefer taking action to knowing what one is doing. As with all resolutions of our concerns, the side one takes reflects the kind of person one is and what one thinks he wants. Students are reminded that what people *say* they want is not always what they *behave to get,* and that what results from their wanting, saying, and doing always deviates at varying distance from their ideals.

General Concerns

The specific content of these concerns and a measure of their generality are described by the survey conducted by Cantril and his associates (1965) during the early 1960s. These investigators sampled the aspirations and anxieties of people in twelve nations[4] who represented almost one-third of the world's population. The researchers combined the spoken concerns of these twelve samples and weighted them according to the size of the population represented by each sample. The results give an ordering of some 129 concerns for oneself and one's nation, each of which was mentioned by samples representing at least 4 million persons. Tables 1-1 and 1-2 present the reported hopes and fears for self and nation, respectively, by millions of people represented.

These tables present a pattern of concerns about two general issues: *keeping alive and living well.* The concern to live well includes thoughts about how to attain and maintain some standard of living and how to be healthy and happy. Being happy, in turn, includes such separable spheres of pleasure and despair as having congenial work, achieving security and status, enjoying some leisure, and being appreciated by friends and lovers.

These *hopes* for the good life are countered by possibilities that threaten them. These *fears* are, in large part, of the harm others may do us and our country, and, to a lesser extent, of the injury from such natural calamities as accident, climate, and physical deterioration.

It will be noted from Cantril's list of concerns that there is a division and yet a connection between hopes and fears that are personal and those that are

[4]The states sampled were, in order of size of population, India, the United States, Brazil, West Germany, Nigeria, the Philippines, Egypt, Yugoslavia, Cuba, the Dominican Republic, Israel, and Panama.

Table 1-1   Rank Order of Personal Concerns*

Concern	Rank order (millions)
Hoping for improved or decent standard of living	549
Hoping for welfare and opportunities for children	262
Fearful of deterioration of present standard of living	259
Fearful of ill health, accident, death of self	222
Hoping for good health of self	144
Fearful of ill health, accident, death in family	133
Hoping for good job, congenial work	132
Hoping for a house of their own	124
Hoping for own land or farm	123
Fearful about children's welfare or opportunities	109
Hoping for happy family life	99
Fearful of war	83
Hoping for own business	62
Hoping for health of family	62
Fearful of unemployment or inability to work	58

Table 1-1 Rank Order of Personal Concerns*

Concern	Rank order (millions)
Hoping for happy old age	47
Hoping to be useful to others, public service	46
Hoping for modern conveniences	45
Hoping for welfare of relatives, being with relatives	44
Hoping for recreation, travel, leisure	40
Hoping for self-development and improvement	40
Fearful of separation from relatives, not living up to expectations from them	36
Hoping for employment	36
Fearful of unhappy family life	35
Hoping for resolution of religious, ethical problems	34
Hoping to lead good, decent life	32
Fearful of poor or uncongenial work	32
Fearful of being dependent on others	28
Hoping for peace in international situation	26
Fearful of not having own business or improving it†	26
Hoping for acceptance by others	26
Hoping to maintain status quo	23
Hoping for emotional stability and maturity	23
Hoping for success	23
Hoping for wealth	18
Fearful of not owning land or improving it†	18
Fearful of being unable to provide dowry for daughters†	18
Hoping to be able to marry daughters and provide dowry†	18
Fearful of not being able to get a house	18
Fearful of being alone	15
Fearful of general economic instability	15
Fearful of no self-improvement or development	14
Resigned to Fate or God's will, nothing worse can happen†	13
Fearful of not being accepted by others	11
Fearful of being a failure in job or work	10
Fearful of being emotionally unstable and immature	9
Fearful of inadequate standard of living for whole nation	9
Fearful of becoming antisocial, taking to crime	8
Fearful of inequality of opportunity based on race, color	8
Hoping for social security	7
Hoping to achieve sense of own personal worth	7
Hoping for equal opportunities	6
Fearful of lack of freedom	6
Fearful of militarism and armaments	6
Fearful of not being useful to others	5
Fearful of achieving no sense of personal worth	5
Fearful of aggression or domination by Communist power	4
Fearful of no social security	4

*Reprinted from Hadley Cantril, *The Pattern of Human Concerns* Table XIII:1. © 1965 by Rutgers the State University. Reprinted by permission of the Rutgers University Press.
†Refers to special problems added to original code.

Table 1-2   Rank Order of National Concerns*

Concern	Rank order (millions)
Fearful of war	372
Hoping for improved or decent standard of living	182
Hoping for technological advances	154
Hoping for peace	126
Hoping for employment	106
Fearful of Chinese aggression†	96
Fearful of dishonest government	91
Hoping for better education throughout nation	88
Fearful of economic instability	87
Hoping for economic stability	79
Hoping for agrarian reform	62
Hoping for improved sense of social and political responsibility on part of the people	58
Fearful of disunity among people of nation	50
Fearful of Communism	49
Fearful of unemployment	46
Fearful of political instability	44
Fearful of no improved or inadequate standard of living	42
Hoping for better public health	40
Fearful discrimination will not be eliminated	36
Fearful of Kashmir-Pakistan problem†	35
Hoping discrimination will be eliminated	33
Fearful of threat, aggression, domination by Communist power	32
Fearful of lack of moral, ethical standards among people	31
Hoping for honest government	30
Hoping for social justice	30
Hoping for national unity	29
Fearful of lack of national independence	28
Hoping for national independence	27
Hoping for national prosperity through planning†	26
Hoping for better moral, ethical standards	25
Hoping for better world re international situation	25
Hoping for reunification of the country†	25
Fearful of population problem	25
Hoping for efficient government	23
Hoping nation will enhance its status and importance	21
Fearful of threat or aggression by some foreign power	21
Hoping for political stability	21
Hoping housing situation will be improved in country	21
Fearful standard of living in country will deteriorate	20
Hoping for improved labor conditions	19
Hoping for democratic or representative government	18
Fearful of social injustice	17
Hoping to maintain status quo	15
Fearful no technological advances will be made	14
Fearful about lack of freedom	13
Fearful about lack of law and order	13
Fearful planning may fail†	13
Fearful there will be no rural development†	13

Table 1-2 Rank Order of National Concerns*

Concern	Rank order (millions)
Hoping nation will become a world power	13
Hoping for increased foreign trade	11
Hoping for law and order	11
Hoping for modern amenities for people	11
Hoping nation will be militarily strong	10
Hoping for fewer taxes†	10
Hoping cold war will lessen	10
Hoping for social security for nation	10
Fearful of poor or unfair working conditions	9
Fearful of inefficient government	9
Fearful of consequences of Nehru's death†	9
Fearful of inadequate educational facilities	8
Fearful of no democratic or representative government	8
Fearful of high or increased taxes	8
Fearful of continued armament	7
Hoping for friendly relations with all countries	7
Hoping for disarmament	6
Fearful of no sense of social and political responsibility	6
Hoping for freedom	6
Hoping for socialist government	5
Hoping Tito will maintain health and position†	5
Hoping country will provide moral or ideological leadership	4
Fearful of natural disasters†	4

*Reprinted from Hadley Cantril, *The Pattern of Human Concerns* Table XIII:2. © 1965 by Rutgers the State University. Reprinted by permission of the Rutgers University Press.
†Refers to special problems added to original guide.

national. These concerns run together because our purely individual concerns depend upon a social order for their resolution. The sample of concerns addressed in the following chapters run from those that are most individual, like being happy, to those that are more global, like reducing war.

EVALUATING PRESCRIPTIONS FOR OUR SOCIAL CONCERNS

The pages that follow will describe, in some part, the quality of modern social concerns, the probable correlates of these behaviors and conditions, their disputed causes and embattled resolution. It is recognized throughout that concerns include interpretations, that interpretations define and evaluate, and that, therefore, the responses recommended for one's concerns are never made solely from "the facts of the matter." The feasibility and palatability of prescriptions for concerns depend also upon the associated definitions of the world to which they are addressed. These definitions are burdened by morality as much as they are illuminated by information.

The world, however, is not just a matter of definition. There *is* a "real" world, and in it there *are* discernible consequences of human decision and action. It makes sense, then, to ask how the differing remedies of our troubles are apt to work. There *is* knowledge to guide us. The knowledge is imperfect, however, and one of its imperfections is that it is always a knowledge of some past.

Meanwhile, a hazard of being concerned is that, when concern gets armored with zeal, it tends to deny history. It loses the "memory of mistakes," becomes immune to facts, and promises unhistorical futures—a new humanity and New Jerusalems.

The present goal is to preserve our memory of mistakes in reacting to our concerns while attending to the possibilities of new worlds. The task is that difficult one of simultaneously reading the continuities while evaluating the promises of novel relationships. My personal attitude is to strike a balance in response to our social concerns so that one is neither paralyzed by the past nor frenzied by the future.

We shall ask questions about some of the hopes and fears that appear to be near-universal. Some of these questions can be answered with information. Other questions, the moral ones, are probably not soluble in facts.[5] We shall not evade the moral issues. Where advice is given, it will be guided by this maxim: *For people you love, what would you advise?*

---

[5]You may wish to dispute this. There is a large literature on the nature of morality that struggles with the question of whether moral preferences can ever be made rational. A personal opinion is expressed more fully elsewhere (Nettler, 1973).

Chapter 2

Being Happy

The signs of concern are recognized as worry, fear, misery, and despair. Their opposite sign is called happiness. If the general conditions of happiness could be described, the description would illuminate some sources of concern. The first question is whether we can talk sensibly about being happy.

WHAT IS HAPPINESS?

Everyone knows what happiness is until he or she begins to talk about it. Then, suddenly, we hear statements about happiness being an unknowable quality, about its being something that cannot be measured but only felt, or about its being too subtle an emotion for the psychologist's crude tools.

We do have conceptions of happiness, however. At least we have some idea of what it is we are talking about when we use the word. If we can agree what the word points to, then we can gauge which kinds of people are more and less happy, and we can study the conditions that seem associated with felicity and misery.

Precisely this has been done at various universities by scholars interested in such diverse matters as business success, marital adjustment, altruism, occupational satisfaction, power, and the fate of people with high IQs. These differing studies have been concerned with happiness as a *steady emotional state.* This state seems to be a compound of self-respect, physical well-being, and contentment with one's lot. It is found among people who do not stew in their lost pasts but who live in the present with plans for their futures. Not surprisingly, happy people enjoy time; unhappy people seek to kill it. Happy people make more long-range commitments, are more punctual and efficient, and tend to *over*estimate how much time they require to do their work (Wessman and Ricks, 1966).

Happy people are not without worries, however. They sometimes feel inadequate and they suffer tensions and disappointments (Bradburn and Caplovitz, 1965). In short, happiness is not a condition free from care; that is apathy or death. Happy people differ from unhappy ones in the way they respond to their anxieties and to their failures. The happy person responds with a mixture of action and patience; the miserable individual retreats from life.

CAN HAPPINESS BE MEASURED?

"Of happiness and despair we have no measure," Ernest van den Haag tells us (1957). In one sense, he is correct. There is no measure of these states if by "measure" one means a ruler with units that are standardized and equal. Yet even without such a fine ruler, we *do* form opinions about our own and others' satisfactions and miseries. Some people *are* happier than others. We see it in their faces, hear it in their voices, watch it in their walk. We even believe it, with reservations, when people answer our questions about their lives.[1]

Judgments of human contentment have been collected by social psychologists. These ratings have been tested for their reliability, for the association among multiple indicators of satisfaction, and for the degree of agreement among judges who are acquainted with the persons being assessed. While such measurement is too crude for the poet, it is accurate enough to tell us something about the conditions of contentment, particularly when we are comparing groups of people rather than analyzing particular persons.

How Has Happiness Been Measured?

An assortment of behaviors have been counted as signs of happiness. Professional observers have lived with their "subjects" and recorded their words and movements (Lewis, 1959, 1966). Other students have examined diaries and suicide notes, administered lengthy questionnaires, and engaged in detailed interviews. Wessman and Ricks (1959), for example, had their assistants rate themselves on an "elation-depression" scale every night for six weeks so that daily highs and lows and swings in mood could be estimated.

---

[1]It is notable, incidentally, that sociologists seem more willing to believe people when they say they are unhappy than when they say they are happy. I have no "hard data" on this; it is an impression gathered from living with sociologists and from critics' reviews of these pages. It is an impression that is bolstered, as a hypothesis, by the proposal that people of "liberal" attitude are sensitive to what Minogue (1963, pp. 6–9) has called "suffering situations." For persons of such humane attitude, suffering is more readily perceived, is more real and more pervasive, than is happiness.

Nonverbal behaviors have also been counted as indexes of relative happiness. Suicide is the extreme example. Alcoholism and drug rates are another index. School truancy and employee absenteeism are indicators of dislike for the classroom and the job respectively. Even the migration of people tells us something about the conditions under which human beings find their lives more and less satisfying. We vote with our feet when we can. The net balance of movement between regions is a measure of the relative goodness of life. Thus people find life better in Hong Kong than in the People's Republic of China, and they find life better in Canada than in Hong Kong. Similarly, Jews find life better in Israel than in the Union of Soviet Socialist Republics.

Maps of migrations have been drawn that describe differences in the quality of life on an *aggregate level*—that is, for people in general as opposed to any particular individual. The descriptions given us by these maps can be supplemented by asking people questions about their movements and their wishes to move. For example, a recent Gallup poll (1971) reports that while some 41 percent of British subjects would like to leave their country, only 12 percent of Americans expressed this desire.

Voting with our feet and wishing to be where we are not constitute an "operational definition" of happiness, according to Hart (1940). He calls happiness "any state of consciousness which the person . . . seeks to attain or to maintain, and . . . the opposite of any state which the possessor seeks to change or from which he seeks to escape or withdraw" (p. 183).

The most popular way of assessing happiness is to ask people about their lives. The questions asked range from the direct query to complicated checklists. An illustration of the direct question is one asked by the National Opinion Research Center of a sample of Americans. "Taking all things together, how would you say things are these days—would you say you are very happy, pretty happy, or not too happy?" (Bradburn and Caplovitz, 1965, p. 7). An example of a more complicated instrument is the one Hart invented (1940) in which you are asked to underline adjectives that describe "the way you have felt a good deal of the time" and to cross out with an "X" each word that does not describe your feelings. Thus an unemployed engineer whose wife had run off with another man began his self-description like this:

miserable thrilled frustrated cheerful jolly <u>disappointed</u> bored successful <u>dissatisfied</u> elated <u>despondent</u> jubilant [Hart, 1940, p. 115]

Investigators who have studied human satisfactions have attempted to separate temporary swings of mood from more enduring emotional states. Obviously there are times in our lives when we are more or less pleased with our condition. Some of us do get into miserable situations—and out of them. Most human beings, however, do not experience great reversals in their careers. We are today what we have been a long time becoming. For adults at least, there is more continuity than variation of estate. The important point is that however we measure happiness, and whether we are describing a temporary elation or a more enduring satisfaction, there is a *generality* among the conditions associated with being happy and, conversely, with being unhappy. That is, we can describe the contexts in which people lead more and less contented lives.

WHAT ARE THE HAPPINESS ZONES?

Sigmund Freud was once asked what it meant to be a healthy personality. He replied, "To have the ability to love and the ability to work." *Loving and working* define two of the principal regions of action in which we find ourselves happy or miserable. These "uses" of the self constitute most of our lives. There is, of course, time for play and meditation, for sex, and for eating and sleeping. However, we are not apt to relish these times if our connections with others and our feelings about ourselves are unpleasant. Then we play without fun, eat without appetite, have sex without satisfaction, and sleep without rest. Loving and working are the major ways in which we know ourselves and through which we receive our pleasures and pains.

If we are or have been unhappy in one of these ways, we like to think that some other activity may compensate. Aldous Huxley once claimed that most work was dung-digging and recommended that, when one was through shoveling his load, he should "go home, wash his hands, and be a man." Some people tell us as much: "So I've got a crummy job, and I do my nine to five, but I've got good kids and a good woman." We also hear it put the other way about, "She was bruised in love. That's why she's pouring herself into her work."

These compensations are sometimes there. Some people experience them. Compensation is not the rule, however. If any generalization applies, it is that "those who have, get." Good things go together and miseries accumulate. Life is more compact than partitioned. More accurately, *miseries seem more closely correlated than pleasures.* For example, Bradburn and Caplovitz (1965) found this skewed association of pleasures and pains when they asked 2,006 Americans about their anxieties, their job satisfactions, their marital tensions, and their involvement in social life. "There appears . . . to be a cumulative quality to maladjustment," the investigators report. "The more the unmerrier" (p. 39).

This is to say that compensation is less possible in the lower depths and more possible as a person "has something going for him." A low-skilled job provides little balance to a miserable marriage, while interesting work may make up for the displeasures of home. Conversely, one of those rare, shared, fulfilled families may make it possible to tolerate a dull job, whereas a so-so union of appetites does not do so.

IS EVERYBODY HAPPY?

The answer to this question depends, naturally, on where we look—on the angle of our lens. It depends, too, on our standard of comparison. We are reminded that the standards of contentment are quite different among the Hottentot and the suburbanite, and we are cautioned against imposing our demands for happiness upon other people.

A second reminder is required before this question is answered. The proportions of people deemed to be miserable or content must always be taken as estimates, since the figures will vary with the questions asked. If we use these figures, however, not as finely calibrated statistics but as magnitude indicators—as signs of "more and less"—then we can say something about the social location of happiness. With these qualifications in mind, societies can be roughly mapped for their highs and lows in human contentment.

How Many Are Happy?

Henry David Thoreau believed that "most men lead lives of quiet desperation." This statement probably represents a projection of Thoreau's personality rather than an observation of people. When we *ask* people in the Western world about their pleasures and displeasures, most such citizens tell us that they are "pretty happy."

Gurin and his colleagues (1960) interviewed 2,460 Americans representative of people over the age of twenty-one living at home. These persons were asked their "general feelings about how things are today." Thirty-five percent of this sample said they were "very happy"; 54 percent, "pretty happy"; and 11 percent, "not too happy."

Bradburn and Caplovitz (1965) asked similar questions of people living in an economically depressed area. Allowing for this economic situation, their figures are not greatly different from the Gurin calculations. Twenty-four percent of the Bradburn-Caplovitz respondents reported that they were "very happy"; 59 percent, "pretty happy"; and 17 percent, "not too happy."

In 1971, the Survey Research Center at the University of Michigan asked a representative sample of Americans a modified version of the happiness question: "All things considered, how satisfied are you with life in the United States today?" Over 75 percent of the respondents said that they were "satisfied" or "very satisfied." Only 9 percent claimed to be "dissatisfied." In February 1972, a Gallup poll of Americans revealed that three-fourths of the population was satisfied with its housing, 78 percent with its standard of living, and 84 percent with its work (Watts and Free, 1973, p. 20).[2]

This picture of general contentment does not deny that there are pockets

---

[2]If there is some validity to such polls—if they are just *pointing* in the right direction—then they demonstrate what others have told us about the "image makers" in modern societies: that intellectuals, like television, prefer dramatic presentation and crisis thinking to plain reporting (McLuhan, 1964; Shils, 1972). A result of this preference is a separation between privileged thinkers and the people about whom they so frequently express concern (H. Kahn, 1973). There is increasing notice of the failure of the "intellectual elite . . . to imagine as real people, large segments of our population unlike themselves." (Alpert, 1972, p. 72). Alpert's point is well illustrated by the comment of one intellectual after 1972's landslide national election in the United States. "I live in a rather special world," said the movie critic Pauline Kael during the Christmas meeting of the Modern Language Association. "I know only one person who voted for Nixon. Where they [i.e., the Nixon supporters] are, I don't know. They're outside my ken. But sometimes when I'm in the theater I can feel them" (Buckley, 1973, p. 167).

of despair in the best of modern societies. Some of the chapters to follow describe such enclaves of misery.

Was the Past Better than the Present?

Some part of our contentment depends upon our standards of comparison. As individuals we often compare our present state with our past and with our expectations. Whether the past appears better than the present depends upon how far back one looks, from where, and when. The answer to this question varies, too, with whether one is examining his personal career or that of his world.

Public opinion polls in Western countries show that individuals feel their personal lives have been improving in recent years. They do not always believe, however, that things in general have been getting better. The "state of the person" seems to have been improving, but not the "state of the nation."

The Gallup organization has used a "ladder of life" measure developed by Kilpatrick and Cantril (1960) on which individuals can rate the quality of their circumstances on a scale from zero (terrible) to ten (great). Recently at least, Americans have been optimistic about themselves and their country, although they believe that as individuals they have made more progress than their country has (Table 2-1).

If we ask people about life in the more distant past, a different picture is apt to emerge. Although most people in industrial countries seem content with the present, they believe that people were happier during preceding generations. This glamorization of "the good old days" can be illustrated in general and in particular. If we ask a general question like "Do you think people were happier during horse-and-buggy days than they are now?" about two-thirds will say yes (AIPO, 1939). If we go on to inquire whether these respondents would rather have lived then than now, as high or higher a proportion say no (AIPO, 1939). We may think people were happier in the past, but we do not want to return there.

A similar effect is obtained if we ask individuals about their own pasts. Most of us report pleasant memories of childhood and adolescence. Barschak (1951), for example, studied the recollections of young women in Switzerland, Germany, England, and the United States. More than 91 percent of her Swiss

Table 2-1 Visions of the Past, Present, and Future from June 1972*

	State of the person	State of the nation
Past†	5.5	5.6
Present	6.4	5.5
Future†	7.6	6.2

*Data taken from W. Watts and L. A. Free (eds.), "Progress or Decline: The Public's Evaluation," in *State of the Nation*, Chap. 1. © 1973 by Potomac Associates. Reprinted by permission.
†Five years from date.

samples recalled a happy childhood and adolescence. Some 84 percent of an American sample recalled happy pasts, 82 percent of an English sample, and 74 percent of a sample from Gottingen, West Germany. Only in Berlin, where World War II hit home, did the proportion—48 percent—recalling pleasant memories of childhood become less than a majority.

Reports of happier pasts must be taken with a grain of caution because there is a strong tendency to forget the unpleasant (Gilbert, 1938; Meltzer, 1930; Waldfogel, 1948). There are, of course, neurotics who cannot forget their past failures, but they are an exception to our rule. The rest of us healthy personalities tend to remember the good times rather than the bad ones. Incidentally, this is a reason why so many of us repeat the same mistakes. Forgiveness has a strong friend in weak memory.

Are the Happy People Really Happy?

Artistic observers of the social scene do not believe these happy statistics. The dramatic life preferred by the artist contrasts with the routines in which most of us are immersed. Tension is lacking, and zing. Or so it seems. Thus the distinguished drama critic Pauline Kael finds a movie (*Limbo*) about the wives of Vietnam prisoners banal (and it may be). Kael writes (1973, p. 77):

> The film is a representation of a form of actual suffering, but everything in it seems synthetic. And the synthetic begins to seem *true*. The words spoken are pitifully simp-ordinary: "nice," "a lot of," "You're a wonderful woman," "You have wonderful kids." The scriptwriters might have worked for the astronauts. "Limbo" has a frightening superficial realism—it's the same kind of fright we feel when we walk into a suburban supermarket and see customers who look just like the people who polish and spray in TV commercials . . . It's apparent that the mediocrity of their lives—the rooms devoid of reading matter, the absence of any sign of taste or thought—is meant to guarantee the audience's sympathetic identification with them [emphasis hers].

Whether or not one agrees with Ms. Kael's taste, the preference for a more stimulating life ought not to be confused with the conditions under which most people find contentment. The advice, again, is to avoid imposing one's own requirements for the good life upon others. If we avoid this imposition and recognize that we are looking at people in general rather than at particular individuals, it is possible to list the circumstances of lives that are more and less happy.

CONDITIONS OF HAPPINESS

An outline of the conditions associated with happiness must be read without yielding to the temptation to interpret each correlation as causal. What goes with being happy is only sometimes the *cause* of felicity and is frequently but part of the *description* of the happy state.

Money Is an Accompaniment of Happiness

Note that this does *not* say that money will *make* you happy. All that is said is that, *within particular societies,* people who have more money more frequently report contentment with their lives than do their fellow citizens who have less. This seems so whether we study developed or less-developed countries or industrialized or more rural lands. Having more money is associated with other good things rather universally, good things like better health, longer life, more friends, more civic involvement, wider recreational activity, self-respect, honor, prestige, and satisfaction with one's work. Merely to list these accompaniments is to describe happiness.

A popular and wrong conclusion from this fact is that money *produces* happiness. This is a good example of the logical error of inferring causation from correlation. Just *having* money, or, worse, *acquiring* money, does not necessarily make people happy. An opposite effect is conceivable and is, at times, observed.

Furthermore, what is true of individuals within societies is not true for societies as wholes or for a society changing with time. Increasing the wealth of nations does *not* raise the happiness level of their citizens. Expectations rise with riches, so that the increasing postwar affluence of Western countries cannot be said to have increased contentment. Easterlin (1973) has summarized data from thirty investigations conducted among nineteen more- and less-developed lands on the relation between reported happiness and income. His conclusions, with his emphases, are that, *"In all societies, more money for the individual typically means more individual happiness. However, raising the incomes of all does not increase the happiness of all.* The happiness-income relation provides a classic example of the logical fallacy of composition—*what is true for the individual is not true for society as a whole"* (p. 4).

We are additionally cautioned against the easy assumption that money is the cause of happiness when we note that there are contented poor people and miserable rich ones. The point has been amply illustrated. For instance, Baughman and Dahlstrom (1968) interviewed youngsters in a poor section of the rural southern United States. The researchers found few complaints about life in this rustic setting, little animosity toward parents, no awareness of racial problems, and good adjustment in school. The authors report, "Many of [these youth] have yet to learn that they are poor" (p. 411).

On the opposite side of the financial spectrum, there are prices paid for wealth. At least one psychiatrist, Wixen (1973), believes that there are specific disabilities associated with being a "rich kid." Whether or not this is so, there are the productive and creative rich, the happy ones, and the "filthy rich," the miserable ones. It is possible to be happy when one is rich *if* one is exercising a vocation. This need not be a job in the middle-class sense, but it is an absorption. It is a use of talent. Without such interest, boredom becomes the occupational hazard of too much money. The idle "son of the rich" has a difficult time finding joy.

Allowing for these interpretive qualifications, the relationship between socioeconomic status and happiness is positive. What counts, however, is *what goes with* financial success—what one has *done,* and what one *is,* when he is making more money. Money helps, and most of us would like more of it, but money alone is no guarantor of happiness.

Age

The psychiatrist Thomas Szasz (1973, p. 36) tells us that happiness is "now usually attributed by adults to children, and by children to adults." He is correct in suggesting that one can be happy or miserable whether youthful or mature. Happiness is not strikingly associated with age except that old people—those over sixty—say they are less happy. For example, the National Opinion Research Center study yields proportions as shown in Table 2-2. Unfortunately, these data do not reveal possible variations in happiness among teen-agers and people in their prime twenties.

The "golden years" may have their comforts, but they are outweighed by their pains. The older years are made less happy than the younger ones by the failure of health and the end of hope.

Education

Schooling has been correlated with income in Western lands and, as with money, more schooling has meant greater contentment. The association is modest, however, and it must not be interpreted as causal. The slight correlation is subject to thinning out as more people go to school longer. Again, the relation is most apparent at the extremes, as Table 2-3 illustrates.

Religiosity

Participation in religious functions is associated with happiness. Going to church, being religious, and having been reared in a religious environment are all moderately related to reports of happiness (Bradburn and Caplovitz, 1965; Hart, 1940; Wilson, 1967).

There are two interpretations of this association. One interpretation reads religiosity as but another link in the chain of social connections; and being

Table 2-2 Age and Reported Happiness*

Age group	Percent "very happy"	Percent "pretty happy"	Percent "not too happy"
Under 30 years	30	58	11
30–39	24	66	10
40–49	25	62	13
50–59	23	59	18
60–69	21	54	24
70 and over	18	52	30

*Adapted from N. M. Bradburn and D. Caplovitz, *Reports on Happiness*, Table 2.1. © 1965 by Aldine Publishing Company. Reprinted by permission.

Table 2-3 Schooling and Reported Happiness*

Schooling level	Percent "very happy"	Percent "pretty happy"	Percent "not too happy"
Eighth grade or less	19	56	25
Less than high school graduate	25	59	16
High school graduate	27	61	12
Part college	22	67	10
College graduate or more	29	60	10

*Adapted from N. M. Bradburn and D. Caplovitz, *Reports on Happiness*, Table 2.1. © 1965 by Aldine Publishing Company. Reprinted by permission.

socially connected is, as we shall see, a strong determinant of our contentment. A second interpretation looks at what religious activity *does,* quite apart from its friendship function. Among other things, religions explain the mysteries. They answer the unanswerable questions. Religions respond to the moral questions that cannot be resolved with facts. They tell us *why* things ultimately are as they are, where a science can only describe *how* things are and may have been.

Religions give these satisfactions, moreover, through practices and rituals as well as with words. These cultic actions are dramas that unite their participants. Thus religions persist, although their forms change. Today's renaissance of occultism, for example, is but a substitute for more conventional faith (*Newsweek,* 1973a, 1973b). Those who kill old gods invent new ones.

The Social Bond

A strong correlate and probably a cause of happiness is being connected to others. Traveling the solo route is rough. Few do it in comfort. Despite all the miseries others give us, people are also a principal source of our pleasures. Most of us feel better about our lives when we live with others and for them. There is a rich inventory of fact to be sampled in illustrating this point.

Marriage and the Good Life   When we ask people about the satisfactions and dissatisfactions in their lives, *married persons more frequently tell us that they are content than do single persons.* Of course, age, sex, and money intrude upon these reports, as does the culture in which marriage is embedded.

It is easier, for example, to be a single young person than a single old one. Being single by choice or with the anticipation of a connection is a different matter from involuntary solitude. Furthermore, sex makes a difference. Contrary to some popular conceptions, unmarried men say that they are more unhappy and show more signs of dissatisfaction with themselves than do married men. The evidence concerning the emotional states of married and unmarried women is mixed, however. Some studies show only slight differences between married and single women in their reports of happiness and psychic distress. Other research indicates that single women, at least single white women, may be happier than married women, and that this remains true when one controls for age (Gove, 1972). Black women in the United States may be an exception to this finding (Gove and Lester, 1974).

Facts such as these come out of studies that have asked people *directly* about their happiness (Bradburn, 1969; Bradburn and Caplovitz, 1965; Gurin et al., 1960), and they appear also in research that has assessed happiness *indirectly* through measures of mental health (Gove, 1973; Gove and Lester, 1974; Srole et al., 1962). Psychic distress is an indirect measure of discontent. It is possible to be neurotic and happy, but people who experience numerous "nervous symptoms" are less happy than more healthy persons. When such symptoms are carefully counted, as in the research by Srole and his colleagues, married men and married women do not differ significantly in the number and gravity of their psychic complaints. However, when bachelors—men who have never married—are compared with their married counterparts and with single and married women (holding age constant), striking differences appear. These differences are apparent after twenty years of age, they tend to increase with age, and they indicate that persistent bachelorhood is correlated with psychic "dis-ease" (Table 2-4).

A map of our ailments, such as Table 2-4 provides, provokes these causal questions: Were the perpetual bachelors "sick" to begin with, or did their solo state make them more "peculiar," or does a bad start get reinforced by the solitary condition it promotes? This fascinating issue need not be debated here. The present point is simply that there is a moderate association between being *maritally disconnected* and *being psychically ill, particularly for the weaker sex, the male.*

As suggested earlier, the relative contentment of married and unmarried women seems more varied and questionable. For example, Table 2-4 shows that, except for those in their forties, married women report more psychoneur-

Table 2-4 Proportion of Impaired† Respondents among Single and Married Men and Women of Like Age in Midtown Manhattan (Percent)*

Sex and	Age group			
marital status	20–29	30–39	40–49	50–59
Single men	20.5	30.4	37.5	46.1
Married men	11.7	19.6	19.0	25.7
Single women	11.2	12.1	24.6	25.6
Married women	13.4	22.1	18.1	30.6

*Adapted from L. Srole et al., *Mental Health in the Metropolis: The Midtown Manhattan Study*, Tables 10-1 and 10-2. © 1962 by the McGraw-Hill Book Company. Reprinted with permission.

†"Impaired" is a composite category of individuals diagnosed as suffering from "marked," "severe," and "incapacitating" symptoms.

otic symptoms than single women or married men, age for age. This qualified finding is further refined by data Gove and Lester (1974) provide. Their study indicates that insofar as married women report more emotional distress than unmarried women, this may apply more strongly to white women than to black women in America (Table 2-5).

The possibility that marriage may be more strongly associated with the happiness of men than of women is also illustrated by the self-reports of the widowed and the divorced. "Widows and widowers are more unhappy, worry more, [and more often] anticipate death in the near future . . . than married people of the same ages," say Gurin and his researchers (1960, p. 237). These investigators provide evidence that widowed men are more distressed than widowed women. This is an additional datum that fits the fact that women are more viable than men. They are more durable. At all ages including the intrauterine ages, more females survive than males (Dublin et al., 1949, pp. 39–59).

Separated and divorced persons are also less happy than married people of the same age. It is debatable whether women suffer more from these disruptions. Some studies report greater maladjustment on the part of women than of men who have been divorced (Goode, 1956; Gurin et al., 1960, p. 236). Table 2-6 finds differently. It is notable, however, that divorced women feel their futures will be brighter than their pasts (Gurin et al., 1960, p. 236). This means, for most of the optimists, the anticipation of remarriage; and this optimism is realistic. In recent years in Western lands, young widowed and divorced women have been remarrying at a high rate (Bernard, 1956, p. 51). A summary example of the relationship between marital status and professed happiness is given by the National Opinion Research Center findings charted in Table 2-6.

Findings such as these seem to run counter to the sophisticated complaints about marriage, to the fact of high divorce rates, and to recent attempts at other forms of union. The resolution of this seeming contradiction is the ancient one:

Table 2-5 Psychiatric Symptoms and Self-Esteem by Sex, Marital Status, and Race (Percent)*

	Men		Women	
	High on psychiatric symptoms	Low on self-esteem	High on psychiatric symptoms	Low on self-esteem
Whites:				
Unmarried	39.5	40.6	42.5	29.9
Married	29.5	25.6	51.6	40.2
Blacks:				
Unmarried	31.5	38.4	41.8	30.1
Married	18.8	24.0	31.5	25.1

*Adapted from W. R. Gove and B. J. Lester, "Social Position and Self-Evaluation," Table 2. © 1974 by the University of Chicago Press and the *American Journal of Sociology.* Reprinted with permission.

Table 2-6   Marital Status and Misery by Sex*

Marital status	Percent "not too happy"	
	Men	Women
Married	14	11
Single	31	15
Divorced or separated	38	26
Widowed	43	39

*Adapted from N. M. Bradburn and D. Caplovitz, *Reports on Happiness*, Table 2.4. © 1965 by Aldine Publishing Company. Reprinted by permission.

Difficult as it may be to live with a man or woman, living without him or her carries its own price. Changes in marriage forms, if they do come about as advocated and predicted (Elliott, 1970; Mead, 1973), will probably not affect the correlation we have been describing between being intimately connected to others and being happy.

Sociologists prefer to explain this bondage as having social—that is, learned—sources. Learning affects the *form* through which we express our need for others, but the roots of this longing are biological. We are organisms with physiological drives that move us into social relations. Learning provides the channel in which these urges run. The attraction between male and female has an evolutionary history and an obvious survival value for the species. As Wickler (1972) demonstrates, *the social bond is tied with sexual cords.* Men and women complement each other. Many signs show that we need each other. Contrary to the claims of those minorities that dislike the opposite sex, exclusive or predominant homosexuality *is* an abnormality. It is a statistical abnormality and, from an evolutionary point of view, a biological abnormality as well.[3] To make such a statement of fact says nothing, incidentally, about civil rights or the legality of the private uses of our sexuality.

Social Participation and Contentment

The marriage tie is only one thread in the social bond. There are other indicators of our involvement with people, and these signs are also correlated with direct and indirect measures of happiness.

When the social behaviors of more and less happy people are compared, the happy ones are found more frequently engaged in a variety of recreational activities, in civic affairs, and in the artistic and religious functions of their communities. Happy people are more frequently joiners. They belong to more clubs and they have wider circles of friends. Their telephones ring more often (Burgess and Cottrell, 1939; Phillips, 1967; Wilson, 1967).

[3]Calling behaviors abnormal alarms some people who confuse being deviant or rare ("deviating from the ordinary rule or type," as the *Oxford English Dictionary* puts it) with being pathological or immoral. To avoid this confusion, the adjectives "statistical" and "biological" have been used to signify the kind of abnormality meant. Such usage is neutral as regards the morality or psychic health of homosexuals.

WHAT KINDS OF PEOPLE ARE MORE AND LESS HAPPY?

Locating happiness and misery on the social map describes some of the conditions of our satisfactions. Individuals differ, however. As we have noted, the social map shows us where greater and lesser *proportions* of people are content. Within each such "isothermic belt," there are individuals who illustrate the trend, exaggerate it, or buck it. Our constitutions and our personalities make a difference in the way in which we handle our environments and hence in our possibilities for happiness.

It is part of the professional bias of social scientists to discount the role of personality as a determinant of our destinies. This discounting becomes greater as other scholars locate the roots of our personalities in our temperaments and the determinants of our tempers in our genes. This issue will bet met in Chapter 4, when we discuss the genetic basis of mental disorder. For the present it is enough to suggest that there *are* constitutional differences that raise or lower the prospects of our being happy. We are not born equally able to cope with what life deals us. Some of us are resilient and some are brittle; the conditions that challenge the one are fatal to the other. For material illustrative of this point, read how we behave in extreme situations (Bettelheim, 1943) and compare such suicides as Marilyn Monroe, Michael Wechsler (1972), or Sylvia Plath (1971) with individuals who have emerged more happily from similar circumstances.

A first, personal conditioner of happiness is *health*—physical health. We have seen that mental health is almost synonymous with happiness, but physical health underwrites happiness although it does not define it. It is the physical decay and pain that account for much of the misery of older people.

Physical health varies with how we live, but it is also a function of the materials of which we are made. Our bones, muscles, glands, and nerves are part of this physical constitution. We are *not* biochemically or neurologically equal (Williams, 1956). Our different neural "wiring" builds the temperament that helps or hinders our adjustment.

The origins of our differing personalities need not be debated, however, in order to read the evidence of the kinds of individuals who are more and less content. To summarize generally: The happy person tends to be healthy, extroverted, optimistic, religious, compassionate, independent, productive, self-approving, work-happy, and ambitious within the limits of his possibilities. Sex differences make little difference to contentment. IQ, too, seems unimportant (Block, 1961; Wilson, 1967).

This description of the characteristics of the happy person is almost a definition of happiness. In science, much of what we know is circular. At least, so it seems *after* we know.

IS HAPPINESS AN ACHIEVEMENT OR A BY-PRODUCT?

Happiness is a state that is seldom achieved but more frequently *realized as a by-product.* It is doubtful whether anyone can intend to be happy as he can intend to learn French, fly a plane, or make more money. Happiness is one of those objectives that slips away when we try to aim for it directly. The contented state is a *result,* but not a result that can be planned.[4] It is an effect of what we are and how we live. These whats and hows have been described by their social locations and in individual tempers. It is popular to phrase these descriptions as prescriptions. It is comforting to be told what to do, and it is assumed, particularly in North America, that if people *know* what to do, they *can* do it. This assumption is weak, and our translation of the conditions of contentment into recommendations is made with the acknowledgement that our abilities to change ourselves are limited.

THE HAPPINESS PRESCRIPTIONS

For Yourself and for Others

Happiness requires self-love. One has to appreciate oneself. It also requires the love of others, and it involves living one's life not just for oneself but also for some concerned others. The love of self and the commitment to others is a web. It is futile to ask which comes first, me or thee. In the happy state, we go together.

People who do not like themselves are not apt to be liked by others. People who like only themselves are in a similar fix. We do not gain the love of others—which makes us happy—by asking for it. We get it from being a "person," which, in this sense, means one who can stand alone.

There is nothing new in this prescription. According to the Talmud (Auerbach, 1944), the Rabbi Hillel said it 2,000 years ago:

> If I am not for myself,
>   Who will be?
> If I am for myself alone,
>   What am I?
> If not now, when?

Relations and Proportions

Happiness sometimes rests upon a contrast effect. It varies with where we are as compared with where we were and where we hope to be. This is a reason why some people who have gone through hell seem happier than others in similar present circumstances. It is a reason why refugees from oppressive states are so often greater patriots in their newfound land than the natives of the host country.

The contrast effect provides one way of observing that happiness is relative. Contentment shifts with what we want relative to what we are apt to

---

[4]Some intelligent people continue to find this surprising. So the novelist Virginia Woolf (1921) exclaims, "And the other way about it was equally surprising—that is, when everything was arranged—music, weather, holidays, every reason for happiness was there—then nothing happened at all. One wasn't happy. It was flat, just flat, that was all."

get. Two people climb the social ladder and arrive at similar social positions. One, however, has come to believe that more is due him. When that "more" is beyond his reach, he turns sour. *Opening opportunities increases discontent.* More accurately, opening opportunities increases discontent when

The actors operate in an ideological climate that denies the rules of the game under which differences in reward are achieved.

The achievement that is possible requires abilities that the aspirant does not have.

A neighbor's luck is better.

Past achievements have been divorced from merit, that is, have been *given* rather than *earned.* This condition describes the process of producing a "spoilt" child.

These statements, today, have an unpleasant ring for many persons. This does not deny their validity, of course. Sociologists since the great Emile Durkheim have noted an association of contentment with fixed social position and an increase of discontent with raised horizons. The quotation from Baughman and Dahlstrom concerning poor children in the rural South (p. 22) is an illustration. Industrial and military research confirms the example. For instance, Stouffer and his colleagues (1949) studied the factors affecting military morale during World War II. These investigators discovered that dissatisfaction with promotions was *greatest* where the probability of promotion was *highest* (in the Air Force) and that discontent was *least* where the chance of promotion was *lowest* (in the Military Police).

This sentiment of relative deprivation underlies another fact: That social revolutions more frequently occur when social conditions have been improving rather than when they have remained constantly poor (Brinton, 1938; Davies, 1962).

Such patterns of relative discontent have been produced experimentally as well as observed historically. For example, "game theorists" have demonstrated that the schedule of outcomes—how rewards are distributed—makes a difference in players' satisfactions. In these laboratory games, people who win *the same amount of money* experience different degrees of satisfaction depending upon how their winnings have been apportioned. Within a range of possible gain, those who win in smaller units are less happy than those players who win the same amount but with some bigger portions. However, the players who extend their expectations to include high but rare gains—the long-shot bettors—have a lower average level of satisfaction. From a survey of research on such games, Parducci (1968, p. 90) concludes that "If the best can come only rarely, it is better not to include it in the range of experiences at all. The average level of happiness can be raised by arranging life so that high levels of satisfaction come frequently, even if this requires renunciation of the opportunity for occasional experiences that would be even more gratifying."

Here is an experimentalist's answer to the old question: "Will you be happier with a few rare ecstatic moments or with more frequent but less intense pleasures?" The answer favors the ancient Greek recommendation of moderation. It is an answer that has found its way into the French proverb which says that "The better is the enemy of the good."

The historical and experimental findings can be converted into a generalization: *The happier person is one whose needs are proportional to his means.* Stretching our talent is good for us; wanting the improbable makes us sick.

Health

Health is a fount of happiness. Much of our health is given us. It remains for us to guard it. There is more to this than training physicians, building hospitals, and extending medical insurance. These instruments doctor us once we have fallen into disrepair. They do not significantly affect the health of a population (Cassell, 1973). In the context of modern sanitation and control of communicable disease, how we live becomes more important to our health and our longevity than how we are treated after we are ill.

The prescription for health is part of folk knowledge. It should be no novelty to people who have gone to school. The recipe starts with the advice of that durable baseball pitcher "Satchel" Paige, who used to urge, "Go lightly on the social ramble; 'tain't restful." The prescription goes on to recommend a balanced diet and a routine of physical exercise. It advises caution about using the "comforting chemicals" (Chapter 8), and it recommends abstention from the habituating drugs. In the Western world, the opportunity for health that affluence provides is rejected by considerable numbers of people who eat too much, smoke too much, and exercise too little.

Pasts and Futures

One way to remain miserable is to live in the past. Many neurotics walk backwards into their futures, regurgitating their sad pasts. It is difficult to turn such people about. The turnabout is recommended, however. The future is going to happen to us anyway; it happens best when we confront it face-forward. We may then have a chance of steering events instead of merely having them happen to us. The advice is pleasantly rhymed in a German proverb:

Glücklich ist	Happy is he
Wer vergisst	Who forgets
Was nicht anders ist.	What cannot be changed.

Happy people live in the present, but they consider their futures. They make plans, but without counting on every one. Like the wise investor, the happy person does not put all his resources in one spot. There is, again, a balance between his investment in the future and his enjoyment of the present.

Cracked Mirrors

The sociologist C. H. Cooley (1902) described how much of our feeling about ourselves depends upon the reflections we see in those "mirrors" that others hold up to us. We learn something about ourselves from the way others treat us. Their regard or disregard works like a looking glass in which we see ourselves as better or worse individuals.

There are some intimates—parents, spouses, lovers, and enemies—who hold up distorting mirrors in which we see ourselves as incompetent, immoral, useless, annoying, stupid, and ugly. It makes us neither healthy nor happy to live with people who reflect only our failures and never our accomplishments. In such cases, a change of mirrors is recommended. There *are* some people, even those with whom we may be "officially connected," who are not good for us.

VOCATION

It is difficult to be happy if one feels useless, and it is difficult to feel useful unless one *is*. A vocation is a calling. It is work that exercises the individual's talents and interests while it satisfies the needs of some others.

Upon his retirement, the prominent psychologist E. L. Thorndike remarked, "I am a fortunate man. I have been paid all my life for doing what I would just as soon have done anyway."

That is the prescription: Find out what you enjoy doing and then ascertain how these interests might be channeled into activities that others will reward you for doing.

IN SUMMARY

The person who is able to follow this sixfold path is happy. He appreciates himself and loves others as well. His goals are proportioned to his means. He balances work with play, the present with the future, and he protects his body, the vessel of all pleasure. He is able to distinguish friend from enemy and sickening intimates from sound ones. His work expresses his interests and contributes to the satisfaction of other people's needs. Such a person is apt to find himself loved. He may be close to realizing happiness as it was defined by our Athenian cousins centuries ago: "The full use of one's powers along lines of excellence."

Chapter 3

Meaning of Mental Health

Being happy can be thought of as a state in which our concerns are manageable. The description of this state has shown it to overlap specific concerns such as worries about money, personal identity, work, and health. The overlap is particularly noticeable between health and happiness, and what has come to be called mental health is almost the same as being happy. The main questions are: "What are the styles of mental disorder, what are their sources, and what can we do about them?"

WHAT ARE MENTAL HEALTH AND MENTAL DISORDER?

To be sane is to be "sound." To be healthy is to be "whole."

These words imply a standard. The standard of health is *proper function*. There is little difficulty in applying this standard to the assessment of *physical* health because there is agreement about the proper functioning of our organs. We tend to agree about the soundness of a limb or the health of a heart. We have fairly standard conceptions of how these physical units ought to act. More to the point, both physicians and patients are likely to agree about the *mal*function of our bodily parts.

The situation is different, however, when disorders of the mind are considered. The mind is *not* an organ. *"Mind" is a word referring to a complex of emotions, thoughts, and actions.*

Although the mind is not an organ, it is, in practice, given an inexact physical address. The convenient, but imprecisely designated domicile of the mind is the central nervous system, more particularly the brain, and, even more narrowly, that portion of the brain, the cerebrum, that is the most recent development in the evolution of the nervous system.

If we do not attend too closely to how the words "mind" and "mental" are used, it is a convenient first approximation to call the brain the home of the mind. If, however, we listen to people talk about their minds and if we read a manual of mental disorders such as that prepared by the American Psychiatric Association (1968), it is apparent that the disturbances called mental range from those immediately and narrowly determined[1] by a deficiency or an injury in the central nervous system to behaviors that are part of "the total personality." In the "personality disturbances," the causes are unknown or disputed and, while the causes include the operation of the brain, of course, they may also lie beyond this location in glands and other tissues.

A Definition of Mental Disorder

These considerations permit no more exact definition of "mental disorder" than this: *A mental disorder is a deviation from some standard of behavior, thought, and feeling (1) for which the cause is either a developmental defect or an injury in the central nervous system or (2) for which the cause is unknown but is attributed to activity of the central nervous system.*

This definition has several implications. It implies:

1   That some standard of right action underlies our conceptions of mental health and illness.

2   That not all differences in behavior are called disease.

3   That our responses to bizarre behaviors differ as we define such behaviors as illnesses rather than as moral defects.

4   That our responses differ, also, as we define the *causes* of the bizarre behaviors as mental rather than physical.

5   That the disorderly behaviors that concern us differ in their course, in their quality, and by degree.

Standards Are Required

There must be some standard of how people ought to feel, think, and act before one can be judged mentally ill. There are such standards, and some of them have rather universal application. But as we move from considering extreme behaviors toward the middle range of conduct, there is dispute about how abnormal an act must be in order to be abnormal enough to be called sick. In this border land between "far out" feeling and thinking and more standard conduct, cultural differences intrude to define what is normal and acceptable

---

[1]"Immediate and narrow" determination means "is sufficient to cause." That is, there is little need to look for additional causes. The physical injuries are enough to account for the behaviors being studied and our curiosity rests.

and what is crazy. Thus "getting the power on you" at a Wednesday night prayer meeting is a sign of religiosity among the participants. The hallucinations, fits, and trances experienced "under the power" are "normally abnormal." The celebrants, at least, do not believe their actions or those of their brothers and sisters to be sick. If, on the other hand, one behaves the same way alone on Main Street, his acts receive a different interpretation.

The standard by which behavior is judged as sane or insane is *efficiency.* This includes efficiency in getting along with other people and in coping with reality. Individuals who exhibit similar symptoms are judged to be more or less sane depending upon their intelligence, that is, depending upon their competence (Hamlin and Ward, 1973). Pathological symptoms appear more sick when demonstrated by dull persons that by bright ones.

Every group of people who persistently live together shares some conception of reality and some conception of its effective grasp. Those who are grossly deficient in knowing this reality and in handling it are considered to be mentally aberrant. Again, at the extreme of inefficient conduct, there is close to universal agreement about sanity. There is more leeway in definition, however, as we get closer to normal behavior. Here cultures differ. They differ in the range of behaviors considered normal, in their tolerance for peculiar manners, and in the kinds of efficiency they require. Along this border, definitions of behavior make a difference. For example, Hsu (1951) showed that normal Chinese behavior was more neurotic by American standards than normal American conduct. On American tests of neurotic traits the mainland Chinese studied by Hsu scored as more disturbed. Hsu concluded that "A trait may be called 'neurotic' in one culture because it hinders the happiness and efficiency of living."

Deviation Is Not Necessarily Disease

To talk about mental disease and mental illness is to encourage the idea that a particular physiological malfunction can be specified for each category of disturbance of thought and feeling. This is possible for only a limited number of abnormalities—cases in which organic injury can be shown to account for the behavioral deficiency, as, for example, when a syphilitic infection can be demonstrated to have damaged the central nervous system. Such *organic* damage has been identified for only a small portion of those abnormal states called mental illness,[2] and there remains a great range of deviant behavior for which no specific physiological malfunction has been isolated. These nonorganic disturbances are usually distinguished from the organic defects by the title *functional.* They must have a physiological basis, of course, despite our inability to identify it, since there can be no mental activity without physiological activity. There is no mind without body. However, given the uncertainties about the physical bases of many aberrations, it is wiser to regard these

---

[2]While *some* mental disorders can be traced to brain damage, *not all* brain damage results in behaviors considered to be psychopathological (Werry, 1972).

extremely unpleasant and inefficient ideas, emotions, and behaviors as signs of mental disorder or mental disturbance rather than as symptoms of mental disease. This labeling helps discourage the false hope stimulated by the notion of disease—namely, the assumption that if there is an illness, there are doctors with cures. The idea of a disease contains the notion that there is a specifiable, singular cause. Thus tuberculosis is said to be caused by the tubercle bacillus.[3] *Disorders,* on the other hand, have less definable causes than *diseases.* They are, therefore, less open to rational manipulation. This conception better accords with the present state of the psychotherapeutic arts.

Moral Attitudes and Treatments Vary with Definitions of Deviations as Diseases or Disorders

Despite the fact that many mental disturbances cannot be identified as diseases, there is a *moral consequence* of the attempted definition of deviance as a medical problem. We do not ordinarily blame a person for contracting a disease. Consequently, calling the offensive behaviors of others "sick" tells us to treat these people rather than to punish them, restrain them, or ignore them.

Moral Attitudes and Treatments Vary With Definitions of Deviations as Physical or Mental

Notice that the popular usage of the word "mind" *contrasts it with* "body." There is a tendency to speak of behaviors as mental when the source of feelings and beliefs cannot be accurately and immediately traced to the function of a specific organ or group of organs. This can be tested by listening to everyday speech and by observing the differential treatment given physical as opposed to mental illness. Thus a depression that can be traced to a thyroid deficiency is less likely to be called a mental disorder and more likely to be spoken of as a symptom of the physical disease. Similarly, defective behaviors that result from brain injury are perceived to be physical deficiencies and, although one may speak of the patient's mind as having been affected, the treatment and the regard given him acknowledge his physical impairment. We do not exhort a brain-damaged person to "be better."

A contrary impulse is provoked, however, when a disturbance is called mental. The concept of the mind is allied with the notion of free will, with the assumption that a person can control his mind, change his or her attitude, and think differently, quite apart from anything that is going on in his physiology. It is assumed that one can wish or will to think differently and that, in doing so, one behaves differently.

It is not denied that we can "talk to ourselves" and change some behaviors. We can "decide" to hold our breath, relax an arm, or count to ten. The important question concerns the *range* of feelings, thoughts, and acts that can be thus consciously controlled by the actor. The answer to this question is

---

[3]This is not entirely true, since other agents are involved in determining the illness of those whose bodies are invaded by tubercle bacilli. In such cases, the TB germ is *necessary* for the diagnosis of the disease, but it is not always *sufficient* to produce the illness.

embedded in ideologies, in competing faiths. *Westerners with more schooling and greater privilege have more faith in the power of positive thinking than their less educated and poorer fellows.* People of higher social status are more aware of psychological problems than are lower-class persons, and they more frequently attribute abnormal behavior to "mental" sources. By contrast, lower-class persons tend to see emotionally unpleasant behavior as due to "unhappiness, tough luck, laziness, meanness, and physical illness" (Hollingshead and Redlich, 1958, p. 175).

It is no surprise to find that lower-class people are more likely, therefore, to want and to receive physical treatment for their mental disorders while middle- and upper-class people have been the principal recipients, and advocates, of the "talking therapies" (Brill and Storrow, 1960). This may well be another case in which schooling has been misleading and where folk knowledge is more accurate than sophisticated belief.[4] Persons with more schooling tend to believe that people who behave in a disturbed fashion do so because their thought is disordered. They come to this conclusion because people who *behave* peculiarly also *talk* that way. Since how one *speaks* is used as a principal indicator of how one *thinks* and since bizarre behavior without known physical cause has been defined as mental disease, middle- and upper-class logic calls for treatment of the disordered person's mind. The therapy that follows from this logic tries to correct how one thinks by reasoning, persuasion, and insight. This kind of therapy has a remarkable record of failure— remarkable in that so much time and money have been spent on the verbal procedures and remarkable in that schooled people continue to have faith in such healing despite its poor record. Summaries of the failures of the talking therapies can be found in Eysenck (1966) for adults and Levitt (1957) for children.

A reason for the wrong conclusion about "mental illness" more frequently drawn by middle- and upper-class persons is that they have confused a *part* of the disorder with its *causes*. Talking and thinking crazily are *part* of being disordered, but they are probably not its causes (see Chapter 4). Here again, there seems to be a confusion of a correlation with causation. Nevertheless, whichever side one takes in this debate, it is clear that defining abnormal behaviors as mental diseases lends them a different coloration and a different treatment from defining them as neurochemical disturbances or even as the consequences of sin, as one psychologist has urged (Mowrer, 1964, 1967).

Disorders Differ in Their Careers, in Their Qualities, and by Degree

The state of our mental health fluctuates somewhat. There are situations that distress us or buoy us, and there are longer segments of our lives during which "the condition we are in" may be depressing or exhilarating.

---

[4]There are other situations in which education (or, at least, schooling) seems irrelevant, if not inimical, to better judgment. For example, guessing how the world operates and what the future will be is unrelated to amount of schooling. When schooling is associated with an optimistic view of the world, it produces *poorer* estimates of what is apt to happen (Avison and Nettler, 1975).

If we allow for these situational variations, however, *a continuity of temperament* is discernible. The *career* of our emotional lives is more likely to remain as it has been becoming than it is to show dramatic change. The evidence of continuity is impressive. It includes long-term observations of individuality in temperament (Honzik, 1966; Thomas et al., 1970; Sontag, 1963), in "cognitive style" (Mischel, 1969; Schimek, 1968; Witkin, 1973), in social adjustment, and in other personality dimensions (Kelly, 1955; Roff, 1961; Zax et al., 1968).

It takes time, naturally, to identify a pattern, and the course of our lives becomes more clear the longer we observe each other. This explains why older people tend to see more continuity in personality than do younger observers. It is a fact, too, that underwrites the idealism of the young and the skepticism of the old.

The careers of our mental lives are themselves a variable. There are tempestuous individuals who go through cycles of mood. Others slide continuously downward into despair with, at times, bright moments of "remission." A few individuals become better than they were, more in control of their lives and more sound.

These differences in the course of our mental well-being complicate its description. So, too, does the fact that there are qualities to our careers. That is, the content of our mental disturbance may differ. We are not equally prone to the same style of disorder. Some of us withdraw from conflict and retreat from life. Others are vulnerable to physical symptoms and become immobilized by their "nerves." Some individuals have difficulty containing their rage or making it efficient. They are inclined to attack their imagined or real miserable worlds with damaging consequences but feeble results. Still other persons are injustice collectors. They feel constantly put upon, and they persistently have problems with people. They go through life "demanding to see the manager."

These differences in the *quality* of disorder and in its *career* are further complicated by the variations in *degree* of disturbance. We are better or worse by more or less.

These are three dimensions along which we may be described as less than sane—by the *quality* of our disorder, by its *career,* and by its *degree.* The fact that we can be less than whole in this combination of patterns has important implications for how we define each other.

On Verbal Categories

A first implication is that *it is more accurate to describe ourselves with adjectives or verbs than with nouns.* Nouns are substantial; they drop us into categories which fit us more or less well but from which it is difficult to escape. When, for example, we say that, "She *is* a schizophrenic," the *is*ness obscures the degree, the quality, and the pattern of that individual's difference. When we say, instead, that "She is schizoid" or that "He behaves 'schizally,'" the adjective and the verb connote degree and possible variations in quality. Most of us who are moderately disturbed are not that way every day all the way. We fluctuate a bit. This fluctuation by degree leads to a second implication: *The fact that we are more or less disordered tends to give a moral credit to those we love and a moral debit to those we hate.*

The preceding chapter noted that we tend to forget the unpleasant. This is particularly true when the unpleasantness has come to us from some loved one. There is, then, stronger motivation to forgive and to define the damage as accidental, situational, or otherwise uncharacteristic. A contrary impulse may be generated toward those whom "we did not like anyway" (Nettler, 1974, pp. 139–140). In the case of the disliked person, we are more apt to see continuity in his or her disorderly conduct, which we blame upon this person's disposition (Regan et al., 1974a).

If our concern is with personal protection, the first impulse is the more dangerous. Those who are hurt by ones they love have difficulty believing it. Since there are degrees of craziness and periods of sanity apart from the lunacy, these disturbances tend to be attributed to—blamed upon—something outside the actor. In support of this attribution, one can always find a counselor who will contend that the injury inflicted by the disturbed person was "caused," and that "the cause" is something transient, uncharacteristic, understandable, and hence, with hope, removable.

An Advice Each person's response to these implications will vary with the price he or she is willing to pay for love and hate. The only *impersonal* counsel that can be given, then, is predictive: *The more frequently someone has hurt us, the higher the probability that this person will do so again.*

On Calling Names Sociologists have sensitized us to the injustices committed by hanging labels on people. It is recognized that some part of our treatment of others depends upon the images evoked by the names we call them. The sociologist's warning is that these labels may be wrongly applied. The word "stereotype" has been borrowed by social psychologists from journalists to refer to those images of others that are caricatures—partly true, partly false, but always exaggerated. More recently, under the influence of the popular "labeling school," it has been claimed that the *behavior* of those to whom we attach titles is itself determined, to some unknown degree, by the differential way we behave toward them as we call them good or bad names.

There is truth in this suggestion. There are also disadvantages in assuming that this sociological hypothesis is nothing but the truth. Three disadvantages can be summarized briefly:

1 *Stereotypes are true as well as false.* The error in stereotyping has been assumed, but it has not been adequately tested (Nettler, 1970, pp. 29–30). When folk images of others are examined for their truthfulness, they seem to be more accurate than inaccurate (Mackie, 1969, 1973).

2 While it is possible to give illustrations of the damaging effect of stigmatic labels, as, for example, Shoham (1970) has done so well, *we do not know the degree to which, or the conditions under which, applying the label*

(making the diagnosis) does affect the behavior of the labeled. The evidence thus far does not support the assumption that bad names cause much bad behavior (Hagan, 1973).

3 Last, and most important for the present concern, *labels are both indispensable and useful.* We may change the tags, but we do not eliminate them. We may substitute adjectives and verbs for the sticky nouns, but we continue to categorize people. There is a survival value in doing so, and the sensible attitude is not to try to eliminate categories but to make them more accurate.

Names function as a psychological shorthand. They provide abbreviated descriptions of what a person has been doing, of what goes along with that doing, and of what we can reasonably expect. More accurately, the label may tell us what *not* to expect.

This is a way of saying that *diagnosis* carries with it a *prognosis.* The names we call each other may do us good, therefore, as well as harm. Everything hinges on the validity of the diagnosis, and diagnosis is always less than certain. This uncertainty characterizes all our judgments about how to behave—from whether to carry an umbrella today, to whether to marry him or her, to how much to invest in what kinds of care for the mentally disturbed.

The present point is that, while there are risks in diagnosis, *the risks are always taken,* whether by omission or by commission, whether by believing a diagnosis or by rejecting it. We have called a caution by recommending that we appreciate each other with adjectives or verbs rather than with nouns, but the adjectives and verbs are still diagnostic categories even though they have greater flexibility than nouns. *There are times in our lives when learning the name that fits what we, or others, have been doing yields a predictive advantage, an economy, and a relief.*

An illustration is provided by the distinguished journalist James Wechsler (1972). Wechsler, in collaboration with his wife, Nancy, and their daughter Holly, has done us a service in describing their efforts to save the life of his son Michael, who committed suicide after years of treatment and the ministrations of eight expensive psychiatrists. At one period in the struggle, the father tells us what everyone who has suffered knows: *That a definition, even a vague one, may be better than continued fumbling in the dark.* Wechsler writes, "Up until this point the word *schizophrenia* had rarely been applied to Michael in our presence by the long succession of therapists we had encountered, but now Dr. Sixth employed it freely. In a way it seemed a relief to have a diagnosis offered. Schizophrenia was not considered incurable. Unfortunately, as we were to discover later, neither is it very precisely definable—sometimes it appears to be a code word expressing psychiatric bewilderment over the failure of usual methods" (p. 113, emphasis his).

Despite our reluctance to call names and our acknowledgement that every label carries a risk of being wrongly used, we continue to categorize people and actions. We may shift from nouns to adjectives and verbs and we may change the labels, but some nomination will persist. It is important, then, to look at the names commonly given to categories of mental disorder.

WHAT KINDS OF MENTAL DISORDERS ARE THERE?

Western psychiatrists tend to classify mental disorders into ten broad groups, following the system of the American Psychiatric Association (1968). Each of these ten categories has subclasses, some of the more common of which are listed below:

I   Mental Retardation: "subnormal intellectual functioning [originating] during the developmental period" (APA, 1968, p. 14)

II   Organic Brain Syndromes—with or without psychosis: "disorders caused by or associated with impairment of brain tissue function" (ibid., p. 5)

III   The Psychoses—not attributable to brain damage:
1   The schizophrenias
2   The affective psychoses, such as melancholia and manic-depressive illness
3   Paranoid states

IV   The Neuroses:
1   Anxiety neurosis
2   Hysterical neurosis
3   The phobias
4   Obsessive-compulsive neurosis
5   Neurasthenia
6   Hypochondriasis

V   Personality Disorders and Certain Other Nonpsychotic Mental Disorders:
1   Personality disorders
a   Paranoid personality
b   Schizoid personality
c   Explosive personality
d   Antisocial personality
2   Sexual deviations
3   Alcoholism
4   Drug dependence

VI   Psychophysiological Disorders: physical disturbances that are presumably psychological ("mental") in origin

VII   Special Symptoms:
1   Speech disturbances
2   Special learning disabilities
3   Tics
4   Disorders of eating, sleeping, or evacuating

VIII   Transient Situational Disturbances

IX   Behavior Disorders of Childhood and Adolescence:
1   Hyperkinetic reaction
2   Withdrawing reaction

   3 Overanxious reaction
   4 Runaway reaction
   5 Unsocialized aggressive reaction
   6 Group delinquent reaction
X Conditions without Manifest Psychiatric Disorder:
   1 Marital maladjustment
   2 Occupational maladjustment
   3 Dyssocial behavior

These categories have been listed to illustrate the gamut of behaviors that are considered to be indications of mental disorder. They run a range from organic defects to personally discomforting symptoms of probably mixed organic and sociological causation to difficulties in living with others. The mental disorders cover a wide spectrum of the miseries we experience, excluding only the miseries produced by our physical environments, our social systems, and those injuries we receive from rational, human predators (about which see Chaps. 13, 14).

A detailed discussion of each of these disturbances can be left to textbooks of clinical psychology and psychiatry. However, our social concerns are addressed in some part to keeping ourselves and our loved ones sane and, as citizens, to making an informed response to the severely disordered. These ends require definitions of some of the major mental disorders and consideration of their possible causes and cures.

Some Interesting Disorders Defined

Several of the ten categories of disorder we have outlined need no further definition for present purposes. However, three of these styles of disturbance deserve description here because they are common abnormalities that may affect our private lives and about which we have some concern as citizens. It is worthwhile to distinguish *psychotic* from *neurotic* behavior and both of these modes of conduct from an intriguing kind of antisocial character, that of the *psychopathic personality.*

    On Being Psychotic   The principal criterion for calling behaviors psychotic is their *divorcement from reality.* Again, this criterion becomes less clear as we get closer to normal behavior and dispute among ourselves how things "really are." At the extremes of abnormal conduct, there is less disagreement that an individual has broken with reality. When a person tells us, for example, that he is God and acts in accordance with this delusion, granting us great favors like bits of his feces wrapped in gift tissue, most of us will agree that he is crazy. When Michael Wechsler tells his psychiatrist that FBI agents and others are watching him from the tops of buildings and that he suspects his mother of being an FBI emissary (Wechsler, 1972, p. 113), there is consensus that this person is not living in our "real" world. The definition of lunacy is that, to a greater degree than our group can tolerate, such individuals have lost contact with reality.

In addition to this sign of psychosis, the deranged individual usually suffers marked *emotional disturbances,* such as extreme depression, frenzy, or "flat affect." Flat affect or *anhedonia* is a lack of pleasure in living, the inability to feel enthusiasm, to take joy, to "do" anything. These moods are accompanied by *intellectual deterioration* (an inability to "think straight") and by *social regression* (behavior that we consider more appropriate to a child). There is *loss of that control* over one's emotions, thoughts, and behaviors that is required if we are to live together. Sexual appetites and hostile impulses are not restrained. They are expressed beyond the limits of our group's tolerance.

On Being Neurotic   The neurotic person is distinguished from the psychotic by the fact that he sees reality as most of us do. He is still functioning in the "real" world although he does not function as well as he should. The neurotic may imagine other worlds, as do the rest of us, but he does not believe that he lives there.

The hallmark of neurotic behavior is *anxiety.* The psychotic person may also experience anxiety, so that we tend to reserve the label of neurosis for those anxious persons who do not demonstrate an organic basis for their symptoms and whose intellectual functioning is not grossly impaired.

Anxiety is abnormal concern. It is often described as a "freefloating" fear, objectless except as it is attached to a specific condition or thing as in a phobic state. A popular way of designating the neurotic is to call him inefficient. He performs less competently than we think his talents might allow.

We all may be somewhat insecure in a particular circumstance, but, as a matter of degree, the neurotic lives with a more persistent tension, the physiological signs of which are similar to those produced in a frightened person. A neurotic experiences more strain, particularly in interpersonal and competitive situations. The strain is notable in a variety of signs such as speech disorders, uncontrollable worries, headaches, the inability to sleep, compulsive eating, sexual impotence, wet and trembling hands, bitten nails, shortness of breath, dizziness, the weeps, inexplicable fatigue, and an abnormal fear of failure and an accompanying demand to be right.

One heavy-drinking neurotic patient described the tension succinctly when she said, "I never have a waking, relaxed moment unless I'm loaded."

"You mean," she was asked, "that when you go to the beach with your husband, and you're all alone at some picnic spot, and the sun is shining down warm, you can't relax then? Just shut your eyes and zonk out?"

"No," she replied, "never." Her movements support her report. There is constant, quick motion. Strain. Discomfort.

Some neurotics are *obsessed* as well as "merely" anxious. They have silly ideas that they cannot get rid of. The ideas are silly by their standards as well as ours. They may then act *compulsively,* that is, in accord with the annoying idea. For example, the obsession might be the notion that, if one does not count the stairs one climbs, something awful will happen. The compulsion is to count. "Disobeying" the obsession produces anxiety. A sometimes correlated state has been termed *psychasthenia* or *neurasthenia.* It refers to exhaustion without discernible cause—feelings of fatigue, weakness, irritability, and lack of initiative.

It is apparent from these brief descriptions of psychosis and neurosis that the signs overlap. They overlap each other and normal behavior. This makes diagnosis difficult; but, again, at the extremes definition becomes clear. At these extremes, the basis for regarding people as neurotic or psychotic is social. *The standard is incompetence.* The inefficiency is measured by the sufferer himself, who feels that he cannot do what he wants, and it is measured by those others who live with him and who are disappointed or wounded by his lack of control.

On Being Psychopathic   These neurotic and psychotic disabilities contrast with a third mental disorder, the diagnosis of which is again social. Some individuals appear sane, or at least not crazy, and they do not seem neurotic. They live in our world. They are competent, particularly along the lines of persuasion. They may even be charming. They do not suffer the anxiety of the neurotic or the strange feelings and ideas of the psychotic. They look like us, yet they suffer from a dangerous disability. By our standards, *they have no moral sense.*

People with this defect have been called various names. The most popular current term is *psychopath.* The psychiatrist Cleckley (1964) studied such individuals in depth and described them by the title of his analysis as wearing *The Mask of Sanity.* According to Cleckley, the mask of sanity covers a damaging combination of such characteristics as these:

1   Average or superior IQ
2   Freedom from the "cognitive slippage" and the "irrationality" that marks the psychoses
3   Freedom from anxiety
4   No sense of responsibility
5   Disregard for truth
6   No sense of shame
7   Antisocial behavior committed without compunction
8   Inability to learn from experience; repeats the same escapades and injuries
9   "Poverty of affect," that is, the subject does not feel the sympathy and empathy that we regard as normal
10   Lack of insight, that is, the subject does not seem aware of others' conceptions of him or her
11   Little responsiveness to special consideration or kindness

12 No history of sincere attempts at suicide
13 Sexual peculiarities: sex is either regarded casually or the drive is weak
14 Impulsiveness
15 Onset of these characteristics appears no later than the early twenties

There are many ways in which this combination of characteristics can be packaged. The philosopher Davie (1973, p. 58) provides this description:

> Scott is a great charmer. He is always easy to talk with, always interested in doing something. He has a bright, friendly, almost puppy-like quality about him—a bit mischievous, fun-loving, not at all malicious or secretive. Scott always exudes self-confidence. There is never a sign of nervousness or insecurity in him. If you were to meet him, you would immediately sense that he has a high grade intelligence. Despite his obvious intelligence, however, Scott dropped out of high school after his second year and never went back.
>
> You wouldn't have to know Scott for long in order to discover that he is a glib actor. He is able to sound so sincere that it is hard to believe at first that he would intentionally tell you a lie. But in fact he lies often, easily, and earnestly.
>
> Scott is extremely showy when he is in public. He will, for example, feign fierce anger whenever he has an opportunity. But in truth Scott's feelings, whether of anger or affection, always turn out to be rather shallow and fleeting. His anger never lasts for long, neither do his feelings of love or affection. One time at a Christmas party Scott said frightful things about his wife—in public—not ten minutes after he had displayed the greatest affection for her. He likes to be the center of attention.
>
> The really remarkable thing about Scott is his propensity for getting into trouble. He finds trouble wherever he goes, with family, neighbors, police, "friends." Scott drinks to excess and when drunk, or pretending to be, he is liable to do almost anything. He has no compunctions about fights, theft, vandalism, obscenity, and so forth. Later he will plead that he is deeply sorry for all the trouble he has caused, that he is certainly going to turn over a new leaf. Naturally, people believe him.

As an antidote to "intern's disease," or the catching of symptoms by reading about them, it must be remembered that all behaviors and their combinations are matters of degree. Furthermore, although Davie's example, Scott, is a man, it should not be inferred that only males are psychopaths. As far as we know, psychopathy is not sex-linked and women may be as vulnerable as men to this disorder.

Some attention has been given here to the psychopathic personality as a category of mental disturbance because this class of conduct illuminates the *social* conception of disorder, because it is relevant to theories of the sources of mental and emotional abnormality, and because the psychopath is involved in some of the styles in which we kill each other, which are described in Chapters 13 and 14.

THE RISK OF BECOMING MENTALLY ILL

It is difficult to estimate the risk of becoming mentally deranged because the statistics of disorder vary with the severity of the symptoms used to define "mental illness" and with the sensitivity of the diagnostic instruments. If, however, admission to a mental hospital is taken as the measure of risk, it is probable in Western countries that as many as one in every ten babies born each year will be hospitalized at some time during its life (Goldhamer and Marshall, 1949). For the United States in recent decades the annual hospital admission rate for the psychoses has been running around 20 per 100,000 population (Felix and Kramer, 1953).

If we count the prevalence of disabling psychological symptoms rather than just hospital admission rates, it appears that at least one in four persons and perhaps as many as one in three experiences a lessened efficiency from discomforting thoughts and feelings for some considerable segment of his life (Leighton, 1955; Srole et al., 1962).

In short, a large minority of us are hampered by annoying doubt, tension, worry, and feelings of insecurity. These emotions have their physical signs and their social and financial costs. In the United States, for example, over \$1 billion in public funds is spent each year for the care of mental patients. This sum is undoubtedly much less than that spent privately for psychological counseling and for chemical relief. The care of psychic disabilities is a multibillion dollar industry in advanced nations.

THINKING ABOUT MENTAL DISORDER

When we think about abnormal behavior, we tend to think about its causes. The search for causes is often futile, but the motivation to inquire about them is built into our language, a language that is saturated with causal terms. The inquiry is also moved by the assumption that finding causes will provide cures. It is important, then, to look for the causes and cures of derangement, as the next two chapters do.

Roots of Derangement

Our efforts to understand ourselves and our world are marked by an often futile attempt to locate the causes of what ails us. This is not the place to enter into a detailed philosophical discussion of what is meant by causation or of how causes can be known. The interested student will find that these questions are tangled and more difficult to answer than is assumed by our easy talk about what causes what.[1] However, as an introduction to a consideration of the causes and cures of mental disorders, some general principles concerning the nature of causation deserve attention.

KNOWING CAUSES AND GETTING RESULTS

In outline, these principles are that:

1 It is not necessary to know causes in order to make predictions.
2 It is not necessary to know the causes of behaviors in order to control the behaviors.
3 The search for causes sometimes produces poorer prediction than operating with "experience tables."

---

[1]Some of the styles of causation and the political uses of these styles are described by Nettler (1970, pp. 145–170).

4 The search for causes is often morally and politically motivated.
5 Knowing the singular or few causes of events in a "closed system" increases our efficiency.
6 Knowing the *necessary* cause of an event may not be sufficient to give us control of that event.

Each of these principles can be explained briefly.

1 *It is not necessary to know the causes of behaviors in order to be able to predict conduct better than by random guessing.*

The forecasts we make in everyday life are built upon projections from the regularities we have observed. This kind of prediction can be formalized. It then becomes "actuarial," based upon experience tables, and it allows us to improve our guesses about what is likely to happen *without* consideration of the causes of those events.

2 *It is not necessary to know the causes of events in order to control them.*

We can and do put out fires without stopping to quarrel about their causes. We behave similarly in response to other of our concerns, including those concerns that are generated by human behavior. History is full of illustrations of our ability to repress the undesirable actions of others without attention to the alleged causes of their behaviors. We may or may not approve of these controlling responses, but the present point is only that control need not wait upon knowledge of causes. See, for example, how the Thugs, a hereditary religious sect that lived by robbery followed by ritualized strangulation, were repressed in India (Bruce, 1969). Or notice how the Mafia was at one time controlled in Italy (Pantaleone, 1966).

3 *Searching for the causes of actions sometimes produces poorer predictions, and less control, than "mere" bets from experience.*

This is another way of saying that many causal theories about human behavior are incorrect. Insofar as this is so, an actuarial prediction—one that draws a trend line or makes bets based on past performance—is more accurate than a theoretical prediction—one based on hypotheses about causes.

This proposition has been variously tested. For example, Fancher (1966, 1967) has shown that abstract conceptions about people ("theories," in this sense) lead to poorer predictions of behavior than estimates drawn from the assumption that people will continue to behave as they have. Thus Fancher finds a *negative* association between accuracy in judging others and the number of courses taken in psychology ($r = -.17$) and with course grades in abnormal psychology ($r = -.31$). Additional evidence that "too much theory" about the causes of behavior decreases accuracy in judging it is provided in research by Kelly (1952) and by Weiss (1963).

4   *In the social arena, the search for causes is strongly motivated by moral and political preferences.*

One reason why causal theories may be incorrect is that our ethicopolitical preferences often find some evidence unacceptable.

When we are morally motivated, we seek not all the causes or the most powerful causes of the events that concern us but, more congenially, only those causes that we wish to change. Our desires influence our choice of causes (Nettler, 1973). *Truth* (how things really are) is consistently at war with *utility* (what agrees with our morality or how we want things to be).

The history of science is pocked with illustrations of the human inability to accept "immoral evidence" despite its validity and of the human proclivity to change one's "scientific conclusions" to accord with one's morals without there having been any change in the facts. For example, Provine (1973) demonstrates the latter tendency among biologists studying the genetics of racial mixture. In Provine's demonstration, the *morals* of scientists changed their *beliefs* without there having been any change in their *knowledge.*

5   *Where singular causes or a few causes can be isolated operating in a closed system, we can increase the efficiency of our manipulation of the environment.*

This is the case, for example, when we "treat" a "sick" automobile engine. We know what makes engines work, the system of causation is fairly closed (not influenced by many external events), and we can therefore isolate and repair the cause of a faltering motor.

By contrast, much of the human conduct that concerns us does not occur in such a compact field of force. There are multiple and linked determinants of our behaviors. What affects our lives is better thought of as a *web of causes* than as a *chain of causes.* We are therefore less able to do any one thing or to find the necessary source of most of the conditions that concern us.

This principle tells us to beware of intellectual salesmen with pat solutions. If the causes of our miseries are not well known, neither are the cures. If the search for the causes is heavily influenced by what we *want* rather than by how things *are,* we are even more likely to be persuaded into social action that "does something," but not what it promises.

6   *Knowing the necessary cause of an event is not the same as knowing the sufficient causes.*

That which is *necessary* to produce a behavior may not be *sufficient* to produce it. Moreover, the necessary cause may be relatively unimportant in the web of causes. This sounds contradictory, but it is not. For example, a physician who had spent years studying tuberculosis once commented that he thought that the tubercle bacillus (the *necessary* cause of the illness) was the least important factor in its production. There are apparently a host of other conditions that must go with the presence of the bacilli before one succumbs to tuberculosis.

IN SUMMARY

These six points should be borne in mind as we consider the mental disorders, but they also pertain to our analysis of other concerns. The debate about the causes of mental disturbance is as much influenced by our morals and our politics—by what we would like to see done—as it is by reasoning from data.

WHAT CAUSES THE MENTAL DISORDERS?

There are three broad locations in which we search for the causes of human behavior, including disordered behavior:

    In the constitution of the actor
    In the impact of his social environment
    In some combination of the two

    Within each of these regions of causation, there are, of course, more particular sites that can be selected as determinants of the way we are. The *constitutional* search may focus upon our genes, our prenatal environment, the function of our hormones, or the "wiring" of our frontal lobes. The *sociopsychological* search may look at family environments, institutional arrangements, or the conditions under which we make a living. Last, these particular causal locations can be *combined* in more patterns than there are chess moves.
    To complicate matters, the importance of any of these possible causes will vary with the kind of disorder studied. We believe, for example, that genetic constitution is more determinative of schizophrenia than of neuroticism.
    All of these qualifications should be applied as one reads the hypotheses advanced to explain the mental disturbances.

THE GENETIC BASIS OF MENTAL DISORDER

There is abundant research demonstrating that how we are is strongly influenced by our physiologies and that the physical materials with which we function are principally given us through genetic transmission. Although genes, the chemical source of our constitution, have now been photographed in action (Miller, 1973), the evidence for genetic transmission of the mental disorders has not been based on knowledge of specific gene contributions. Research is moving closer to this possibility, however (Wyatt et al., 1973). To date, the evidence of genetic determination is largely *statistical,* a matter of comparing the incidence of a class of disturbances among relatives of varying degrees of hereditary distance. The probability of a disorder appearing among kinfolk of varying hereditary closeness is then compared with the risk in a general population of being diagnosed as suffering from a particular mental disability.

With refinements, this procedure has been employed in the study of the genetics of a broad spectrum of disorders ranging from the functional psychoses and neuroticism to types of criminality, homosexuality, and addiction (Eysenck and Prell, 1951; Gottesman, 1963; Kallman, 1938; Rosenthal, 1971; Slater, 1953). The logic of such investigations can be illustrated, along with a summary of their findings, for schizophrenia, one of the more distressing deficiencies. This disability accounts for half or more of all hospitalized mental patients in Western industrialized countries. In turn, mental patients occupy from one-third to one-half of the hospital beds in such nations. Rosenthal (1971, p. 64) gives a figure of 40 percent for the United States. Such statistics mean that, at any one moment, between one-sixth and one-fourth of hospitalized patients in affluent lands are suffering from schizophrenia.

The fundamental fact with which genetic and environmental theories contend is that *the risk of becoming schizoid increases with schizophrenia in the family.* For example, Zerbin-Rüdin (1967) has calculated the chance of a person becoming schizophrenic from the results of twenty investigations encompassing varying periods between 1928 and 1964 in six European countries. He gets an overall estimate of the expectancy of schizophrenia for the European general population of 0.85 percent, a figure slightly higher than the psychiatric rule of thumb of 0.80 percent at risk. When this expectancy is compared with the risk among relatives, it is apparent that the hazard increases with the genetic proximity of schizoid kinsmen. Slater and Cowie (1971) present a chart of these increased risks adapted from Zerbin-Rüdin's extensive summary and reproduced in Table 4-1.

It is notable that the probability of a schizoid person having a schizoid parent is much lower than the probability of his having schizophrenic siblings or children. This results from the fact that schizophrenics rarely produce children after the onset of their disturbance. This fact requires statistical adjustments for the age of parents at the time of birth of a schizoid case, the logic of which need not delay us here but which can be read in Essen-Möller (1955).

Twin Studies   A sensitive method of testing the genetic contribution to mental disorder is through a comparison of monozygotic (MZ) and dizygotic (DZ) twins. The MZs develop from the splitting of a single fertilized egg—one ovum and one sperm. Such twins are invariably of the same sex[2] and so much alike in appearance and temperament that they are commonly called identical twins. By contrast, the DZs are more like brothers and sisters who happen to arrive together. DZ twins develop from separate ova and separate sperm. Their genetic composition is therefore more variable than that of the identical pairs.

---

[2]There have been rare cases reported of intersexed MZ twins in which sex differences were noted between the pair (Edwards et al., 1966).

Table 4-1   Expectation of Schizophrenia in Relatives of Schizophrenics*

Dates	Number of studies	Relationship	Size of sample	Number schizophrenics	Expectation, percent
1928–1962	14	Parents	7,675	336	4.38
1928–1962	12	Siblings	8,504	724	8.51
1932–1962	10	Siblings (parents free of schizophrenia)	7,535	621	8.24
1932–1962	6	Siblings (parents not free of schizophrenia)	675	93	13.79
1921–1962	5	Children	1,226	151	12.31
1930–1941	4	Uncles and aunts	3,376	68	2.01
1916–1946	3	Half-sibs	311	10	3.22

*Reprinted from E. Slater and V. Cowie, *The Genetics of Mental Disorders*, Table 4. © 1971 by Oxford University Press. Reproduced by permission.

The logic of twin studies, as applied to the explanation of mental disorder or any other reliably observed behaviors, is to compare the *degree of concordance,* the amount of similarity, between the appearance of the behaviors in MZ and DZ pairs. As Slater and Cowie (1971, p. 348) put it,

> Where there is a high degree of concordance . . . within MZ pairs and a much lower concordance within same–sexed DZ pairs, the hereditary predisposition plays a major role. Where concordance is high in pairs of both kinds (e.g., in some infections, such as measles), the environment common to both twins is the predominant factor; where concordance is low in both (e.g., multiple sclerosis), neither genetical predisposition nor early environment are [sic] important, and factors which operate more randomly in later life (e.g., poisons, infections, somatic mutation) must be the main ones.

An enormous pool of data has been accumulated from twin studies of the mental disorders, particularly with regard to schizophrenia. This research must be read with the consideration that there are age and sex differences in the risk of schizophrenia—males are at higher risk at early ages and females at higher risk at later ages. It is also necessary to consider the differences in standards of diagnosis in different countries at different times, because it is likely that the evidence of genetic effect will be more clear in the more severe disabilities (Slater and Cowie, p. 20). With these provisos, one can summarize years of research in several nations as showing a concordance of schizophrenia in MZ pairs that is *five times* as great as the concordance in DZ twins. The differences in expectancy of schizophrenia between MZ and same-sexed (SS) DZ twins is charted in Table 4-2. It is a difference that provides strong evidence of a genetic component in the production of this disorder.

Controlling for the Environment A popular criticism of twin studies argues that the environments of twins are more similar than those of other relatives and that, therefore, environmental factors are not excluded as possible explanations of mental disorder. This argument does not plausibly account for differences in risk of disorder between MZ and DZ twins, but it has been answered, nonetheless, by additional data.

Follow-up studies have been conducted of the incidence of schizophrenia among MZ twins who were separated at birth or in early years and reared apart. The number of such cases is small, but the concordance rate runs around 65 percent. That is, in almost two-thirds of the cases of *separated* MZ twins, the onset of schizophrenia in one of the pair was associated with the development of the disorder in the separated twin (Slater and Cowie, p. 41).

Another way of controlling for the possible impact of the environment in the production of schizophrenia is to compare the incidence of this disorder among children in foster homes and foundling institutions where it has been possible to get information about the presence of schizophrenia in their parents. Heston (1966) began such a study by following the children of hospitalized, actively schizophrenic women. These babies were separated from their mothers at birth and placed in the care of members of the fathers' families or in foundling homes. Heston then selected a control group from the institutions and matched them with his index cases, individual by individual, by sex, age, type of eventual placement, and length of residence in child care institutions. Of the children (five) who became schizophrenic, *all* had schizophrenic mothers, while *none* of the control group developed this disorder. The age-corrected expectancy of schizophrenia among the index group was close to 17 percent, a rate that is similar to the rates reported for children who have *not*

Table 4-2   Degree of Schizophrenic Concordance in MZ and SS DZ Twins*

Investigator	Date	Number	MZ pairs, percent concordant	Number	DZ pairs, percent concordant
Luxemburger	1928	19	58	13	0
Rosanoff	1934	41	61	53	13
Essen-Möller	1941	11	64	27	15
Kallmann	1946	174	69	296	11
Slater	1953	37	65	58	14
Inouye	1961	55	60	11	18

*Reproduced from E. Slater, "A Review of Earlier Evidence on Genetic Factors in Schizophrenia," in D. Rosenthal and S. S. Kety (eds.), *The Transmission of Schizophrenia.* © 1968 by Pergamon Press. Reprinted by permission.

been separated from their schizophrenic parents. Further, other disabilities were more frequently found among the experimental group. The children of these schizophrenic mothers, when compared with their controls, were more frequently mentally retarded, convicted of felonies, "never" married (that is, unmarried by age thirty), and they were more frequently diagnosed as suffering from "sociopathic personality" or "neurotic personality disorder."

Rosenthal and his colleagues (1968) conducted a comparable investigation in Denmark. They started with about 11,000 biological parents who had put up their children for nonfamilial adoption. Omitting the approximately 1,000 cases in which the fathers could not be identified, the researchers examined the hospital records of the remaining 10,000 parents. These were separated into those diagnosed as schizophrenic or manic-depressive and a group without a psychiatric history. From the pool of adopted children whose parents had no record of mental disorder, the investigators drew a control group, matched case by case with the index group by sex, age, age at transfer to the adoptive parents, and the socioeconomic status of the adoptive family. The examiners who studied these children during two days of testing and interviewing did so "blind." They did not know which was the index child and which the control. Furthermore, the children themselves did not know their own familial histories.

This research is still in progress, but some preliminary findings are available. Rosenthal reports (1971, pp. 81–82):

> Among the 39 index adoptees examined, three were diagnosed schizophrenic, but only one of these had been hospitalized. Seven were diagnosed as borderline schizophrenic. Among the 47 control adoptees examined, none was schizophrenic, one was a clear borderline, and two were near or probable borderline cases . . . In addition, the more severe cases cluster clearly among the index cases, 10:1. There could not have been any biasing tendency based on knowledge of which subject was an index case or a control since the diagnostician did not have this information. Therefore, the data provide strong evidence indeed that heredity is a salient factor in the etiology of schizophrenic disorders.

Still another procedure for testing the relative impact of biological heredity and social environment upon the development of schizophrenic disorders has been employed by Kety and his coworkers (1968). This Danish investigation began by following *all* children (some 5,500) given up for *nonfamilial* adoption at an early age. All these adopted children who had been admitted to a psychiatric agency and diagnosed as schizophrenic after reaching the age of risk comprised the index group. From the remaining healthy children, a control group was drawn matched individual by individual with the index group by sex, age, age at transfer to the adoptive home, pretransfer history, and socioeconomic status of the adoptive parents. Then *all* parents, adoptive and biological, as well as siblings and hilf-sibs of both the experimental and the control groups, were identified and the national psychiatric registry studied to find which of these relatives had ever developed a mental disorder. Diagnoses of the disorders were again made "blind." The diagnosticians did not know which were the index relatives and which the control.

A *genetic hypothesis* would predict that the relatives of schizophrenic children would themselves be disproportionately schizoid. An *environmental hypothesis* would predict that the adoptive relatives of the "sick" children were more frequently disturbed. The data in Table 4-3 clearly favor the genetic hypothesis. The biological relatives of schizophrenic children were *four times* as likely to be schizoid as were the biological relatives of the healthier children. When the researchers considered only those children separated from their biological parents within the first month after birth, they found that almost 10 percent of the schizophrenic children had schizoid biological relatives while none of the control children was so handicapped. Among the adoptive relatives of schizophrenic and normal children, no significant differences were found in the incidence of schizoid disturbances.

Comparable findings are reported by Gottesman and Shields (1972) from their intensive study of schizophrenia in twins in London, England. These investigators were careful to control for a wide range of factors that might distort the interpretation of their findings—factors such as the reliability of diagnosis, the determination of zygosity, variations in environment, and the relation between severity of symptoms and degree of concordance. This research is a model of objectivity. It concludes that schizophrenia is "the outcome of a genetically determined developmental predisposition."

Table 4-3   Distribution of Schizoid Disorders among the Biological and Adoptive Relatives of Schizophrenic Index Cases and Control Subjects*

	Biological relatives		Adoptive relatives	
	Total	Sz spectrum	Total	Sz spectrum
All index cases (N = 33)	150	13	74	2
All controls (N = 33)	156	3	83	3
Index cases separated within one month of birth (N = 19)	93	9	45	2
Control class separated within one month of birth (N = 20)	92	0	51	1

*Reproduced from S. S. Kety et al., "The Type and Prevalence of Mental Illness in the Biological and Adoptive Families of Adopted Schizophrenics," in D. Rosenthal and S. S. Kety (eds.), *The Transmission of Schizophrenia.* © 1968 by Pergamon Press. Reprinted by permission.

IN SUMMARY

This sample of studies of the genetics of a mental disorder could be expanded. As we have noted, such research is statistical, and people who are disinclined to accept the *causal* possibility in such correlations argue that a "mere" correlation, even a repetitive and high association, does not prove causation until a disease agent, or agents, is discovered.[3] Research on the chemistry of the nervous system gives promise today of isolating some of the predisposing physical sources of schizophrenia (Wyatt et al., 1973). However, since the genetic structures that might differentially predispose individuals to mental disorder have not yet been mapped, the hypothesis of a biological basis of such disturbances remains in dispute. This hypothesis is particularly opposed by social-environmental theories.

ENVIRONMENTAL EXPLANATIONS OF MENTAL DISORDER

There are two breeds of environmental explanation of mental disorder—as well as of other deviant conduct. The older family of explanations assumes *social stress*, variously defined, as producing the unpleasant behaviors. The newer style of environmental explanation is *political*. It holds that how we behave is less important in determining our fate than is the fact of who has the power to define us and to treat us. These arguments will be considered separately.

Social Stress and Mental Disorder

Environmental explanations of behavioral differences assume that biological differences are negligible and that, in the production of our behavior, *what happens to us* is more important than *how we are*. How true or false this assumption is depends, of course, upon the behaviors to be explained and upon the extremes of environments and of conduct taken into consideration. Some associations that hold at the extreme ranges of circumstance do not obtain as we move toward the middle regions of our lives.

The image employed by stress theories in regarding environments as more and less healthful has been borrowed from engineering. "Stress" refers to the demanding characteristics of the environment to which the person is subjected. "Strain" refers to what the person feels (Freeman, 1960). This model allows for some slippage between the quality of an environment and individual response to it. Given the same stress, not all of us need experience the same strain. However, as we approach some extreme condition—as stress becomes enormous—everyone is strained.

In research practice, this distinction tends to get lost because strain is difficult to measure independently of the behaviors to be explained. If, for

---

[3]As we shall see in Chapter 8, a similar argument has been advanced against accepting the statistical association between prolonged inhalation of tobacco smoke and respiratory and cardiovascular disease.

example, we are testing the hypothesis that social stress produces a psychological strain that results in neurotic conduct, we do not usually have a measure of strain other than the fact that the person is neurotic. As a result of this blending of measures, studies that have used the stress model look for indicators of what are *presumed* to be stressful circumstances and then infer that both the stress and the strain must have occurred if the disordered behavior appears disproportionately under such circumstances.

The Ecological Distribution of Mental Disorder

The major evidence used to support stress hypotheses examines the ecological patterning of disturbances. In the behavioral sciences, the term "ecology" refers to the study of the relations between environments and human behavior, with particular emphasis upon the effects of the spatial and temporal distribution of people. Ecological studies of mental disorder begin, then, with an attempt to map *the social locations* of greater and lesser disturbance. These social locations have been examined principally as *social-class sites,* defined, in turn, by the usual criteria of money, education, and occupational prestige. However, it is possible to employ other ecological criteria, such as how people are physically spaced (Galle et al., 1972) or, more strongly, how they are related to the broader web of their environments (Barker, 1968, 1969; Willems, 1972). The latter type of study, "ecological psychology," is in its infancy.

Ecological studies conducted in a number of American cities agree in showing higher rates of a variety of psychiatric disorders nearer city centers and declining rates toward the suburbs (Faris and Dunham, 1939; Green, 1939; Hadley et al., 1944; Mowrer, 1939; Queen, 1940; Schroeder, 1942). This distribution holds more true for the psychoses, with one exception, than for the neuroses. The exception to this distribution of the psychoses is the manic-depressive (affective) disorders, which are more randomly spaced through urban locations.

This kind of distribution in itself says little about the causes of mental disorder, although it is suggestive of a social-class link. The zones of higher psychotic breakdown tend to be the poorer areas, while neurotic and affective disorders are less clearly correlated with status.

Interpreting the Distribution   It is difficult to assign any causal significance to ecological maps of the mental disorders—in particular, in a way that might test the stress-strain hypothesis—because the interpretation of these maps suffers from at least five intertwined troubles:

1   These maps do not tell us whether the zones differ in *stress*. This can be assumed and debated, but it is not usually measured.
2   In themselves, such maps do not relate the presumed *stress* to the sense of *strain,* nor do they relate either stress or strain to the formation of mental disturbances.

3 These urban portraits are drawn from *reported* disorders rather than from all disturbances. There is room, then, for differences in rate of report among city areas.

4 Ecological distributions alone do not tell us whether something in the status area *produces* disorder or whether disordered individuals or their forebears drift into social niches by reason of their disturbance.

5 Ecological maps are not always plotted from the same tallies. Many do not distinguish between the *incidence* of disorders and their *prevalence.*

Incidence and Prevalence   If one counts the number of first admissions to private and public mental hospitals during a specified time span, he is measuring incidence. If one counts people who have been in hospitals during a particular period, he is measuring prevalence.

An incidence rate is computed from a tally of new cases occurring during a particular time. This measure should not be confounded with a prevalence rate, which is based on an enumeration of all active cases during a period regardless of when they were first reported. An incidence rate can be subdivided into (1) those new cases occurring during the observation period and still active at the end of it and (2) those new cases that are no longer active at the close of observations. Similarly, a prevalence rate includes (1) cases that began before the observation period, that continued through it, and that were still active at its conclusion, and (2) cases that began before the observations but that were terminated during the period.

When the prevalence of disorders is being counted, their incidence is being counted also. However, prevalence rates include other factors than just who is disturbed during a particular time span, since such a measure is affected by differential recovery and mortality rates. That is, some kinds of people who fall ill and are counted in a prevalence statistic may recover or die at a different pace from other kinds of persons enumerated in a health census. This becomes important in interpreting class-linked rates of mental disorder, because once lower-class people are treated for the psychoses, they tend to remain in treatment longer than middle-class persons except, again, in treatment for the affective psychoses (Hollingshead and Redlich, 1958, pp. 295–297). This fact, if it is general in many locations, *inflates* the lower-class *prevalence* rate.

The New Haven Survey   An attempt to disentangle incidence and prevalence statistics and to improve upon earlier ecological studies has been made by a psychiatric census that set out to count all persons in the New Haven metropolitan area who were "in treatment with a psychiatrist or under the care of a psychiatric clinic or mental hospital between May 31 and December 1, 1950" (Hollingshead and Redlich, 1958, p. 19).

This study was addressed to two questions unanswered by earlier research on the distribution of the mental disorders: "Is there an association between social position and mental disturbance?" "Does psychiatric treatment vary with social status?"

Social status was measured with a weighted index composed of ratings of residence, occupation, and education derived from interviews with a representative 5 percent sample of households. The index was then cut into five segments, as follows:

Class I "The upper class," which constitutes about 3 percent of the population. It is made up of families living in expensive residential areas whose heads are college graduates and who are either professionals or executives of large companies. There is considerable inherited wealth at this level.

Class II "The upper middle class," which includes about 9 percent of this community. It is composed of people who have had some education beyond high school, who live in the better residential districts, and whose heads are managers or in the lesser-ranking professions. This class has less inherited wealth than Class I and fewer graduates from the elite private schools. According to the researchers, "this is the most status-sensitive stratum in the population" and it experiences "a continuous strain" to maintain a social front (ibid., pp. 85–95).

Class III "The lower middle class," which constitutes a little under 21 percent of the community. The women in this stratum frequently work and their husbands are semiprofessionals, foremen, or skilled workers, or they own small businesses or work as salaried white collar employees.

Class IV "The working class," which accounts for almost half the households. About half the men here are semiskilled workers; 35 percent are skilled manual employees. One percent are "petty proprietors," and the remainder are clerical and sales workers. Median years of schooling is 10.5 for the wives and 9.4 for the husbands.

Class V "The lower class," which constitutes just under 18 percent of this community. About half the employable adult males are semiskilled workers, while 46 percent are unskilled. Two percent of these men have never had a regular job. Most of the adults in this class have not completed elementary school and they live in tenements, flats, and semirural slums.

Along with these indexed differences in status go differences in ethnicity, religion, and attitudes toward the world—differences that are richly described by the investigators.

The Findings: Is Social Status Associated With Mental Disorder?   The investigators report that "the lower the class, the greater the proportion of patients in the population" (p. 216). This finding remains true when sex is held constant, but the relation is "less intense among females than males" (p. 200). The association becomes more true after age twenty-five than during younger years, and a similar pattern of class-linked disorder is exhibited by blacks and whites. Further, the general picture of greater disturbance as one descends the class ladder holds up whether one measures incidence, reentry into treatment after a previous release, continuous treatment during the research period, or whether one combines these measures into a prevalence rate adjusted for age and sex. The authors conclude, "Even though the age and sex corrected rate per 100,000 for each component [of the prevalence rate] is related significantly to class status, the dramatic differences in rates from the higher to the lower classes are highlighted by the cases in continuous treatment" (pp. 215–216).

A Qualification Critics of the New Haven study have argued that it is misleading to interpret its findings to mean that there is a uniform increase in mental disorder as one goes down the status ladder. Miller and Mishler (1964) reanalyzed the New Haven data and demonstrated that the association of mental disorder with social class is different for the neuroses and the psychoses and that the conclusions drawn depend upon whether one is looking only at prevalence rates or at those rates along with incidence, reentry, and continuous treatment rates. The important result of the Miller-Mishler reassessment has been to show that *it is Class V, sometimes called the underclass, that differs significantly from the remainder of the population.* It is this class that "pulls" the distribution. Ignoring the gap between Class V and the other strata conceals the lesser differences among Classes I through IV. From their analysis of the Hollingshead-Redlich figures charted in Table 4-4. Miller and Mishler conclude,

> There are *no* significant differences among social classes I–V in the incidence of new cases of neuroses. There are *no* significant differences among classes I through IV in the incidence of new or old cases of neuroses *or* psychoses. Class V has significantly different and higher rates of new and old cases of psychosis (and the inclusion of Class V in the computations suggests that Class IV has a *lower* rate of reentry of neurotics than the other classes) [p. 30, emphasis theirs].

Social class and treatment. The New Haven research is a better study of who is being treated and how than of who is mentally disturbed. The findings

Table 4-4   Incidence, Reentry, Continuous, and Prevalence Rates per 100,000 for Treated Neuroses and Psychoses by Class (Sex- and Age-Adjusted)*

Class	Incidence	Reentry	Neuroses Continuous	Prevalence
I–II	69	44	251	349
III	78	30	137	250
IV	52	17	82	114
V	66	35	65	97

Class	Incidence	Reentry	Psychoses Continuous	Prevalence
I–II	28	44	117	188
III	36	38	217	291
IV	37	42	439	518
V	73	88	1344	1505

*Reproduced from A. B. Hollingshead and F. C. Redlich, Social Class and Mental Illness: A Community Study, Table 16. © 1958 by John Wiley & Sons, Inc. Reprinted by permission.

are straightforward. The higher the social status, the more likely is the patient to be treated in private hospitals and by physicians in private practice. The lower the status, the greater the use of veterans' and state hospitals. Public mental health clinics are seldom used by Class I and II persons. For both the neurotic and the psychotic disorders, patients of higher status tend to receive psychotherapy while lower-class patients are more frequently given custodial care and organic therapy (shock, surgery, drugs).

This pattern of treatment will be considered "just" or "unjust" depending upon (1) whether one has more or less faith in psychotherapy and (2) whether justice is judged from *outside* the doctor-patient relation or from the point of view of the patient and his family. Our doubts about the effectiveness of psychotherapy will be discussed on pages 87–91. Here it need only be noted that Hollingshead and Redlich surveyed patients' conceptions of mental disorder and their attitudes toward treatment with the finding that patients tend to get the kind of help they want and understand. "The need and value of insight therapy is not appreciated by lower-class patients," say Hollingshead-Redlich.

> Class IV and V persons seek material help in the form of pills, needles, obscure rays, and ritual; some actually seek support and sympathy [p. 346]. Less than two percent of the Class V patients understood the aims or techniques of psychotherapy . . . Even among the Class III's who were able to talk about their problems, there were some who never grasped the meaning of psychotherapy and hoped that after "all the talking" comes the "treatment" [p. 339].

The authors regard these lower-class attitudes as grounded in ignorance and as obstacles to treatment. However, given the poor record of the psychotherapies, the plea from Class I–II researchers for more psychotherapy for Class IV–V patients (p. 378) raises the ancient question, "Who guards the guardians?"

The Midtown Manhattan Survey　A different way of studying the social distribution of mental disorder has been employed by a team of researchers in social psychiatry (Srole et al., 1962). This investigation, to which we referred in Chapter 2, was designed to test the hypothesis that "biosocial and sociocultural factors leave imprints on mental health" (p. 31). The hypothesis was tested by counting *symptoms* in a representative sample of urban households rather than by counting patients in treatment. Care was taken to ensure the reliability of data recorded from interviews with 1,660 individuals. The symptoms reported by these persons were grouped by their severity into four health categories: "well," "mild symptom formation," "moderate symptom formation," and "impaired." The distribution of these ratings appears in Table 4-5.

The investigators provide reasons for believing that the high "impaired" rate discovered, almost one person in four, is not excessive. It does not seem to be a distortion attributable to peculiarities of the people in New York or their living conditions, nor is the figure out of line with other surveys of the prevalence of psychic symptoms.

**Table 4-5   Respondents' Distribution
on Symptom-formation Classification
of Mental Health***

Well	18.5%
Mild symptom formation	36.3%
Moderate symptom formation	21.8%
Impaired	23.4%

*Reproduced from L. Srole et al., *Mental Health in
the Metropolis: The Midtown Manhattan Study.* © 1962 by
McGraw-Hill Book Company. Reprinted by permission.

Symptoms and Social Class   Using six strata of socioeconomic status, the
Manhattan survey finds a distribution of these signs of mental disturbance that
accords well with other research and with what we think we know about the
conditions of health and happiness. The class distribution of symptom categories is shown in Table 4-6.

*For that majority of people (58.1 percent) who experience mild to moderate
signs of disturbance, there is no variation among the social classes.* The
proportion of "well" people is highest in the upper strata and lowest at the poor
levels. As with the New Haven data, there is a *striking break* between the two
lowest strata and the other classes. Conversely, with one small inversion
between strata A and B, there is an increase in impairment as one descends the
status ladder.

IN SUMMARY

The sociological maps of mental disorder draw a boundary between the
majority of citizens in modern societies and an underclass at the bottom of the
status ladder. This poor stratum suffers disproportionately from the schizophrenias and from the more disabling psychic signs. Upon crossing the frontier
from this impaired stratum into working society, however, it becomes difficult
to find any striking differences in the distribution of the psychoses and
neuroses among the social classes.

**Table 4-6   Distribution of Respondents (Ages 20–59) in Mental Health
Classification by Parental-SES Strata in Midtown Manhattan, Percent***

Mental health category	Parental-SES strata					
	A	B	C	D	E	F
	(High)					(Low)
Well	24.4	23.3	19.9	18.8	13.6	9.7
Mild symptoms	36.0	38.3	36.6	36.6	36.6	32.7
Moderate symptoms	22.1	22.0	20.1	20.4	20.4	24.9
Impaired	17.5	16.4	24.5	29.4	29.4	32.7

*Reproduced from L. Srole et al., *Mental Health in the Metropolis: The Midtown Manhattan Study.* © 1962 by
McGraw-Hill Book Company. Reprinted by permission.

Where Is the Stress? Who Feels the Strain?

What is confusing for the stress-strain hypothesis in these sociological maps is, first, that we have no adequate measure of differences in stress or strain up and down the status rungs. Second, while investigators may call the causes they are looking for stresses, that does not make them such. At least, such a title does not convert a stress into a strain, and many persons who are supposed to be under stress from the investigator's point of view report no strain. One of the investigators in the Midtown Manhattan study puts this phenomenon in these words, "Many respondents verbalized the mitigating effects of the wide prevalence of a stress factor" (Langner, 1963, p. 318). This means that many of the people studied said that conditions that were supposed to be distressing did not bother them when they were perceived to be *general* conditions.

There is a converse to this point too, namely, that some individuals who do *not* appear to be under stress exhibit strain. This characterizes the multitude of neurotics of whom we say things like, "Why should such a talented, good-looking girl feel so insecure?"

Last, the stress-strain issue is confounded by the fact that, depending upon the researcher we read and what he has been studying, we can find stresses described for every style of life. Hollingshead and Redlich have told us that it is the upper middle-class that experiences a particular strain, the anxiety of the status-striver. On the other side, there is the reported stress of poverty and the tension of being reared in an unruly household. Even here, however, we can find experts who reverse the location of stress.

We have seen, for example, that Wixen holds that it is sickening to be born rich. Green (1946), on the other hand, finds distinctive possibilities of neurosis among middle-class boys who are reared in a bind between submitting to parental demands and being independent achievers. Green goes further. He holds that while the "good" middle-class family makes neurotics of its boys, the children of working-class Polish immigrants remain sound in their brawling, authoritarian environment because they are not emotionally involved. A not dissimilar picture is portrayed by Vidich and Bensman's study (1958) of life in Smalltown, U.S.A. In this rural backwater, it seems that the only psychologically healthy persons may be the underdogs, "the shack people [who] live a private code of pleasure, relaxation or debauchery" (p. 290).

This babel about who is under stress becomes more confusing as one hears messages from authorities who tell us that stress may be valued (Langner, 1963, p. 139) and even that *stress is good for us.* Here, for example, is an exchange between the late Senator Robert Kennedy and the psychiatrist Robert Coles in testimony before a U.S. Senate subcommittee on urban problems:

Senator Kennedy: Going into some of these areas and looking at the faces of the children between the ages of 6 and 12, and then comparing, walking along Fifth Avenue and seeing the faces of children between the ages of 6 and 12 who come from very wealthy homes, my impression, strong impression, is that the ones who come from these ghetto areas are much, much happier than the ones who are being pushed along in their programs. Do you think that is true or not?

Dr. Coles: This is a very touchy point and one, of course, immediately runs the risk of being called a romanticist and everything else, but this has been the most puzzling kind of experience for me, because I treated upper middle class children.

How do you tell the contented American middle class that craves every kind of new method of child training and that has elevated us [psychiatrists] to a position of secular lay priesthood that their children need suffering and stress? No, you don't tell them that.

Anna Freud, Sigmund Freud's daughter, at times I think has a little more sense than her father, particularly these days: I think that after she had worked with children facing the blitz in London, she commented . . . that perhaps the mind under suffering develops strength, that the mind that is in luxury not only does not develop but cannot develop, and progressively loses its ability to develop this kind of strength . . . I think the objective at times of school administrators and even teachers, certainly I know people like me, is to kill that, to say we don't want that. It is inappropriate. It is too much for us. There may even be envy . . . (Coles, 1967, p. 45).

What Should We Conclude?   A personal advice is to stick with the data. The data do *not* measure stress. They count diagnoses or reported disabilities. The data tell us that mental disturbance is rather generally distributed among rich, poor, and middling people who are in the work force. It is only as we cross the border into extreme poverty and separation from working society that there is a quantum jump in the amount of mental disorder. The unanswered question is why? One kind of answer holds that there must be some sickening influence in our civilized way of living. Another kind of answer says insanity is a matter of politics, of who has the power to apply diagnostic labels. A third reply combines the genetic and environmental points of view. Each of these replies will be described.

Civilization and Its Discontents

One way of coordinating the ecological findings with the stress-strain hypothesis is to claim that there are stresses in civilized society that hit the lower classes particularly hard. This assumption gains support from the observation that poverty in the rural areas of modern societies seems *not* so strikingly associated with disabilities as it is in the urban jungles. It is then reasoned that perhaps it is "civilization" that drives us insane, and references are made, always in vague terms, to the hectic life, personal insecurity, and competitive pressures that allegedly affect the denizens of capitalistic, industrialized societies. In this vein scholars have called Western culture "schizoid" (Bain, 1935) and Western societies "sick" (Frank, 1949).

The thesis that it is industrial, urban civilization that makes us sick is popular. However frequently it is debunked, it revives. It is, nevertheless, *false.* The *content* of symptoms varies with culture, but recognizable disorders paralleling those in modern societies have been described for societies at all levels of complexity—including stable and isolated primitive communities. The literature on primitive psychopathology is extensive and, while there are reports of populations relatively free of psychosis, there are innumerable accounts of neurotic and psychotic behaviors among preliterate peoples (Demerath, 1942; Laubscher, 1937; Winston, 1934).

Furthermore, *within* industrial societies, even those ethnic enclaves that have resisted the allegedly stressful elements of the competitive world around them are not free of mental disorder. Thus we have reports of high proportions of mental disturbance in isolated Norwegian and Swedish communities (Essen-Möller, 1956) and among rural, religious communities in North America. Eaton and Weil (1953, 1954, 1955), for example, conducted a careful census of the symptoms of mental disorder among Hutterites in Canada and the United States. These people are descendants of German sectarians who migrated to North America from southern Russia in the late nineteenth century. They live in colonies in the Dakotas, Montana, and the prairie provinces of Canada where they practice pacifism and communal ownership of property. Their social life is harmonious and their history shows no record of murder, serious physical attack, sex crime, or arson. A high standard of living is provided with guaranteed economic security. Luxurious living is taboo, including such sinful temptations as overstuffed furniture, radios, cars, television, movies, and jewelry.

The Eaton-Weil survey found no psychopaths among these people and only a few cases of schizophrenia. There were, however, significant numbers of neurotics and manic-depressives. The authors conclude that "although our data on the Hutterites' mental disorders clearly demonstrate the inadequacy of a purely sociological approach to the problem of mental health, they do show that culture has a large influence in shaping personality" (1955, p. 237).

Substantiation for this type of finding is provided by Goldhamer and Marshall (1949) who analyzed rates of hospital admissions for psychosis in Massachusetts. These investigators compared rates in the nineteenth century from the 1840s on with rates a hundred years later. Despite the increased urbanization during the period of their study, Goldhamer and Marshall did *not* find any increase in the rates of the functional psychoses except possibly for increases among the elderly.

Civilization may have its discontents, as Sigmund Freud told us (1930), and there may be unpleasant consequences of our disaffection, but neurosis and psychosis are not among them.

The Politics of Mental Disorder

A popular sociological idea has been promoted during the past decade under the title of the "labeling" or "societal reaction" school. This way of regarding social phenomena shifts attention from how abnormally people *behave* to how groups *respond* to the abnormality. It assumes that, at some starting point, we are equally prone to peculiar or disturbed behavior, but that some of us, usually those of lower status and lesser power, get caught and singled out for stigmatization. A "scarlet letter," the label of some shameful difference, is hung upon the miscreant, and he or she is marked for life. It is assumed, than, that a "secondary deviance" is generated (Lemert, 1951), and that, cut off from participation as a normal person, the labeled deviant is forced into the role of the abnormal. It is assumed that if the stigmatizing title had not been applied, the deviant could have been saved from a life of peculiarity. Once applied, however, the label sticks and identifies a difference. The identification, it is held, makes a difference in the way others regard the deviant, and this allegedly reinforces the deviant in his difference. "Being cast out means being outcast and makes it comfortable for the stigmatized to band together in defense of their egos and in justification of their 'peculiar' interests" (Nettler, 1974a, p. 203).

This thesis is appealing because it sides with the underdog and sees injustice in the application of shameful labels to abnormal people. It is appealing, too, because there is some truth in it. There is no doubt that this process, which Tannenbaum (1938) called "the dramatization of evil," occurs. There is no doubt that some stigmatized people have their options closed by the reaction of those who read their labels. This seems particularly true in the case of a person labeled criminal. However, sociologists have been busy pointing out how other behaviors *might* be molded into roles assigned actors by the label-applicators. This possibility has been used to explain paranoia and stuttering (Lemert, 1962, 1967), physical illness (Lorber, 1967), mental retardation (Mercer, 1965), and, of course, neurosis and psychosis (Braginsky et al., 1969; Plog and Edgerton, 1969; Scheff, 1966).

The logical conclusion of the labeling hypothesis is that there are no *real* individual differences. There are only *perceived* differences, the perception of which is motivated by interests (personal gain), imposed by power, and justified by the discriminatory label. "Insanity" becomes merely another such label which, according to this school, does not reliably or universally mark off sick behavior from healthy. Thus madness may be more sane than sanity, and neurosis, including the involuntary soiling of one's trousers, may be, in the words of a British essayist, "a form of obscure social criticism, not stupid at that, and needing interpretation" (Nott, 1964, p. 91). Ms. Nott is joined in her view of neurosis by an English psychiatrist, R. D. Laing (1967, p. 100), who claims that "there is no such 'condition' as 'schizophrenia,' but the label is a social fact and the social fact a *political event*" (emphasis his). In similar vein, an American psychiatrist, Stern (1972), argues that reality, like beauty, is in the eye of the beholder, and that "what is tragic is not that the average madman believes in his delusions, but that he does not believe *enough* in them" (p. 37, emphasis his).

This attack on the idea of mental illness has been motivated, in part, by abuse of the notion of mental disease. The term has been stretched, by kind people, to cover any bad behavior that is supposedly not the actor's fault. Calling the bad behavior sickness removes the blame and the urge to punish and tells one to treat or help the "sick" bad actor. Thus, at the height of psychiatry's popularity in Western countries, almost any malfunction or misery was called sick. People who divorced were thought to be sick because they had failed at marriage (and one is not supposed to fail in this arrangement). Delinquency and criminality were also considered to be signs of illness, as were racial prejudice, prostitution, homosexuality,[4] and "authoritarianism." The roster of mental disorders grew so large that some psychiatrists rebelled and began to speak of "the myth of mental illness" (Szasz, 1961). This reaction, as taken over by the labeling school, has now reached the point at which some students claim that there is no such thing as lunacy. This unsound idea has been publicized recently by an interesting research that has been widely misinterpreted and which, therefore, requires comment.

Can Psychiatrists Tell the Difference Between the Sane and the Insane?

The idea that hanging bad names on people condemns them to the roles inscribed on the labels has been given favorable publicity by a clever experiment conducted by Rosenhan and his associates (1973). Rosenhan and seven men and women had themselves admitted to twelve mental hospitals in five American states by faking symptoms. These "pseudopatients," as Rosenhan calls them, told the admissions office that they had been hearing voices. When asked what the voices said, the "crazy" actor replied that "they were often unclear, but as far as he could tell they said 'empty,' 'hollow,' and 'thud'" (p. 251).

After being admitted to the asylum, each pseudopatient immediately stopped faking any symptoms of disorder. Apart from falsifying names, vocations, and employment, no further alterations of "person, history, or circumstance" were made.

Rosenhan found that despite the sane behavior of these simulated patients *after* they had been admitted for psychiatric help, none was found out. What is worse, many normal acts were given an abnormal meaning in the hospital. In three cases pseudopatients were observed taking notes on their experiences. This was recorded on their nursing charts as "Patient engages in writing behavior" (p. 253). Another man was found pacing the hospital corridor. A kindly nurse inquired, "Nervous, Mr. X?" "No," he replied, "bored."

Rosenhan concludes that "a psychiatric label has a life and an influence of its own" (p. 253).

This study does a service in describing the depersonalizing effects of asylums. It also provides additional evidence of the ideological elements in psychiatry and of the way in which diagnostic labels adhere. However, in league with others who have made a sociological school out of such observa-

---

[4]By a split vote, the American Psychiatric Association, 1974, removed homosexuality from its *Manual of Mental Disorders*.

tion, Rosenhan concludes too much. He concludes that "we cannot distinguish the sane from the insane in psychiatric hospitals" and that "we cannot distinguish insanity from sanity" (p. 257).

Evaluating the Politics of Reality

Something called reality is at the heart of the sanity issue. A principal test of mental health is how one defines reality and how one responds to it. The societal reaction school operates with the assumption that reality is always "constructed" and never perceived[5] and that, therefore, being sane or insane is only a matter of who has the power to apply the labels and never a matter of how people really behave. This is a political philosophy, one that runs against common sense (which need not make it incorrect) and one that is not helpful in our search for the sources of derangement and its cure. The inadequacies of the labeling hypothesis can be outlined by saying that:

1   There *are* discernible differences that allow us to distinguish extremely disordered persons from more sane individuals. Rosenhan's conclusion is incorrect.
2   Applying the label of sickness does *not* cause the disturbance.
3   The ethicopolitical preference of the societal reaction school *reduces* predictive power.
4   The recommendations of the labeling school do not help people change their unwanted behavior.

1   *Can We Distinguish the Sick from the Sane?*

The major psychoses and neuroses seem universally to have been recognized as abnormalities—as inefficiencies—although tolerance levels for these differences have varied, as have beliefs about causes and cures. Contrary to Laing and others, there *is* a recognizable condition called schizophrenia. Diagnosis is difficult, of course, and particularly so when it seeks fine categories. At the extremes of behavioral malfunction, however, it is less difficult. A psychiatric diagnosis represents a complex weighing of a patients' history, symptoms, signs,[6] and his performance on standardized tasks (Hoch, 1972). The reliability of psychiatric diagnosis is less than perfect, as is all medical diagnosis. However, when psychiatric diagnosis is confined to broad categories of functioning and is concerned with screening people as relatively psychotic or nonpsychotic, sane or insane, competent or incompetent, there is considerable agreement on the reality of these differences (Lorr et al., 1962; Schmidt and Fonda, 1956; Zigler and Phillips, 1961). How adequate psychiatric diagnosis is

---

[5]There is widespread confusion about the meanings of and the difference between *perceiving* the world and *conceiving* it. The confusion allows some students to write as if they believed that "reality" were only conceived and never perceived. This issue deserves seminar discussion. Some heuristic attitudes toward this issue are expressed by Nettler (1974b-i and Ratliff (1965, Chap. 5).

[6]A symptom is a subjectively experienced abnormality as reported by the patient. A sign is an objective indication of malfunction.

judged to be depends on what one wants to do with the diagnosis. The diagnoses that are good enough for prediction of the patient's behavior, for self-protection, or for legal purposes may not be good enough to facilitate cures.

The Trouble with Rosenhan's Research   The Rosenhan study does not justify his conclusion, congenial to the societal reaction school, that "we cannot distinguish insanity from sanity." This conclusion jumps from the fact of "did not" to the supposition of "cannot." Because psychiatrists and their nurses *did not* later see the sanity in pseudopatients who had complained of abnormal symptoms, Rosenhan concludes that they *could not*. However, the picture of asylums given us by Rosenhan and other observers is one of places geared to custodial care and marked by a harried lack of attention.

The correct conclusion is not that we cannot tell the difference between sound and psychotic people. The correct conclusion is, as we have already noted, that middling degrees of difference are more difficult to identify as sick or well, but that at the extremes of abnormal behavior, there is higher reliability and even universal agreement as to who is living in the real world and who is not. There is more agreement also as we approach the extremes of neurotic behavior, and there is little quarrel about the relative inefficiency of such neurotic feeling as the phobic reports (fears of flying, elevators, clouds, and open spaces) and such neurotic actions as defecating in one's pants.

The very investigators who propose the idea that we cannot tell the difference between sanity and lunacy cannot adhere to their proposition. Thus Rosenhan concludes his research paper by asking, "How many people . . . are sane but not recognized as such in our psychiatric institutions?" (p. 257). The question makes no sense, of course, if "we cannot distinguish insanity from sanity."

Common Sense and Mental Health   The attempt to politicize sanity goes against the grain of people's good sense. At least six major investigations were conducted in the United States during the 1960s that asked samples of the population about their attitudes toward the mentally disordered (Dohrenwend et al., 1961; Dohrenwend and Chin-Song, 1967; Kentucky Mental Health Planning Commission, 1964; Lemkau, 1962; Lemkau and Crocetti, 1962; Meyer, 1964). In these surveys, brief descriptions were presented of the behavior of the paranoid, the schizophrenic, and the alcoholic. Crocetti and his colleagues (1972, p. 3) summarize this research as showing that "none [of these studies] reported less than 90 percent of their samples as identifying the paranoid schizophrenic as mentally ill; no study reported less than 67 percent as identifying the simple schizophrenic as mentally ill, and only one study . . . reported less than 63 percent as identifying the alcoholic as mentally ill." Even among a relatively *poor and uneducated* sample, 91 percent identified the paranoid as suffering from a mental disorder; 78 percent, the simple schizophrenic; and 62 percent, the alcoholic (Lemkau and Crocetti, 1962).

Identifying mentally disturbed people is a social act, but it is not just a "political event" in the sense in which Laing uses the phrase.[7] The identification of mental disorder is not "merely" a perception imposed by the powerful upon the powerless. The categories are in everyman's eyes, and they perceive real differences in behavior.

2 Does identifying the "mentally ill" produce or intensify their behavior?

It is doubtful whether applying the label of sickness causes mental illness. Research addressed to this issue does not support the belief that *identifying* deviants, whether they be mentally disturbed or criminal, significantly alters their behavior. For example, Gove (1970a, 1970b) has reviewed numerous studies on the reactions of intimates to their friends and loved ones hospitalized for mental disorders and on the process by which people come to be mental patients. The data show that the majority of commitments to mental hospitals is voluntary; that is, that the patients themselves seek relief. In this majority of cases, the person is *not* disturbed because others have said so but because he feel so. Furthermore, only a minority of those who seek commitment are accepted, and, when they are, it is on the basis of specific criteria of disorder rather than as a result of a political process based on power differentials. Even in the cases in which others do ask for the commitment of some intimate, the road traveled to this decision is usually long and painful. It is a route marked not so much by "secondary deviance" as by *real* behavior. The real behavior that leads to the mental hospital is not merely peculiar and uncomfortable. It is also frequently dangerous, like repetitive wife beating and threats to kill (Yarrow et al., 1955). Contrary to the labeling hypothesis, research on this matter reveals considerable reluctance on the part of intimates to define a loved one's behavior as pathological (Sampson et al., 1964; Schwartz, 1957; Yarrow et al., 1955). In addition, it does not seem that the behavior of a mental patient upon release is markedly affected by the alleged stigma of hospitalization (Angrist et al., 1968; Freeman and Simmons, 1963).

Again, it is not denied that how others treat us affects us. The crucial question is *to what extent* such treatment determines our sanity *and when.* The answer is, once we have become neurotic or psyehotic or psychopathic, not much.

The overall contribution of the societal reaction school to our understanding of the causes of undesirable behavior is slight. Hagan (1973) draws such a conclusion from his review of the general application of the labeling hypothesis and suggests that this point of view became popular among theorists not so much because it was true but because it was interesting. This theme has been interesting because, as Davis notes (1971), it stands common sense on its head.

[7]There can be political uses of the charge of insanity, of course. Thus both the Soviet Union and the United States have been accused of using mental hospitals as substitutes for prisons for persons distasteful to the regime (Bukovsky, 1972; Gorbanevskaya, 1972; Medvedev, 1971; Szasz, 1957, 1958, 1963).

The common sense that says that some people are more disturbed than others and that this is why we respond to them differently—this good sense is turned upside down and made intriguing by the labeling theorist's argument that we are all equally mad but that only some of us are found out.

A Moral Opinion The interpretation of mental disorder given by the societal reaction school demeans the suffering of those neurotic and psychotic persons who seek our help. It locates the causes of such suffering in how people respond to the sick rather than in what troubles them. It provides, thereby, yet another denial of the authenticity of the other person's experience.

3 *Do the assumptions of the labeling school increase or decrease our predictive accuracy?*

If the societal reaction school were correct, behavior ought to be significantly changed when it is differently identified. Changing the label ought to change the conduct.

While differential response might have an impact during formative years, there is little reason to believe that differential response markedly affects the course of adolescent and adult mental disorder. The labeling theorist's implicit prediction is that giving the abnormal person's difference a better name and a better response will alter it. This prediction disregards or denies the significance of personality differences and their continuity. Causal force is attributed exclusively to the social environment, and it is predicted that deviance will diminish or disappear if our attitudes toward it are changed. There is much of Christian forgiveness in this idea, an idea that encourages such optimistic risks as believing that

> He will be honest if I trust him.
> She will be reasonable if you are.
> He will be pacific if we are.
> Her psychosis is not "in her" but in her situation. When the mirrors in which she sees herself are changed, she will change. [Nettler, 1974a, p. 208].

It does not have to be argued that the labeling theorist's prophecy is never true in order to claim that it is more often inaccurate than accurate. Predictions are probability statements. The odds involved depend upon our knowing how much of the behavior to be forecast is *conditional,* varying with circumstances, and how much is *dispositional,* a function of the way the organism is. As regards the psychopath and the impaired neurotic and psychotic, there is no good reason for believing that loving the madman, being kindly to the phobic, or being friendly to the paranoid will alter their thoughts, their feelings, or their behaviors.

4 *Is the attitude of the labeling school therapeutic?*

If the societal reaction school locates the generator of disorder in the wrong place, it is not likely to find the most efficient therapy. The assumption that is implicit in the labeling perspective is that if differences are not acknowledged and not assigned titles and roles, then behaviors will change. The question of who has cures for which disorders will be discussed in the next chapter. However, it is of moment here to note that there are therapies, with as fair a record of success as any others, that operate with the *explicit* assumption that the patient will *not* change until he admits to the *correct identification of what he is and what he does.*

Alcoholics Anonymous began with this assumption—that the compulsive drinker can *not* control his addiction until he admits that he is sick or has an "allergy." The wording of the label is not so important as is the admission of the difference. Synanon, which specializes in the group treatment of opiate addicts, works with the same principle, as does the more recently formed Families Anonymous, which treats childbeaters (Kempe, 1972). For these attempts at therapy, calling oneself the appropriate name is part of the cure.

IN SUMMARY

Two locations have been described in which scholars have dug for the roots of derangement: in the genes and in social environment. Probably the best way of making the search successful is to combine these locations.

HEREDITIES IN ENVIRONMENTS

It is now a cliché of the behavioral sciences to say that no genes function without environments. It follows, then, that what genes produce depends upon the environments in which they operate. The continuing question remains: "How much?" And the answer to this question varies, in turn, with the kind of behavior to be explained.

Those extremes of incompetence and unpleasantness that are recognized as neurosis, psychosis, and psychopathy have a well-documented genetic foundation. The fact of this genetic basis has been more clearly demonstrated than has any specific environmental cause of mental disorder. This does not mean, however, that our constitutions determine our fates.

The Idea of Predisposition

The medical model of an illness that has been employed to understand mental disorder has been criticized, as we have seen. It has been criticized because a "disease," in the medical sense, is a disturbance of proper function for which a specific cause has been isolated. However, in the medical model, a specific cause is not everything that is *sufficient* to produce the illness. It is only that which is *necessary.* Thus there is no syphilis without the spirochete and no tuberculosis without the tubercle bacillus, but not everyone whose body is invaded by such organisms runs the same course or the full course of the disease. The necessary cause does not always produce the disease, does not fix its career, and need not be the most important factor to be attacked in its treatment.

Physicians employ the word "diathesis" to refer to those constitutional differences that make individuals more and less immune to disease. *Diathesis is a constitutional predisposition.* The idea of predisposition is a useful one in understanding mental disorders, and it allows us to bring heredity and environment together in their explanation. This way of thinking about mental illness has been clearly expounded by the psychologist Paul Meehl (1962) with regard to the explanation of schizophrenia. With differences in the possible relative contributions of constitutions and environments, it is a style of thinking that applies also to other functional psychoses and the neuroses.

Neural defect, personality, and mental disorder In brief, Meehl shows, first, that there is agreement as to what is meant by being schizophrenic. The giveaway symptom is disordered thought, what Meehl calls cognitive slippage. The patient makes wild associations such as saying, "Naturally, I am growing my father's hair." In addition, the schizoid person is withdrawn, self-referential, anxious, distrustful, hostile, and unhappy. The schizophrenic cannot think straight, has little fun, confuses his wishes with reality, feels unloved, and, of course, hates people.

Meehl claims that such evidence as we have examined urges the inference that people are differentially disposed to such bizarre thoughts and feelings, that underlying their exhibition is a "neural integrative defect" which Meehl terms *schizotaxia* and "which is all that can properly be spoken of as inherited" (p. 830).

It is then held that the environments in which schizotaxic individuals are reared tend to produce a universally recognizable personality, labeled *schizotype.* Meehl believes that being schizotypic is learned by the schizotaxic individual, but he also believes that, under any social learning schema we know, the translation from genetic predisposition to personality type is highly probable. At this point, other causes may enter to determine whether the schizoid person becomes recognizably ill. If the social mirror is sound and if, says Meehl, "the schizotaxic person also has the good fortune to inherit a low anxiety readiness, physical vigor, general resistance to stress and the like, he will remain a well-compensated 'normal' schizotype, never manifesting symptoms of mental disease. He will be like the gout-prone male whose genes determine him to have an elevated blood uric acid titer, but who never develops clinical gout" (p. 830).

The Schizophrenogenic Mother If we ask what in the environment seems most likely to push a schizotype into schizophrenia, the burden of blame has been placed upon the schizophrenogenic mother. She may, of course, be a schizoid personality herself. The clinical literature is full of descriptions of a mother of such patients who is inconsistently rewarding and punishing, who loves and rejects, and who puts her children into the "double bind" of being wrong if they do and wrong if they do not.

Some scholars have advanced the idea that it is rearing in the double bind that is the strongest determinant of schizophrenia (Bateson et al., 1956). The weight of the genetic evidence does not justify such a conclusion for the more disabling psychoses and neuroses. Such a hypothesis may be more applicable, however, to the explanation of the milder disorders and antisocial behavior.

Deficient Rearing and Mental Disorder   The human shares with all mammals a need to be nurtured, to be "brought up." Being brought up in the double bind of love and hate, of mixed signals, is only one of the ways by which the young are injured. Mammalian infants are made incompetent also by neglect, by isolation, and by consistent rejection.

Three methods have been used to chronicle the effects of inadequate nurturing upon human development: *comparative studies,* in which the emotional status of children reared in institutions and foster families is compared with that of children nurtured by their parents; *retrospective studies,* in which the backgrounds of well and ill adults are analyzed for differences in child-rearing experiences; and *longitudinal studies,* in which children from varied nurturing environments are followed into adulthood to observe the effects of differential rearing upon mental health.

The results of such research can be summarized as follows:

1   The earlier the deficiency in child rearing, the greater the psychic damage.

2   All children are vulnerable to such mental wounding. As a rule of thumb, the first six or seven years seem crucial.

3   Extreme deprivation, isolation, and lack of love result in a mixed package of incompetent behaviors, including anxiety, sadness, withdrawal, passivity, and inappropriate aggression (Goldfarb, 1955).

4   There are marked individual and species differences in response to early deprivation (Fuller, 1967; Orlansky, 1949).

5   The human functions *most* readily affected by deficient nurturing are *cognitive,* in particular, the ability to speak and to understand speech (Bowlby, 1952).

6   The human functions *least* affected by defective rearing are *neuromuscular,* such as walking, manual dexterity, and other aspects of physical coordination.

7   The *social responses,* the ability to get along with others, lie *midway* between these extremes in sensitivity to defective nurturing.

8   Once a child has been injured through such early defects in his rearing, rehabilitation is difficult and it is only partly compensatory. If the therapeutic objective is *full* restoration to what the child might have been had be never experienced extreme deprivation, the rehabilitative effort is futile. In the development of our emotional and cognitive capacities, there are critical periods during which deficiencies in rearing leave damage that is never fully compensated (Lenneberg, 1967).

This summary shows a range of incompetence that may be caused by defective child rearing. Not all these disabilities are called mental disorder, however; and, as we turn our attention from "socially maladaptive" behavior toward the more disabling neuroses and psychoses, we are probably moving the blend of genetic and environmental causes from the environmental toward the genetic.

DOES LOCATING THE CAUSE DETERMINE THE CURE?

A recurring theme of our study of social concerns has been the idea that the search for their causes is strongly influenced by what the seeker wishes to see done. If the investigator wishes to reform society, in part because he or she believes it to be sickening, it will be discomforting to read the evidence of a genetic contribution to mental disorder. The assumption is that if a behavior is constrained by inherited materials, then nothing can be done to change it and social reform must be limited to genetic engineering. This assumption is another weak one. The *necessary* cause of a disorder is not always the *strongest* cause, and the necessary cause need not be attacked in order to modify the course of an illness.

Acknowledging the importance of the human material upon which environments operate sets a limit to our wishes. We agree with Freud, however, that the recognition of our limitations is one definition of freedom. This recognition provides the radical meaning, the root meaning, of Epicurus's belief that knowledge can make us free: *Knowledge frees us of false hope.*

Chapter 5

Therapies

Efforts to heal sick souls are as old as medicine and magic. The treatment of disordered feelings and thoughts has long been part of the expert practice of witch doctors, as it is today of a variety of doctors of divinity, psychology, and medicine. It cannot be said, however, that psychotherapy has kept pace with physical therapy, and the alliance in "advanced" countries between the professions that heal *bodies* and those that would heal *minds* lends a false coloration of science to our treatment of the mental disorders. This is not news to some physicians who themselves have commented on the parallels between the moralist and the psychiatrist (Szasz, 1961) or the shaman and the psychoanalyst (Torrey, 1973).

The question of who knows best how to heal disordered thought and feeling is clouded by the confusion of counseling with therapy and "feeling good" with getting better.

Is Counseling Therapy?

Most persons who are troubled enjoy talking about their worries. "Having someone to talk to" is an important source of relief when we are burdened by grave decisions or desperate emotions. Any person we respect, who listens to us with sympathy, makes us feel better (Sommer et al., 1955). If our auditor has an informed competence, we may use him or her as a counselor. It is assumed that counsel is based on knowledge or, if it is not grounded in knowledge, that it is founded on good judgment.[1]

Counsel tends to be cognitive rather than emotional, although its appeal frequently mixes information with moral prescription. The point is that counseling is distinguished from therapy by the presumed *greater control* over his decisions on the part of the counseled client as opposed to the treated patient.

The counselor can help us clarify our situation and he may give us information about the likely consequences of different courses of action, but the *decision* is ours. As Harry Truman used to say when he was President of the United States, after listening to his counselors, "This is where the buck stops." The responsibility for decision, after all the advice, rested with him. Similarly, in vocational, financial, or marital counseling, our advisers can assist us in defining our difficulties. They can provide us with information we may not have had. The choice of actions, however, is ours, and acting upon our choice is deemed our possibility.

Now, by degree, the therapies move away from counseling as defined toward situations in which the helper intends to change the patient in ways in which the patient cannot seem to change himself. Thus a disturbed person asks for a change in his conduct that he feels helpless to effect. He *cannot* do what he says he would like to do—be unafraid and confident or stop stuttering, gambling, or drinking. Here we cross a vague border between the offering of advice and the effecting of a cure. It is important to recognize this transition from counseling to therapy, however, because the success of counseling ought not to be confused with the results of therapy. This difference suggests another.

Is Feeling Better the Same As Being Cured?

People who voluntarily enter "helping" programs rather generally report that they feel better. This becomes more true as people stay in such programs. It does not matter what the program is. It can include musical therapy, physical therapy, meditation, sensitivity training, or "group-grope." As long as we *choose* it and find ourselves among like-minded persons, we are apt to find that we feel better.

Feeling better is important, of course, but it should not be confused with the cure of mental disorder. If the troubled person seeks only friendly counsel, relief from loneliness, or a "philosophy of life," there is a vast cafeteria in which to choose one's help. The psychotherapy boom today largely represents a search for identity and a flight from boredom (London, 1974). In this search there is *help*, but most of it does not *cure* neurosis, psychosis, or psychopathic personality.

---

[1]There are differences between having information, having experience or acquaintance, having knowledge, having know-how, and having sound judgment. The differences are spelled out by Nettler (1972, 1973).

TYPES OF THERAPY

Just as there is a range of ways of "finding oneself," there is also a broad spectrum of therapy employed against the mental disorders. What is used, what is recommended, and what works vary with the patient, his disorder, and the therapist. The styles of therapy may be grouped as follows:

1 Magic

The heart of magic is an appeal to an unseen power that will work the cure. The magical practitioner may claim special techniques for focusing the unseen power upon his patient, but the agency of the cure is outside the material world. The appeal to unseen forces may be ritualized, as in an organized religion that defines faith healing as part of its justification, or it may be personalized, as when a particular person is believed to have distinctive competence in using the spirit world to effect his cures.

   The word "magic" as it is applied here is not a denigrating label but an exact and neutral term. Magic is an accompaniment of all medical practice among preliterate people and it remains a prominent treatment among literate groups. As with many other attempts to treat sick souls, magic is often used in combination with physical therapy such as herbs, rest, massage, and hot and cold baths. The practitioners of magic, the medicine men, undergo extensive training to learn the ceremonials of their people and, in some tribes, there is even a specialization of function as between the diagnostician and the healer.

   There is no doubt that for the believer, magic does something. A nine-day-and-night Navajo ceremonial may be expensive—a recent one cost $600 plus eighty-five sheep and three cows—but the attention, the companionship, and the recital of the faith in song and dance provide at least temporary relief from depression and anxiety. McDowell (1973a) reports that the demand for native treatment in the United States has never been higher and that to meet the need, a branch of the federal government has financed a training program for medicine men in Arizona.

   No one has scales with which to weigh the amount of magical practice among industrial societies in comparison with so-called primitive societies, nor has anyone objectively tested the relative rate of magical cure compared with other therapies of thought and feeling. However, the prominent philosopher-psychologist Karl Jaspers (1948) believes that a comparison of the results of faith healers and modern psychotherapists would prove the former more effective. Jaspers finds it "self-evident that the greatest success has been achieved, not by neurophysicians, but undoubtedly, as in earlier times, by shamans, priests, founders of sects, miracle-workers, father confessors, and spiritual leaders."

   In all societies today magic continues to be a popular and hence important mode of response to mental disorder.

2 The Psychotherapies

As its title suggests, a psychotherapy is an attempt to change behavior by changing the mind. The attempt may be employed with individuals or with groups. The assumption of any psychotherapy is that "thinking better" will produce better feeling and better behavior. The thesis is that if one finds out "what is troubling him," he will then be able to free himself of his undesirable behavior. "Understanding" and "insight" are key terms in psychotherapy, and they describe the operative assumption that once we "understand"[2] the sources of our difficulties, we are in a position to remove them.

Beyond this, the definition of psychotherapy becomes vague, as does the specification of its method. The unsatisfactory state of the art has never been better summarized than by the recording secretary of a psychological congress devoted to this matter. At the end of the meetings, Lehner (1952) concluded that "we have left therapy as an undefined technique which is applied to unspecified problems with nonpredictable outcome. For this technique we recommend rigorous training."

Since the principal instrument of this kind of effort is words, these attempted cures—and there are many types of them—are often called the talking therapies. Until recently, they have constituted the most popular form of treatment for the mental disorders in Western countries. As with the magical remedies, the popularity of the psychotherapies is as much a manifestation of faith as it is a consequence of results.

The psychotherapies undergo fashions and their great variety need not be described in detail here. It is sufficient to note that these treatments run a range from "warm understanding," reasoning, and persuasion—near the counseling end of the spectrum—to analyzing "the games one is playing" (Berne, 1964), urging patients to shriek and throw things (Janov, 1970, 1972), forceful massage as a means of breaking down "the muscular armor" of neurotics (Reich, 1973), insulting patients (Stern, 1972, pp. 101–102), and, not surprisingly, having sexual intercourse with them (Wolf, 1974).

Apart from these kinds of "cures," two major modes of psychotherapy deserve description, recognizing that there are varieties within each mode. One group of practices, frequently a form of counseling, we may call *the honesty therapies*. The other method, *psychoanalysis*, purports to be less of a counseling service and more of a medicine.

The Honesty Therapies   These attempts to help disturbed people assume that a person's difficulties may arise from his mistaken conception of what he and others are doing and of what the world is like. The objective of these

---

[2]"Understand" is placed in quotation marks because it has no clear meaning. "To understand" in the therapeutic sense is *not* the same as "to be able to say" or "to have information" or "to know" something. People who "know" things about themselves without appropriately changing their behaviors are said by their psychotherapists to have "intellectual understanding" but no "emotional understanding." The meanings of these phrases are also comfortably vague.

remedies is to assist the patient to think clearly, to be honest about his feelings and his actions, and to develop a more realistic image of his social environment. Such therapies include what has been termed "rational psychotherapy" (Ellis, 1962, 1964) and "reality therapy" (Glasser, 1965).

The effectiveness of persuasions to rationality depends upon a rapport between the therapist and his patient, a feeling of trust that is stimulated by the therapist's show of concern and his reluctance to blame. Once such confidence is built, the therapist becomes much like a counselor or teacher who helps the distraught person face up to what he has been doing, to see his intimates more realistically, and to comprehend the probable prices of optional courses of action. At this stage the adviser may suggest other ways of living and give practical assignments toward a manner of being that may provide the patient with a better sense of himself and more of what he wants at lower cost.

A considerable number of disturbed persons who undergo psychotherapy are not psychotic or severely neurotic. They are, rather, persons who are morally troubled. No one has counted this, but it is a personal opinion with some warrant that a significant proportion of individuals who seek psychological help in modern societies are in moral quandaries. They are torn between what they are doing, what others tell them they are doing and should do, and what kind of moral identity they themselves should seek. From such inquirers one gets the impression that our rich countries are populated with many persons who do not know right from wrong, literally and personally. They do not know, that is, how they should define right and wrong in living their own lives (Mowrer, 1960). Many of these seekers are looking for moral direction. They commonly ask their "rational therapist" for moral advice and the counselor provides this, but usually in a relativistic context. He shows his questioner different moral definitions of the difficulties the patient is having. At this point, the patient frequently asks the moral question directly: "What do you think is right?" Help here lies in the counselor's having a morality that can be modeled.

Psychoanalysis   Of the many psychotherapies, the most widely publicized procedure in the Western world has been psychoanalysis. This expensive and prolonged treatment involves dredging up the patient's memories of adolescence, childhood, and even infancy (Lindner, 1944) and analyzing what is recalled, along with other "freely associated" ideas, in an effort to ascertain the presumed *conflict* between conscience and desire that has produced the illness.

Although this method has been outlawed in some lands—in communist countries, for example (Kiev, 1968; Wortis, 1950)—it has dominated North American psychiatric training and practice until the 1970s. In the United States, the government agency responsible for spending millions of dollars annually to promote research and training in psychiatry, the National Institute of Mental Health, "recently had as its director someone who had been psychoanalyzed; the deputy director had been psychoanalyzed as well; and even the research director had been put on the couch" (Sargant, 1964, p. 90).

As we shall see, the curative powers of this and other psychotherapies have been far from demonstrated. Indeed, one of the fathers of psychoanalysis, Sigmund Freud, believed his invention was principally a research tool and of limited value as a treatment of the serious disorders. Freud himself reported the detailed therapy of only five patients and, by his own admission, some of these select few did not improve. The poverty of this procedure has moved the British psychiatrist Sargant (1964) to suggest that "Freud's work may be one of the great hoaxes of the century."

3 Behavior Therapy

This family of treatments of mental disorders attempts to change the undesirable *behavior* rather than the mode of *thinking* that is supposed by psychotherapy to cause it. It attempts to alter unwanted behavior by changing the setting in which it is stimulated and reinforced. This kind of therapy does *not* assume that the distant sources of the inefficient conduct must be known or that the patient and his therapist must "understand" these causes in order to change behavior. As opposed to most of the psychotherapies, behavior therapy works with explicit hypotheses about how people learn.

Learning by Teaching and by Training There is more than one way in which we learn. We can conceive of this range of learning procedures as running from the most intellectual kind of learning—the learning of logical principles, for example—to the most physical kind of learning, in which habits are unthinkingly acquired. There are, of course, skills that we have acquired, like writing shorthand or playing tennis, that were learned through a moving mixture of *apprehended principles* and *trained habits.* Hilgard's diagram (1962, p. 280) illustrates the kinds of things learned blindly, rationally, and as a mixture (see figure below).

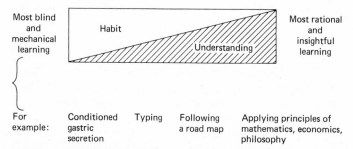

Learning processes and learned results. The scaling of learning tasks according to degree of understanding involved. Most learning involves a mixture of habit and insight. (*Adapted from* Introduction to Psychology, *3d edition, by E. R. Hilgard, Figure 9.25. © 1962 by Harcourt Brace Jovanovich, Inc. Reproduced by permission.*)

The behavior therapist distinguishes between *teaching* and *training.* Teaching uses words and other symbols to transmit information and expressions of approval and disapproval. It operates on the right-hand side of Hilgard's diagram. Training uses reward, punishment, and models to mold behavior. It operates on the left of the diagram. Teaching is a more intellectual process than training. In the teaching situation, both teacher and learner are more aware of what the teacher is teaching. In the training situation, the learner is not necessarily aware that his behavior is being shaped. Teaching characteristically results in the acquisition of cognitive skills—how to use algebra or bake a cake. Training is the process by which we acquire moral values, aesthetic tastes, and motor habits. In learning a skill, both teaching and training come into play. The teaching tells what should be done; the training smooths the motor skills and makes them automatic.

The behavior therapist employs any one or a mixture of three training procedures: *respondent (classical) conditioning, operant (instrumental) conditioning, and modeling.*

Respondent conditioning is a form of learning by association in which a stimulus that is inadequate to produce a response becomes adequate through simultaneous or nearly simultaneous association with an adequate stimulus. The classic example is that of a dog that is trained to salivate to the sound of a bell which is rung, repeatedly, just before the hungry animal receives its food. In such a training situation, the experimenter looks for stimuli that "unconditionally" produce a response. He can then train the animal to behave on command by associating some other stimulus—a hand clap, a gesture, a word—with that response.

Since some kinds of undesirable behaviors, particularly fears, have been learned through such conditioning, it is possible to train persons out of their unpleasant emotional habits by "counterconditioning." The principle, which Wolpe (1958) has christened "reciprocal inhibition," involves placing the patient in situations in which more desirable responses are stimulated that conflict with and thus inhibit the "bad" behavior. Gradually, a new response is conditioned to the stimuli that previously provoked inefficient behavior. The desensitization to a frightening object—be it water, trains, or snakes—is accomplished by associating the conditional stimulus with other stimuli that elicit an antagonistic response.

Operant or instrumental conditioning is one of the most powerful ways of guiding behavior. It differs from respondent conditioning in that the organism is changed by the *consequences* of its acts. Whereas in classical conditioning a new stimulus is "hooked up" to an adequate stimulus *before* the organism behaves, in operant conditioning the organism acts and is trained by what *follows* upon its action.

Operant conditioning works with the commonsense notion that reward and punishment powerfully affect behavior. The difference between common sense and the use of reward and punishment in behavior therapy lies in the greater awareness of the psychologist to the fact that neither reward nor punishment has a uniform effect. A pain or a pleasure is but one event in a stream of happenings, and the consequences of reward and punishment vary with their *intensity,* their *timing,* their *consistency,* and the organism's *experience.* Rewards and punishments also come in different *styles*—there are different kinds of pleasures and pains. Furthermore, the *balance* between reward and punishment also affects behavior. The inventory of research on this subject need not be reviewed to acknowledge that what happens when we act influences how we act.

The interesting and difficult question asked of psychologists is how to apply a schedule of reinforcement, a mixture of reward and punishment, to improve incompetent behavior. While there are subtleties in the answer to this question, the principles of behavior modification are sufficiently clear that they can be taught parents who then become therapists for their own children (Allen and Harris, 1966; Hawkins et al., 1966; Wahler et al., 1965). For certain classes of behavior disorder, particularly those in which a limited target can be set for behavioral change, mixtures of respondent and operant conditioning have probably the best recorded rate of success among the therapies. This is especially true of the treatment of phobias (Chapel, 1967; Kennedy, 1965), toilet difficulties (De Leon and Mandell, 1966; Hundziak et al., 1965; Lovibond, 1963), hyperactivity (Patterson et al., 1965), speech defects (Hewett, 1965), self-injury (Lovaas et al., 1965; Tate and Baroff, 1966), and withdrawal (Allen et al., 1965).

Modeling, or "social learning," refers to the age-old observation that human beings and their mammalian cousins learn by imitation. If we can acquire habits, including bad ones, by watching others, then again it is possible that we can remove some habits by associating with better models. For example, a desensitization technique has been used by Bandura and his associates (1967) by having children who were afraid of dogs watch other children play with a dog. In this experiment, a control group of children was reasoned with about the dog's harmlessness and told that they need not fear the animal. The children who received this talking therapy did *not* lose their fear, as did the children who observed the fearless model.

Objections Despite the success of the behavior therapies with a limited range of troublesome behaviors, there is strong resistance to the employment of this method. The resistance comes from persons who resent the manipulative character of the therapy and who feel that cures of mental disorders should come from a cognitive change willed by a reasoning sufferer rather than from an "animal trainer."

There are two sources of this objection. One is religious—at least Christian-religious—and the other is ethical. The religious foundation for objecting to behavior therapy is based on the idea that undesirable behaviors that have no apparent physical or structural causes ought to be corrected through reform of the will, through a change of "heart and mind." This is particularly true when the undesirable behaviors have unpleasant social consequences, so that they may be regarded as sins. "Redeeming" the sinner by manipulating his rewards and his pains seems not so satisfying to the religious reformer as improving him through an appeal to his conscience. For example, in Burgess's *Clockwork Orange* (1962, p. 67), the prison priest voices the religious objection to behavior therapy in advising the thieving, raping, ultraviolent Alex against submitting to Ludovico's [conditioning] Technique.

"The question," says the priest, "is whether such a technique can really make a man good. Goodness comes from within. . . . Goodness is something chosen. When a man cannot choose he ceases to be a man."

Another version of the ethical reluctance to employ behavior therapy has political significance. It raises the most important of political questions: "Who has the right to control whom?" Individuals who value freedom are alert to the possible imposition by others of their unwanted "help." There is, however, *no escaping some kind of social control.* Living together requires some expectations that limit our actions. As the psychologist B. F. Skinner (1955, 1956, 1972) repeats to many deaf ears, "the problem is to free [us], not from control, but from certain kinds of control." The behavior therapies that free us from disabling fears and incompetent habits that are beyond our "mental control" deserve a better appreciation than that of a Frankenstein.

An Interpretation   For a limited but important range of disorders, the behavior therapies work, and work better than the psychotherapies. There are many reasons why this should be, but a simple reason is that *psychotherapy attempts to change by teaching what has been learned by training.*

To the extent to which learning is involved in the production of mental disorder, it is *not* the learning on the right side of Hilgard's diagram (page 81). It is not rational, cognitive learning that underwrites neurosis or psychosis. If there is a learning that makes us more or less sane or sick, it is a learning of which we are little aware. It is the training received in our conditioning and from our models.

In this sense, cause ought to influence the choice of cure, and we should not spend much time, money, or hope in trying to cure heads and hearts of what originates in nerves and glands.

4   Encounter Groups, T- (for Training) Groups, Sensitivity Training

It is more than coincidence that a style of therapy that mixes the treatment of attitudes and beliefs with some desensitization procedures and strong elements of faith should have originated in the summer camp of one of America's leading relogous denominations. From its start in the late 1940s in an Episcopal retreat in Bethel, Maine, sensitivity training has become a minor social movement. There are classes and schools throughout Europe and North America applying variations on the theme of this therapy. It has been adopted by business organizations as a means of increasing productivity and reducing interpersonal friction. It has been employed as a method of rehabilitating delinquents, reforming addicts, "sensitizing" bureaucrats, and, even of improving the quality of legal judgment among jurists.

The working assumptions of this style of therapy are at least these:

1   That much of what troubles us is inhibition, a fear of our emotions and a failure to express them

2 That "being open" to our feelings, to their expression, and to others' feelings releases impounded talent and makes us happier, healthier, and more "creative"

3 That we often do not get along well with others because we do not see ourselves accurately, and that misperceiving the way we act encourages misperception of the other person

4 That correct perception of ourselves and others heals our wounds

The encounter procedure brings people together under the direction of a "counselor" or "facilitator" whose role is largely neutral but who may, in some sessions, serve as an interpreter to the group. The therapy calls for an "unfreezing" of old attitudes, a change or acquisition of new perceptions, and a "refreezing" or consolidation of new perceptions and values.

The method is a group therapy in which the participants are encouraged to tell what bothers them, to express their reactions to others in the group, and, depending upon the mode of training, to engage in desensitizations techniques that run a gamut from the verbal report of the unbearable to holding hands, feeling bodies, and nude group-grope in warm pools. One book in praise of the method is appropriately titled *Please Touch* (Howard, 1970).

This form of group therapy differs from traditional psychoanalytic group treatment not only in its employment of desensitization procedures but also in the length of the session. Encounter groups often live together for weeks, meeting daily for two or three sessions of several hours each, and marathon encounters are sometimes engaged in in which the participants are together for an entire day or longer. For example, Church (1973) reports that the cosmetics and house-care company for which he worked urged him to sign up for a four-day course, at a fee of $1,000, in which the first session lasted thirty-nine hours.

What Are the Results?   As with any social movement, the *voluntary* participants are likely to report benefits. The reports are anecdotal, seldom checked for the endurance of the alleged improvement, and rarely validated against objectively observable changes in behavior.

The use of desensitization techniques—a form of behavior therapy—lends theoretical credibility to the program. For example, it is conceivable that sexually shy individuals may be relieved of their inhibitions by prolonged touching sessions. There may be other facets of interpersonal relations in which a person is trained through desensitization. However, the question of the healing efficacy of the therapies and, in particular, of the encounter treatment suffers from a lack of outcome research.

When results *are* checked against outcomes, the findings are inconclusive. For instance, in business, more research has been addressed to the effects of T-groups than to those of any other management training technique (Argyris, 1964). After surveying a mass of such research, Campbell and Dunnette (1968) conclude that it is difficult to get encounter enthusiasts to specify treatment goals in objective terms (an "existential" language is preferred) and that, while many participants *say* that they have changed, differences in their *performance* on the job have not been adequately documented.

Does Sensitivity Training Hurt?   There are indications that the pressure for self-disclosure that is the basis of sensitivity training is harmful to some individuals. The procedure is a form of "brainwashing" in which one's peers are used as inquisitors to bring one to "the truth." In the process, some individuals are hurt.

On an objective level, Underwood (1965) shows that T-groups sometimes produce changes in on-the-job performance but that the proportion of *detrimental* changes is greater for the "sensitively trained" than for those who recive no such treatment.

On the anecdotal level, there are numerous accounts of individuals who have been made anxious and desperate by the "brutal truthfulness" of this search for "sensitivity." Odiorne (1963) lists some of these ugly encounters, as do Church and Carnes (1973) and Stafford (1973). Stafford is particularly bitter. She asks:

> Do you know that there are "encounter bums"? Well, there are—going from one mare's nest to another hurting total strangers' gut-level feelings, punching that old sensitivity-training dummy tackle to a fare-thee-well, relating it up like hell's angels. It seems an odd hobby. Indeed, it seems the oddest hobby I have ever heard of. You take old ladies who make the round of funerals every day, weather permitting: *that* makes some sense—gives them a reason to fix their hair and dress up and get a little exercise by walking to the mortuary parlors. But packing a valise and going off to pay money to encounter a collection of malcontents or self-improvement buffs seems about as profitable as dead-heading back to the car-barn just for the ride [p. 32, emphasis hers].

A Personal Opinion   If our concern is with mental health, each of us will take the help he needs where he can find it. If one feels better after a good cry in a mortuary or after a marathon encounter, so be it. This personal taste should not be confused with the remedy of psychosis or neurosis, however, and companies and governments that *require* attendance of their employees in T-groups, as some do, ought to be sued for violation of civil rights.

There is a tradition in both Oriental and Occidental cultures that recognizes the healthful effects of silence and privacy. Privacy places a limit upon questioning and disclosure. It is guaranteed by manners, the etiquette that is a social lubricant. The demand to tell everything one thinks about everyone, and to express everything one feels about both friends and strangers, erodes manners. It will more probably increase personal friction than reduce it. Sensitivity training cannot be recommended as a program for improving one's mental health.

5 Milieu Therapy

This phrase describes any planned change in the environment as a means of healing emotional wounds. There are people and situations that are sickening and, assuming that the hurt person does not carry some psychic infection with him, getting away from these persons and places is helpful.

The difficulty in recommending a more healthful environment as therapy lies in the uncertainties about the sources of a person's disturbance. There are neurotics who try "to run from themselves" and who find misery wherever they flee. On the other hand, there are persons, insulted and injured by "loved ones," for whom any change of scene is an improvement. There is no perfect advice to be given about milieu therapy. Judgment is involved, and it is always fallible.

6 Somatotherapy

Treatments that would heal the mind by affecting the body are called somatotherapy. Again, there is a repertoire of such physical therapies of sick thoughts and emotions that include weight reduction, hormone ingestion, shock treatment (chemical or electrical), brain surgery, and chemotherapy (the use of mood-changing drugs).

These treatments all produce temporary relief. The most drastic of these procedures, cutting into the nervous system, runs a high risk of irreversible damage. Depending upon the kind of surgery, peace is brought to the disturbed patient, but at the cost of a great reduction in his contact with the world.

Of the somatotherapies, the most promising general treatment is chemical therapy, the use of tranquilizers, stimulants, and other pharmaceuticals for the control of moods. Those who work in chemotherapy expect that by the 1980s nonnarcotic drugs will be widely used and socially accepted as means of controlling undesirable feelings and behaviors (Gordon and Helmer, 1964).

ON EVALUATING TREATMENT

Not all treatment helps. Some hurts. It is important to recognize this possibility, although particular cases of harm will be debated, especially by those whose occupation it is harmfully "to help."

For example, some disorders go away if left untreated but are exaggerated if attended to. Dement (1972), one of the world's leading students of sleep disorders, tells us that some of these disturbances, notably the "drug-dependent sleep disorders," are *produced by their treatment*. Furthermore, as regards sleepwalking and related annoyances, especially among children, Dement writes, "It is our strong opinion that these conditions should not be treated. I cannot overemphasize this point. Most treatments are ineffective and generally only make the child anxious for no good reason. In the end, patience is the only cure" (p. 5).

The most doubtful of the "cures" are the psychotherapies, particularly those that require prolonged regurgitation of the past, analysis of oneself, and public exposure of feelings. There is no census of the harm such treatment has done, just as there is little evidence of its merits. It must be considered an open possibility, however, that a psychotherapy that influences people may harm some individuals as much as it helps others.

On an anecdotal level, Walsh (1961) claims that he has observed "a number of individuals who were frightened into chronic maladjusted states as a result of their encounter with psychotherapy," and he believes that "the day will come when psychotherapy will be as outmoded as blood letting."

Cross (1964) reviewed a series of studies of psychotherapeutic effects in which a control group was compared with the treated group. Considering the great investment of time and money in psychotherapy, such controlled investigations of outcome are surprisingly few. At the time of his writing, Cross found nine such studies. Six of these experiments showed some positive effects of psychotherapy. This finding is tentative, however, because the treatment in this research was brief and more like counseling than therapy, the measuring tools were of questionable validity, and, in some of the research, the control groups were not well matched with the experimental groups. From his survey, Cross concluded that "while psychotherapy is probably *the most popular* single area of specialization within psychology (not to mention psychiatry), its efficacy has *not* been scientifically demonstrated beyond some reasonable doubt" [p. 416, emphasis added].

A more hazardous effect of psychotherapy, the *deterioration effect,* has been suggested by Bergin (1966). Bergin analyzed seven well-designed investigations that used objective measures of personality change and that compared changes of treated groups with changes among untreated persons. He found that:

> although there tends to be no difference in the average amount of change between experimentals and controls, there tends to be a significant difference in *variability* of change. The . . . change scores for treatment groups attain a much wider dispersion than do those of control groups. . . . Typically, control subjects improve somewhat. . . . On the other hand, experimental subjects are typically dispersed all the way from marked improvement to marked deterioration. Now frequently documented, this information is alarming to say the least. Psychotherapy can and does make people worse than their control counterparts! [pp. 118–119, emphasis his.]

These doubts and these risks are well summarized by the psychiatrist Wheelis (1958, p. 231), who says of the analyst:

> With his interpretations he writes in water. His patients get better and get worse. Most of them derive some benefit from his efforts, but of structural alterations and radical character change he sees little. He is forced reluctantly toward the

conclusion that psychoanalysis is not what it is represented to be, and he begins to be troubled by a vague sense of fraudulence.

What Is Required to Evaluate Treatment?

The scientific test of a therapy requires at least the following conditions:

1 Adequate base-line measurement of the target behavior

This means that the kind of behavior to be treated—stuttering, let us say—must be measured in such a way that one has a fair estimate of its severity. All stutterers are not equally handicapped, and if there is to be a worsening or an improvement in the treated behavior, it must be gauged from a base-line of the individual's performance before treatment (Gelfand and Hartmann, 1968).

2 A control group

There is such a phenomenon as "spontaneous remission." Some people get better without treatment. There are ups and downs in the state of our mental health. It is as La Rouchefoucauld said centuries ago, "The soul's maladies have their relapses like the body's. What we take for a cure is often just a momentary rally or a new form of the disease."

There are reports of the spontaneous remission of the milder neurotic disorders—the annoying feelings of insecurity, incompetence, and nervousness—in from two-thirds to three-fourths of cases seen over a two-to-three-year period (Eysenck, 1967, p. 40). One long-term study of the less severe psychic complaints found that 90 percent of patients were relieved of their symptoms at the end of five years (Dencker, 1947).

To assess the value of a cure requires, then, that there be a comparison with a control group that is equal to the experimental group in all ways conceivably related to the possibility of spontaneous remission—equal, for example, in age, sex, severity, and duration of the same type of disorder.

3 Objective examination procedures before and after therapy

The assessment of base-line behaviors and the measurement of change should *not* be performed by the therapist. These measurements should be the work of independent clinicians who are themselves ignorant of which tested individuals belong to the treated or untreated group. That is, the measurement of pre- and posttreatment behaviors should be "blind." Furthermore, the measures must be objective. There must be some record of publicly observable change in behavior beyond the usual claims of therapists and reports of patients that they "feel better."

4 Rigorous follow-up examininations of both experimental and control groups

Since individuals differ in their histories of aggravation and remission of mental disorder, an adequate test of the value of a therapy requires follow-up examinations, objectively and "blindly" performed, for some years after therapy.

IN SUMMARY

There have always been therapies of the mental disorders. This does not mean that there have been cures. It does mean that there has been faith and experiment.

The scientific test of the therapies is lacking, as we have seen. On the individual level, this may not matter much, except, of course, as individuals are gulled or hurt. Each of us when troubled will take what help he can find. If there is a choice of treatment, the best we can do is to be informed. Being informed means knowing what is *not* so as well as what is. It means knowing what has *not* been proved as well as what might be.

The cures of the mental disorders are, at present, mostly palliative. The popular comparison of "psychological help" with *medical* competence is misleading, for the treatments of the mind do *not* have the efficacy of, say, penicillin or an appendectomy.

On the level of social concerns, this matter becomes important. The impotence of the psychotherapies means that as citizens we should be slow to advocate the "treatment" of undesirable behaviors. Sending the Boston Strangler (Frank, 1967) to a psychiatrist may be more humane than executing him or placing him in prison, but we should *not* recommend this kind of public policy on the grounds that it works. Similarly, while we are concerned for the adequate care of the mentally ill, we ought not to have our hopes elevated toward the probability of cures if only more money is spent.

A Personal Opinion It is one thing for me to spend my own time and money improving myself. It is quite another matter for me to advocate the expenditure of *your* funds in the cure of what ails you or others in our society. The ethic in this shift of responsibility becomes more clear—is more easily resolved—as the results of the social programs are seen to be *unreliable.* When the results of such programs are as uncertain as are those deemed to improve a public's mental health, it becomes but another case of fraudulent advertising to propagandize for more money, as have some mental health associations.

The majority of beds in mental hospitals are occupied by schizophrenics who suffer from a disorder which is, at present, incurable. A considerable number of additional beds are occupied by persons suffering from organic dementia, a deterioration of mental function induced by brain injury. For these classes of mental disorder, the best that can be provided is custodial care. In the competition among our concerns for public monies, the political question is whether more money should be spent for "better hotels" for the mentally ill (Hanley, 1973), for more research, or on other issues. The decision should be based on facts rather than on hopes.

CULTURE, IDENTITY, AND MENTAL HEALTH

Part of our concern with mental health is a concern with identity. *How should we be?*

The search for identity is particularly noticeable among those who feel worthless and pointless. This sense of the absurdity of life is the curse of rich countries. It is unheard of among those people whose lives retain that most universal of meanings: survival. Relieved of the necessity to struggle for existence, many citizens of modern societies find themselves without stimulating interests and without good reasons for getting out of bed.

A Diagnosis   This illness, a compound of boredom and meaninglessness, is a result of the breakdown of *culture*. "Culture" is a difficult word. It refers to a way of life of a people who have a sense of common history, a sense of being a "we" as opposed to a "them," and who, usually, live within a bounded territory.

In Eliot's phrase (1948, p. 57), "Culture is a peculiar way of thinking, feeling, and behaving." Culture describes the pattern of our lives together, a pattern that is discernible in our art; in our diet, dress, and customs; in our religion and values; in our obligations to each other; and in our language. Dialect, a distinctive way of using a language, is one of the most sensitive indicators of cultural membership.

Culture means regulated behavior. It draws the difference between *conduct* and just acting. Being reared in a culture means being trained toward *how we are supposed to be.* If we do not receive this training, if we are left to find out for ourselves what kind of person to become, we are, at the minimum, made uncomfortable and, at the maximum, made vulnerable to self-destruction.

This diagnosis assumes what some may dispute: that, from some cosmic stance, our lives on this lesser planet are absurd. As the skeptic Mencken (1920) once put it, "The cosmos is a gigantic fly-wheel making 10,000 revolutions a minute. Man is a sick fly taking a dizzy ride on it. Religion is the theory that the wheel was designed and set spinning to give him the ride."

Astronomically, at least, we *are* insignificant. Everything passes—our hopes, our works, our efforts to help ourselves and others. It is as the Emperor Septimius (A.D. 146–211) said, looking out upon his Roman conquests, "I have been everything and it is worth nothing."

There is no *objective* meaning to life. Meaning is *given* to our lives. It is transmitted by that culture that defines for us who we are and how we should become. When there is a strong culture, there are models, and we receive an education in why we are here and how we should bear ourselves. Without this training, we are lost. While some of us may succeed in finding or developing an identity, it is difficult work and hazardous.

Cultures have been carried by small groups of people—bands, tribes, and, more recently, nations. These groups have a sense of *kinship.* The word "nation" comes from the Latin "to be born of." Today's popular term "ethnic" derives from the Greek for "nation." Both words refer to a people who consider themselves related by blood ties.

States Are Not Nations   In recent times, however, bodies of people have become citizens of states that attempt to rule many nations. This is one source of their disorder and of the breakdown of culture.

A *state* is a governmental agency with a monopoly of power. A *nation* is a people with a common heritage. States today do not necessarily represent a culture, and states can neither create a culture nor command it.

Each of the states called Canada, Great Britain, Belgium, Switzerland, Spain, the Union of Soviet Socialist Republics, the Republic of South Africa, and the United States of America is attempting to govern more than one nation. Where the nations within such states are regionally isolated, their cultures may be preserved and may continue to be effective. Examples are the survival of the Basques and Catalans in Spain. Where nations meet and mix, however, even though it be under the bond of a common citizenship, their cultures are apt to be broken, their ways of life challenged, and the identity given by the culture is apt to be diluted by other influences. Commerce, the mass media, and, to a lesser extent, public education are substitutes in modern countries for the cultural indoctrination that has normally occurred within nations. They are poor substitutes.

Religion and Culture   This description is a diagnosis. It details what ails us. The culture-free person in "denationalized" states is subject to the unpatterned and conflicting lessons of his schools and the mass media. These substitutes for culture have thus far been unsatisfactory. Their poverty as culture bearers is attested by the disharmony of their lessons, by the great rate at which we steal from each other and kill each other, and by the continuing "quest for identity" among persons who feel estranged from the larger societies within which they live (Nettler, 1957) and who subscribe to a potpourri of social movements promising consolation and salvation.

The nature of this quest bespeaks the fact that the functions of religion are a constant. Human beings need some nonrational (that is, unproved) style of being. So-called countercultures and the many ethicopolitical enthusiasms are sought by *deracinated* persons, by persons who have lost a cultural heritage. These people are *uncultured* in the exact sense of that word. They are individuals who have not been reared in a distinctive, patterned lifeway.

It is notable that the movements they join parallel in form, but not in content, the activities of all religions. There are heroes and originators who gave *the Word*—Buddha, Jesus, Marx, or Mao. There is a *cosmology,* a theory of how the world is. There is a *theology,* a description of what makes the world that way, whether the gods be in a heaven or in the laws of history. There are *rituals* and *guardians of the rituals,* be they called priests or boo-hoos. There is a *definition of justice,* of morality, and of the proper model of manhood-womanhood. Last, as with all religions, the modern movements in search of meaning give a *promise* of what will happen in some near or distant future if we live by "the Word."

The Antidote   If this diagnosis is correct, cures may be prescribed—without any assurance, of course, that the patient will take them.

It is a commonplace to attribute the alienated sickness to something vague called "social change." The question is seldom asked, "*What* has changed that sets men 'free,' rootless, and meaningless?" A good answer is, "Anything that breaks culture." A better answer is, "When peoples meet, cultures break."

People are meeting, however, and moving, and the person of good will wants this congregation to proceed without friction—without costly side effects—and to end in amity. In the Western world the prevalent academic doctrine from the 1930s until about 1970 was assimilationist. The image was that of the melting pot, a cultural broth that would develop its own flavor as a result of the happy blending of diverse peoples.

The image has proved inaccurate. Glazer and Moynihan (1963) believe it to be a myth. The late 1960s and early seventies have seen a renaissance of nationalistic claims, what Alpert (1972) has called "a fever of ethnicity." These claims to a cultural identity are seen by their advocates as conducive to their personal dignity and self-esteem, in short, as good for their mental health. In North America, many black people have ceased trying to adopt white culture and have sought to revive African traditions. Native Indians, French Canadians, Mexican Americans, Japanese, Chinese, Jews, Poles, and innumerable other ethnic groups have urged the value of their separate identity. In Europe the Tyrolese wish to be free of Italy, the Basques of Spain, the Protestant Irish of Ireland, Scotsmen of England, the Flemish of the Walloons, and on. The scene is repeated, with variations, in Africa and Asia.

"Good" governments are beside themselves. On the one hand, they advocate "equal rights with separate identities." This is an unstable accommodation, as all accommodations are, but it is at least a way for nations to live together within a state that does least damage to their cultures.

Some governments with good intentions follow another course. This course, exemplified by the United States, is an inconsistent mixture of "equal rights with separate identities" and coerced congregation. There is political pressure, not only in North America but also in Europe, to use state power to *force* disparate peoples to live together in at least some phases of their lives. School busing of quotas of ethnic groups in the United States is one version of this assimilationist policy. Another version demands that public housing be used to relocate income groups as well as ethnic groups to achieve a "better mix" of citizens.

Being Moral versus Being Rational   It must be remembered that the debate about these issues is relevant to questions of identity and, hence, to our concern with happiness and mental health. The debate, however, is normally confused. The thinking person who participates in this quarrel is often in a predicament, the predicament of reconciling what he wants with how the world is. Being a professional thinker, an "intellectual," does not relieve the tension but may, on the contrary, increase it insofar as the intellectual recognizes that how he would like people to be is some distance from how he knows they are.

The conflict is produced by the need to give reasons for our moral preferences. There is, at least, an attempt to make our morality appear reasonable and even rational. Being reasonable, being rational, and being moral are, however, different characteristics of behavior. *To be reasonable* is to be open to reasons, willing to listen, able to comprehend the other person's arguments as well as one's own. *To be rational* is quite another matter. To be rational is to employ efficient means in the achievement of one's objectives. It may therefore be rational for a person to be unreasonable, and neither being rational nor being reasonable is the same as *being good*. A moral person may be unreasonable, although he gives reasons for his stand. He may also be irrational while he is being moral. It is possible to be moral *and* irrational when one is not clear about his objectives or has not calculated the likely consequences of his acts. It is also possible to be moral and irrational because one's moral preference is so commanding that the morally motivated person is blind to evidence that acting upon his ethic may be inefficient or productive of costly by-products. There *are* ethics that are suicidal.

A Personal Conclusion   Some philosophers believe that the assessment of consequences cannot be disentangled from a moral preference. If this were so, there would be little point in asking sociologists to know anything (Nettler, 1972, 1973). We could simply take sides on moral grounds, as we ordinarily do when disputing emotionalized social issues. The logical end of this taking of sides is as the late Justice Oliver Wendell Holmes, Jr., described it. "Pleasures are ultimates," he wrote (1926, p. 862), "and in cases of difference between oneself and another there is nothing to do except in unimportant matters to think ill of him and in important ones to kill him."

Holmes's statement can be translated, "Moralities are ultimates." Moralities are *justified* by reasons, but they are not *caused* by those reasons nor are they much *moved* by new reasons. Moreover, moralities are neither adopted nor abandoned through an assessment of their consequences. It is both inappropriate and ineffective to criticize the other person's religion because it is based on faith rather than on evidence.

The personal advice that follows is to know what you are doing. If your morality calls for the enforced congregation of diverse cultures within a state or around the world, examining the consequences of your advocacy will be both ineffectual and irrelevant. However, if your morality is less demanding on this issue and if you are concerned with those disaffections that flow from rootlessness, meaninglessness, and boredom, then you will not advocate culture breaking.

On Being Isolated and Useless   Our discussion of happiness and health has illuminated two major signs of sickness which, on their reverse sides, are sources of health. Being isolated and being useless are correlates of mental illness. They accompany the process of becoming sick, and they suggest their remedy in vocation and social connection. Thus far in our history, being connected to others and having a sense of vocational utility have been most effectively given when we have been reared in a community that teaches us a way of life. The culture thus acquired evolves. It is not invented. Governments cannot create cultures, although they can damage them.

To the person who is still sane but sick of life, the difficult recommendation is clear: *Find a calling and a tribe if you can.*

Loving, Marrying, and Divorcing

Our concern with being happy and healthy is intertwined with our interest in loving and being loved. It may not be *impossible* for human beings to be happy and mentally healthy without loving, but it is *difficult.* The difficulty in keeping sane and contented without a strong emotional tie to others describes another predicament about which we are concerned, a predicament that some have called "the tragedy of human relations." The tragedy is that other persons, particularly those we love, are at once the greatest source of our joys and of our miseries. This fact is sufficient to answer those who ask, "If loving (or marrying) is so risky, why do people do it?"

Every affectionate connection is hazardous. The hazard is the possibility of disappointment. This possibility is a price paid for what we need. Calculating the risk of disappointment—which is one reason for thinking about our concerns—is complicated by the fact that the hurt we give each other is not always intended, nor is it necessarily the product of vice. It is a possibility that arises from *how we are:* a kind of animal that thinks but does not always know; that often wants what it cannot have; and which, even with the purest of hearts and the clearest of minds, makes mistakes. The situation is as the Navaho moralist Bidaga described it to the philosopher John Ladd (1957, p. 333):

But we always make mistakes. You're going to get mistake next few minutes or tomorrow—a little—but you don't know where mistake is. You just run into it. Or somebody puts you into it. By taking your own care you think you're good care of yourself. You don't want to lie somebody—but you get into that just the same.

THE QUESTIONS WE ASK ABOUT LOVING, MARRYING, AND SEPARATING

The questions we ask about the intimate human connection are at least these:

1 What does it mean to love?
2 Whom do we love?
3 Is sex a help or a hindrance to the loving connection?
4 Why do we marry and how well?
5 Why do marriages succeed or fail?
6 How well does loving without marriage work?
7 Who divorces and why?

THE MEANING OF LOVING

Loving you grows out of liking you. The difference is not sharp. The roots of attraction are joined and, by degree, what makes me like you makes me love you. Conversely, the opposites of these sources of attraction are the conditions of our disliking each other and, again by degree, of our hating each other.

Objects of Love and Qualities of Love

To love is to be concerned with the "well-being"[1] and continuity of the love object. One has to speak of an "object" because it is possible to love oneself, other persons, cats and dogs, trees and flowers, the opera, sports cars, surfing and skiing.

Not only may the *object* of one's love vary, but the *quality* of love takes many forms. There is love linked with sexual feeling and love divorced from erotic emotion. There is love that admires the other's difference, although that is not common (pp. 99–103), and love that aspires to become like the other. There is love that appreciates the equality and independence of the lovers and love that intends to absorb the other.

Of these and other possible qualities of love, the kind of loving that is most universally called love is *behavior that regards the loved object as oneself.* This is the strongest evidence of love. In the words of a Mexican peasant, "Love is a force that makes a person seek the well-being of those he esteems" (Maccoby, 1964).

To this minimal definition, philosophers, psychologists, and lovers have

---

[1]"Well-being" has to be placed in quotation marks because the lover's conception of "what is good" for the loved one may *not* be a blessing as seen by the loved person or by dispassionate observers. On love that damages, see pp. 98–99.

added their own statements of what love means. A sample of these definitions illustrates the range of feeling and human connection that has been called "loving":

> That famous condition of love, the most radical of attempts to escape solitude [Ortega, 1958, p. 77].
> Love is surrender, and sex is victory [An American teen-ager, 1966].
> To an ordinary human being, love means nothing if it does not mean loving some people more than others [Orwell, 1954, p. 182].
> Love is a great force in private life, but in public affairs it does not work [Forster, cited by Harrison, 1964].
> Only if I know a human being objectively, can I know him in his ultimate essence, in the act of love [Fromm, 1956, p. 31].
> Loving . . . entails wanting to make oneself known to the loved one [Jourard, 1958, p. 77].
> The beloved person is a substitute for the ideal ego. Two people who love each other are interchanging their ego-ideals. That they love each other means that they love the ideal of themselves in the other one. When people are entirely satisfied with their actual selves, love is impossible [Reik, 1944, p. 62].
> Love is an expression and assertion of self-esteem, a response to one's own values in the person of the other [Rand, 1963, p. 5].
> [Envy and hostility] . . . are the unconscious prerequisites for deep affection. In other words, if you cannot hate, you cannot love. If you cannot bite, you cannot kiss [Reik, 1944, p. 105].
> Love is pleasure [Hinsie and Campbell, 1970, pp. 440–441].
> *Love:* A temporary insanity curable by marriage [Bierce, 1958].

These added meanings of love may be debated, but two important conclusions can be derived from the debate.

The first is that there are individuals who cannot love, just as there are persons who cannot live without loving.

Hurtful Love   A second conclusion is that there are qualities of love that are as *harmful* to the loved object as hate or indifference. This is the love that "eats the other up." It is the loving that becomes an *absorptive concern* and that denies the dignity of independence to the loved person. "Smother love" is one of its common varieties.

The idea of harmful love runs against the grain of much of what we have been taught. Many of us have been reared in a culture that *advocates* love and *sells* it. The quality of love that is advertised is *romantic.* It is the notion that there is only one special person in the whole world who is made for us and that we can recognize our "true love" by the "right vibrations." It is the notion that love is *compelling and absorptive,* and that it has a right to be such. The idea of romantic love bears the additional peculiar notions that love conquers all and cures all. "TLC"—tender loving care—is even part of our medicine.

That love heals need not be denied if, at the same time, we are reminded that there are qualities of love that hurt. The principal form of this harmful love is that which would make two people one. Against this romantic impulse, we are better advised by the Middle-Eastern poet Kahlil Gibran (1923, pp. 19–20), who urged that "there be spaces in your togetherness" and that we should

> . . . stand together yet not too near together: For the pillars of the temple stand apart, And the oak tree and the cypress grow not in each other's shadow.

"Love" is a glorious four-letter word and a resonating prescription for what ails us, but when we look at the many qualities of relation called loving, it is apparent that neither to love nor to be loved is a benefit without cost. Loving is exhilarating, vitalizing, rejuvenating—and always risky. Most of us are unhappy without love, but we are only uncertainly happy with it.

WHOM DO WE LOVE?

There are two magnets that attract us to some people rather than to others. The first is the magnet of similarity and rewarded ego. The second is the magnet of "need," an attraction that is more difficult to define and which, therefore, requires the defense of quotation marks.

The Magnet of Similarity and Rewarded Ego

When we meet people, an immediate element in our appreciation of them is their similarity to us. People who appear to be similar to us are people we tend to like (Byrne and Griffitt, 1966). Conversely, people whom we like are thought to be similar to us (Berkowitz and Goranson, 1964; Fiedler et al., 1952; Lundy, 1956).

In addition, we are attracted to persons who give signs that they like us and whose regard of us does not offend our own self-conception (Lott and Lott, 1965). The more others agree with us about the good things we think of ourselves, the easier it is to like them (Newcomb, 1956). Since it is easier to reflect an appreciation of persons who are similar to us, the elements of *rewarded ego* and *social similarity* may be regarded as one source of attraction.

Birds of a feather do flock together. When psychologists and sociologists observe how people choose people—in situations as far-ranging as how individuals seat themselves in strange rooms to how friends are selected—the unsurprising finding is that we select associates who give *apparent* indication of their similarity to us and who are also *objectively* similar (Evans, 1962, chap. 4; Lundberg and Dickson, 1952; Sommer, 1969). In short, the assumptions we make about our similarities and differences are not just works of imagination. They have an accuracy. For example, Byrne and Griffitt (1966) show that actual similarity of belief is associated with attraction to strangers, and that what is true of adults is also true of children.

On Homogamy The fact that likes attract likes is not the whole story about whom we come to love. It is a first step, however; and the power of the magnet of similarity is observed, again, when we marry. Studies of mate selection repeatedly reveal a tendency toward *homogamy,* the marriage of similar kinds of people.

These studies have significance for loving because, in Western societies, the choice of a mate is "free" rather than arranged, as in some other cultures (Kapadia, 1958). It is assumed, then, that Western marriages are conceived, at least, with love, whether or not they persist in love. Conversely, the arranged marriage that is entered without love may yet yield affection as a result of the homogamous principle on which the arrangement is made (Freeman, 1958).

The phenomenon of homogamous mating has been repeatedly recorded, particularly in North American research. This research has used both the sociologist's broad categories of kinds of people and the psychologist's narrower network of personality traits. The findings show that we tend to love and to marry people who are similar to us in race, religion, occupational and educational status, and who live nearby (Bossard, 1932–1933; Catton and Smircich, 1964; Centers, 1949; Davie and Reeves, 1938–1939; Dinitz et al., 1960; Freeman, 1955; Kennedy, 1942–1943; Koller, 1948; Marvin, 1918–1919; Peach, 1974).

There are reduced but yet significant tendencies for us to seek mates who are similar to us in intelligence (Richardson, 1939) and who share our interests, beliefs, and temperament (Burgess and Wallin, 1944; Kelly, 1937, 1940, 1955, 1960; Schellenberg, 1960; Schooley, 1936). There are indications that spouses resemble each other in neurotic behaviors (Willoughby, 1936) and that there is a tendency for people of similar body build to be attracted to each other (Burgess and Wallin, 1953; Cattell and Nesselroade, 1967). For example, Clark (1963) found correlations of .39 for height and .20 for weight among a sample of married university students.

The fact of homogamy can be interpreted as saying that it is easier to love people who are culturally similar to us. The degree of such *ethnocentric* mating fluctuates in time and among societies, but there is a consistent pull toward preferring "people like us."

There are worldwide illustrations of this ethnocentric appeal and of the variations around the theme. For example, Ruppin (1913, p. 159) reports that at the turn of this century there was no intermarriage among the 6,700 residents of the Dutch island of Shokland in the Zuyder Zee, half of whom were Protestants and half Catholics. A parallel situation is observed in the American Southwest, where, after an early period of mixture between the Spanish colonists and the native Indians, interbreeding and intermarriage between Spanish-Americans and Amerindians has been negligible despite the proximity of these people (Burma, 1949).

The fluctuating fate of intermarriage is well illustrated in the history of that dispersed yet continuing people, the Jews. Jewish intermarriage has been formally forbidden to the orthodox since at least 400 B.C. (Ruppin, 1913, pp. 157–158). Yet in recent times, Jewish intermarriage has varied widely in time and place as a function of the proportion of Jews in a population and the political climate of the country in which they have resided. Thus for Germany as a whole between 1904 and 1908, the proportion of interfaith marriages between Jews and Christians was about one intermarriage for every five Jewish marriages (Ruppin, 1913, p. 163). This rate varied dramatically by region; it was low in Catholic Bavaria and higher in the Protestant and urban north of Germany. By 1930, before Hitler's regime, one in four Jews in Germany who married did so with a non-Jew. In specific European cities, the proportions of intermarriages differed, but the pre-Nazi trend was similar. In Berlin, Jewish intermarriages increased from 15 percent to 29 percent of all Jewish unions during the first thirty years of this century. Outside Germany, the assimilationist tendency during this period is evidenced by an increase of interfaith marriages from 22 to 32 percent in Copenhagen and from 18 to 56 percent in Trieste. This is an extremely high rate of intermarriage. It represents both the cultural assimilation of European Jews and their small proportions among continental populations. The Nazi and Soviet persecutions have reversed this assimilationist trend (Weinstock, 1970).

In the United States interfaith and interracial marriages continue to constitute but a small proportion of all marriages, despite removal of the legal restrictions formerly applied by some states against interracial unions. California, for example, used to have an antimiscegenation law that was declared unconstitutional in 1948. In the thirty months after repeal of this law, the proportion of interracial marriage license applications in Los Angeles County amounted to slightly more than one-half of 1 percent (Risdon, 1954).

During the 1960s, a period of civil rights ferment in North America, the proportions of racial intermarriages did not change appreciably. In general, less than 1 percent of Blacks and Caucasians chose persons of the other race as marriage partners. The census tabulations are indicated in Table 6-1.

A similar but reduced ethnocentric pattern is observed in the United States among persons of different religions. Kennedy (1952) studied the trend in such interdenominational marriages in New Haven for the period 1870–1950. While there was less tendency in 1950 for people to marry someone of the same religion than there had been eighty years before, still 70 percent of Protestants

Table 6-1   Percent of All Husbands and Percent of All Wives with Cross-Race Spouses, United States, 1960–1970*

	1960	1970
Percent of all black husbands who had white wives	0.1	0.1
Percent of all white husbands who had black wives	0.8	0.7
Percent of all black wives who had white husbands	0.8	1.2
Percent of all white wives who had black husbands	0.1	0.1

*Source: 1960 and 1970 U.S. Censuses of Population, *Marital Status*.

who married did so within the faith, as did 73 percent of Catholics and 96 percent of Jews. Winch (1963, pp. 328–332) compared the actual mating behavior of Americans as of 1957 with the pattern that would have existed if mating among the major religious denominations had been purely random, that is, if no homogamous attraction had been at work. He shows that for all couples in which the spouses were members of a religious group, 94 percent belonged to the same faith; whereas if mating had not been pulled toward homogamy, the chance figure would have been 56 percent. For the three principal denominations, the comparisons of the degree of actual homogamy with the amount that would be expected if mating were random are:

Protestant	67	percent homogamous against
	48	percent expected by chance
Catholic	23	percent homogamous against
	7	percent expected by chance
Jewish	3.4	percent homogamous against
	0.1	percent expected by chance

A Canadian study of interfaith marriages over a thirty-year period has shown an increase in Jewish-gentile and Protestant-Catholic marriages (Heer, 1962). It is assumed from this and other research that denominational religion is becoming less significant as a cultural marker. It is worth noting, however, that among those *interfaith marriages that survive,* there is a strong tendency for one spouse to adopt the faith of the other (Babchuk et al., 1967). Given the recent history of swings between assimilation, accommodation, and conflict, between the death and rebirth of religions, and between loving and hating "other kinds of people," it would be foolish to draw a fixed trend line into the future.

What Affects Homogamy?   The attraction of like for like varies somewhat with broad sociological categories like race or religion. The variations move also with the degree of ethnic identity, with social status, and with the relative proportions of "different people" in the population.

The more closely knit the ethnic group—which is one way of saying the more it satisfies—the greater the pull for its members to love and to mate within "the tribe" (Thomas, 1951). Groups that take pride in their identity have lower rates of intermarriage than groups characterized by "self-hate" (Barron, 1951). Factors that produce a loss of faith or a lessened ethnic identification reduce the homogamous attraction (Goode, 1964). Conversely, as intermarriage occurs, the unity of the original ethnic groups disintegrates (Anderson, 1958). Another way of looking at the association of ethnic cohesion with *endogamy,* that is, with marriage within the tribe, is to note that the less a person identifies with his parents and the more unhappy his relations with them were, the more likely is he to marry outside his group (Heiss, 1960; Hunt and Coller, 1957).

Social status is part of this picture. The more similar the ethnic groups are in social position and the more they interact, the more readily do they love each other (Barron, 1951; Hunt and Coller, 1957; Merton, 1941; Talmon-Garber, 1956). Furthermore, as an ethnic minority moves up the class ladder, it intermarries more frequently (Broom, 1956; Burma, 1963; Thomas, 1951).

The risk of gaining or losing social status through a mixed marriage is an additional consideration that affects the tendency toward or away from endogamy. Religious intermarriage between persons of the same class is more frequent among persons of higher socioeconomic status than among persons of lesser status (Chancellor and Burchinal, 1962; Thomas, 1951). However, interethnic marriages decline as more status is at stake, as in interracial marriages. Thus, even where there is much ethnic intermarriage, as in Hawaii, there is more cross-cultural mating among persons of lower social status and less intermarriage among persons of higher occupational-educational position (Schmitt, 1965).

Finally, assimilation—loving and marrying *across* the categories—is easier the smaller the "other" group (Heer, 1962; Thomas, 1956). There are two related interpretations of this fact. One interpretation is that the scarcity of prospective mates within a small minority encourages intermarriage (Thomas, 1951, p. 489). An additional interpretation is that minorities are conceived to be less threatening and less different the smaller they are in relation to the majority. Thus one alien in our tribe of 200 is more likely to be loved than are 50 such bearers of foreign culture. In short, *ethnocentrism increases with the relative size of the minority* (Lundberg and Dickson, 1952).

What Homogamy Means   The fact that there is a pull to marry people like ourselves has been well documented when the similarity has been measured in terms of race, ethnicity, religion, and socioeconomic status. There are fluctuations, as we have seen, in the amount of homogamous mating in time and among different segments of a society. However, the fact of a homogamous tendency signifies two things.

It means, first, that we tend to associate with people who are "more like us," and, of course, we marry people with whom we have been acquainted (for the most part). So, in the first place, the categories of ethnicity and social class operate like screens. They filter the kinds of people we meet and hence the kinds of people among whom we are likely to find a mate.

A second meaning of the tendency for people to marry within these broad social categories is that these social strata are very much like cultures or subcultures. They betoken some patterning of preferences. They signify similarities among "our group" in styles of doing things, in the daily habits of others that make life comfortable when those customs are like our own and uncomfortable when they are markedly different. Mating among people "like us" thereby reduces the risk of conflict, a risk that is always present when two or more people live together intimately.

Needing You and Loving You

If similarity is one magnet that draws us together, needing is another. Here, of course, *personal* factors enter and account for some of the variation within the social determinants.

Personal factors are those individual differences, those quirks of taste and temperament, that make some people easier to abide than others, whether or not they are socially similar. These idiosyncrasies are reflected in differences in personal tempo, in the rapidity or lethargy with which we move. They are seen also in the physiological rhythms that affect whether we are "night people" or "day people" and whether we awaken sullen or smiling. These individual differences are exhibited in our preference for noise or quiet and for what, in general, has been called stimulus seeking. These personal quirks have been measured along many dimensions of reliable individual difference that have a strong genetic component; they seem more inherited than learned. Such measured dimensions include those of dependency and self-sufficiency, shyness and adventuresomeness, sobriety and enthusiasm, and sensitivity to stimuli (Burt, 1938; Claridge et al., 1973; Cortes and Gatti, 1965, 1966; Goldstein, 1964; Gottesman, 1963; Petrie, 1967; Sales et al., 1974).

These differences in individual temperament can be analyzed as though they required different things of the environment, including the people in it. However, the concept of need is difficult to define independently of the behavior that it is used to explain. The trouble with invoking needs as the causes of our conduct is that we are likely to prove the existence of the need by the fact of the act.[2] Worse, if the actor says he does *not* need what we think he does when we try to explain his behavior, we are apt, in this post-Freudian age, to go underground and to speak of the other person's unconscious needs. This is to say: "He is not aware of his needs, but we are."

The Hypothesis of Complementary Needs   Despite these difficulties with the concept of need, the term is used here—cautiously—because a prominent hypothesis about loving and mating has been advanced under the title, "the theory of complementary needs" (Winch, 1958). Winch follows Ohmann's thesis (1942) that "we fall in love with those whom we need to complete ourselves." The theory of complementary needs says, then, that we seek mates who give the greatest promise of satisfying our needs. People who fall in love are said to have complementary needs if (1) they have the same need, but one of the pair has more of it than the other, or, what is more interesting, if (2) they have opposite needs that give mutual gratification. Examples of the type 2 complementariness are the sadist who finds his masochist, the Milquetoast who finds his Mama, the dependent woman who finds her brute, and so on.

---

[2]The vagueness of the idea of a need as employed by psychologists to explain our behavior can be seen in a prominent definition. Murray (1938, pp. 123–124) writes that "A need is a construct . . . which organizes perception, apperception, intellection, conation, and action in such a way as to transform in a certain direction an existing, unsatisfying situation."

The evidence for this hypothesis is intriguing but infirm. It is enough to allow us to say that such things happen without specifying how much of our loving results from the meeting of complementary needs. The bulk of the evidence is clinical, that is, it consists of reports from psychiatrists and others about the cases they have seen. Winch (1958), however, tried to test the hypothesis more objectively through an intensive study of twenty-five young married couples who, at the time, had been married about one year. The assessment of their needs was attempted through interviews and from an evaluation of the stories they told on the Thematic Apperception Test.[3] Assuming the validity of the interpretation of need from these interviews and stories, Winch made 388 predictions of the kinds of correlations to be expected among the needs of the spouses if complementarity had brought them together. Two-thirds of these predictions were fulfilled, a fact that allows Winch to report his hypothesis confirmed.

An Alternative Idea   It seems as true, but more simple, to translate the theory of complementary needs into the facts of *exchange.* We expect something from each other. We do so as strangers driving our cars on a freeway or as lovers debating marriage or trying to stay married. These expectations, whether or not we call them needs, are sometimes well met, sometimes compromised, and sometimes so disappointed that the original attraction turns into aversion. Whenever we know someone, we are engaged in a running process of rewarding and disappointing and, in turn, of being pleased and pained. The continuity of our acquaintance, and its intensity, depend on this moving balance of reciprocated satisfactions and dissatisfactions.

It is part of the definition of others "being like us" that they have similar or complementary anticipations. Similar or matching expectations are conventions that are most successfully taught during the acquisition of a culture. It follows, then, that social changes that challenge conventional ways of living make loving more difficult. It will be our thesis (pp. 113–115) that modern marriage suffers as expectations break loose from culturally embedded roles. This freedom means that how we are to behave together is put up for negotiation. Negotiation substitutes debate and bargaining for trained and reciprocated expectations. This freedom, like all freedoms, has a price.

IS SEX A HELP OR A HINDRANCE?

One of the major needs that we seek to complement and that seems to drive us toward and away from love is the sexual appetites. This need is referred to in the plural, as "appetites," because the sexual urgency has more than one

---

[3]The Thematic Apperception Test is a "projective" measure. This means that the stimuli to which the subject responds are relatively unstructured, allowing the respondent to project his personality upon them. The test consists of pictures for which the subject is asked to tell "what is happening." The interpretation of this test is subjective, its retest reliability is modest, and its validity uncertain (Adcock, 1970).

stimulus and more than one style of satisfaction. As with other tastes, sexual preferences are varied.

It is apparent that the sexual drives are satisfied in and out of marriage and with and without love. The persistent questions are whether love needs sex and whether sex strengthens love. The answers to both questions are yes and no.

Love may fuel sex, but sex thrives without love. Love is particular; sex is diffuse. We are more particular about whom we love than about whom we have sex with.

The Freudians tell us that sexual appetite is the energy behind all love, even that between parent and child. It is impossible to prove or disprove this idea, but the normal use of the word "love" to refer to a concern for the other is applied in many cases where no sexual attraction is apparent.

Feeling sexually attracted is an accompaniment of much loving, but it is not necessary for loving. Conversely, love sometimes accompanies sex, but it is not tied to sex. For example, there is evidence that unhappily married couples, even those on the verge of divorce, have sexual intercourse about as frequently as happy pairs (Dickinson and Beam, 1931; Terman, 1938).

Sex has its own urgency. There is no census of such matters, but it is probable that the overwhelming preponderance of sexual acts is *unloving.* One has only to make an inventory of the awesome array of things people *do* sexually to demonstrate this point. For instance, human beings achieve sexual gratification by masturbating, dreaming, looking, hitting, rubbing against strangers and inanimate objects, exposing themselves, setting fires, stealing, being insulted, and communing with their gods. The "sexual partners" used by humans—principally but not always without love—include a variety of inanimate objects and other animals from dogs to ducks. Both observations and interrogations reveal that people are sexually aroused by wrestling (of course), playing football, driving at speed, quarreling, fighting, climbing ropes, doing chin-ups, hearing martial music or "rock," and seeing flags fly (Barclay and Haber, 1965; Hirschfeld, 1956; Kinsey et al., 1948, 1953; Krafft-Ebing, 1959; Sorensen, 1973; Terman, 1938). Human beings can even be sexually satisfied by machines in front of a professional audience (Masters and Johnson, 1966).

All this may be no news to the sophisticate, although it continues to astound the novice. A conclusion to be drawn is that increasing the "sex level" need not increase the "love level." The popular slogan of the sixties, "make love, not war," translates more accurately, in action, into "have sex, don't fight."

A paradox arises from the apparent connection between sexual desire and love and the many instances of the separation of these impulses. The paradox is compounded as we see sex used to express *hate.* One has only to note the quality of our rude gestures or listen to street language to be impressed with the common link between having sex and despising its object. The four-letter words for the "love act," for example, indicate abuse and exploitation, not concern, and no one mistakes "screw you" for "love you."

Attending to Sex and Corrupting Love

There are many indications that at least the urban, educated young in Western countries have experienced a "sexual liberation" since World War II. We say "at least the urban, educated young" because young people of lesser affluence and schooling have long had fewer inhibitions against premarital heterosexual intercourse (Kinsey et al., 1948, 1953). In short, the better-off youth had more room to change.

The inflated attention to sex is visible in the mass media, in the popularity-of "how-to-do-it" manuals, and in the increase in illegitimacy and venereal disease rates (American Social Health Association, 1968; Clague and Ventura, 1968; Sklar and Berkov, 1974; Statistics Canada, 1972). This change in the climate of sexual activity has not relieved us of sex problems. It has only shifted their location from the sufferings of life without sex or of sex with guilt to confusion about how one should regard himself and his sexual partners and one's anxiety about sexual competence.

If mutual affection rather than mere sexual outlet is our concern, then today's question becomes, "Does better sex make for more love?" The answer is, obviously, "not necessarily."

While sexual union is one of life's great pleasures and while it enriches a loving relation, a risk is run in promoting sexual athleticism. The risk is that anxiety about sexual performance may become the modern's neurosis, replacing the Victorian's frigidity. The extreme of either attitude—glorifying sex or denying it—detracts from love and makes living together more difficult.

WHY DO WE MARRY AND HOW WELL?

In industrial lands where marriage is less frequently arranged and more frequently voluntary, the norm is to marry for love. This expectation is supported by social inducements and by mating patterns that allow love to determine the choice of a spouse (Goode, 1964; Winch, 1958). Fulfilling love, which includes building a household, becomes the major reason for marrying. It is a good reason, but, as we shall see, a fragile one. The fragility of love as a basis for marriage puts us in a bind: there is risk if we do and risk if we don't. The dilemma is nothing new. Benjamin Franklin recognized it over two hundred years ago when he wrote in his *Poor Richard's Almanack:*

> Wedlock, as old men note, hath likened been
> > Unto a publick crowd or common rout,
> Where those that are without would fain get in
> > And those that are within would fain get out.

Despite the hazards of marrying principally for love, taking the risk is apparently preferable to remaining unloved or single. The proof lies in the rate at which we marry. It is *normal* to be married. It is normal in the statistical sense—most adults are married—and it may be normal in an *evaluative* sense—it is healthier to be married. In the Western world almost everyone marries sometime. Only 3 or 4 percent of North Americans, for example, never marry (Carter and Glick, 1970, p. 323). Furthermore, married people of either sex have lower death rates than single, widowed, or divorced persons of like age (Carter and Glick, 1970, p. 345).

The preference for marriage is attested not merely by the fact that the overwhelming majority of citizens in "developed" countries are married but also by the fact that the majority of marital failures are followed by remarriages. Age for age, both divorced males and divorced females have high marriage rates, rates that frequently *exceed* those of single or widowed persons (Dublin, 1951, pp. 46–47; Glick and Norton, 1970; Kuzel and Krishnan, 1972). These differences vary, of course, with age, race, sex, and social status. However, the popularity of marriage is notable in the fact that those who "fail" in marriage leap back into wedlock at such high rates. Some wit, looking at such statistics, has called this the triumph of hope over experience.

In Canada and the United States about three-fourths of divorced men and two-thirds of divorced women remarry, and the recent trend has been toward an *increase* in the proportion of all marriages that are remarriages (Glick, 1949, 1958; Kuzel and Krishnan, 1972; Schlesinger and Macrae, 1970). More than one marriage in four that is now contracted north of the Rio Grande involves a spouse who is, in the vernacular, a "retread." A representative figure for North America is that among spouses aged thirty-five to thirty-nine, about two-thirds of all marriages are remarriages. Furthermore, the probability of early divorce and early remarriage is greater among persons of lower social status than among persons who are better off (Glick and Norton, 1971).

Such statistics show that modern marriage involves a considerable amount of serial monogamy. There is at least a minor norm for a person to have one spouse at a time but more than one in a lifetime. There is even some reality underlying the optimism in this repetitive attempt to be happily married. A recent American survey reveals that "persons who remarry are more likely to remain in their second marriage than persons married only once are to remain in their first marriage" (Glick and Norton, 1971, p. 314).

Since so many of us take the gamble of getting married against the current North American odds that "one-third of the whites and one-half of the Negroes [now entering marriages] will eventually end their marriages in divorce" (Glick and Norton, 1970, p. 6), two questions arise: (1) what factors raise or lower the odds of happy marriage and (2) why do these factors operate that way?

FACTORS IN MARITAL SUCCESS AND FAILURE

Over the past forty-five years there have been numerous attempts to isolate the factors associated with success and failure in marriage. Hamilton (1929) started this kind of research in the United States using questionnaires and interviews to find out what made the difference between happily married people and others. His early effort was followed by several large-scale investigations. The sociologists Burgess and Cottrell (1939) studied couples in the Chicago area, while psychologists under the direction of Terman (1938) conducted parallel research in California. Locke (1951) added to the findings of these studies by comparing the characteristics of divorcés in Indiana with a comparable group of happily married persons, and Burgess and Wallin (1953) contributed to our knowledge of American marriage by following 1,000 engaged couples through the mating process and into the first five years of their marriages.

A Portrait of the Happily Married

The findings of these investigations are quite uniform. Considering people in general, rather than particular individuals, those who are conventional, sociable, and homogamously mated are more likely to be happily married. The "interesting, difficult" people we know are just that—interesting and difficult. They may be creative and valuable, but they are not good marriage bets.

The factors associated with marital success are largely fixed before marriage. It is what one *brings to* the marriage more than what *occurs in* the marriage that determines its success. For example, having happily married parents and having had a happy childhood are both prognostic of better chances of marital success. So, too, are a home discipline that was firm but not harsh and that resulted in an attachment to one's parents without an absorption by them. People who are reared in bickering households by parents whom they cannot respect are apt to experience discord themselves when they marry. Other good signs—that vary, of course, in importance—are agreement between spouses concerning marriage ideals, with the odds favoring those couples that prefer taking their vacations together rather than separately, that allow the husband to be the leader, and that apply a single moral standard to the partners' sexual behavior. Couples whose parents favor their marriage have a running start on those whose families disapprove it, as do couples who know each other for some time before marriage. Hasty marriage may be romantic, but it is not a recommended way of reducing the risks of this investment.

As we should expect, there are psychological factors as well as sociological ones that affect the chances of marital happiness. The Terman study, for example, finds overlapping yet significant clusters of personality traits associated with being happily or miserably married—or divorced. According to this research, there are tendencies (and only that) for happy husbands to be "cooperative, conservative, cautious, and emotionally stable" (Johnson and Terman, 1935). On the other hand, unhappy husbands are described as "neurotic, irritable, seclusive, and timid," while divorced men are called "gregarious, willful, daring, and more gratified by admiration than by achievement." The happy wives in this research were found to be "kindly, docile, placid, methodical, cautious, and conformist" in comparison with the unhappily married women who were termed "relatively neurotic, careless, lazy, tactless, and unsympathetic." The divorced women were characterized as "self-reliant, self-assertive, and tolerant."[4] Both male and female divorcés showed more signs of *intellectual interests* than either the happily or unhappily married groups.

Tharp (1963) summarizes research on the personal characteristics of the happily and unhappily married with this tabulation:

Happily Married	*Unhappily Married*
Emotionally stable	Emotionally unstable
Considerate of others	Critical of others
Yielding	Dominating
Companionable	Isolated
Self-confident	Lacking self-confidence
Emotionally dependent	Emotionally self-sufficient

In keeping with our two-step hypothesis about how one falls in love and out, Tharp notes several studies that show marital success to depend on a *meeting of expectations.* Individuals are more likely to be happily married when a husband's regard of his wife agrees with her conception of herself, and similarly for the wife's regard of her husband. In Western marriages, at the time of Tharp's study at least, it seems particularly crucial that the wife's perception of her husband agree with his view of himself. It seems less important that the husband's perception of his wife be in accord with her view of herself.

A Qualifying Note   Findings such as these have a common sense to them. They should be read, however, with an awareness that the differences described are those found among aggregates of individuals and that they may *not* apply to a particular person.

Furthermore, it should be remembered that the samples from which these portraits have been drawn are limited in time, place, and size and that some of the correlations we have noted may be expected to change somewhat with changes in marital style. For example, as more people become divorcés, the differences between divorced persons and unhappily married persons may be expected to blur. It is impossible to predict in which direction these differences may shift with the duration of the marriage. As divorce becomes more popular and less stigmatized, it is conceivable that those who remain married though unhappy may be even more sharply distinguished from those who divorce.

An additional qualification is this: if marriages become more egalitarian and the relations between sexes more "unisexual" (more single-standard oriented), then there may also be changes in such findings as Tharp's about whose expectations, the husband's or the wife's, are the more important for marital adjustment.

---

[4]Some readers have criticized Johnson and Terman for using trait names that sound more value-laden than objective. This is an additional reason for placing their descriptive adjectives in quotation marks.

On Validity Whenever behavioral scientists attempt to measure the influences working upon our emotional lives, they are open to the criticism that their tools are too crude for the sensitive job of perceiving what makes two people love each other and what allows them to live together satisfactorily. The criticism is often voiced as the complaint that much is left out of the sociopsychological description of how we do or do not get along. This criticism is true but unreasonable. It is unreasonable because *every* way of describing our lives leaves something out. The practical question is, "How much can you do with the data you've got?"

The marital adjustment studies have been criticized because the data come from reports given by the subjects themselves. The social scientist's measures, then, not only leave something out, but they may also put things in that are not there. The pragmatic answer to this accusation is to test how much one can do with his imperfect tools. Terman and Wallin (1949) show, for example, that marital adjustment tests allow one to predict better than by random guessing which couples will divorce. Furthermore, adding a prediction of *marital unhappiness without divorce* to the criterion of "ended in divorce" increases the predictive utility of the social psychologist's blunt instruments.

If it is recognized that the sociopsychological portrait of the happily married is a group picture and that it lacks fine individual detail, then these research findings are useful as cautionary guides for our lives and those of our loved ones.

MARRIAGE PRO AND CON

We are faced with a puzzle. On the one hand, we approve of marriage in both word and deed. The majority of us think marriage is a moral and sensible arrangement, and we North Americans marry at one of the highest rates of any people in the world. We also marry at younger ages, which bespeaks some eagerness. Furthermore, at the cost of considerable pain, we marry more frequently within a lifetime now than in the past.

At the same time that we demonstrate this approval of being married, we view the state skeptically—sometimes with humor, sometimes with hostility, but always as a condition fraught with danger.

Two questions arise from this puzzle: the first is, "How many marriages work out well?" and the second is, "What accounts for the failures?"

How Many Enjoy Being Married?

The answer to this question depends on whom you ask and how. If you ask the middle-class white North Americans (who have been the subjects of most of the marital adjustment studies) to rate the happiness of their unions and if you ask their friends also to rate them, the results run along these lines: between 60 and 70 percent say that they are happy or very happy in their marriages, between 15 and 30 percent call themselves average in their marital adjustment,

Table 6-2   Ratings of Marital Happiness, American Samples*

"Would you say that your marriage has been successful or not very
successful?" (March 25, 1950)

	Very successful	Fairly successful	Not very successful	Don't know
National total	68%	23%	6%	3%
Men	70	22	5	3
Women	66	24	8	2
College educated	83	14	3	–
High school education	71	24	3	2
Grade school education	62	25	9	4

"Knowing what you do now, if you had it to do over, is there a chance you
might not marry the same person, do you think you probably would, or are you
certain you would?" (February 26, 1949)

	Certainly	Probably	Might not	Don't know
National total	49	28	10	13
Men	52	27	8	13
Women	47	29	11	13

*Adapted, with permission, from American Institute of Public Opinion polls.

and between 15 and 25 percent are rated as unhappy (Burgess and Cottrell,
1939; Lang, 1932; Popenoe and Wicks, 1937; Terman, 1938).

When similar questions are asked of more representative samples of North
Americans through public opinion polls, the results are not greatly different,
although the answers do vary a bit with the kind of question asked. For
example, slightly more than two-thirds of Americans in 1950 called their
marriages very successful, but when the question was phrased, "If you had it to
do over, would you marry the same person?" the proportion of favorable
responses dropped to about one-half. The details are shown in Table 6-2.

These figures are a generation old, but they seem to have held up quite
well. The University of Michigan's Survey Research Center asked similar
questions in 1971 of a representative sample of Americans. This study of "the
quality of life" (Campbell et al., 1975) finds 86 percent of married persons to be
"satisfied" or "completely satisfied" with their marriages. Seven percent feel
"neutral" about the matter while only 6 percent report themselves to be
"dissatisfied" or "completely dissatisfied." Sixty-eight percent of these people
say that they have *never* thought of getting a divorce and 71 percent say that
they have *never* wished they had married someone else.

IN SUMMARY

We need not ask of a social science that it give an exact number to the
satisfactions and dissatisfactions with marriage. For present purposes it is

enough to note that while most people seem content in marriage, a considerable segment of our married population is unhappy with the arrangement.

Here again, it is well to remember that an evaluation of our own marriage or that of others is a function of our expectations. There are different ways of living together and of getting along, and our judgment of the goodness of life always varies with the standards we apply. Many marriages are satisfactory to their participants although they fall short of the romantic ideal of the fully shared, mutually fulfilling companionship, nourished by the sexual bond and stimulated by intellectual ties. Just as there are different *expectations* of how marriage should be, there are also different *accommodations* to how it is to be lived, and these varying expectations and adjustments need not be put on one scale that ranks people by degrees of marital happiness.

We are left with conclusions like these: marriage has its discontents, but the record of our marrying and remarrying indicates that, whatever its liabilities, we prefer being married to staying single. Our concern, of course, is that our marriages and those of our children should be successful. About the conditions of success we know some things. We have good reason for believing that misery in marriage, like misery in general, increases in urban settings with poverty and low education. We have also seen evidence that unhappy people, the children of unhappy parents, are carriers of a discontent with which they infect their own unions. On top of all this, there is a cultural reason underwriting much of present dissatisfaction with marriage.

A Hypothesis: The Cultural Roots of Marital Misery

It is not just being married that is difficult. All living together is difficult. In real life as opposed to the hopeful ideologies, conflict and disappointment are as probable as peace and harmony. From observations of natural scenes, it is apparent that egoism is at least as strong an impulse as altruism. Go to the nursery and watch the little ones at play. There is cooperation, but it is a weak impulse readily succumbing to competition, rivalry, and junior warfare. The teacher and the parent stand on constant guard against the expression of selfishness, the urge to exploit, and the ventilation of hatred. What each child wills is opposed by what others want, and it is only slowly and gradually that our cubs are humanized—that is, that they learn to behave as we expect human beings of a certain age and sex to act and that they learn the etiquette of response to a *reciprocal* relationship.

This learning process is most successful when there is a clear *culture,* an agreed upon style of life that defines and reinforces how we should behave toward each other. These cultural definitions tell us how boys are thought to be different from girls, how children should act toward their parents, how parents should rear them, and, finally, what is expected of boys and girls when they become men and women and form new reproductive unions.

All societies attempt to transmit these expectations. Where there is a strong culture rather than disputed ones, these expectations are reinforced by social pressure, by example, and by institution. Without a well-defined culture and without its reinforcement by model and institutional practice, how we act toward each other is thrown open to negotiation. Negotiation is itself a form of fighting that bespeaks lack of agreement about the rules of the game. Such lack of agreement has been called many names. The most popular title given it by sociologists is borrowed from the French scholar Emile Durkheim, who called such relative rulelessness *anomie.*

This view of the function of culture in reducing discord says nothing about the *content* of that culture. The institutions that do this work need not be the ones you and I prefer. The marital arrangements that such institutions defend need not be those we approve. In fact, the kinds of union that work in most areas of the world are *not* the kinds idealized by feminists and their representatives in the United Nations.[5] It is a mistake to believe that our own preferences describe the only workable arrangements between men and women or that what we are accustomed to is without disadvantage, risk, and its own peculiar costs.

An Illustration   We are in a mountain town deep in southern Mexico. Seated about the pool one afternoon are two of the pueblo's lovely young ladies and some tourists from the United States. The Mexican misses are engaged, and their marriages are to take place within the year. One of the tourists—a caricature of the gringo with his loud voice, demanding manner, and incredulous gape at the "foreigner"—begins to tease the señoritas about the prospects of their marriages. His final jibe, and one he thinks will be most telling, is to remind these young ladies that after marriage, their husbands will undoubtedly have *casas chicas,* that is, mistresses, in the big city. For the American this possibility is supposed to be the clincher. It is intended to raise doubts in the hearts of the señoritas, to lead them to defensive protests, and, of course, to result in an unfavorable comparison with the gringo's own definition of marriage.

The señoritas, however, are neither disturbed nor defensive. There is no denial that mistresses are probable. There is simply no importance attached to this possibility. Calmly, one señorita puts it this way, "The home will be mine." *Her* marital expectations will not be grievously offended by her future husband's infidelity; in fact, they include this likelihood. Her marriage is to be held together by other considerations, by other definitions of what the family is and why one forms such a group. To the gringo, a man who has "progressed" beyond such traditional definitions of marriage and who has embraced the ideology of romantic love, the señorita's attitude is indeed foreign.

The Import   This story is told not to praise Mexican marriage or to recommend *casas chicas* but rather to indicate that arrangements other than

---

[5]Advocates of "women's liberation" are quite correct in perceiving the family to be one source, but only one, of sexual inequality. The ideology of the Israeli kibbutz also recognizes that the development of an egalitarian commune requires the deemphasis, if not the elimination, of the family and the individual. However, in such communal situations it is instructive to note that women themselves take the lead in reaffirming the value of the family and the individual. This is one of the observations of the long-term (1955–1966) research conducted by the late Yonina Talmon (1972) in Israel.

ours work. They work because they are embedded in a social fabric of understood roles and complementary marital expectations.

With this view of things, a source of the difficulty with many modern marriages becomes apparent. The trouble is that such unions have been individualized, deinstitutionalized, and romanticized.

Freeing Marriage from Institutions   In the urbanized areas of western Europe and North America, the assured styles of marriage have been challenged. Mate selection, traditionally protected by elders, has become subject to individual taste and the accident of a meeting. The reasons for forming a family are not always clear and, as a consequence, the expectations that lead us into marriage are often fuzzy, unrealistic, and ultimately disappointed.

The rites of passage that formalize the transition from childhood to adulthood are now nonexistent or but hollow ritual, and in many Western societies we find a group of quasi adults, people called teen-agers, who live in a biocultural no-man's-land, adult in body but children under the law, and, consequently, often in a quandary about how they should behave.[6] These adolescents are prepared for marriage principally by their appetites, their TV-fed dreams, and the questionable example of their parents and peers.

Furthermore, the form of the contract between men and women entering matrimony has been altered and in the process left ambiguous, a matter of individual interpretation. The marriage itself is protected against the personalities of the union not by social preparation, social pressure, and socially prescribed functions but by the couple's good sense and emotional maturity—qualities that are not so common as we should wish.

In place of institutionally defined roles for husband and wife, in place of well-learned expectations to be fulfilled in marriages, many modern unions depend upon romantic love and the cult of personality to make things work. These are fragile sentiments upon which to base an enduring and pleasant friendship. Marriages so contracted place a heavy burden upon the bare meeting of two individuals romantically attached but culturally abandoned.

This morning's press carries a picture of a famous entertainer, age fifty-five, who has just married for the third time. His bride, age twenty-five, is also a marital repeater. The question that is asked from both left and right, a question raised by both innovators and traditionalists, is "Why are they doing it?" Her motives may be spelled "fame and fortune," but his? However well we may wish these newlyweds, their marriage is a prominent illustration of the freeing of this estate from culturally defined objectives. Their freedom makes everything depend on them, and that is a heavy load for a long haul.

Ways Out   Different arrangements have been, and are being, attempted. The old idea of trial marriage, advocated by numerous distinguished thinkers

---

[6]Adolescents themselves recognize their ambiguous state. A recent survey of a representative sample of American teen-agers found almost three-fourths of them agreeing that "I'm not a child any more, but I'm not an adult yet, either" (Sorensen, 1973, Table 254).

from Lord Bertrand Russell to Judge Ben Lindsay, is being renovated. It is seen in the middle-class version of common-law marriage—"living together"—and it has been a long-time practice in Iceland under the title of "engagement marriage." Such trials are also seen in the efforts to establish urban communes, and it is witnessed among those couples who formally marry, but with the understanding that their union is an experiment for which an expiration date is set. Some of these experimental pairings illustrate our point that the loss of a culture throws relations open to negotiation, as when some young couples write their own contracts, noting in detail what used to be understood from the religious ceremony. Thus, when M. L. and J. G. married, "they signed a two-year agreement spelling out who does what around the house. The contract is three pages long and includes specifications" about combining the couple's last names, about doing the housework, and about an expiration clause (*U.S. News & World Report,* 1973, p. 74). According to this news account, "The two say they place little value in the institution of marriage. They got married because they felt their friends and relatives expected it of them."

Do the Ways Out Work? Such data as we have about these experiments do not indicate that they work any better than conventional marriages. There are different styles of satisfaction, of course, but each set of satisfactions carries its own costs.

Urban communes tend to be heterosexual dormitories, maintained because of their economic utility and subject to high personnel turnover. The rural communes that have been studied in North America (Berger et al., 1971; Downing, 1970; Kinkade, 1973) develop their own brand of interpersonal tension and have not succeeded in achieving equality of the sexes, as some of them had promised.

Just living together relieves one of the awesome thought that this relationship is forever, but it does not remove the difficulties that arise when two people with different expectations try to get along. There are feminists who believe that, at least in the present climate of marital expectations, women living with men outside of marriage are apt to get the worst of the deal in that they provide the usual conveniences of marriage without a reciprocal responsibility on the part of the man. No one has scales in which to weigh this possibility. However, it is a possibility that our sisters and daughters ought to consider, and do consider, before they try this way out. For example, Hobart (1974) found Canadian university women to be more skeptical of trial marriage than their male peers on the ground that they might be "used." The women in this survey were as agreeable as men to experimental marriage *if* they believed the trial would lead to conventional marriage.

Measuring the success of alternative styles of living together is as difficult as measuring marital happiness, and the research findings on this topic are tentative. If "breaking up" is a measure of success, then the record thus far does not show these trial arrangements to have improved greatly over "regular marriage." Trost (1972) reports that cohabiting unmarried couples in Scandinavia have about ten times the "divorce" rate of conventionally married pairs. Of course, many participants in alternative ways of living together do not regard endurance as a virtue, and hence for them "breaking up" is not a fair test of the satisfactions of cohabitation without marriage.

There is evidence, again tentative, that the recent swing toward cohabitation outside marriage has been accompanied by a rise in emotional difficulties among young people who are placed in poorly defined but intense relations with the opposite sex. Katz (1974) reports this for a sample of American university students, and his finding is supported by statements from psychiatrists and psychologists who counsel students (Bowen, 1973; Halleck, 1967; D. G. Kahn, 1973). The psychiatrist Bowen believes that his detailed clinical experience with relatively affluent graduate students in an eastern American university allows him "to predict that students who are 'living together' in college will have less stable marriages than average, that they will do less well than average as parents, and that their total lives will be more problem-prone than average."

However correct or incorrect such a forecast may prove to be, present indications are that experiments in living together work no better, and possibly worse, than the culturally embedded, institutional forms by which the sexes have traditionally shared their lives.

What Is Required?   When institutions that remind us of how we should be bound to others lose their force, when they become subject to argument and experiment, there yet remains a last resort if we are to get along with each other. The last resort and first requirement is *manners*. Manners are a social lubricant. Etiquette reduces friction and keeps our individual wills within limits. However, the trouble with much modern marriage is that its celebrants view manners as "formal" and "artificial." Today there is a strong attitudinal current running against formality. Rudeness on the domestic scene is epidemic and hilariously advertised by television. Spouses shout at each other, slam doors, break promises, tell lies. Finally, unmannered themselves, parents transmit their rudeness to their young. Parents who shout at each other may be expected to scream at their children. Inevitably the children will shout back, and so is ensured the circle of insult. Here, at our cultural roots, lies the source of our discontent.

We do not know how to rebuild cultures, but we know how to say goodbye. Divorce ends a present misery, although it may provide no permanent cure for what ails us.

DIVORCING

It is not news that divorce has become an increasingly popular way of adjusting to marital disappointment. At least among the "developed" countries, the trend over the last forty years has been toward higher divorce rates. Thus far, Japan has been an interesting exception to this tendency. Divorce rates in that land have not fluctuated much since the early 1930s (Carter and Glick, 1970, p. 28). Other rich states, however, have experienced a doubling of their divorce rates in the past two generations, and some countries have had fivefold increases. For twelve affluent societies, Table 6-3 shows the shift in the number of countries experiencing high and low divorce rates in 1965 as contrasted with 1932. Whereas in 1932 six of these countries had divorce rates of between 0.1 and 0.3 per 1,000 population, by 1965 none of these countries was in that low bracket. Meanwhile, the number of these states experiencing high divorce rates of one or more per 1,000 population had increased from one in 1932 (the United States) to four in 1965.

The countries with the greatest relative increases in divorce are those that had the lowest initial rates, indicating that some portion of their movement may have been a result of changed divorce laws that liberated unhappily married couples from their bondage. These more rapidly changed lands are Austria, Canada, Finland, Sweden, and the United Kingdom.

Who Divorces?

Within these rich lands people of different categories have different probabilities of divorce. The tendencies are for persons of lower socioeconomic status to divorce at a higher rate than those with more money, schooling, and prestige. In addition, as we should expect from the marriage adjustment studies, divorces are more frequent among those couples that had but brief acquaintance and short engagements before marrying. Too, divorces are more likely among couples that are dissimilar in education, occupation, religion, and ethnicity (Goode, 1956, 1962; Kephart, 1955; Monahan, 1970).

**Table 6-3 Changes in Divorce Rates among Twelve Rich Countries†
1932–1965***

	Number of countries with specified divorce rates in—	
Divorce rate per 1,000 population‡	**1965**	**1932**
0.1–0.3	0	6
0.4–0.6	2	3
0.7–0.9	6	1
1.0 and over	4	1

*Adapted from H. Carter and P. C. Glick, *Marriage and Divorce: A Social and Economic Study*, pp. 28–29. © 1970 by Harvard University Press. Reproduced by permission.

†These states are Australia, Austria, Canada, Finland, France, the Federal Republic of Germany, Japan, the Netherlands, Norway, Sweden, the United Kingdom (England and Wales), and the United States. West Germany is omitted, of course, from the 1932 tabulation.

‡A divorce rate per 1,000 population is a crude rate. Rates become better indicators as they are refined to include in their denominators *all those cases and only those cases* that are at risk of appearing in the numerator. Since only married couples can divorce, a better rate would be the number of divorces during a year per 1,000 married couples in the population that year. The utility of this table depends, therefore, on the assumption that the age and marriage structures of the populations being compared did not differ greatly among these countries.

Those who marry for the first time when they are teen-agers have a higher probability of divorce than those who first marry in the more conventional years. For American white men, for example, recent divorce rates per 1,000 of their population in the first five years of their first marriages run 16 for those who married when they were in their teens, 14 for those who first married when they were twenty to twenty-four years old, and 11 for those who did not marry until they were over thirty (Glick and Norton, 1971). These rates contrast with a divorce risk of *five* per 1,000 for white men who first married when they were twenty-five to twenty-nine years of age, a finding that correlates, of course, with the relation between school completion, career orientation, and successful marriage. A survey covering a twenty-year span of the marital histories of a representative sample of American adults in 28,000 households finds that one-fourth of the white men and nearly one-half of the black men who first married in their teens had experienced divorce (Glick and Norton, 1971).

As more people have divorced, the stigma attached to divorce has diminished. The reduced shamefulness of divorce may, in turn, account for the fact that the average duration of marriages that end in divorce has decreased in recent years (Goode, 1963, p. 85).

Still another change in the characteristics of people who divorce may be anticipated. In past decades the probability of divorce was higher for childless couples than for parents, holding constant the number of years they were married. However, this distinction may also be expected to be reduced or to disappear as divorce becomes a more acceptable solution to domestic misery. Looking at the world scene, Goode (1963, p. 85) concludes that with the reduction in the stigma associated with divorce, "the consequences of divorce have become less harsh for the children as well as for the husband and wife."

Why Do We Divorce?

The answer to this question has already been given in general: we divorce because we differ, and the difference is largely in what we expect of each other.

The possible balance of the pleasures and pains we are to give each other in marriage is made more difficult to foresee today because the decline in the institutionalized functions of the family has left so much of marriage "up to us." We now have to *negotiate* how we shall be; whereas, among our tribal cousins, it is *known* how men and women living together should act.

This is the general answer to our question. It is of interest, however, to listen to the specific complaints of those who divorce. These complaints may or may not be the causes of estrangement, but they are the reasons given.

For example, lawyers tell us in private what they cannot shout in court—namely, that the legal grounds for divorce have only a loose connection with the real reasons for separation. A research among a sample of Idaho lawyers asked these professionals what, in their opinion, were the causes of domestic disruption as opposed to the legal grounds given. The lawyers listed financial difficulties as the major bone of contention, with infidelity, drunkenness, and "basic incompatibility" following in declining order (Harmsworth and Minnis, 1955). "Basic incompatibility" is, of course, a blanket phrase covering all the facets of spoiled expectation which we see as the general underwriter of loss of love.

In another study of domestic complaints, Levinger (1966) compiled the results of interviews with 600 couples applying for divorce in Cleveland. The women in this sample had twice as many complaints as the men. The men complained significantly more frequently than the women about only two sources of trouble: sexual dissatisfaction and meddling in-laws. Table 6-4 diagrams the differences in the complaints made by husbands and wives. It is notable that spouses agree in naming their most common disappointment "mental cruelty." "Mental cruelty" is a residual category of disaffection that refers principally to depreciating the other, to devaluing who the spouse is, how he behaves, and what he stands for. It covers the range of unloving practices from criticizing, nagging, and quarreling to making unfavorable comparisons of one's spouse with other men or women.

What Is Recommended?   It is notoriously difficult for people in love to use their heads. On the personal level, it is possible to advise those one cares for to minimize the hazards of choice by attending to what we know about the sources of marital discord. Sometimes, however, need outranks knowledge. At this point, facts have small voices, and the sociologist's correlations provide no certain prescriptions. Choosing against the odds is not recommended; but as Las Vegas reminds us, it will be done.

No-Fault Divorce   There is, however, one recommendation that seems sensible and that can reduce the pain of separation. It is no-fault divorce.

The laws of many industrialized countries place divorce under the control of the state in such a way that an adversary proceeding must be engaged if a

Table 6-4   Marital Complaints of 600 Couples Applying for Divorce*

Complaint	Proportion of all complaints† Wives	Husbands
Mental cruelty	0.40	0.30
Neglect of home or children	0.39	0.26
Physical abuse	0.37	0.03
Financial problems	0.37	0.09
Drinking	0.27	0.05
Infidelity	0.24	0.20
Verbal abuse	0.24	0.08
Lack of love	0.23	0.14
Sexual incompatibility	0.14	0.20
In-law trouble	0.07	0.16
Excessive demands	0.03	0.04

*Adapted from George Levinger, "Sources of Marital Dissatisfaction Among Applicants for Divorce." © 1966 by the *American Journal of Orthopsychiatry*. Reproduced by permission of the author and the journal.

†Each spouse may have mentioned more than one complaint.

miserable marriage is to be dissolved. The adversary procedure assumes guilt and innocence, a wrongdoer and a victim. It assigns blame and hence allocates reward and punishment. The legal model for a divorce action under such a procedure approximates a criminal trial. This is an unfortunate parallel. There seems no good reason today for insisting that there be a plaintiff and a defendant in a divorce suit. The process of marital dissolution—what we do to each other behind the walls of our domiciles—can never be truthfully told in a courtroom. *A court has no scales adequate to weigh the balance of hurts spouses have given each other.*

The law is not only *incapable* of judging fault in a disorderly marriage, but it also appears *unnecessary* for it to do so. Justice can be achieved without assuming that there is a balance of blame to be assigned to husband and wife. The protection of discordant spouses, the division of property, and the allocation of responsibility for the support of children can be mediated by domestic courts without engaging in the false drama of establishing who is at fault.

As long as we have private property and private children, the state ought to license marriage and divorce. Come communism, a condition in which there is neither privacy of property nor of parenthood, licensing may lack a rationale. Such a "termite society" may be man's fate in the twenty-first century, as some predict and others hope, but modern states will continue to control marriage and divorce by law and its force. It is recommended that this legal exercise be freed of the inappropriate assumption of blame and the trappings of a trial.

WHERE DO WE GO FROM HERE?

Crystal balls are always cloudy. There seems no good reason, however, to prophesy the end of marriage in the near future. It may be increasingly difficult for those who marry to conceive of themselves as entering upon a lifelong commitment. The fact of living in a world of divorcing people raises the prospect of impermanence for every thinking person who marries. Nevertheless, there seem to be sufficient promise and sufficient satisfaction in marriage to make most of us prefer "real marriage" to its substitutes. On this score, it is notable that homosexuals, like heterosexuals, today demand the right to be married legally as well as erotically and domestically.

We will continue to marry for two good reasons: the family is a major way to reproduce and care for our young and the family remains a source of emotional gratification. There are other ways to nurture our young, of course, as in communal arrangements, but the development of urban *kibbutzim* in Western centers does not seem likely. Similarly, despite our disappointments in love, most adults continue to look upon marriage as a way of securing affection, of making a commitment, and of "building a nest."

The fact that marriage does not work as idealized leads some of us to look elsewhere for love. There are even some disgruntled souls who have tried love and didn't like it and who have renounced the attempt at enduring, intimate connection. They, like the poet Gregory Corso (1959), find "love as odd as wearing shoes." These are minority positions, however, and marriage, with its risks and its discontents, still exerts a powerful attraction.

The person who expects foolproof insurance against the hazards of loving and marrying expects too much. Such a person is apt to view the difficulties that confront us when we live together as problems that have solutions in knowledge. Such an individual should be advised, again, that our knowledge is imperfect and that difficulties can be anticipated, accommodated, and overcome without being solved.

Chapter 7

Lying, Cheating, and Stealing

Other people are the greatest source of both our satisfactions and our disappointments. A major concern is to reduce the disappointment.

Disappointment comes in many styles, of course, but a timeless and worldwide concern is not to be deceived. We prefer, most of the time,[1] to be treated honestly. This means not to be lied to, stolen from, or cheated. These are not the only ways in which we are disappointed, but they constitute three principal dimensions of the abuse we give and take.

THREE DIMENSIONS OF DISAPPOINTMENT

Lying, cheating, and stealing are distinctive ways in which we hurt each other. These harms run together, but not always in harness.

To lie is to write or speak falsely with the intent to deceive, but it is also to convey a false impression.

To cheat is to deprive one of something of value by deceit, but it is also to break the rules of the game, as when one cheats at cards.

To steal is to take dishonestly, that is, in violation of our group's definition of property. Stealing connotes stealth, taking things secretly, but it also refers to open theft, as in robbery; and to causing a loss, as through trickery.

---

[1]There are exceptions to this. There are comforting lies, and some dishonesty we recognize as courtesy. Courteous exaggerations and reservations serve as social lubricants.

We recognize differences in the *methods* of deception and in the *gravity* of various kinds of cheating, but the idea underlying these varieties of disappointment is that someone takes away something of value that, by the code of our tribe, is deemed to be rightfully ours. The thing of value can be time, trust, happiness, or property. Thus the discovered lie breaks trust, reduces happiness, consumes time. It may or may not be part of a fraud that takes property as well. It has to be added, however, that some lies that are *not* discovered or that are conventional do people good (Ludwig, 1965). Hypocrisy has its uses as well as its abuses (Warriner, 1958).

Judging the Gravity of Deceit

Lying, cheating, and stealing may be personal or impersonal hurts. They may be committed face to face, in which case there is a clear victim; or they may be committed against anonymous others, like corporations, governments, or particular segments of a population, in which case a victim is more difficult to discern. It is apparent that if the victim is sufficiently depersonalized and distant, even "good" men and women can cheat that victim without feeling guilty (Smigel, 1956; Smigel and Ross, 1970). It is no surprise to find that individuals who will not steal directly from individuals will steal indirectly from "people," since people are an anonymous and dispersed aggregate. Examples of such conscience-free thieves range from students who "rip off" their college bookstores and libraries, to "nice ladies" who cheat on their long-distance telephone calls, to politicians (and other advertisers) who make false promises.

The Difference Distance Makes   Conscience varies with moral distance, where "moral distance" refers to the degree to which one regards others as similar or different from oneself. The less distant others are from us morally the more guilt we feel about cheating them; the greater the distance, the less the resistance to deceiving others.

The attribution of moral distance reflects an attitude. It is a matter of definition and of expectation. Thus deception is *expected* in Latin countries, where only persons within the family are morally close and everyone else is a moral stranger (Banfield, 1958). There are also, individuals called psychopaths for whom everyone is a stranger, including "loved ones."

Fashions in Deceit

There are not only degrees of deceit, as defined by the moral distance of the victim, but also continuities of style and changes in fashion. This means that there are enduring patterns of theft, although the specific techniques may change with circumstances. For example, that style of fraud known as the con game operates, now as always, on the two principles of trust and lust: the victim's trust in the con man's promise and his lust for larcenous gain. The specific "games" by which confidence and greed are converted into theft are many, but the underwriting principles persist (Maurer, 1940, 1964).

Another illustration of persistent style and changing fashion in theft is the variety of fraud committed by falsifying business records. Defrauding investors and tax collectors by concocting false reports is an ancient art. Technological change refines the art, but its principle remains the same. Thus when modern businesses put their accounting records on tape and process them by computer, they create new opportunities for stealing by computer jockeying (Dirks and Gross, 1974; Pearlstine, 1974). "Cooking the books" is as old as commerce; chicanery by computer is its technological "improvement."

PATTERNS OF HONESTY

In trying to protect ourselves against theft and deceit, we create assumptions about who is honest and about the conditions that promote deception. A first question asks whether honesty is one thing or many. Are people *generally* more or less honest or only *particularly* so?

We ask this about one kind of virtue at a time, as when we wonder whether, if she cheats me, she will cheat you too. Or if Alpha lies to Beta, is he likely also to lie to Gamma? In addition, the question about the generality of honesty is asked about the relations between styles of deceit. For example, are thieves more likely to be liars and cheats? Are cheats more likely to be thieves and liars too?

The answer is yes, somewhat. There is some generality in honesty. However, being honest or dishonest is not so tight a bundle as moralists would like. There are dimensions of deceit and gaps between the dimensions. Situations make a difference, and the consistency with which we are honest or crooked varies not just with us but also with the circumstances we are in.

Studies of Deceit

The consistency of our character depends not just on us but also upon the consistency of the situations in which we are tested. The *more similar* the kind of tempting situation in which we are observed, the more apparent is the *generality* of our moral conduct. As we are confronted with different opportunities to lie, cheat, or steal, with varied support or urging from our peers, with different risks of getting caught, with different values attached to what the deception will earn us or what the shame of getting caught will cost us—as all these situational aspects vary, there is less consistency in our honesty.

Cheating, Lying, and Justifying In illustration of this, MacKinnon (1938) studied one kind of circumstance in which graduate students were tempted to cheat on a problem-solving task. For this relatively uniform kind of temptation, there was considerable consistency of character. That is, those who cheated also tended to lie about their behavior. Furthermore, the cheaters justified their action by calling the assignment unfair and, as a result of this justification, they exhibited little guilt. On the other hand, the more honest students blamed themselves not the task, for their inability to solve it. MacKinnon's research is a demonstration of the consistency of character within a limited tempting circumstance.

The Hartshorne-May Studies   A more challenging test of the generality of honesty is found in a series of studies conducted among American schoolchildren by the psychologists Hartshorne, May, and their associates (1928–1930). These investigators used a variety of opportunities to lie, cheat, and steal in their measurement of honesty. They gave children the chance to cheat on tests of reading, spelling, arithmetic, information, and grammar, on puzzles, and in parlor games. They also devised ingenious ways of tempting children to steal coins without being observed but in a manner that allowed the theft to be recorded. Last, opportunities were given children to make false statements on questionnaires where the lying[2] had two kinds of motive: to win approval and to escape disapproval.

Hartshorne-May Results   All these measures of deceit run together, but with varying degrees of closeness. There is, for example, a higher association of one kind of cheating with another, and between lying and cheating, than there is between cheating or lying and stealing. The more similar the style of deceit, the greater the consistency of conduct.

Furthermore, Hartshorne and May found what seems obvious—that the amount of cheating, for example, increased as it became easier to cheat, with less risk of getting caught, and as a little cheating produced success.

When the results from the cheating tests are calculated as a "cheating ratio" (the number of cheating acts divided by the number of opportunities to cheat for ten tests), the distribution of students is close to "normal." Table 7-1 shows that 3.2 percent of the children cheated whenever they had a chance, while 7.0 percent never cheated. Most students, however, cheated some of the time; more than half (53.5 percent) cheated between one and two times out of every three chances to deceive.

Hartshorne and May thought that while the correlations among the various tests of honesty were positive, they were too low to allow one to speak of a general trait of honesty. However, Burton (1963), another psychologist, recalculated the Hartshorne-May data, omitting from his analysis those tests that were unreliable. Among the reliable measures of behavior, Burton found a *general tendency* for children to be more or less honest. "There is," he concludes, "an underlying trait of honesty which a person brings with him to a resistance to temptation situation" (p. 492).

This general disposition to be more or less honest shows interesting variations in its *consistency* and in its *correlates.* For example, on the tests given the Hartshorne-May schoolchildren, honest individuals tended to be

---

[2]The "false statement" tests are not direct measures of lying since the notion of lying includes the *intent* to deceive, something the psychologists could not measure.

Table 7-1 Distribution of Cheating among Schoolchildren*

Cheating ratio†	Number of students	Percent of students‡
1.00	78	3.2
0.90	105	4.3
0.80	178	7.3
0.70	231	9.4
0.60	252	10.3
0.50	308	12.6
0.40	310	12.7
0.30	439	17.9
0.20	231	9.4
0.10	140	5.7
0.00	171	7.0
	Total 2,443	

*Data collected by H. G. McCurdy, *The Personal World*, Table 31, from findings reported in Hartshorne and May (1928–1930). © 1961 by Harcourt, Brace, Jovanovich. Reproduced by permission of the publisher and Professors Hartshorne and May.

†Cheating ratio = $\dfrac{\text{number of cheating acts}}{\text{number of opportunities to cheat}}$

‡Percentages are rounded to nearest tenth

more consistently honest while dishonest persons were less consistently dishonest. Furthermore, the brighter the child the more likely he was to be honest and to be consistent in his behavior. This tendency is based on moderate correlations and therefore exhibits exceptions, but the tendency is there for this range of behaviors.

Social status is also associated with honesty. Within any one society, people of lower social status tend to be less honest than those of higher status. This has been found true in *behavioral* tests of honesty, as in the Hartshorne-May experiments, in *verbal* tests of moral judgment (Aronfreed, 1961; Boehm, 1957; Bronfenbrenner, 1962), and in the greater expressed *approval of stealing* among people of lower status (Smigel, 1956). This finding is substantiated by additional measures of crime and delinquency in worldwide settings (Nettler, 1974a, pp. 106–117).

Age interacts with socioeconomic status so that, for these schoolchildren, there was increasing consistency of character as they grew older, with the higher-status children becoming more honest and the lower-status children more dishonest.

Sex, too, seems to make a difference. Girls are generally rated as developing a conscience earlier than boys and as being more honest (Aronfreed, 1961; Krebs, 1969; Sears et al., 1957). On verbal measures of moral judgment, girls tend to score better in a way that Brogden (1940) has called "acceptance of the moral code." They are more concerned than boys with the display of "being good." However, the degree to which this verbal morality is correlated with conduct is questionable.

On the Hartshorne-May tests girls tended to cheat more than boys. Furthermore, girls tended to be more *consistently deceptive* and boys more *consistently honest.* Investigators of this phenomenon have not explained it adequately, and some later research on smaller samples has not found such sex differences in cheating (Johnson and Gormly, 1972; Krebs, 1969).

It is to be expected that sex differences in honesty, and the persistence of any such difference, will vary with the cultural setting. If one looks at sex differences in official crime rates, for example, it appears that the more closely men and women approach equality in their cultural roles, the more similar they become in criminality. Ordinarily, men have higher official arrest and conviction rates than women, but the size of this sex difference diminishes as men and women move toward equality in their general rights and privileges (Nettler, 1974a, pp. 102–105).

It has been suggested that there may be a biological source of sex differences in moral conduct. At least a series of studies in widely different cultures indicates that girls and women are more dependent than boys and men on "external definitions of moral consequences" (Aronfreed, 1961). Females, more frequently than males, look to others in determining how to judge and how to act in ambiguous circumstances (Farber and Wilson, 1963; Witkin et al., 1962). This is true of the judgment of space and position as it is of right and wrong.

The debate, of course, is whether these observed sex differences in judgment are culturally determined or biologically rooted. Sociologists prefer the assumption that sex differences in physical and moral judgment are the result of culturally assigned roles while geneticists consider such differences to be at least *biosocial,* the result of an interaction between differing biologies and their environments (Scheinfeld, 1943). This debate can be opened here, without being resolved, since we know little about the conditions under which possible sex differences in the physiology of judgment become translated into sex differences in conduct.

Two other findings from the Hartshorne-May studies are of interest. They concern the effects of association upon deceit.

Birds of a Feather   The Hartshorne-May research supports the common observation that "birds of a feather flock together." Friends have more closely related scores on measures of honesty than do children paired at random. Additionally, putting friends together in a classroom increases their tendencies toward honesty or dishonesty.

Clubs and Character   A last finding of interest is that membership in so-called character-building organizations such as churches or the Boy Scouts has no relation with honest behavior when socioeconomic status is held constant. Apropos of this point, the journalist Bridge and his colleagues (1974) report that some directors of Boy Scout troops in the United States cheated during a national recruitment drive sponsored by federal funds. They padded their membership rolls with fake members ("paper Scouts") doubling the true enrollment in some instances.

IN SUMMARY

The Hartshorne-May research and related studies demonstrate that *deception is a common way of dealing with conflict.* Homo sapiens is not the only species that tells lies, but human beings are the greatest deceivers in the animal kingdom.[3]

Lying, cheating, and stealing are *normal* procedures for defending one's interests and for getting what one wants in a world where wills clash. Calling deception normal does not call it moral but only statistically frequent. Deceit in its varied styles occurs with different probability in different settings, but it remains a well-used way of adapting to our social environment.

We cheat and steal when doing so gets us what we want at low cost and when we have not been specifically trained against the temptation. We are less than honest sometimes because we can't remember the truth, but we also deceive to make a good story better or to avoid hurting someone's feelings. Then, too, we tell lies to save face and to get something from our victim. We lie, finally, to give ourselves and others *hope.* This is not merely the kind of lying heard at deathbeds; it is also the kind of lying familiar to political arenas and it is, perhaps, the most dangerous of all the styles of falsehood.

The associations observed between *behaving* honestly and *talking* morally and between these kinds of conduct and one's rearing suggest that moving people from treachery to honesty is seldom accomplished by words. Preaching and teaching are of little avail against temptation and the rewards of deceit. Honesty is learned, which means, among other things, that it is most practiced where it has been best modeled and most consistently successful.

The fact that there are good reasons for lying, cheating, and stealing means that a kind heart is no defense against telling lies or believing them. We deceive each other out of malice sometimes, but also out of goodness. The cynic may lie, but so does the idealist. To date, we have no scales with which to weigh the relative honesty of good and evil intention.

Then too, the fact that there are good reasons for lying, cheating, and stealing should mean that dishonesty is prevalent. It is, but *how* prevalent depends on what we have assumed about human beings and where we look.

HOW HONEST ARE WE?

The answer depends on the assumptions with which the question is asked. If one has been reared among honest people and treated honestly, he is likely to

---

[3]Other animals, from insects and fish to dogs and apes, give false signals. Deception is a common defense against predators, but animals also "lie" to gain attention and affection (Eibl-Eibesfeldt, 1970, pp. 113, 282–283). Lying to one's *own* species, however, as opposed to deceiving *enemy* species, is more characteristic of human beings than of other mammals.

believe that dishonesty is an abnormality. If, on the other hand, one has been reared among liars and cheats and if one has been both the victim and the practitioner of theft, he will see more deception around him. Career thieves believe in theft—that everyone has his "hustle"—just as consistently honest individuals believe that most people are trustworthy unless some unusual circumstance pushes them into treachery (Ball, 1957; Gough and Peterson, 1952; Hathaway and Monachesi, 1957).

The answer varies, too, with where one looks and what one counts as deceit. In general, rich societies that provide much to steal and that bring together people of unequal wealth from different backgrounds with different loyalties—such urban places stimulate larceny. By contrast, some communities of religious persons, isolated from "contaminating influences," have little theft or assault within their groups. Examples are the Hutterites and the Amish in North America.

Allowing for these qualifications, if one looks out upon Western societies and tries to count lying, cheating, and thieving, the tallies do *not* justify "faith in humanity." They *do* indicate that we are burdened by deceit and that we defend ourselves against the great variety of fraud at high cost.

An appreciation of the prevalence of public honesty can be gained from a sample of tallies of popular probity.

Counting Honesty

Over two hundred years ago the Scottish philosopher David Hume (1758, p. 101) advised us that "A man who at noon leaves his purse full of gold on the pavement at Charing Cross may as well expect that it will fly away like a feather as that he will find it untouched an hour after." Modern descriptions of public honesty in a variety of settings show how correct Hume was. For example:

1   "Shoplifters in U.S. discount department stores (where self-service is the rule) stole at a record annual rate of nearly $1 billion last year. The loss represented almost 2.6% of annual sales, more than the majority of store operators earned after taxes. The thefts, according to the stores' reckoning, resulted in price increases of $21 for each family in the country" (*Newsweek,* 1973c).

2   An American investigation of reports of "unidentified flying objects" found that about one-fourth of the photographs submitted as "evidence" had been fabricated (Morrison, 1969).

3   Intensive interviews conducted on a false-name basis with 1,400 boys in London, England, revealed that *half* had been caught stealing. Of these, 13 percent had been caught by the police and 37 percent by someone else (Belson, 1968).

4   "In only nine months, Defense Department employees stole 60,000 pieces of silverware from the Pentagon cafeteria, the equivalent of one place setting for each worker in the building" (*Esquire,* 1974).

5   *The Wall Street Journal* (1972, p. 12) provides this picture of its recent

move into new offices while the building was still under construction. A spokesman reports:

> They stole us blind. As much as $10,000 worth of office equipment and furnishing was taken, despite the presence of uniformed guards on each floor.
>
> Among the items taken:
>
> A 15-by-20 foot piece of carpet ("It was glued to the floor and they peeled it right up," the spokesman says).
>
> A 20-foot long walnut counter-top ("I don't know what anyone wanted with the Payroll Department's counter—maybe someone needed a bar").
>
> At least 30 chairs, worth about $200 each ("We had the guards sitting in them").
>
> In addition, so many telephones were stolen, the spokesman says, that "the phone company threatened to stop installing them. Not because they're so expensive but because they were running out of phones."

6 ". . . all employees of a chain-store were run through his (Keeler's) polygraph (lie-detector) when the company complained it was losing more than one million dollars annually through petty thefts. Polygraph records indicated that fully three out of four employees were pilfering funds. This and subsequent experiences led Keeler to pronounce a rather cynical dictum generally held by lie-detection experts today: '65 percent of people who handle money take money. . . .'" (Deutsch, 1950, pp. 154–155).

7 *Reader's Digest* (Riis, 1941a,b,c) conducted a survey among a sample of small businesses in the early 1940s. A man and a woman were employed by this magazine to tour garages and radio and watch repair shops in the United States. The automobiles, radios, and watches that they submitted for repairs had been deliberately "jimmied" to make them appear to be out of order, and the test employed was to observe how many shops made charges for false "repairs." According to this survey:

> Of 347 garages visited, 63 percent were dishonest.
>
> Of 304 radio shops, 64 percent were dishonest.
>
> Of 462 watchmakers, 49 percent were dishonest.

"Normal" Crime

The popularity of crime among otherwise law-abiding citizens has been recorded in a variety of situations in which investigators have questioned people confidentially about their off-the-record crimes. Wallerstein and Wyle (1947) did this among a sample of predominantly middle-class persons in New York. Ninety-nine percent of the 1,700 respondents admitted anonymously to having committed, as adults, one or more offenses against the criminal laws of their state. Some of these offenses were minor, but almost two-thirds of the men and one-third of the women acknowledged having committed a serious crime (a felony). The average number of confessed crimes committed during adult years was eighteen for the men and eleven for the women.

A similar pattern of results was obtained among a sample of 515 Californians who were without official criminal records (Nettler, 1959). Everyone in this sample confessed to some adult lawbreaking.

Even exceptionally talented and mentally healthy individuals reveal pockets of hostility and treachery when we get to know them well. Thus Barron and his colleagues in the University of California (1955) found that the eighty graduate students with whom they lived during intensive assessment periods "numbered among [them] those who had committed arson, larceny, assault and battery, and wanton destruction of property. In short, almost the whole catalogue of human folly and disorder in human life could be read in the histories of these normal and currently well-functioning persons."

A similar description of the normality of some kinds of deceit is provided by tests of people's accuracy in answering interviewers' questions.

Can We Believe What People Say When We Ask Them Public Questions?

The answer depends on who is asking what question of whom. It depends, too, on whether people understand the question (Klare, 1950) and whether they feel their answer somehow reflects on them. The more prestige attached to the answer, the less accurate it is apt to be (Hyman, 1944–1945).

For example, when census takers ask people their age, they get "funny" answers. Ages ending in *zero* are reported far more often than any other age. In fact, ages ending in zero are reported *twice* as often as ages ending in five, the next most popular digit (Stockwell, 1966; Stockwell and Wicks, 1974; Zelnik, 1964).

We lie about more than our age, of course. When poll takers ask people a variety of questions *in situations where the accuracy of their answers can be checked,* we find a wide range in the honesty of their answers. This occurs, in varying degree, when we ask people about their income, the amount of their schooling, their job seniority and pay changes, their recent purchases, their receipt of welfare benefits, and their information about public issues (Haberman and Sheinberg, 1966; Hardin and Hershey, 1960; McCord, 1951; Neter, 1970; Weiss and Davis, 1960; Weaver and Swanson, 1974; Withery, 1954). As an illustration of the range of honest answers to questions of this nature, Parry and Crossley (1950) asked a representative sample of citizens in Denver, Colorado, such things as the following:

Their age
Whether they had registered and voted in recent elections and, if so, their party affiliation
Whether they had contributed to the Community Chest (United Fund)
Whether they possessed a valid Public Library card
Whether they had a valid driver's license
Whether they owned an automobile and if so, its make and year
Whether they owned or rented their residence, and
Whether they had a telephone at home

The proportion of honest answers ran from highs of 98 percent about having a telephone and 96 percent about home ownership to lows of about 50 percent for voting behavior.

Interpreting the Results

Two kinds of response are common after reading such research. One is to lay the blame for dishonesty on others "not like us." The second response is to catch "intern's disease." With appropriate qualification, we should guard against both tendencies.

    1 Blaming "Those Others" When we read about human wickedness, a popular tendency is to blame the cheating and stealing on "other kinds of people" and not on "our kind." There is some validity in this shifting of the blame, depending on who is doing it and how. We are not equally prone to the same wrongs with the same frequency. Some people *are* more dangerous than others.

    The present point, however, is Leo Tolstoy's: that "the seeds of every crime are in each of us." Probably everyone has intentionally given some kind of injury to others; the *motivation* to deceive and to steal is common rather than rare. This does not mean that we are equally malicious but only that lying and larceny are universal proclivities against which we struggle with the training of conscience and the imposition of law.

    2 Catching "Intern's Disease" Another response to reading about the popularity of crime is to catch "intern's disease." This is the feeling that one is contracting the sickness he is studying. Thus the young physician reading about the symptoms of smallpox begins to itch, and the young criminologist discovering the "normality" of theft begins to see crookedness everywhere.

    The antidote for this ailment is a balanced point of view. Evidence of widespread deceit and thievery need not lead to their exaggeration—to the belief that no one can be trusted, ever. On the other hand, such evidence should provide protection against the opposite error—the folly of unquestioning trust. This folly wears two faces: that which doubts the reality of malice and that which assumes that good intentions cannot lie. Those who cannot believe in the authenticity of malice and treachery are ill-equipped for survival. Like Desdemona and Billy Budd, such people are innocents whose own goodness blinds them to the evil in others. The other side of this mask of innocence is the belief that deceit flows only from ill will and never from good hope. On the contrary, ideals, our own as well as others', generate an urgency toward deception. This kind of deception is insidious, since it may require fooling oneself as well as others.

    Between these opposing pulls of faith and skepticism, we struggle for equilibrium.

CONVERTING WRONGS TO CRIMES

In response to the constancy of the damage we do each other, three impulses have been universally exhibited: the impulse to flee, to fight back, and to trust a just mediator to right our wrongs.

1 Flight One impulse in the face of persistent injury is to flee it. The flight maybe solo, as is the hermit's retreat to the wilderness, or it may be communal, as are the many attempts to build segregated communities free of sin. Yet other forms of flight are chemical—as when one seeks to "put up with it all" by killing his consciousness of it—and *total,* as in that chosen ending called suicide.

2 Revenge as Justice A second response to wrongdoing is personal and vengeful. It seeks personally to return damage to its giver or "his kind." The impulse to revenge, to the balancing of harms, to seeing that wrong does not go unpunished—this impulse underwrites the oldest conception of justice, as written, for example, in the Code of Hammurabi (1792–1750 B.C.).

The personal response can be one man's revenge, or it can be a "class action" type of retribution as in a feud. Furthermore, the personal style of response can use substitute enemies—not the persons who originally hurt one, but their symbols, as when one hates policemen or presidents because he dislikes his father (Feuer, 1969).

All personal forms of retribution are damaging to the society in which they occur—whether the attack be in the form of man-against-man revenge, family vendetta, or riot and rebellion.

3 State Control Because of the destruction inherent in a personal response to wrongdoing, a third mechanism has evolved. It is the process of law which seeks to minimize the flight from society and the direct confrontation between the wounded and the hurtful by substituting *an allegedly neutral agent of justice and control.* To be effective, this neutral agent must have a monopoly of power within the society in which it operates. In modern countries, the agency with a monopoly of power is called the state. To say that the state has a monopoly of power means that its actions are relatively unchallengeable. They are relatively unchallengeable because the force it can wield is overwhelming, or because the state's power is accorded legitimacy, or because of some changing mixture of force and legitimacy.

Legitimacy is the sense of a people that the power of their state is just. Legitimacy, therefore, is never absolute or permanent. Differing proportions of populations accord differing degrees of "rightness" to their states, and these proportions change. The delicate task of statesmen becomes, then, the maintenance of legitimacy so that the monopolized power of the state may be exercised with a minimal show of force.

When the state intervenes to punish wrongs, a different coloring is given those injuries: They are then called crimes.

The Meaning of Crime

Wrongs that are punished by the state rather than by their victims are crimes. Unfortunately, the word "crime" refers to other wrongs as well, and in the stretched, literary use of the term, any injury or mishap may be called a crime, as when one says, "It's a crime the way he treats her," or "It's a crime it had to rain on your holiday."

In its *legal sense,* however, a crime is "an intentional violation of the criminal law, committed without defense or excuse, and penalized by the state" (Tappan, 1947). By this restricted definition, there is no "crime" without a law and a state to punish its violation. This means, for example, that "war crimes" are not legal crimes, since there is no state with the power to penalize such acts.

In addition, the legal definition of crime attempts to restrict crime to "intentional acts" as opposed to "accidents." However, in practice, it is difficult at times to separate intention from accident, and Anglo-American law still holds people responsible for wrongs they did not "intend" if the injury was caused by "negligence."

The legal definition of crime is narrowed further by its permitting certain defenses and excuses against being held accountable for wrongdoing. Thus one may not be held responsible for homicide if it is legally defined as justifiable, and one may be excused from responsibility if he is mentally incompetent or under age.

The definition of crime, in its legal sense, is *political.* It refers, as we have noted, to wrongs defined as such by a state whose citizens (or subjects) accord the definition fluctuating amounts of loyalty. Making laws and unmaking them, enforcing them or ignoring them—these become political acts. That is, legislation and enforcement impose power.

The political nature of law means that, in heterogeneous societies in particular, there is a constant struggle to maintain and to change definitions of crime and justice. A sample of this conflict illustrates its character.

1   Changing Crimes   Mass societies are under pressure to change the *content of crime.* It is urged, on the one hand, that many acts now illegal be "decriminalized,"[4] and, on the other hand, that new classes of wrong be made criminal. Thus some interest groups have suggested that "crimes without victims" be removed from legal attention (see Chapter 8), while other wrongs, whose victims are deemed defenseless, be "criminalized."

---

[4]The verbs "to criminalize" and "decriminalize" will not be found in dictionaries, although sociologists have been using them with increasing frequency. In sociological use, "to criminalize" means two things: (1) to bring an act or a situation within the scope of the criminal law, that is, to make it a crime, and (2) to confirm a person in a criminal career, as when one says, "Prisons criminalize." The negative form of the verb, "to decriminalize," is used only in the first sense, i.e., to remove an act from legal definition as a crime.

The idea of crime without victims is itself a matter of definition and hence subject to conflict. At various times it has been urged that such sometime offenses as abortion, homosexuality, and drug addiction be decriminalized (Schur, 1965). It has also been advocated that prostitution, incest, keeping a bawdy house, statutory (noncoercive) rape, and the production and distribution of pornography be removed from legal sanction. In addition, other voices are arguing for the elimination of the crimes of suicide and attempted suicide, gambling, drunkenness, disorderly conduct, vagrancy, some kinds of speeding, and the sale and possession of gold where that is still illegal.[5]

On the other side of this conflict, there are pleas to criminalize acts that are not now legal offenses. Thus there are advocates who recommend that new categories of victims be defined and protected by the criminalization of such heretofore lawful acts as driving without a seat belt or polluting the environment by emitting noise, fumes, or liquid and solid waste—whether this is done by corporations, governments, or by individuals and their animal pets. It has been urged, too, that the publication and dissemination of hate literature be made a criminal offense, as it is now in some jurisdictions, and that the manufacture, sale, and use of "harmful" products also be made criminal. These harmful products run a range from alcoholic beverages, aspirin, and tobacco to detergents, insecticides, some kinds of cosmetics, and "ill-designed" automobiles. Given the concern with population increase, some people have advocated that bearing more than two children be made a crime. Willing (1971), for example, would enforce laws against "excessive fertility" by tattooing and sterilizing offenders.

In addition to these advocacies, many styles of "discrimination"[6] are now criminal that once were not, and there is demand that new forms of discrimination be punished by the state. In the United States in particular, it is urged that "unfair treatment" in housing, education, occupation, or any public service by reason of age, sex, race, creed, national origin, income, or tested traits of personality and intelligence be made criminal. In this vein, Williams (1974) would have

> a bold, Federal regulatory law, a truth-in-testing law, . . . formulated and enacted . . . and vigorously enforced. . . . Sanctions, ranging from stiff fines, suspensions, dechartering of the corporations, colleges, or universities, or even more severe criminal penalties should be leveled against the testing corporations, state departments of education, local school districts, colleges and universities. . . . Black communities should file class-action law suits that demand an end to testing of black children for whatever reason. [p. 41].

---

[5]Gold hoarding was a crime in the United States from the early 1930s through 1974. During this period, keeping gold was not a crime in Canada or in many other industrialized countries.

[6]"Discrimination" is placed in quotation marks to indicate its vagueness. The determination of discrimination in its legal sense requires agreement upon some standard of fair treatment. It also requires the assessment of *motive*, since as the word is used sociologically, to discriminate is to *intend* some unfair result. The difficulties of ascertaining the standard of justice operative when discrimination is charged and of inferring motive from result has led one student to suggest that the term cannot be given an exact meaning for sociological use (Hagan, 1975).

Similarly, Thomas (1972) would extend the penalties of the law to "certain acts committed by school people" which he believes can be linked as *"accessory to whatever crime the child commits in later life* as a result of a teacher's or administrator's cruelty" (pp. 179, 182, italics added).

The number of wrongs recommended for elevation to crimes seems endless, particularly in social environments that favor using the power of the state to improve our lives. Improving our lives includes righting wrongs and, given the broad spectrum of injuries we can be deemed to inflict upon ourselves and others, the tide seems to be running toward the invention of more crimes rather than toward a reduction in their number.[7] Thus, in the Soviet Union, the State Sports Committee recently found "the passion for playing bridge to be socially harmful" (UPI, 1973a). It is now illegal to organize bridge tourneys in that land. In Canada it has been urged that physicians be charged with crime if they do not report childhood wounds that could represent instances of child abuse (van Stolk, 1972), and others, concerned with "public apathy," have recommended that the failure of a citizen to report a crime be made a crime (CTV, 1974).

2 Changing Justice   In addition to these demands to add and subtract from the roster of crimes, modern states, particularly the more "open" ones, confront claims to change the conception of justice. This demand is connected to that which would change the content of crime because the legal definition of crime rests on a moral sense. It rests on a moral agreement about what is fair play, about what is and is not the government's business, and about what constitutes private property.

Challenges to this moral foundation demand that the burden of criminality be erased or that it be shifted from one group to another. This challenge is given by every nonpenitent offender—that is, by most of us—when we are caught. It is a challenge that would cleanse current offenders of their crimes by laying the blame elsewhere. The common justifications for this "shifting of the load" are that

The *intention* was not criminal.

This "crime" is not "really" a wrong.

This crime is not terribly wrong when it is compared with other deeds that go unpunished.

This act is not a crime when one considers the "circumstances." The popular form of this defense is, "I did it for the good of . . ."

In the dotted space one may place any noun one likes—"the nation," "the corporation," "our gang," "my family"—as long as it is *not* one's "self."

Illustrations of this challenge to conventional justice show its variety:

---

[7]No one has counted the claims made upon modern states to criminalize and decriminalize acts. It would be an interesting research to attempt to balance these advocacies.

Bad environment makes crime just (1):

Wrong was my only salvation. . . . Don't be telling me what is right. . . . There ain't no such thing as right or wrong in my world. Can you dig? Right or wrong is what a chump chooses to tell himself. And I chose to tell myself that stealing is right. I had a choice:[8] to be a poor-ass, raggedy-ass mothafukker all my life or to go out into the streets and steal me some money. . . . I ain't ashamed of what I did or who I am [Hassan, a several-time loser, 1972].

Bad environment makes crime just (2):

One thing that the judges, policemen, and administrators of prisons seem never to have understood, and for which they certainly do not make any allowances, is that Negro convicts, basically, rather than see themselves as criminals and perpetrators of misdeeds, look upon themselves as prisoners of war, the victims of a vicious, dog-eat-dog social system that is so heinous as to cancel out their own malefactions: in the jungle there is no right or wrong [Cleaver, 1968, p. 58].

Illegality is not criminality:

Gov. Reagan said yesterday those involved in the Watergate break-in and bugging should not be considered criminals because they "are not criminals at heart." Reagan noted that the electronic bugging of the Watergate Democratic party headquarters was illegal but said "criminal" was too harsh a term to use [*UPI*, 1973b].

Property is theft:

They want us to study the people who commit crimes against their property, but the real crime is their property! [Barbara Dudley, interpreting disturbances at the University of California's School of Criminology (Berkeley), as reported by *Newsweek*, 1974a]

Racism is crime:

Protesters who prevent academic racists from lecturing take the position that the very expression of racist theories is a crime to be physically stopped in much the same way as the burglar must be stopped [Adams, 1974, reporting the disruption of lectures in the Universities of Chicago and Toronto].

Fraud is not crime if there is no criminal intent:

She said that neither of them would have become involved in the hoax if they had regarded it as criminal [Edith Irving, wife of Clifford Irving, quoted upon her

---

[8]A comment on Hassan's language is relevant. Note that Hassan speaks repeatedly of his choosing. He does not view himself as a pawn, something manipulated, but as a rational actor. His conception contrasts with a popular sociological interpretation of offenders as objects rather than as agents, as "caused" rather than as "causing" (cf. pp. 141–143).

release from prison after a failed attempt to defraud a publisher of about three-quarters of a million dollars, *Reuters,* 1972].

Inequality of wealth is crime:

I think that if we look around us we see that somehow or another a very small minority of people in this country have all of the wealth in their hands and to top that, we don't even see them out working. We do not see them in the factories. We don't see them in the fields. . . . That tells me that something is *wrong* and it tells me that maybe *the real criminals* in this society are not all of the people who populate the prisons across the state, but those people *who have stolen the wealth of the world* from the people. Those are the criminals. And that means the Rockefellers and the Kennedys, you know, that whole Kennedy family, and that means the state that is designed to protect their property, because that's what Nixon's doing, that's what Reagan's doing, that's what they're all doing. And so every time a black child in this city dies, we should indict them for murder, because they're the ones who killed that black child [Angela Davis, 1970, p. 27, emphasis added].

Social Concern with "Crime"

Claims such as these, which demand a redefinition of crime and of justice, make governing difficult. If a society were to accord equal weight to every claim for a change in the notion of crime or the sense of justice, the result would be the end of responsibility. Every person charged with an "offense" could contend that his wrong ought not to be a crime (or not so great a crime), that other people's wrongs should be made crimes, and that the system that judges him is itself unjust.

Debates about whose sense of offense should or should not be made the criterion of a crime are moral debates. The citizenry takes sides in these quarrels, but its concern with crime exhibits a generality and a durability that discounts many of the particular advocacies of special interest groups. The more general social concern with crime is with those serious offenses against person and property that have long been considered wrongs in themselves. The concern of most citizens when they think about crime is personal first and societal secondarily. The concern is to protect one's person and belongings and, after that, to protect those institutions and public properties that citizens value. Where a state and its laws receive the consent of the governed—that is, where they are accorded legitimacy—public concern is conservative. The question it asks about crime is how it can be reduced *within the framework of present social relations.* This is a different question from that asked by radical critics of a society who are concerned to create new orders of social relations in which crime is abolished and in which people can be different without being criminal. "The task," say the English sociologists Taylor, Walton, and Young (1973, p. 282), "is to create a society in which the facts of human diversity, whether personal, organic or social, are not subject to the power to criminalize."

There never has been such a society, of course, and it is doubtful that anyone knows how to create it. Insofar as people in modern countries have been questioned about their concern with crime, their vision is practical rather than utopian (Erskine, 1974; *Life,* 1971). Within the context of this practical concern, people ask for an explanation of crime.

EXPLAINING CRIME

The explanations of crime, like explanations of other behaviors, are more or less adequate depending upon the questions to which they are addressed. The questions asked about crime may be divided into psychological issues and sociological ones. Psychological questions ask for explanations of the behavior of individuals—"Why did she do it?" Sociological questions ask for explanations of the behavior of aggregates—"Why are rates of this kind of crime higher in one society than another?" For the most part, social concerns ask the sociological type of question.

Explanations of Crime on the Sociological Level

Every sociological explanation of the production of crime looks to something in *the pattern of relations* among people as the cause. This means that unlearned variables, such as the natural environment or biological differences, are not considered to be important sources of difference in crime rates between societies or within a society in time. Such unlearned variables may have triggering effects, as may be noted in the increase in street crime with hot weather, but no sociological explanation of crime accords primary influence to such noncultural factors. Today, the only persuasive theories of crime causation see aspects of the social environment as more or less crime-productive. These theories differ only in the aspects of social relations they emphasize. What is emphasized is important for political reasons because the emphasis suggests doing *this* rather than doing *that*. However, each facet of social relations used to explain crime reflects some truth.

If one were to ask a congress of Western criminologists, "What causes differences in crime rates?" one would receive the following answers, some of them passionately proposed as part of a larger political program:

1 Subcultures cause crime.
2 Social structures cause crime.
3 Attitudes and beliefs cause crime.
4 Training or its lack causes crime.

1 Subcultures Cause Crime   People who live under the rule of modern states are not of one piece culturally. There are differences among them in ethnic values and social-class preferences, and these differences encourage or discourage behaviors that the majority has legislated into illegality.

This type of explanation documents differences in learned ways of behaving among different groups subject to the same criminal law. It then shows how these differences in preferred styles of being get one into trouble with the law or defend one against such trouble. The argument is that *the very preferences* generated by class or ethnic subcultures produce a conflict with many of the laws prevalent in the societies within which the subcultures live.

   2 Social Structures Cause Crime This is perhaps the most popular explanation of criminality among criminologists. It is a kind of explanation that takes many forms and that lends itself to many emphases. Its substance is that there are situations that make it *rational,* or even *necessary,* to commit crime. In addition, it is held that there are circumstances that affect our human natures uniformly to produce frustration, anger, and hence antisocial sentiment and conduct.

   Durkheim's "Anomie" Today's structural explanations of crime production derive from the teachings of the French sociologist Emile Durkheim (1858–1917). Durkheim thought of human beings as *social* animals as well as physical organisms. The idea of the human being as a social animal suggests more than the obvious fact that he lives a long life as a helpless child depending on others for his survival. To Durkheim this idea implies that human survival depends upon *moral* connections. These connections represent a bond with, and hence a bondage to, others. In the writing of Durkheim and his followers one finds the repeated notion of *social pressure* as a requirement of adequate human functioning. The pressure of this moral environment must be neither too little nor too great. One can be crushed by the excessive demands of others upon his life, but he also falls apart when he lives without the moral restraint that others impose upon him.

   What is required, according to this metaphor, is a regulation of social life so that there be a balance between desires and satisfactions, between our goals and our possibilities. "No living being can be happy or even exist," Durkheim argues, "unless his needs are sufficiently proportioned to his means" (1951, p. 246).

   Social conditions that allow a "deregulation" of social life Durkheim called states of *"anomie,"* from the Greek roots meaning "lacking in rule or law."

   The concept of anomie has been taken up by modern structuralists to depict the strains produced in individuals by the conflicting or impossible demands of their social environment. A popular application of the notion of anomie to the explanation of deviant behavior has been advanced by the American sociologist R. K. Merton (1957). His hypothesis is that a state of anomie is produced whenever there is a gap between the goals of human action and the societally structured, lawful means of achieving them. The proposal is, simply, that crime breeds in the conflict between aspirations and possibilities. The emphasis given to this idea by the structuralists is that both our goals and our means are given by the pattern of social arrangements. It is the structure of a society that allegedly builds desires and provides opportunities for their satisfaction. This structural explanation sees illegal behavior as resulting from goals held to be desirable and possible for all, motivating behavior in a societal context that provides only limited legal channels for their attainment.

Pressuring People into Crime   Structural explanations look at aspects of social arrangements that are described as "pressures" forcing people to behave one way rather than another. For example, classroom cheating is seen as the result of "pressure" to get a good mark where everyone cannot get top marks, and sports cheating is also seen as the result of "pressure" to win. A recent illustration of structures "pushing" people into competitive cheating is provided by Woodley (1974) in his essay, "Training Children to Cheat," an analysis of the frauds committed to win soapbox derbies.

The channels by which young people are led from childhood to adulthood are also portrayed as paths that make crime more or less probable. Thus compulsory schools that are boring to many of their inmates and that abuse their egos with failure are held to be instigators of delinquency (Goodman, 1956; McDonald, 1969; Stinchcombe, 1964). Furthermore, societies that preach equality and practice inequality are described as structures that generate crime. In this vein, it is argued that if everyone is urged to get "more" and to have what others are seen to have—often without "good reason"—and if society provides only limited legal channels for getting this "more," then people who are so motivated will resort to illegal means to attain these valued ends (Cloward and Ohlin, 1960).

The idea of a social structure pushing people into crime is extended to "crimes in the factory," where the necessity to achieve quotas or to maintain difficult standards of quality within time limits pressures both blue-collar and white-collar workers into fraud. This kind of criminality has been described in both capitalist and communist countries (Bensman and Gerver, 1963; Berliner, 1961; Connor, 1972; Moore, 1954; Vandivier, 1972).

The structural style of explanation can be used to explain large-scale business fraud, the corruption of high officials, and predatory street crime. The theme of these explanations is always to show how, *being in that situation,* it is "understandable," and perhaps even justifiable, for a person to cheat.

Whether one justifies what he has thus been given to "understand" depends, of course, on whether or not the theorist's politics and morals sympathize with the offender being explained. Did Bonnie and Clyde *have* to behave as they did? Did Hitler?

The mass media today portray a variety of liars, cheats, and thieves as sympathetic characters. One needs only to understand the situations that "forced" them to become frauds (the Irving case), burglars (*The Anderson Tapes*), whores (*Klute*), dope peddlers *(Easy Rider),* bank robbers *(The Getaway),* and gangsters *(The Godfather).* All these stories "explain away" the corruption these people display by showing how "circumstances" make their behavior understandable.

It should be noted that this sort of explanation can be given in favor of *any* offender. The theme is the same whether it is applied to persons in high places or low. Thus the structural explanation has been applied, but with little popularity, by defenders of the United States President, in 1974, against his impeachment. It is argued that, given the circumstances of "leaks" of state secrets and given the President's mandate to defend his country, the use of "dirty tricks" and burglars becomes understandable. What we "understand" in this way often becomes what is justified.

The attribution of crime rates to social structures may or may not provide true descriptions of how things are. However, the description that is offered as an explanation carries with it the most common of criminal justifications:

"Others are doing it."
"If conditions weren't so lousy, he would not have needed to do it."
"Anyone in the same situation would have. . . ."

The flavor of this explanatory justification can be sampled in the words of a rich (by world standards) American, enterprising blue-collar worker, as related by Mayer (1972):

> Richie is an electrician, working on a high-rise office building now under construction. In an average week he takes home about $250; in a good week, with overtime, up to $400.
>
> But it isn't always enough. "I don't have to tell you how tough it is to make ends meet," says the 42-year-old father of five. To support his family (two of his sons are in college), meet the mortgage on his Staten Island house and make payments on his two cars, Richie supplements his income on weekends: He wires basements for homeowners trying to beat the high cost of regular contractors.
>
> It's a booming business. Right now, Richie is booked up for the next 2 1/2 months. "They call me because I can do the work a lot cheaper than a regular electrician," he explains.
>
> The secret of Richie's low prices: "I don't have to pay for materials or tools. I just take what I need from the site I'm working on."

Richie's justification is the common one: "You steal it instead of letting them steal it."

The structural explanations tell true stories, but the truth they tell is only part of everything that is happening that causes us to behave as we do. We know something is missing in the structural account because *not everyone* in the same situation behaves the same way. Other explanations of crime attempt to accommodate this fact.

3   Attitudes, Interpretations, and Ideas Cause Crime   The fact that everyone does not behave similarly in apparently similar circumstances leads social psychologists to look for things that might make a difference. A leading school of social psychology, the symbolic interactionist, emphasizes that how we *interpret* our circumstances determines how we respond to them. Thus, between *where we are* and *how we act,* meanings intrude to guide our behavior. These meanings are called various names such as "attitudes," "beliefs," and "definitions of the situation." Whatever their title, these interpretations are held to be crucial in explaining how one responds to his world.

These meanings that guide our actions can be studied as they are attributed by the *offender* in coping with his world or as they are attributed by *lawmakers* who "criminalize" particular kinds of acts.

In the first instance, the sociologist is looking at the different ways in which offenders and nonoffenders interpret reality. The differential association theory, a prominent version of this sociopsychological outlook, explains crime as resulting from a balance of definitions of the situation favorable or unfavorable to breaking the law. When the balance swings toward defining the situation as justifying a violation of the law, criminal conduct ensues (Sutherland and Cressey, 1970, p. 75).

A second way of applying a social psychology that emphasizes the causal power of interpretation has been called the labeling or societal reaction school. Instead of studying how offenders differentially define the world, this school studies how prosecutors, legislators, and their publics define people who are caught in some deviation from proper conduct. The people with the power to make the rules and to define their violation have themselves been labeled "moral entrepreneurs" (Becker, 1963).

The labeling school claims that the way in which moral entrepreneurs respond to rule breakers and the names they call them involve interpretation, and that this interpretation of the behavior of deviant others is often at variance with how the others "really" behave. It is further claimed that the label that the majority applies to some minority *causes* the minority to behave in a different way. It allegedly does this by changing the apprehended deviant's interpretation of himself.

The difference between these two versions of symbolic interactionist explanations of crime is that the differential association theory assumes that offenders are motivated toward criminality by different definitions of their situation. On the other hand, the labeling school assumes that, initially at least, everyone is pretty much the same, but that some people get caught violating some norm and that the social response that stigmatizes an offender pushes him from a casual delinquency into an offensive career.

Again, both of these styles of explanation point to something true. How we interpret our situation makes a difference in how we behave. How others treat us as we behave well or ill has some effect upon the future course of our conduct.

Questions remain, however. A first question is, "Which of us under which circumstance is pushed how much in which direction by the attitude of which others toward us?" A second question is, "How are the interpretations of ourselves and others acquired?"

A fourth mode of explaining crime attends to these issues.

4   How We Are Trained Causes Crime   Another type of sociopsychological explanation studies the effects of different programs of training upon adolescent and adult behavior. This kind of explanation has been given the unfortunate title of "control theory" because it emphasizes *how* behavior is learned. It assumes that human beings, like their primate cousins, have to be reared, and that the rearing requires socialization, that is, a guidance and a practice in how to behave.

This theory turns the usual question about crime causation around. It does not ask, "Why do some people cheat and steal more than others?" although it answers that. It assumes that *without training* against the temptation to take what one wants, cheating and stealing come naturally. There are, we have seen, good reasons for deceit and predation. Control theory asks, therefore, "How do people learn to be honest?"

Advocates of this theory do two kinds of things by way of research. They study how learning occurs and they compare the behavior of individuals who have been differently trained.

Psychologists study the difference it makes to the behavior of animals, including the human one, if they are trained one way rather than another. As every owner of animals has learned and as every parent assumes, reward and punishment and the models we provide guide behavior. Psychologists have attempted to make more exact our knowledge of how different *balances* of reward and punishment—their timing and intensity—and the presence or absence of models affect behavior.

Sociologists and anthropologists conduct comparative research to ascertain the differences in behavior that occur with different kinds of nurturing. This kind of investigation has compared child-rearing practices and behavioral consequences in widely different societies, among different classes of people within the same society, and among children reared lovingly or coldly, with or without parents. A review of these socialization studies as they pertain to criminality is given by Nettler (1974a, Chap. 9).

The conclusion of this kind of research supports the basic assumption of control theory: that the human organism, if left alone, does not just grow up naturally cooperative, considerate, and honest. The conclusion is that how we are to behave toward each other has to be learned and that how we are trained makes a difference in how we behave. The value of such research that ends in such ordinary conclusions has been to show *how much* this is so and to illuminate the *different ways,* varying in their efficiency, by which we are trained.

IN SUMMARY

All these explanations of variation in the amount of crime are somewhat true, it has been said. If one tries to pull them together to make a coherent story, the theme that binds these different emphases is that *anything that breaks community increases criminality.*

A community is a group of people who live together with a shared interpretation of the world. A community shares, also, a pattern of performances, and it agrees how this pattern is to be transmitted to succeeding generations. When this pattern of lessons is distinctive and when there is some continuity to it, we speak of a *culture*.

Cultures regulate the expression of self-interest. They prescribe rights and duties. They define limits to the intrusion of one ego upon another and, at the same time, they define the occasions on which obligation is expected. Cultures teach their participants "right and wrong" and train them in habits that make the recognition of right and wrong second nature. The fact of such training makes control by law and the police less necessary.

Where people try to live together under the laws of one state but as carriers of diverse cultures, higher crime rates are probable. The conflict of cultural prescriptions is exemplified in the different definitions of the situation. It is exemplified in the different definitions of justice and in the demands for changes in the power to "criminalize" and "decriminalize."

The conflict of cultures, and hence the production of crime, is assured, too, when any significant number of people who live in the same society train their offspring well or ill and with different moral lessons. In some zones of Western countries, it can even be said that children grow up almost abandoned. These abandoned ones exhibit behaviors approximating those expected of feral children, those imaginary creatures born of human parents but suckled by dogs or wolves.

To repeat, whatever challenges a culture and weakens community increases criminality. Communities and their cultures are weakened and sometimes broken by cultural contact and conflict and by social change that presents new situations to which a culture must respond.

This interpretation of the many stories about crime causation explains why treating any *one* aspect of our social arrangements—such as educational and vocational opportunities, or poverty, or stigmatization—has no effect, or a barely perceptible effect, on crime rates. These minimal effects are to be expected because treating such singular aspects of our living together does not restore community.

Saying this neither commends nor condemns community. It only describes the fundamental condition of crime production. This qualification is given because it is a recurring theme of our study that everything we value exacts a price. For those of us who have grown accustomed to freedom, community exacts the price of conformity. On the other hand, crime is one of the costs of freedom.

Chapter 8

Comforting Chemicals

The concerns with being happy and healthy, which include being loved and loving and being treated honestly, get entangled with pleasures, our own and others'.

We run into conflict between one person's pleasure and another's as, for example, between wilderness lovers and ski developers or rock festival promoters and neighborhood protectors. However, a major social concern is with the pleasures that *hurt ourselves* primarily and others secondarily. In particular, there is public anxiety about those wounding habits associated with the use of "the comforting chemicals." Surveys in Western countries reveal worry about drug abuse to be among the three or four most pressing public issues, with concern expressed for both the *practical* and *moral* consequences. These surveys report that large segments of the population find the use of comforting chemicals morally offensive. For instance, in the United States, 40 percent say this about the use of alcoholic beverages while 64 percent say this about marijuana (Shafer et al., 1972, p. 133).

The Practical and Moral Bases of a Social Concern

The practical and moral sources of concern are intertwined, of course, but separable. The practical concern is with some apparent *damage,* physical or psychological, inflicted upon oneself or others. This concern becomes enlarged when the impairment seems associated with a preferred but different way of life.

The practical concern is interwoven with a moral attitude. "Harming oneself" is not defined only by reference to some physical or psychological disability. The moral element in a concern with harming oneself derives from some strongly valued conception of how human beings ought to be. Quite apart from any practical consequences our habits may have for ourselves and others, there is regard for the effect of particular practices upon *the way we are.*

It is important to recognize this entanglement of practical and moral issues because some of the ways in which we harm ourselves are pleasurable. Insofar as pleasure is its own good, achieving it is rational. Therefore, the idea of doing ourselves "wrong" when we give ourselves pleasure can only be conceived against an ethical background. To speak of harming oneself in more than just a physical sense is to employ a moral notion of being human. This moral idea defines *virtue:* a model of how one should live. Such a model usually includes a description, as well, of how one should die.

There are cultural differences in the models of virtue, but there is also a universality in the concern to live long and to live well. The cultural differences are largely in the stories told to justify our tribe's definition of virtue. The justifications of virtue have a religious significance. They are embedded in a set of beliefs about how the world works and why we are in it. The religious justification of virtue may be illustrated by an example from another culture. The Stoic philosopher Epictetus (A.D. c. 50–c. 138) claimed that we should care for our minds and bodies because the gods gave them to us. In his *Discourses* (1925, pp. 124–125), Epictetus argues as follows:

> But now because Zeus has made you, for this reason do you care not how you shall appear? Being the work of such an artist do you dishonor him? He has delivered yourself to your own care, and says, "I had no one fitter to entrust him to than yourself: keep him for me such as he is by nature, modest, faithful, erect, unterrified, free from passion and perturbation. . . ."[1]

The Practical Significance of the Moral Meaning of Harming Oneself

The practical and the moral bases of a concern with harming oneself interact, of course. They move together. It is important, however, to note that there are these *two* sources of concern. It is a mistake, therefore, to try to reduce social concern with vice[2] to some measure of its practical effects.

There *are* these practical effects—the physical damage one person's vice does himself or another—but there is also concern with the moral meaning of our habits. It is this dual nature of our concern with vice that makes it difficult

---

[1]Epictetus was neither the first philosopher nor the last to confuse how man is "by nature" with how the philosopher would have him be. The appeal to "nature" is, of course, part of the justification of a model of virtue.

[2]The very words with which we describe self-damaging practices reflect the moral basis of our concern. "Vice" means "defect," "failing," "depravity." Brock (1960, p. 34) adds that "Vice has been defined as unconsciously choosing something which is bad for yourself or for society, and sin as consciously choosing it. Vice becomes sin as soon as the person concerned knows it is vice."

to treat habitual modes of self-destruction as problems for which there are rational solutions. The difficulty lies in how a free society can justify intervening in other people's lives when, most immediately, their practices primarily injure themselves. Suppose that one finds pleasure in eating himself toward an early death, or enjoys his addiction to alcohol or heroin, or "gets his kicks" by selling his sexual services to anonymous buyers. Should society object?

A "mere" assessment of the physical injuries these vices may inflict upon practitioners and innocent others will not answer the question. Such an assessment does not answer the question because there is a moral presupposition underlying our asking it. The moral assumption is that people should not behave that way. The moral premise is that people should not behave that way even if they enjoy it. A test of the *moral* basis of this concern—as distinguished from any *practical* basis—is this: that we finally run out of practical responses to the addict's customary argument while yet disagreeing with him.

His argument says, "It's my life. If smoking gives me pleasure, why shouldn't I take the pleasure even if it shortens my life a bit?"[3]

At this end of the debate, the only answer possible is a moral one that describes how, among "our people," we believe a person should be.

The Peculiar Character of a Social Concern   This entangling of morals with pleasures make the social concern with self-inflicted injuries a peculiar one. It is peculiar because it tends to be an "unselfish"[4] concern. It is not so much our own vices but those of others that bother us. The vices you and I have we rather enjoy. It is the defects of our loved ones that most concern us. Secondarily, it is the depravity of distant others that troubles us for fear it may become epidemic.

It is this "peculiarity" of the concern with harming oneself that makes it difficult to know what to do about it. It should be noted, however, that this difficulty is faced only in *free* societies. Tyrannies do not have this problem because totalitarian regimes are bolstered by an ideology, and the ideology includes moral conceptions of how people should behave. Modern tyrannies therefore have no hesitation in punishing activities they define as immoral— from homosexuality and prostitution to drunkenness and the use of narcotics. There is no freedom to be a "drag queen," a whore, or an addict in Cuba, the People's Republic of China, or the Soviet Union, and there is no public debate in those countries about whether people *should* be free to choose such forms of morally defined self-destruction (Blum, 1969, 1971; Connor, 1972; Tuchman, 1972; Zeitlin, 1967, p. 125).

---

[3]Estimates of the shortened life-span produced by prolonged cigarette smoking are complicated by the different ways of living that are associated with smoking and nonsmoking. However, calculations in Western countries estimate that heavy cigarette smoking (a package or more a day) over a score or more years reduces life expectancy by between seven and twelve years (Best et al., 1961; Doll and Hill, 1964; Dorn, 1958; Hammond and Horn, 1954; Jones, 1956; Pearl, 1938; Retherford, 1974).

[4]"Unselfish" has to be placed in quotation marks because it is a vague term. When I love you, you become part of my "self." Therefore, a concern for the loved one is "unselfish" *only* in the sense that another person is involved.

In such totalitarian regimes, freedom is associated with pleasure seeking. It is given "bad names" such as "individualism" and "liberalism," and it is opposed as the enemy of hard work and devotion to social interests (Mao, 1967, pp. 105–106, 129, 136–141, and Chap. 26).

Vice and crime are prices paid for freedom in societies that are not communities. Each student sets his own value on this equation. A difficulty in trying to assess the value of freedom, given its costs, is that we do not know how much it is worth until we have experienced its lack.

The concern expressed about drugs varies with one's familiarity with them and with beliefs about their physical, psychological, and social effects. It is important, therefore, to analyze the nature of these chemicals.

CATEGORIES OF THE COMFORTING CHEMICALS

Human beings ingest a fantastic pharmacy of mood-altering substances—organic and inorganic, natural and synthetic. We do this in many ways. We eat these substances in food or by themselves. We drink them, smoke them, sniff and suck them. We rub them on our flesh and inject them under our skin and into our veins.

These chemicals are popularly called drugs, but that term is inexact since it connotes several things. For example, "drugs" suggests a medicinal substance used to prevent or cure disease. However, the verb form, "to drug," suggests something that stupefies or poisons. If we use the word "drug" here, it is only for variety.

More exactly, the object of social concern is a wide range of materials that can best be titled "the comforting chemicals" because they are taken principally for the comfort they provide rather than for their nutritional or medicinal value.

There are many ways to classify these chemicals. One useful grouping classes them in part by their chemical properties but also by the kind of effect sought by their users. These drugs may be regarded, then, as (1) *depressants,* (2) *stimulants,* and (3) *psychotropic* ("mind-turning") agents.

1 Depressants

A depressant is a chemical that slows the responsiveness of the central nervous system. In sufficient quantity, it will block the normal nervous responses. The depressants can themselves be classified by their *major* effect, but with some overlap, as *(a)* sedative-hypnotic chemicals, *(b)* analgesic agents, *(c)* narcotics, and *(d)* anesthetics.

    a *Sedative-hypnotics* are calming chemicals. They tranquilize and they promote sleep without inducing intoxication. Examples are the bromides and barbiturates.

    b *Analgesics* are pain-killers. They relieve pain without producing sleep. An example is aspirin.

c *Narcotics,* as their name implies, produce sleep. On the way to sleep, a narcotic is also analgesic. Principal narcotics are opium and its derivatives, morphine and heroin. Other related alkaloids have been synthesized.

d *Anesthetics* produce a progressive, descending depression of the central nervous system. They deaden sensation and, in sufficient quantity, they therefore kill pain and put one to sleep. An anesthetic is said to produce a "progressive, descending" slowing of nervous response because it moves in its effects *cumulatively* from that portion of the central nervous system that was *last* acquired in human evolution—the cortex of the frontal lobes where conscience resides—downward to the more primitive, life-preserving centers that control respiration.

The more familiar anesthetics are ether, chloroform and alcohol. In sufficient doses, alcoholic beverages and the opiates produce narcotic, analgesic, and anesthetic effects.

Some people feel elevated after swallowing a few ounces of alcohol and they therefore speak of a drink as a "pick-me-up." While one may feel psychologically stimulated because tension is relieved, it is incorrect to call alcoholic beverages stimulants. They do not stimulate the nervous system. They are social lubricants because they allay anxiety and self-consciousness, but they do this by deadening the functions of the central nervous system.

2 Stimulants

A stimulant increases the activity of the nervous system. This is a reason for calling one group of stimulants, the amphetamines, "speed." Stimulants vary in their intensity, of course. Caffeine is a mild stimulant; cocaine is a more powerful activator that also has anesthetic effects.

Tobacco functions as a physiological stimulator and a psychological depressant. The active agent in tobacco smoke is a poison—nicotine—that stimulates the nervous system. It increases pulse rate, blood pressure, and cortical activity (Armitage et al., 1968; Dorcus, 1925; Lawton, 1962). It also constricts blood vessels (Lampson, 1935), and some investigators see this combination of increased heart rate and blood pressure and narrowed blood vessels as the possible cause of the higher rate of cardiovascular diseases in heavy cigarette smokers than in nonsmokers (Hammond and Horn, 1954; Levy et al., 1947; Roth, 1951; Roth et al., 1960; Spain and Nathan, 1961).

Tobacco also serves as a tranquilizer, but this effect is psychological rather than physiological. Habitual smokers are more tense and anxious than nonsmokers, and tobacco is used as a tension reducer (Eysenck, 1963; Lilienfeld, 1959; Matarazzo and Saslow, 1960; Thomas, 1960). However, some portion of this tension seems to be a result of the tobacco craving itself, so that tobacco tranquilizes by allaying the discomfort it itself produces (Hammond, 1958; McArthur et al., 1958). "Cigarette smoking causes nervous tension" and "nervous tension causes cigarette smoking"—both statements are true (Thomas, 1968).

There is no contradiction in finding that a physiological stimulant is a behavioral tranquilizer. This is but the reverse of the finding that alcohol is a physiological depressant and, in mild doses, a psychological stimulant.

3 Psychotropic Drugs

Psychotropic chemicals are those whose principal effects are dramatic changes in sensation and impressions of oneself and the world. In small doses they typically induce relaxation and fine feeling. In larger doses they produce a variety of effects, depending on the person and the drug. They have, therefore, been called different names depending upon the effect to be emphasized in the title. For example, the British psychiatrist Humphrey Osmond coined the word, "psychedelic," meaning "mind-manifesting," because he felt that they "enriched the mind and enlarged the vision." However, some of these chemicals produce hallucinations and psychotic manifestations. Thus they are sometimes called hallucinogens, psychotogenetics, and psychotomimetics. Since these drugs do not always induce hallucination or psychosis and since it is doubtful that they "enrich" the mind, whatever that might mean, they seem best called something more neutral and general like *psychotropic*.

The more powerful of these "mind-turning" drugs are the synthetic products, such as STP, DMT, and LSD. Plant derivatives that have similar effects are mescaline and peyote from the cactus, psilocybin from a mushroom fungus, scopolamine from the henbane plant, and nutmeg.

The mildest of these chemicals are the derivatives from the female hemp plant, *Cannabis sativa*. Since at least 3,000 years before Christ, people have made drinks or smoking mixtures from the tops of the uncultivated cannabis weed (Taylor, 1966). The various preparations of this herb are the most widely used illegal drugs in the world, with an estimated 200 to 300 million people taking repeated pleasure from them (Mechoulam, 1970). Crude preparations from the uncultivated weed are known by different names in different cultures: *bhang* in the Far East, *dagga* in Southwest Africa, and *marijuana* in North America. Given the interest in this plant, specially cultivated herbs have been grown that yield a more intoxicating resinous substance. In India preparations from the cultivated herb are known as *ganja*. When the resin from such particularly grown plants is extracted for use, the preparation is called *charas* in India and *hashish* in the Mideast. Pharmacologically, this herb is known as *Cannabis indica*. Hashish is typically five to eight times as powerful as the marijuana usually smoked in North America (Grinspoon, 1969).

All these comforting chemicals have their physical and psychological risks. None is completely safe. The questions we commonly ask about these risks are: (1) Will I get hooked? (2) What are the physical effects of habitual use? (3) What are the social consequences? (4) What, if anything, should be done about drugs?

On Getting Hooked

There is no clear medical definition of "addiction." The idea of being hooked is the notion of being *devoted* to a habit, *subject* to it, *determined* by it to such a degree that a change in the practice produces shock and a struggle to return to it. However, we do not speak of all fixed habits as addictions even when the habit is annoying to its subject and when attempts to remove the habit induce trauma. For example, the habitual fear of high places exhibited by an acrophobic is not spoken of as an addiction, although a change in his habitual avoidance of elevation produces panic. What is added by the notion of addiction is *physiological dependence.*

As the idea is used medically, addiction to drugs has three components. Getting hooked means, first, that a *tolerance* is developed for the chemical so that, up to some limit, increasing amounts must be taken to produce the desired effect. It means, second, that the user shows a psychological attachment to the drug, and we say then that he is *habituated* to it. Last, to be addicted means that habitual use of the chemical has produced *physiological changes* in the user so that he now requires the drug. These physiological changes are difficult to demonstrate; that is, it is difficult to locate the source of the craving in specific biochemical changes. Such changes are assumed, however, from the exhibition of *withdrawal symptoms* when the chemical is removed. The physical signs of distress upon withdrawal of the drug lead us to infer that there are biochemical roots to the craving in addition to the psychological satisfactions given by the drug.

While the physiological roots of the withdrawal distress are difficult to identify, the behavioral mark of the addict is clear. *He behaves as if he could not live without "the stuff."*

The Odds on Getting Hooked   It is this behavioral aspect of using a drug, the compulsion to have it, that is at the heart of what is meant by being addicted. This compulsion becomes the fate of *some* habitual users of alcoholic beverages—perhaps 5 to 10 percent of all regular users (Cahalan, 1970; Hampton, 1947b). Addiction is the fate, however of *all* habitual users of tobacco in cigarette form and *most* of its devotees in other forms.

Compulsive use is also the predictable result for *most* consumers of the amphetamines, cocaine, the opiates, and the barbiturates. The insidious thing about these "heavier" drugs is that they can be tried and denied. However, most experimenters try these "bigger" pleasures again. The experimenter begins to enjoy "chipping"; he uses dope as an amusement. There is the pleasure of the dope itself and the fun of being part of the world of drugs with its "in" language, mutual concerns, and cops-and-robbers excitement. The "chipper" is in control of his appetite for dope and he begins to suffer the conceit that a little more won't get him "strung out." Heroin in particular is dangerous precisely because, to the experimenter, it seems innocent. It is when the "dipper and dabber" loses respect for the power of heroin that he is at risk of becoming its slave.

By definition, the "milder" stimulants and psychotropic chemicals are less addicting in the sense that they do not produce striking withdrawal symptoms and the craving that makes dope a way of life. However, habitual users of these comforts develop a strong affection for them and become *psycho-*

logically dependent upon them. This is true of devotees of coffee, tea, and cannabis.

IN SUMMARY

The risks of addiction to the various comforting chemicals seem clear enough. If it were important for a person to estimate the risk of addiction before he tried a drug—and this does not seem to be a strong consideration among experimenters—then he would stay clear of the barbiturates, the opiates, the amphetamines, cocaine, and cigarettes. He would also understand that the habitual intake of alcohol—let's say six or more ounces of distilled spirits per day over a few years—puts him at risk of becoming an alcohol addict.

The Physical Effects of the Comforting Chemicals

The immediately happy effects of a moderate dose of any of these chemicals should not be confused with the immediately unhappy effects of a large dose, and neither of these effects should be confused with the long-term physical consequences of habitual use.

Physical Effects of Depressants   In the short run, a modest amount of the depressants produces relaxation and usually, but not always, fine feeling. There are occasions when a depressant, such as alcohol, induces gloom rather than joy.

In heavy doses, *all depressants narcotize:* they produce stupor, sleep, and, in sufficient quantity, death.

The habitual use of depressants over long periods has varied effects, and it cannot be assumed that pleasant short-term results will not have their long-term costs. In fact, some of the chemicals that are *less* potent in their short-term physical effects are *more* dangerous in their protracted results. The prolonged use of alcohol, for example, is more damaging to the body than is the prolonged use of the opiates. Long-term habituation to alcoholic beverages is associated with specific alcoholic psychoses—such as delirium tremens and Korsakoff's psychosis, with damage to the intestinal tract, liver, and brain, and with early death. On the other hand, no specific organic damage is attributable to opiate addiction in itself. There are sometimes physical by-products of opiate addiction, as when poor addicts neglect eating in favor of seeking the drug. In such cases, not the drug itself but the way of life associated with drug use has produced the organic damage. In sum, one can be a physically healthy albeit sleepy heroin addict, but one cannot long remain a healthy devotee of alcohol.

In the opiates we have an instance in which potent short-term effects are not associated with damaging long-term physical consequences. Among the stimulants we shall note a reverse case in which a mild short-term stimulant, tobacco, has damaging long-term consequences.

Physical Effects of Stimulants   In moderate amounts, the stimulants in-crease alertness and energy. The stronger ones, such as the amphetamines and cocaine, make a person feel excited, exhilarated, and powerful.

In heavy doses, the stimulants produce irritability and sleeplessness. In addition, large doses of the amphetamines and cocaine induce stomach disorders, convulsions, and psychotic-like behavior, while large amounts of nicotine cause headache and nausea (U.S. Department of Health, Education, and Welfare, 1971).

In the long run, the most insidious of the stimulants in its physical effects is tobacco. This normally legal, popular drug is lethal, and particularly so when smoked as a cigarette rather than in a pipe, or chewed or sniffed. In small amounts, the immediate physical damage of inhaling tobacco smoke appears negligible: irritation of eyes, nasal passage, and lungs. Over the long term, however, inhalation of tobacco smoke is associated, directly or indirectly, with reduced life expectancy and the increased probability of cancers of the lungs, mouth, and lips. Tobacco addiction is one of the contributory agents increasing the risk of emphysema—a condition in which the lung tissue becomes stretched and loses its elasticity—and diseases of the coronary arteries (Hammond and Horn, 1954).

The correlation between heavy cigarette smoking and physical damage is strong and has been repeatedly observed by numerous investigators. The American biologist Raymond Pearl (1938) noticed this association decades ago when he reported the reduced life expectancy of smokers. A few years later, Pearl's study was supported by British findings of a significantly higher incidence of coronary artery disease among smokers forty to fifty-nine years of age when compared with nonsmokers of like age (English et al., 1940). It was not until 1954, however, when Hammond and Horn reported their findings in a large sample of white American men, that researchers and some citizens took seriously the health hazards of tobacco. Hammond and Horn compared the death rates of "heavy cigarette smokers" (one pack or more per day) with lighter smokers and nonsmokers among 187,766 men between fifty and seventy years of age. They found that smokers died *of all causes* at a much higher rate than abstainers. For some specific causes of death, however, the differentials in death rates between smokers and nonsmokers were extremely high. For example, within these age brackets, smokers die almost *two times* as frequently as nonsmokers from heart disease and at about *two-and-a-half times* as frequently from cancer.

A debate persists about whether these kinds of correlations, replicated in at least eighteen studies in five countries (Rutstein, 1957), demonstrate a causal link between smoking and poor health or whether the correlations are only coincidental. As we have seen (pp. 49–50), it is possible that the necessary cause of any disease may not be its sufficient cause, and there are undoubtedly other factors than smoking that account for the observed differences in the health of smokers and nonsmokers. However, given the five to thirty-five times greater risk of lung cancer among smokers than nonsmokers—depending on the amount and duration of smoking—and given the fact that substances in the cigarette smoke have been isolated that produce cancerous changes in tissue, it seems foolish to deny the long-term hazards of the tobacco comfort. After much controversy, some governments have agreed that smoking damages health (Royal College of Physicians, 1962; U.S. Surgeon General, 1964). More recently, investigators in such diverse fields as genetics, pharmacology, medicine, psychology, and sociology pooled their findings about tobacco (Dunn, 1973). The conclusion drawn from this meeting of scientists has been summarized by one of its reviewers as follows:

> . . . the sum total of human disease, disability, death, and lost productivity directly attributable to cigarette smoking is so staggering that a reduction in cigarette smoking may be the single most important health measure open to us for the foreseeable future. In the United States, one-third of all the deaths for men aged 35 to 59 would not have occurred if cigarette smokers had the same death rates as nonsmokers [Jaffe, 1974, p. 1039].

Physical Effects of Psychotropic Drugs   In general, the psychotropic chemicals have pleasant effects when taken in *moderate* doses. Cannabis preparations relax their users, make them feel fine, induce the giggles, lessen inhibitions, and produce fantastic sensations of time, space, and color. The sensations sometimes get tangled so that one experiences *synesthesia*—he hears colors and sees sound. The most apparent short-term physical damages are conjunctivitis (reddening of the eyes), tachycardia (rapid pulse), lessened muscular strength and steadiness, lowered pressure within the eye, and, for some subjects, nystagmus (rapid oscillation of the eyeball) (Nahas, 1973, p. 112; Shafer et al., 1972, p. 57).

Other hallucinogenic chemicals produce more marked effects, even in small doses. For example, 150 to 200 micrograms of LSD takes one far away—a microgram is *one millionth* of a gram and there are 28.4 grams to an ounce. As the title of these drugs suggests, sensation is distorted and the user suffers, or enjoys, hallucinations—he sees, feels, and hears things that have no external substance. Psychotic-like behavior is probable.

Heavy doses of the psychotropic drugs produce anxiety, panic, trembling, vomiting, and psychotic behavior. "Depersonalization" is not uncommon—this is the feeling that one no longer exists—nor does anything else. The habitual use of psychotropic drugs of the stronger variety for as short a period as a few months increases the probability of psychotic episodes. The risk varies, of course, with the chemical used and the amount taken. However, taking repeated "trips of the mind" is not a way of ensuring one's mental health.

There is presumptive evidence that any of the psychotropic drugs can be deadly if taken in large quantity. This seems true even of the relatively benign cannabis. Heyndrickx and associates (1970) report a well-documented account of fatal cannabis intoxication in Belgium, and cases of accidental death have been reported among Egyptian children who inhaled hashish from water pipes (Nahas, 1973, p. 108).

The long-term physical effects of the psychotropic habit are of more concern. It can be said, in summary, that prolonged use of these comforts exacts a physical health cost. How high the cost is and how probable cannot be specified since these results vary with the individual, with the chemical, and with the style of life in which the habit is embedded. However, some of the risks can be described.

Persistent inhalation of any kind of smoke damages the lungs. Where powerful cannabis preparations are habitually used, as in Egypt, India, and Morocco, the drug is reported to cause bronchial irritation, chronic catarrhal laryngitis, and asthma (Benabud, 1957; Souief, 1967). It is not yet clear whether marijuana smoke is as cancerous as tobacco smoke, but carcinogenic agents have been isolated in cannabis as in nicotine (Doorenbos et al., 1971; Magus and Harris, 1971).

Since the psychotropic chemicals have such powerful effects upon thought and feeling, it has been assumed that habitual use might damage the brain. While no specific lesions of the brain have thus far been linked to the repeated use of either the opiates or the "mind-turning" drugs, the possibility of changes in brain function cannot be foreclosed. Some neurochemists hold open the hypothesis that frequent intoxication from marijuana or stronger chemicals may affect the chemistry of the nerves that regulate thought (Nahas, 1973, p. 110). This possibility receives support from a study by Campbell and his colleagues (1971), who examined ten young men who had smoked marijuana daily for from three to eleven years. These men had also taken "speed" and LSD, but their principal psychotropic diet had been marijuana. Campbell and his associates found these men to suffer from brain atrophy, an enlargement of the cerebral ventricles such as is found in deteriorated old persons, sufferers from Parkinson's disease, and "punch drunk" boxers.

All such research findings are tentative because the epidemic of psychotropic habituation in rich countries with research facilities is recent and controlled investigations have only begun. Given such preliminary findings as have been reported, however, a cautionary conclusion seems justified: the long-term habitual use of cannabis and other psychotropic drugs cannot be assumed to be physically harmless.

IN SUMMARY

All the comforting chemicals exact a physical price if they are used long enough in sufficient quantities. This is the same as saying if they are used habitually.

The chemicals vary in their *physical* costs from *low* in the cases of coffee, tea, and the opiates to *moderate and high* in the cases of alcohol, tobacco, cocaine, the amphetamines, and the psychotropic drugs.

This ranking is rough, but it is good enough to show that *there is no necessary relation between the physical damage probably incurred by the habitual use of a chemical and its legal status in modern countries.*

A reduction in the health of a population is a social cost, of course, and one upon which it is impossible to fix a price. There are, however, additional costs of the comforting chemicals.

Some of the Social Costs of the Comforting Chemicals

There is no societal bookkeeping that allows a cost-benefit analysis of our use of drugs. There is no such accounting because we have not counted everything that might be considered a cost of a drug habit. Furthermore, even when we agree what might count as a cost, we have not been able to assign a price to the cost.

For example, the use of tobacco involves a complex of social arrangements that cost something: from the provision of receptacles for smokers in public places, to the necessity for someone to clean the ashtrays, to the public litter of cigars and cigarettes, to the additional fire-fighting services required by the contribution of smokers to residential and forest fires.

Similar difficulties in accounting are met when we consider the social costs of other comforting chemicals. Therefore a description of the *nature* of the costs of using drugs does not constitute a rational assessment of these costs. The fact that there is no such rational evaluation—and that, perhaps, there cannot be—illuminates our original point: that some part of social response to the costs of the comforting chemicals is moral and cannot be reduced to a weighing of prices against benefits.

Social policy in response to the habituating chemicals is therefore always less than rational. This does not make social response unnecessary; it only makes it conflictful.

A Short Price List

For present purposes, it is sufficient to describe in outline the nature of some of the social costs of using the more popular chemical comforts. These social costs include some of the *physical* effects—particularly the health effects—we have discussed, but they also include *psychological* effects—effects on the way people are—that have moral significance.

Two conclusions to be drawn from this short price list can be anticipated. First, there is no pleasure without a price; and second, there is no one-to-one relation between the chemical habits legally allowed or prohibited and their social costs.

These points are illustrated in the legal careers of two of the popular comforts: alcohol and cannabis.

The Social Cost of Alcohol

Alcoholic beverages are the most costly of the depressants. They may, in fact, be the biggest drug problem in Western countries, as Dr. Joel Fort claims (1973). Citizens seem to agree. A study of American drinking practices (Cahalan et al., 1969) finds that a majority, including a majority of the drinking population, believes that "drinking does more harm than good."

It is difficult to measure how many drinkers become impaired and to what degree, either temporarily or permanently. All statistics are estimates, but the estimates give a picture of the probable magnitude of the costs of this pleasurable depressant (Glasscote et al., 1967).

Estimates of the number of problem drinkers and the degree of their disability come from several sources. The World Health Organization employs the "Jellinek formula," a statistic invented by Dr. E. M. Jellinek from the observation that liver disease is reported as the cause of death about ten times more frequently among heavy drinkers than among abstainers. With Jellinek's formula, one can get an approximation of the gravity of drink-related disorders among nations or in time. This measure assumes, of course, that the contribution of alcohol to liver disease remains a constant and that death certificates are equally reliable in different lands. Although the Jellinek formula has been criticized on these grounds, other surveys of problem drinking conclude that Jellinek's calculations may adequately rank populations on the extent of their alcoholism while underestimating the distress caused by heavy drinking (Popham and Schmidt, 1958).

Additional ways of gauging the number of drinkers and the degree of their impairment include the use of surveys by questionnaire and interview, industrial health records, and private and public hospital admissions. From a combination of such measures, the *health* costs of alcoholism can be summarized as follows:

1   Rich, Western countries have higher proportions of alcoholics than do poorer lands. The rates range from highs of three to four alcoholics per hundred adults in France and the United States to two to three per hundred in Switzerland and Scandinavia to about one per hundred in England, Wales, and Australia, to about one-half per hundred in Italy (World Health Organization, 1951, 1952).

2   In Western societies, *almost all adults use alcoholic beverages* occasionally or regularly. The proportions vary with the country, with rural-urban residence, and with socioeconomic status. Higher proportions of drinkers tend to be found in urban areas and among richer people. This does not mean that no rural areas have drinking problems; some do. For example, heavy drinking is a feature of work in timbering areas and among some rural-residing native Indians in North America.

The proportions of all adults who use alcohol range from two-thirds to nine-tenths depending upon country, class, and ethnicity. In the United States and Canada, recent surveys put the proportion of all adults who drink at close to 70 percent. This figure rises to nearly 90 percent in families earning more than $20,000 per year (Cahalan et al., 1969; *U.S. News & World Report,* 1974b).

3   For every 100 people who occasionally or customarily use alcohol, between 15 and 20 become *heavy, habitual drinkers* who are at risk of becoming alcohol addicts. In North America, this proportion seems to have increased in the years since World War II (Hampton, 1947a; Cahalan, 1970).

Of these "excessive drinkers," about half may be considered *alcohol addicts.* This means that 8 to 10 percent of drinkers become compulsive about their habit, so that their use of alcohol causes "physical, psychological, or social harm to the drinker and others" (Cahalan, 1970).

In turn, about half of these addicts—or between three and five of every hundred persons who drink—become *chronic alcoholics,* individuals who have developed physical or mental disorders as a result of their habitual, long-term drinking (Hampton, 1947a; Hirsh, 1949; Riley and Marden, 1947).

These indications of damage to the drinker's health are only part of the social costs of the alcoholic pleasures. In North American cities, for example, about one-third of all arrests are for drunkenness and this figure rises to around half if "alcohol-related" offenses, such as drunk-driving and disorderly conduct, are included (Katzenbach, 1967, p. 8).

In addition, alcohol is strongly involved in violent crime. Wolfgang's (1958) study of killings in Philadelphia from 1948 to 1952 found alcohol in either the victim or his murderer or both in almost two-thirds of the cases. Similarly, Fisher (1951) reports for Baltimore that close to 70 percent of homicide victims had been drinking. Bowden et al. (1958) publish a figure of nearly 50 percent for murder victims in Australia, and Cleveland (1955) finds a similar rate in his study of homicides in Cincinnati, Ohio. Bullock (1955) tells us that almost 30 percent of homicides in Texas occur in bars. Shupe (1954) measured alcohol concentrations by urinalysis among 882 persons arrested during or immediately after the commission of a felony (indictable offense) in Columbus, Ohio, during the 1950s. He concludes that

> Crimes of physical violence are associated with intoxicated persons. Cuttings (11 to 1 under the influence of alcohol), the carrying of concealed weapons (8 to 1 under the influence of alcohol) and other assaults (10 to 1 under the influence of alcohol) are definitely crimes of alcohol influence, even crimes of true intoxication [p. 663].

In sum, alcohol is a *social lubricant,* but it is *not a pacifier.*

Alcohol reduces inhibition and is therefore implicated in additional kinds of crimes than the directly violent ones. For example, Cruz (1943) reports that in England at the time of his study, nearly half of his sample of sex offenders were heavy, habitual drinkers, and that one-fifth were drunk at the time of their most recent offense. Similarly, Selling (1940) finds that 35 percent of his sample of male sex offenders had been drinking at the time of their offenses, and he calls 8 percent of these men "chronic alcoholics."

This sad chronicle is supplemented by the contribution of alcohol to road accidents. Drunk drivers and intoxicated pedestrians account for a high proportion of traffic fatalities. The National Safety Council in America estimates that perhaps *one-half* of those who cause traffic deaths are under the influence of alcohol (Katzenbach, 1967, p. 14). This estimate is supported by studies testing for blood-alcohol concentrations in persons killed in highway crashes. For example, the first forty-three persons killed in vehicular accidents in St. Louis in 1966 were tested for alcohol concentration in the blood. Thirty of these individuals had alcohol blood levels of 0.15 percent or higher, indicating heavy intoxication (Katzenbach, 1967, p. 14). Selzer and Weiss (1965) studied similar records among persons involved in fatal traffic accidents in Michigan and concluded that 40 percent of the drivers responsible for such mortal crashes could be diagnosed as alcoholics.

Drunk drivers are not the only cause of road accidents; drunk pedestrians also make a contribution. Haddon and his colleagues (1960) studied the characteristics of pedestrians who were killed by comparing all such victims over the age of eighteen during a certain period with a control group of persons at the same accident site at similar times. Of pedestrians who died within six hours of their accidents, 74 percent had been drinking, as compared with 33 percent of the control group. Furthermore, the more drunk a pedestrian is, up to some limit, the greater the chance of his being killed. In this research, he found that one in three of the dead pedestrians had been "highly intoxicated"—with blood alcohol levels above 0.15 percent—compared with one in sixteen among the control subjects.

A Failed Experiment: Prohibition   This tentative bill submitted for the use of alcoholic beverages is, of course, incomplete. It has not included the immeasurable costs of damaged careers, wasted talent, and broken families. Recognition of these costs fueled the temperance movement in the United States that culminated in "the noble experiment," Prohibition.

In 1919 the United States amended its Constitution to make it illegal to manufacture, sell, import, or export liquor. This Eighteenth Amendment was to have been enforced under the strict provisions of the Volstead Act, which attached penalties to trade in "intoxicating beverages" (defined as those with more than 0.5 percent of alcohol per volume). The result of this attempt to reform the drinking habits of a country was the widespread manufacture of illegal and often inferior liquor and the invasion of the marketplace by gangsters. The attempt at prohibition ended in 1933 with the passing of the Twenty-first Amendment to the Constitution repealing the Eighteenth.

The lesson learned from this failure is that *legal sanctions cannot economically reduce the demand for a commodity when that demand is relatively inflexible and when it is a demand by a majority or even a significant minority of a population.*

This statement of a lesson learned is necessarily vague because it must include the qualifying phrase "economically reduce." This vague phrase is required because there are several things *we do not know in advance of legislation designed to control other people's behavior:*

How inflexible their demand is for a forbidden product
What proportion of a population will support or break a particular law
How much punishment will be necessary to deter would-be violators
How much punishment we will be willing to inflict

All these unknowns enter decisions about the wisdom of reforming people or controlling them by punishing them. These unknowns illustrate the fact that *laws work best where they are needed least*—that is, where a large majority is imposing its will against a small minority and where the behaviors to be controlled are those about which most of us are flexible, as with our auto driving habits.

We tolerate the high costs of the alcoholic pleasures today because we would rather pay them than the alternative costs of doing without liquor and penalizing those who use it. It may be guessed that a similar fate awaits the "softer" of the illegal comforting chemicals like cannabis—which is not to say that the milder psychotropic drugs are cost-free. They are not.

The Social Cost of Cannabis

As we have seen, there are health risks in the habitual use of cannabis. However, these risks are minor—particularly for the weaker forms of cannabis like marijuana—when they are compared with the health risks incurred by the habitual use of tobacco or alcohol. There are, nevertheless, other social costs.

Intoxication and Accidents   One such probable cost, as yet unmeasured, is that of the accidents that occur under any form of intoxication. Since marijuana use in Western countries has not been as popular as the use of alcoholic beverages, its contribution to road and industrial accidents has been trivial. However, any increase in the customary use of such an intoxicant can be expected to exact some price from "high" drivers, pedestrians, and workers.

Cannabis as a Stepping-Stone   A second cost that nonusers in particular worry about is the possibility that using cannabis leads to the use of more dangerous drugs. This stepping-stone hypothesis is obscured by the vague phrase "leads to." People who employ this language seldom specify whether "leads to" means "necessitates" or "makes more probable." If the latter is meant, then, again, we are not told *how probably* the use of one comfort leads to the use of another or whether this probability varies with individuals and circumstances. There are, however, some facts on this issue that permit us to make a reasonable interpretation.

Some Facts About Multiple Drug Use

1   If any chemical is *the* stepping-stone to multiple drug use, it is tobacco. Almost all tobacco addicts are devotees of coffee, but many coffee lovers are not tobacco addicts. Furthermore, almost all tobacco addicts drink alcoholic beverages, but some drinkers—probably a minority—do not smoke.

2   Almost all North Americans who try marijuana have first tried tobacco and alcohol (Petersen et al., 1972, p. 47). This finding is probably true also of European marijuana users.

3   Young people who use tobacco and alcohol are more likely to try marijuana than those who abstain from the more popular chemicals. For example, a survey of drug use among high school seniors in Michigan (Bogg et al., 1969) reports that among students who drink alcoholic beverages, 20 percent had smoked marijuana at least once. Among abstainers from alcohol, the proportion that had tried marijuana was only 1.6 percent. Similarly, while 24 percent of tobacco users had tried marijuana, only 5 percent of tobacco abstainers had done so. The correlations between using alcohol, tobacco, and marijuana were the most significant associations discovered by this study.

4 Almost all North American users of the opiates, barbiturates, cocaine, "speed," and the stronger psychotropic drugs like LSD have also tried marijuana, but most people who have tried marijuana do not use the more dangerous drugs (Petersen et al., 1972, p. 47).

5 People who use marijuana frequently, and in particular those who become habituated to its use, are more likely to use heavier drugs than those who use marijuana experimentally or casually. For example, a survey among American teen-agers (Josephson et al., 1972) finds that the more regularly one has used marijuana, the more likely he was to have tried heroin, glue, "ups," and "downs." The probabilities increase dramatically, as Table 8-1 shows.

Table 8-1 Smoking, Drinking, and Experimentation with Other Chemicals among Marijuana Users and Nonusers*†

	Marijuana users		
	Nonusers of marijuana (N = 1424)	Experimenters (N = 158)	Occasional and frequent users (N = 103)
Percent who . . .			
Have ever smoked cigarettes	22	91	78
Smoke cigarettes now	13	83	70
Have drunk liquor apart from family	45	91	93
Have tried other drugs:‡			
Heroin	1	0	12
LSD	1	0	55
Glue	3	10	37
"Downs" or barbiturates	1	18	71
"Ups" or amphetamines	1	38	74
Tried one or two of the five drugs	2	35	29
Tried three or more of the five drugs	1	6	51

*Reproduced from E. Josephson et al., "Adolescent Marijuana Use: Report on a National Survey," in S. Einstein and S. Allen (eds.), *Student Drug Surveys*, Table 2. © 1972 by the Baywood Publishing Company. Reproduced by permission.

†This table is based on a weighted sample of 1,701 subjects taken to be representative nationally of youngsters twelve to seventeen years of age. Of this sample, the actual number interviewed was 498. The totals of nonusers and marijuana users do not add up to 1,701 because not all respondents provided information about their behavior with regard to the drug. "Experimenters" where those who had used marijuana one to nine times; "occasional" and "frequent" users were those who had used it ten or more times.

‡Eighteen percent of the occasional and frequent users did not answer the question about heroin use; 12 percent of the occasional and frequent users did not answer the question about use of glue. The proportion of nonusers of marijuana, experimenters, or occasional and frequent users who did not answer questions about other drugs in no case exceeded 6 percent.

6   There is more than one road to H (heroin). Ball and his associates (1968) studied the careers of 2,213 patients admitted for treatment of opiate addiction to hospitals in Lexington, Kentucky, and Fort Worth, Texas. *Two patterns* of opiate use were discovered.

A first pattern shows an association of marijuana habituation with opiate addiction. This pattern is found in 16 of the United States, the District of Columbia, and Puerto Rico. It is largely a metropolitan pattern, and the preferred opiate in this style of drug use is heroin.

A second pattern was discovered for some southern states stretching from Florida westward to Oklahoma and northward to Virginia. This southern pattern of opiate addiction is less frequently associated with marijuana use—only 25 percent of addicts from these states used cannabis. Furthermore, most of the southern addicts used the "softer" opiates such as morphine, dilaudid, and paregoric; only 3.6 percent used heroin and most of these addicts did *not* take their preferred drug intravenously. In the southern pattern, most of the addicts received their drugs from physicians or pharmacists rather than from pushers, and there was less association of their addiction with criminality than was found in the metropolitan pattern.

While there are, then, these different roads to the opiates, an additional finding of Ball's research is important here: "that marijuana smoking has increased among opiate addicts in the United States" (p. 181).

Within the patterns of opiate career that Ball describes, there are still many routes individuals take with drugs. There are different "accidents" by which people are introduced to heroin and there are different styles of its use by which a person drifts into living for dope, using it occasionally, or trying it and dropping it. The multiplicity of these paths is well described by three sociologists and a lawyer (Gould et al., 1974) who lived "on the street" to find out what dope means to its devotees.

An Interpretation of the Facts of Multiple Drug Use   Learning to use the comforting chemicals is, for the most part, a social event. With exceptions—such as the physician or nurse who becomes a narcotics addict through the availability of opiates, through his familiarity with them, and through some pain relieved by them—most people who get "turned on" to tobacco, alcohol, marijuana, and the opiates are introduced to these pleasures by others. The probability of escalating the use of drugs is, then, partly a function of the people one knows. One's choice of preferred people is, in turn, a function of the kind of person one is.

Drug users as well as psychologists *assume* that some people are more addiction-prone than others. This assumption has not been adequately tested by following a cohort of children into adulthood to ascertain the kinds of people who seem more and less vulnerable to the addictions.[5] However,

---

[5]Research attempting to differentiate the personalities of classes of addicts from nonaddicts has been mostly after the fact. *After* addiction, the user is, of course, "different." Thus the personalities of alcoholics and nonalcoholics are distinguishable (Goldstein and Linden, 1969; Goss and Morosko, 1969; Hampton, 1951;

although we cannot now specify in advance which kinds of person are more likely to "need" the comforts of chemicals, we can prophesy that the more one associates with people in the drug culture, the more likely he is to try the more moving chemicals after an introduction to the relaxing ones.

It is not, then, something *in* the marijuana that makes one try LSD or heroin. It is something in the person and in the social climate he chooses.

Cannabis Use and Personality Change   Opponents of marijuana not only fear its possible use as an escalator to harder drugs but also worry about the personality changes that are reported to be associated with its habitual use. Habitual users of hashish in particular, but of marijuana also, are reported to develop an "amotivational syndrome." The amotivational syndrome involves a wholesale "dropping out." Its signs are apathy, fatigue, and lack of ambition. With the flight of motivation, the habitué shows a loss in his ability to remember, to attend to details, to follow a train of thought, and to communicate. Speech is slowed and episodes of confusion are exhibited. There is a loss of interest in school, sports, and work as well as in personal hygiene, diet, and appearance.

Research on the *extent* of the amotivational syndrome is recent and there is room to question how frequently habitual users of cannabis exhibit it. There are questions, too, about the relation between the potency of the drug being used and development of these apathetic attitudes. However, the research to date is sufficiently compelling to call caution to the happy habituation to cannabis. For example, the amotivational syndrome has been noted among chronic users of hashish in Egypt (Souief, 1967), Morocco (Christozov, 1965), and India (Chopra et al., 1942; Chopra and Chopra, 1965).

Some investigators argue that the amotivational syndrome is not an inevitable consequence of habituation to marijuana. Rubin and Comitas (1975), for example, conducted a small-scale study of habitual cannabis users in Jamaica. This research compared thirty habitual users with thirty nonusers on several psychiatric and neurological tests and found no significant differences between the two groups.

Manson, 1949; Marshall, 1947; Overall and Patrick, 1972; Weingold et al., 1968). Tobacco addicts are also different kinds of people from abstainers (Eysenck et al., 1960; Heath, 1958; Thomas, 1960; Thomas and Cohen, 1960; Thomas et al., 1964).

Such findings move us to search for factors that might predispose different kinds of people to learn the habitual use of drugs, quite apart from whether they experiment with them. Identifying these factors requires a cohort analysis, that is, following a group originally unmarked by addiction through several decades and noting who does and who does not get hooked.

The fruitfulness of such research is suggested by the possibility of genetic and constitutional differences between "addictive and nonaddictive personalities" (Blakeslee and Salmon, 1935; Friberg et al., 1959; Segovia-Riquelme et al., 1971; Seltzer, 1963; Thomas and Cohen, 1960). It is also suggested by Berkson's hypothesis (1958) that abstainers from the comforting chemicals may be "biologically self-protective." While Berkson's hypothesis refers to *physiological* factors that defend a person against becoming addicted, our observation of "narcissists"—lovers of their own bodies (such as muscle-builders)—tempts us to add a *psychological* dimension to Berkson's biological one. This psychological feature may be called love of self, and it may be measured by the extent to which one takes care of his health, uses preventive hygiene, and keeps himself in shape. Macmillan (1964) provisionally tested this hypothesis with a questionnaire about habits of self-care and found a significant correlation between love of self in this sense and freedom from tobacco addiction.

However, Rubin and Comitas's results are contradicted by other investigations. For example, Tennant and Groesbeck (1972) made direct medical and psychiatric observations of 720 hashish smokers over a three-year period among American soldiers stationed in West Germany. In contrast with other studies, this research considered the *potency* and the *amount* of hashish smoked. Among the casual smokers, no adverse effects were reported other than minor respiratory ailments. However, 110 of these men had smoked hashish daily for three to twelve months prior to their medical evaluation, consuming over 50 grams each per month. All these soldiers exhibited the amotivational syndrome in varying degree. Seventy of these heavy users had to be discharged for inability to do their work. Tennant and Groesbeck describe *all* these heavy consumers of hashish as

> displaying symptoms of chronic intoxication. . . . Major manifestations were apathy, dullness, and lethargy with mild-to-severe impairment of judgment, concentration, and memory. Intermittent episodes of confusion and inability to calculate occurred with high levels of chronic intoxication. Physical appearance was stereotyped in that all patients appeared dull, exhibited poor hygiene, and had slightly slowed speech. So apathetic were many patients that they lost interest in cosmetic appearance, proper diet, and personal affairs such as paying debts, job performance, etc. (p. 135).

The Tennant-Groesbeck description of the amotivational syndrome has been substantiated by other investigators for smaller numbers of users (Brill et al., 1970; McGlothlin and West, 1968; Smith, 1968).

IN SUMMARY

Our short price list indicates that the comforting chemicals cost something. Two kinds of question arise from our estimates of these costs. One kind of question is *personal:* "What should I do about going into, or staying out of, the 'drug store'?" A second question is *social:* "What, if anything should society do about the 'drug stores'?"

1 Personal Advice

The personal advice is easy to give: *stay free.* This means live without addictions or compelling habits.

This advice is easy to give to people of one's own "tribe." It is irrelevant for those who subscribe to a different model of virtue. In our tribe, however, the model to which we aspire is one of the full use of our talents and the full enjoyment of pleasures that are healthful rather than harmful.

In this tribe, which traces its ancestry to some of the ancient Greeks, one learns to value his body as the vessel of all pleasure. He will not, then, willfully harm it. Our tribal elders have also taught us to seek balance—a moderation in our delights—for we believe that what is good in balanced portions becomes a sickness in excess. Our tribal model seeks a sound mind in a sound body. It seeks *both*, not one or the other.

This model is difficult to sell, of course, to those who live where other styles of being are more strongly encouraged. Most students, however, have some choice about how they will be, and there is room for decision about which tribe to join.

2   Social Advice

Extracting sound social policy from facts is more difficult than giving personal advice. The personal advice follows readily from a moral position. One accepts or rejects this position or remains confused.

Social policy, however, does not follow easily from a moral stance. The thinking person, at least, recognizes that it may be impractical to recommend social policies on the basis of his own morality because others who will implement the policy or be affected by it may not share that morality. In short, a policy that is based on how legislators want people to be is not apt to work if sufficient numbers of others do not want to be that way. However, recognizing the practical limits to the imposition of our morality upon others does not eliminate moral considerations from policy decisions. *Every advocate of social policy rests his advocacy upon moral assumptions.* It is important, then, to know what one prefers in his social arrangements.

A Political Preference: Freedom

Many of us who study in the Western tradition *begin* our inquiries with the wish to maximize freedom. How we end up is another matter, but our youthful morality takes its stand with John Stuart Mill's famous essay "On Liberty" (1859). This essay spells out the proper limits of state power. It objects to the state "pushing people around." It holds that

> The only freedom which deserves the name is that of pursuing our own good in our own way, so long as we do not attempt to deprive others of theirs, or impede their efforts to obtain it. Each is the proper guardian of his own health, whether bodily, or mental and spiritual. Mankind are greater gainers by suffering each other to live as seems good to themselves, than by compelling each to live as seems good to the rest [pp. 75–76].

People who favor liberty, in this Millian sense, used to be called liberals, but this fine label has been so stretched in the twentieth century that one who uses it has to specify which kind of liberal he is. Thus some nineteenth-century small-l liberals who live in the twentieth century have changed their political name to "individualist" or "libertarian" to distinguish themselves from more modern "liberals" who have less fear of state power. The change of title indicates that it is difficult to believe in freedom and to practice consistently what one preaches. It is difficult for many reasons. One is that we cannot ask the state to do things *for* us without inviting it to do things *to* us. If the state is asked to guard our welfare, it will guard our welfare even when we have not asked it to—as in the protection of our health against the use of alcohol, tobacco, and other pleasures.

This is not the only reason why it is difficult to be consistently liberal, however. It is also tough to be a true believer in freedom because we have to live together as people with different tastes. We therefore cannot help intruding upon each other and we are constantly redefining the boundaries—called our rights—of this intrusion. This struggle over the definition of "rights" is illustrated in the debate about drugs.

In the tradition of Millian liberalism, it is argued that it is none of the state's business if people harm only themselves. It follows, then, that "victimless crimes" should be "decriminalized." From this point of view, it is a violation of civil liberties for the state to intrude upon the addict's life *if* he is not seducing others. The fact that we have to add the "if" clause signals that all of us today, like philosophers in the past, continue to wrestle with the question of which freedoms are to be allowed.

To repeat, it is difficult to be consistently liberal. The difficulty deserves comment, and the comment will suggest some research questions.

On the Difficulty of Being Liberal: The Myth of Victimless Vice

We are not, and perhaps we cannot be, consistently liberal. The difficulty in achieving such consistency is illuminated by the notion, central to Millian liberalism, that there are *victimless vices.* Mill did not call them that, but he did try to define personally harmful actions that ought not to be anyone's business but the actor's.

Today's idea of "victimless crime" follows from Mill's teaching. However, the trouble with the liberal notion of "victimless vice" is that *there is always a victim.*

If our spouses wrong *their* bodies, *we* pay a price. If children harm themselves, their parents are victims. If parents are dissolute, their children are victims. If enough individuals harm themselves, then society is the victim.

In brief, there can be victimless vice only when no one influences anyone. As long as someone pays a price for someone else's action, that action is not victimless. The prices paid can be offenses to one's taste or invasions of one's purse. The prices paid can be as varied as insults to eye, ear, and nose; to having to wend one's way on public streets through importunate prostitutes; to having to pay taxes in support of rehabilitation centers for sick addicts; and on. Even our teacher, John Stuart Mill, got himself into this tangle and could not preach his principle with consistency.[6] For example, Mill believed that drunkenness and idleness were none of the state's business *unless* the drunk were violent or the lazy person were supported by the state, but Mill also believed that "there are many acts which . . . if done publicly are a violation of

---

[6]Mill's lack of consistency has recently been analyzed in detail by Gertrude Himmelfarb (1974), who shows us that Mill's essay *On Liberty* contradicts other of his writing and that Mill himself did not foresee the consequences of his liberal prescription.

good manners, and coming thus within the category of offences against others, may rightly be prohibited. Of this kind are offences against decency" (p. 153).

We can all agree with Mill as long as he remains general, but the minute our legislators become specific, as in their attempts to legislate obscenity, we are aware that good manners and decency are themselves up for negotiation when we live as one tribe among many under the power of a single state.

Mill also believed that allowing people to be free did *not* include permitting them to sell themselves into slavery for "by selling himself for a slave, he abdicates his liberty. . . . The principle of freedom cannot require that he should be free not to be free. It is not freedom to be allowed to alienate his freedom" (p. 158).

This argument—that freedom does not mean the freedom to be a slave—can be extended, of course, to other ways of "abdicating our liberty." All that is required is a stretching of the word "slave." Thus moralists have used Mill's principle to oppose the freedom to be a prostitute or an addict. They extend Mill by defining whoring and addiction as forms of slavery. If, according to this liberalism, no one should be free not to be free, then the state has a right to intervene.[7]

We are returned full circle to the theme with which this chapter began: *that conceptions of harming oneself rest upon a model of virtue.* It appears now that ideas of freedom and of civil rights also rest upon such a moral foundation.

The point of it all The point of this digression has been to question whether we can consistently oppose the prohibition of particular drugs on the ground that vice is victimless. Do we really mean it?

Two questions are raised here. One is the philosophic question whether any of us *can* consistently adhere to Mill's liberal principle. A second question is *empirical;* it asks whether any of us *do* consistently adhere to this principle.

The first question about what we *can* do is a matter of argument, but the argument may be partially resolved by tests of the second question about what we do do. The second question, in turn, can be answered by a series of studies:

1 One that counts the frequency and intensity with which people *advocate* controlling others.

2 Another that counts the frequency and intensity with which people *attempt* to control others.

3 A third research on the differential distribution of liberalism among kinds of people. The research question asks "Which kinds of people, under which kinds of political banner, are the most consistent freedom fighters?" Lest one prejudge results here or think them obvious, it should be remembered that in the political forum we hear labels such as "libertarian conservative" and "totalitarian liberal."

[7]The psychiatrist Thomas Szasz (1974) notes the inconsistency in this form of "liberalism." Szasz claims that the state has no right to interfere with a person who wants to shoot heroin or kill himself. Dr. Szasz believes that the only justification for state interference in individual lives is to prevent one person from injuring another. Again, "injury" can be defined so as to include offenses against public decency, as Mill did. Thus Szasz would not allow people to fornicate in public (p. 21).

This research can be conducted by several methods—through question-naires and interviews, through the recording of public behavior, and by content analysis of publications of different political coloration.

A Personal Opinion The studies proposed are based on a hunch. My hunch is that if one scans a wide range of issues on which it is possible to advocate letting people alone or forcing them to do or not to do something, *everyone will be found to believe in enforcing some regulation against someone.* The only exceptions may be the hermit and that rare bird the consistent anarchist. A corollary of this hunch is that one cannot identify a genuine freedom fighter by the political flag he waves.

Proposing a hypothesis such as this angers some people who think that calling attention to a possible inconsistency is the same as advocating some-thing immoral. No advocacy is involved, of course, in making the point that it is difficult to behave consistently on the principle of laissez faire, letting people do what they want. It is only suggested that we find out who, if anyone, is most consistently in favor of state control or lack of control of our behavior.

The answer to this question may help us resolve the oldest of political debates for ourselves—the debate about whom we should entrust with power. My own liberal tendency is to distrust the person who wants it.

Applying Liberalism

The application of a liberal morality to the determination of social policy means that we prefer that people be left to manage their own lives. We prefer that the state stay out of the act. We prefer that legal prohibitions and regulations be minimized, not maximized.

The digression on the difficulty of being liberal indicates, however, that this preference is not an easy one to maintain consistently. This is so because *there is no victimless vice* and because *there is no certain advice that facts can give to policies.*

Modern governments have sought advice about how best to respond to everything, from aspirin and tobacco to alcohol and the opiates. Concerning cannabis alone, there has been a series of distinguished commissions investi-gating this drug in Asia, Europe, and North America. The Indian Hemp Drugs Commission set down a first report in 1894. This study was followed by the Panama Canal Zone Military Investigations, 1916 to 1929, whose report was published in 1933. In 1968 the Advisory Committee on Drug Dependence of the United Kingdom Home Office, under the direction of Baroness Wootton, published findings in agreement with previous committees. Canada published results of its Le Dain Commission in 1972 and in the same year the United States brought out its report from the National Commission on Marijuana and Drug Abuse.

The recommendations of these many committees vacillate between two kinds of societal response:

1 *Prohibiting* trade or use of a particular drug through the criminal law and police action

2 *Regulating* trade or use of a particular drug through state licensing laws

The first response is sometimes called criminalizing a drug and the second legalizing it. There is a third class of response available to us that is never recommended by government commissions. It is

3 *To ignore* a particular drug

Ignoring a drug means either not to legislate about it or, if there is already legislation, not to enforce it. The latter response is a kind of hypocrisy, but it is a procedure commonly used to allow us to live with moral conflict (Warriner, 1958).

Each of these societal responses carries a price.

The price of prohibition includes at least

1 The costs of policing and incarcerating criminals

2 The damage to careers that are criminalized

3 The disrespect for law in general that may be stimulated by attempts to enforce unpopular laws

4 The creation of a black market in the prohibited commodity

The price of regulation includes at least

1 The cost of the bureaucracy needed to manage the regulations

2 The evasion of regulations, as when "minors" get adults to buy their cigarettes

3 The possibility that legally recognizing the use of a drug suggests public approval of it and hence promotes its spread

The price of ignoring a particular drug includes at least

1 The possibility that if there is legislation on the books prohibiting the drug, the law will be unevenly applied

2 The chance that in the absence of its prohibition, the use of a drug will spread

3 The probability that commercial organizations will enter the ignored market, promote the use of its product, and deprive governments of potential tax revenue

What Should Be Done?

All advice is uncertain, subject to unforeseen consequences, offered out of inadequate information, and subject to moral preferences. Yet professors who study these things are asked what *they* would do. As one student put it, "If you were King of Canada, what would you do?"

The personal advice has already been given. The societal advice is to *regulate* the distribution of alcohol, tobacco, cocaine, the amphetamines, the barbiturates, and the opiates. People who are addicted to these chemicals should be allowed to purchase them. In the case of the more powerful drugs, such as the opiates, these should be administered under a physician's prescription as in Great Britain. In Britain, following the recommendations of the Brain Committee (1965), any physician can prescribe morphine or methadone. Addicts who prefer heroin may obtain this drug at low cost from government clinics.

It seems sensible also to repeal present legislation penalizing marijuana use. This need not mean legalizing cannabis, as some students recommend (Brecher et al., 1972, p. 535). For the present, it may be best to "decriminalize" this drug and for Western governments to ignore it.

None of these liberal recommendations should relieve the drug user of penalty for crimes committed while he is impaired by his habit. Drunken driving remains such whether the intoxication is produced by alcohol or marijuana.

Furthermore, licensing or ignoring drugs ought *not* to include the privilege of advertising them. Given the social costs of all the comforting chemicals and particularly the costs of the popular ones, tobacco and alcohol, one can justify the illiberalism of prohibiting the promotion of such nonmedical drugs. In some jurisdictions, it is now illegal to advertise these products by television. To be consistent, advertisement by public display and in newspapers and magazines ought also to be prohibited. Such legislation is not likely, however, given the interests of the tobacco and beverage industries, the need of the press and magazines for space buyers, and the need of governments for tax revenues.

Last, the state should abandon programs called "treatment," particularly where they are coerced. The treatment of addicts has a uniform record of failure. A summary of the failures can be read in Brecher's volume (1972, Chap. 10).

Continuing research is justified, of course, as are programs based on any new findings. Otherwise, it seems both liberal and economical for the state to withdraw from the enforced treatment of addicts. This attitude contrasts with that of totalitarian societies, where treatment is coerced.[8]

If left alone, many addicts "mature out" of their habit or, sometimes, they help themselves. The best record of reform in free societies is not from enforced programs but from voluntary attempts at mutual help. These group-oriented efforts are run, for the most part, by addicts themselves rather than by

---

[8]"A decree of the . . . Supreme Soviet on April 8, 1967 provided for . . . committing a person to compulsory treatment and specified a new variety of institutions for the containment of alcohol offenders. Previously, an offending drunkard had to be on trial for a crime before the People's Court in order for the question of compulsory treatment to be raised. . . . Now, those who violate 'labor discipline, public order and the rules of socialist communal life' (varieties of deviance frequently not containing the elements of crime) are similarly liable. The decree provides for no appeal from the court's decision to compel treatment, and specifies a one- to two-year period in treatment-labor institutions, with a mandatory stay of one-half the sentence period before release of cured inmates can be contemplated. Escape from the institutions, a criminal offense, is punishable by imprisonment" (Connor, 1972, p. 66)

"experts." Such programs presently treat a variety of persons who cannot control undesirable behaviors, including child beaters, food addicts, and individuals subject to the craving for alcohol, tobacco, and the opiates. These groups, such as Weight Watchers, Alcoholics Anonymous, and Synanon, operate on similar principles:

1   The addict *asks* for help; he is not given it unasked.
2   The treatment *costs* the addict something.
3   The addict is pushed by the group toward *honesty* about himself and his compulsion.
4   The addict becomes part of a supportive group that does not condemn his or her past but does criticize any present dishonesty.
5   It is assumed that the addict, and not others, is responsible for his or her own behavior.
6   The addict is given a purpose as a helper of others in similar plight.

The Entanglement of Social Concerns

Our social concerns overlap, it has been said. We pull separate concerns out for inspection, but living well is more all of a piece than these separate analyses suggest. Thus, thinking about drugs has been part of the larger concern with happy survival. Happy survival, in turn, is in part an economic matter, a question of how we make a living and of the level of material comfort attained. Chapters 9 through 12 look at these economic concerns, individually and globally. It bears repeating, however, that being happy, healthy, and useful run together. They are the conditions of our freedom from the debilitating drugs and, at the same time, they are measures of that freedom. Killing oneself slowly with the comforting chemicals is *both a cause and an effect* of misused talent.

Chapter 9

Working

The exercise of human ability is a condition of health and happiness. Doing nothing is at times sweet, as the Italians say, but doing nothing as a career is deadly.

All societies allow time for abilities to be exercised playfully, that is, expressively, without regard for the material utility of the exercise. However, the human being must "make a living," and hence a major social concern is economic. It is a concern with survival and with improving the physical quality of our lives. It is a wish that what we do to survive may be graceful as well as useful and that there may be pleasure in our economic activity. This hope is stimulated by an awareness that gaining a livelihood occupies a major portion of our brief span between childhood and senility. What we do for a living colors our lives.

The activities required for survival have been called many names. A general term for these actions is *work.*

THE MEANING OF WORK

Work is the application of animal energy to transform the environment so that the organism survives. This general activity has been given many meanings, with different titles attached to these meanings. For example, work that is arduous, repetitive, and uninteresting has been called *labor,* drudgery, toil, and travail. On the other hand, work that is deemed of value to others besides the worker, that appears to be inspired or expressive, and that is approved by one's society and its gods—such work is termed a *vocation,* a calling. In our language and our literature such vocational work is associated with both *love* and *play.* It is connected to love because the worker in such a condition exhibits concern for the product of his efforts. The job, then, is done for its own sake as well as for its survival value. When a vocation elicits effort that is enjoyable in itself, when it is activity that the worker "would just as soon do anyway," then work also appears like play. It becomes an exercise that makes one feel better and that is missed when it is not available. Happy work is part of better living. It is also part of longer life. Recent research (O'Toole et al., 1972) finds that "satisfaction with work appears to be the best predictor of longevity—better than known medical or genetic factors—and various aspects of work account for much, if not most, of the factors associated with heart disease." This does not say, of course, that happy work *causes* health but only that it is *correlated* with longevity.

When Work Is Labor   The varied meanings of work tell us that work becomes labor when what one has to do in order to survive does not fit one's interests. The human condition in most societies, apart from a few tropical Edens, has included large allotments of labor. A present concern is to transform survival requirements from the necessities of toil to the pleasure of vocation. This objective has been one of the assignments of industrial psychologists, who try to place people in jobs that fit their interests and who try to redesign some work so that more persons can enjoy it. This objective engages public policy, too, through efforts to provide educational programs for people of all ages so that they may acquire the skills required by the economies in which they live.

WHO LABORS? WHO WORKS?

Almost a hundred years ago one of the fathers of sociology, Karl Marx, did that most typical of sociological acts: he prepared a questionnaire of 101 items and had 25,000 copies distributed to workers' organizations and socialist groups. (One assumes that the money for this research came from Engels's father's factories.) Few workers bothered to reply to this inquiry and the results were never published (Bottomore and Rubel, 1956, pp. 204–212), but Marx's intent was clear. He wanted workers to describe "the evils which they endure."

It has been a major assumption of Marxists that revolution would come to industrialized lands because the organization of work in factories and shops converted it to labor and resulted in an "alienation" of the employee from his "true self" and from the product of his efforts. It has been assumed that this "alienated condition" would result in a general discontent which would lead to a violent overthrow of "bourgeois" institutions and to a new organization of the economy in which workers controlled their destinies.

A difficulty with this angry assumption is that it is based more on theory than on observation. We intellectuals, "professional thinkers," are repeatedly surprised by the chasms between how things are and how they are supposed to be, between how people feel and how they "ought" to feel, and between what people do and what they "should" do (Avison, 1973; Milgram, 1963).

These gaps between hope and reality describe the failure of Marxian prophecy. For example, communist revolutions have *not* occurred principally in advanced industrialized societies, as predicted, but in underdeveloped countries. Furthermore, where such revolutions have succeeded, as in the Soviet Union or Cuba, workers cannot be said to have more control of their destinies. Workers in communist societies may be *called* owners of their factories, but their positions on the assembly line remain the same. The Polish sociologist Szczepanski (1970) comments on industrial workers behind the Iron Curtain that "The socialist revolution does not change their relationship to the machine, nor does it change their position within the technological structure of the factory."

It can be added that neither does the socialist revolution improve the "alienated condition" of the bureaucratic worker. It may, in fact, aggravate it, as many observers have suggested (Axelbank, 1974; Shub, 1969).

Job Satisfaction Research

The Marxian forecast of increasing misery and discontent of workers in bourgeois societies is additionally discounted by the outcomes counted by standard-of-living measures and "employee attitude" research.

Following Marx's early questionnaire, twentieth-century investigators have conducted a host of surveys of job satisfaction designed to find out who likes his work, who does not, and why. The findings are not far different from those yielded by research on marital satisfaction or happiness in general. Most people seem content with their jobs, as they are with their lives.

As with all answers to questions, however, the results depend on the questions asked. Many surveys ask this type of question: "Taking into consideration all the things about your job (work), how satisfied or dissatisfied are you with it?" (Morse and Weiss, 1955). The answers to questions of this nature have been summarized by the industrial psychologist Hoppock and his colleagues, who have reviewed all published research on job satisfaction over the past thirty-five years. A sample of these reports includes work by Hoppock and Spiegler, 1938; Hoppock and Odom, 1940; Hoppock and Robinson, 1949, 1950, 1951; Robinson, 1953, 1957; and Robinson et al., 1964, 1966. The major finding of these reviews is this: The median proportion of Western workers reported to be *dissatisfied* with their jobs runs about 12 to 13 percent, and this figure has not fluctuated over the past three decades (Crites, 1969, pp. 496, 507).

This does not mean, of course, that a one-eighth dissatisfaction figure must be a constant. Times change, and some research is reporting *higher* discontent among *younger* workers. For example, Kornhauser and his colleagues (1965) conducted detailed interviews with factory workers in Detroit during the mid-1950s. While 58 percent of their sample said that they were "completely or well satisfied" with their jobs, this proportion rose to 73 percent among middle-aged workers. "In addition, 25 percent of the young and 16 percent of the middle-aged say 'neither satisfied nor dissatisfied' [leaving] only 17 percent of the young and 11 percent of the middle-aged responding negatively with 'a little dissatisfied' or 'very dissatisfied'" (pp. 157–158). In similar fashion, a national poll conducted in 1969 by the University of Michigan's Survey Research Center reports more discontent among younger workers than among older ones. This survey's figures run *progressively* from a low of 6 percent dissatisfied among workers fifty-five years old and older to a high of 25 percent dissatisfied among teen-age workers.

A finding of a linear, positive association between age and job satisfaction runs counter to previous research that shows happiness at work to vary cyclically with age, with depressions in middle years and elevations among younger and older workers (Super, 1939; Ghiselli and Brown, 1955). There is no evidence as yet that the Survey Research Center's study foretells a trend. It is possible, however, that rising expectations, rather than the nature of the job, may produce more "alienation" in the 1970s than has been recorded for the last three or four decades.

Contentment versus Dreams

A different picture of worker contentment is revealed when questions are asked about *aspiration* rather than about *satisfaction.* If a person is asked whether he is satisfied with his job, he may well say yes because he does not see any other possibility. However, if a person is asked whether he would continue to work in his present job if he were given enough money to live comfortably without working, then one is asking about dreams, and the replies given show greater dissatisfaction. It is a dissatisfaction that varies, as we should expect, with the kind of work one is presently doing. The jobs to which we accord higher prestige, higher income, and more independence tend to be the vocations. As we descend the status ladder, more work becomes labor. Thus, for a representative sample of Americans, Morse and Weiss (1955) find that about two-thirds of professional workers say they would continue in their jobs even if they had enough money to live without working. This proportion falls to a low of about one in six unskilled laborers who says he or she would continue to work without the pressure of necessity (Table 9-1).

A similar finding is reported by Blauner (1960), who has tabulated occupational responses to the question whether a worker would choose the same career if he could begin over again. Blauner shows that only one in six unskilled automobile workers would choose his job if given a fresh start, as compared with about nine out of ten scientists who would select their present careers again (Table 9-2).

Table 9-1   "Would You Continue in Your Work if You Inherited Enough Money to Live Comfortably?" (Responses by Occupational Group)*

Occupational group	Percent who would continue in their present work
Professionals	68
Sales	59
Managers	55
Skilled manual	40
Service	33
Semiskilled operatives	32
Unskilled workers	16

*Adapted from N. C. Morse and R. S. Weiss, "The Function and Meaning of Work and the Job," *American Sociological Review.* © 1955 by the American Sociological Association. Reproduced by permission of the Association and the authors.

Satisfaction, Aspiration, and Indifference

These disparate findings from different kinds of questions suggest the obvious: It is one thing to be adjusted to one's lot in life; it is quite another matter to wish things were otherwise. We can accommodate to being bald, but we wish, if you ask us, that we had hair. So it is with earning a living. It is easy to imagine a different life. Television shows it, politicians promise it, and everyone who buys a lottery ticket bets on it. Meanwhile, survival requires that one come to terms with his possibilities.

There are other ways of coming to terms with one's circumstances than either enjoying them or resenting them. A common response to drudgery is to toil for the paycheck but to pay the job no attention. We are reminded that being indifferent is an attitude at right angles to loving and hating. Some proportion of workers, particularly of unskilled laborers, simply do their jobs without giving a damn about them. For example, Wilensky (1964b) developed a measure of "work alienation" that includes scores on "work indifference." In Wilensky's American sample of 1,156 employed men, "more than one in five of the young white-collar men and one in three of the older blue-collar men score indifferent on *all* attributes" (p. 146, emphasis his). Other sociologists have pointed out that indifference may be adaptive (Dubin, 1958; Hughes, 1958). In every society there is dirty work to be done. Being indifferent, thinking of other things, is one way of staying sane while doing dull work.

Does Modern Work Alienate the Person from Himself?

There is a romantic streak in Marxian thought that seeks to restore "community" where human relations are presently arranged through "contract and the market." Socialists dislike the marketplace and the traders in it.[1] They

---

[1]The socialist's dislike of traders has a long history. It includes attacks upon moneylenders, now called bankers, and upon "trader types." Since the Jew has been a model of the trader in Europe (Baron, 1952; Becker, 1940), it is not surprising to find anti-Semitic sentiment among socialists. One of the most virulent expressions of hatred of Jews, associating them with the sins of commerce, was written by Karl Marx himself under the translated title of *On the Jewish Question* (1926).

would substitute an "altruistic man" who lives to serve others for the "egoistic man" who seeks to maximize personal gain by selling his labor and its product at the best price.

The Marxian argument is that capitalistic commerce and industry "make things out of men" and force people to be other than their "true selves." Given the persuasive arguments of Marx and his followers, investigators have paid particular attention to evaluating the "alienating" effects of work in Western societies. The hypothesis tested is that a "marketing orientation" forces workers in such capitalist settings to be false to themselves and to view themselves as "hands" to be sold in the market rather than as persons to be fulfilled through production. The psychoanalyst Erich Fromm (1947) has written extensively in favor of this thesis. He tells us that "In the marketing orientation man encounters his own powers as commodities alienated from him. He is not one with them but they are masked from him because what matters is not his self-realization in the process of using them but his success in the process of selling them" (p. 72).

Since the notion of the self is slippery (Shuraydi, 1973), it is difficult to test this kind of belief. When social psychologists try to make terms like "self-realization" objective, critics who are disappointed with their findings claim that the measures of self used are insensitive to the kind of selfhood they have in mind. Thus one can continue to talk about "alienated selves" without knowing how such persons could ever be recognized. In addition to the obscurity of the sense of self, the very idea of alienation has taken on so many meanings as to make it useless in rigorous research.

Table 9-2 Proportion in Various Occupations Who Would Choose The Same Work if Beginning Career Again*

Professional occupations	Percent
Mathematicians	91
Physicists	89
Biologists	89
Chemists	86
Lawyers	83
Journalists	82
Working-class occupations	
Skilled printers	52
Paper workers	52
Skilled automobile workers	41
Skilled steelworkers	41
Textile workers	31
Unskilled steelworkers	21
Unskilled automobile workers	16

*Reproduced from R. Blauner, "Work Satisfaction and Industrial Trends in Modern Society," in W. Galenson and S. M. Lipset (eds.), *Labor and Trade Unionism: An Interdisciplinary Reader.* © 1960 by John Wiley & Sons, Inc. Reprinted by permission.

A Comment on the Idea of Alienation   The root of the word "alienation" refers to a separation, a breach. But a gap between what and what? It depends on who is using the term. For example, a group of leftist Hegelians, with whom Marx was for a time associated, introduced the idea of alienation in social psychology and economic theory (Pipes, 1964). The notion of alienation here is the sense of separation between what a worker does and who owns the product of his work. It is therefore the idea of a gap between working and having the pleasure of seeing, owning, and using the product or, at least, of determining how it will be used. However, in Marx's writing, one will also find the idea that the structure of labor in industrial countries estranges workers from their "human nature," their "selves," and from "society" (Marx, 1844).

Freudians, too, have contributed to the confusion by using the word "alienation" to mean a separation between *how we have to be* because of the conditions of work, or of social arrangements in general, and what our *"instincts" require* (Fromm, 1947, 1955; Marcuse, 1955).

From these Freudian and Marxian sources, sociologists have taken the concept of alienation and used it to refer to a host of attitudes such as the following:

A sense of despair, sometimes called anomie (McClosky and Schaar, 1965; Srole, 1956)
A feeling of "powerlessness"
A sense of "meaninglessness"
An attitude of "normlessness," the feeling that there is a lack of connection between means and ends (Seeman, 1959)
Hostility or indifference to the culture that surrounds one (Nettler, 1957)

Given these diverse meanings, it is doubtful whether the concept has much utility today beyond that of expressing emotion (Feuer, 1963; Mouledous and Mouledous, 1964). If we continue to use the word, it is only because it is in the literature; but we recognize that its usual research referent is *discontent*.

Studies of the Alienated Worker

Such studies as have attempted to test for "worker alienation" have not found much of it. Form (1972) tested automobile workers in the United States, Italy, Argentina, and India for their feelings of anomie (despair) and alienation. Automobile workers were selected because their work represents most acutely the technological forces which, according to Marxian hypothesis, turn men into robots. Contrary to this hypothesis, Form found most workers in all four countries to be satisfied with their jobs and with their relations with their workmates. He found no connection between the organization of work and feelings of discontent or between social interaction rates on or off the job and sentiments of despair. Form concludes, "This study of automobile workers in four countries shows no direct relation between social relations in the factory and feelings of anomie. Evidence mounts that we should modify or abandon technological explanations of alienation and anomie" (p. 737).

Wilensky's Research   A more elaborate attempt to test the alienation hypothesis was conducted by Wilensky and a research team (1964b) who interviewed over a thousand American workers. To test for the prevalence of "alienated sentiment," the investigators constructed five measures of workers' "prized self-image, the central attributes of self-concept to which strong positive feelings are attached" (p. 140). Wilensky then compared these valued concepts of oneself with the behaviors required or permitted by the job. When the workers' ideal self-images were placed against the demands of their work, few discrepancies were found. "By our stringent measures," Wilensky writes, "the incidence of alienation is low: only 177 of 1,156 employed men score 'alienated' on even one of the six possible attributes of the work situation; only 51 are alienated on two or more attributes; 11 on three or more" (p. 143).

It is recognized that direct questions about life satisfactions probably uncover a minimum of discontent and are apt to give a misleading picture of "cheerful majorities." Contrary to this interpretation, Wilensky concludes, as we have seen, that "the vast majority of the middle mass and almost a majority of the engineers—swiftly growing categories of the labor force—are generally indifferent to work in the precise sense that their jobs neither confirm their prized self-image nor deny it for most of the attributes analyzed. . . . The majority of Americans are 'playing it cool,' neither strongly wedded to the job nor feeling it to be an intense threat to their identity" (pp. 146, 148).

A "Quality of Life" Study   A more recent test of the "work-alienation" hypothesis is contained in the results of the Survey Research Center's 1971 poll of a representative sample of American adults on the "quality of their lives" (Campbell et al., 1975). In keeping with the reviews by Hoppock and others referred to on p. 176, 90 percent of the respondents say that it is "very true" or "somewhat true" that their "work is interesting," 75 percent say that "the pay is good," 93 percent find that their jobs give them "a lot of chances to make friends," 81 percent that at work "the physical surroundings are pleasant," and 77 percent that "the job security is good."

As regards self-fulfillment, 76 percent say that it is "very true" or "somewhat true" that "I have an opportunity to develop my own special abilities," and 79 percent that "I am given a chance to do the things I do best."

A Psychiatric Study   A team of psychiatrists from the Rutgers Medical School (Siassi et al., 1974) began an investigation of the "alienation" hypothesis with the biased preconception, as they put it, that blue-collar workers engaged in repetitive production-line tasks disproportionately "sing the blues," and rightly so. These investigators examined many facets of industrial workers' behaviors and attitudes, including their attitudes toward the mentally ill, their patterns of alcohol consumption, their contact with mental illness, and their own physical and mental health. In addition, five dimensions of discontent were analyzed: feelings of loneliness, alienation, and depression, and statements about job dissatisfaction and dissatisfaction with life in general. The subjects of this study were production-line workers in a General Motors plant in the Baltimore area and their wives, a total of 888 persons.

Contrary to the psychiatrists' preconception, most workers found their jobs satisfactory and neither tiring nor upsetting. Ninety-six percent of these workers report their jobs to be "satisfactory." Seventy-one percent claim that no part of their work is fatiguing or distressing. When there were complaints of fatigue, stress, boredom, depression, and dissatisfaction with one's job and life in general, these complaints were, in the words of the investigators, "usually part of a broader pattern of emotional illness characteristic of diagnosed patients drawn from the same population" (p. 261).

Alienation on the Farm   What has been found true in the factory has also been observed on the farm. Rushing and his colleagues (1972) interviewed 1,029 male farm workers and 240 farm owners and operators in Washington state to ascertain their sense of social position, their feelings of satisfaction and deprivation, the quality of their ambition, and their moods of despair and power.

The impact of culture upon these attitudes, as distinct from the effect of social class, was assessed by examining separately the results for laborers who were Anglo-Americans, bilingual Mexican-Americans, and non-English-speaking Mexicans. Rushing's objective was to analyze the effects of class and culture on alienation and on the fluctuating relation between alienation, perceived deprivation, and opportunity.

A major finding, but not a surprising one, is that neither laborers nor farmers see themselves as do their sociological investigators. Although these farm workers are at the bottom of the United States income ladder, even the poorest of these poor people do *not* believe, on the average, that "over half of the people are better off than they are." While there are statistically significant differences between farm workers and their bosses in the feelings of "being deprived," the differences are not great. The farm owners, like most other people, believe that many in America "have it better" than they do.

Similar small differences are found in the sense of power over one's life. Although laborers feel slightly less in command than do farm owners and operators, the difference between the two groups is not significant and neither group reports itself as markedly powerless.

Both laborers and owners are greatly concerned with economic matters, but for the laborers this means mostly security, while for the owners it is more likely to mean getting ahead, peace, good government, and a secure retirement.

An Interpretation

The idea that much work, usually that of the other person, ought to be classified as labor seems another example of "projection," that is, of persons in one social station assuming how *they* would feel if they were in the other worker's job. Thus not only factory work but almost every other category of occupation has been charged with alienating its practitioners. The only exceptions seem to be successful and autonomous work in art, science, and the professions, and even among these vocations there is toil. For example, Dr. Albert Sabin (1973), one of the developers of polio vaccine, recently replied to an interviewer's question about the excitement of biochemical research by saying, "Scientific research is drudgery. It is as much drudgery as working on the assembly line."

From a distant perspective and with Shangri-La as a standard, all kinds of work have been called dirty. Salesmen and journalists have been called whores, and the word "prostitution" itself is a synonym for "distorted being." Politicians are commonly demeaned as false operators, while teachers, clerks, and civil servants have been pictured as faceless cogs in bureaucracies rather than as persons. Domestic workers have been depicted as suffering menials and professional athletes as exploited victims, "the new gladiators" (Edwards, 1969). Income is apparently no defense against alienation, as witnessed by the literature that describes the "rat races" run by men in gray flannel suits—the advertising executives and corporate managers. Under Western conditions, mining, construction, fishing, and farming have also been seen as plights rather than as fulfilling occupations.

Yet, contrary to this image of work that views almost every job as labor, investigators who have lived with various kinds of workers and who have themselves performed assorted jobs[2] have described the satisfactions as well as the discontents of widely different kinds of work. For example, Williams (1925) worked in factories, mines, and railroads, interviewing his coworkers and recording their feelings about what made a job a good one or a "bum" one. Fairchild (1930a, 1930b) made similar observations of men in metalwork, while Hall and Locke (1938) interviewed machine operators and box makers. Nettler (1955, 1964) has worked with journalists, salesmen, bill collectors, riveters, sheet-metal workers, movie extras, and lifeguards, and he has collected life histories and psychological test data on career police officials. Anderson (1923) has described the joys of being a hobo, while Chambliss (1972) has recorded the happy career of a safecracker. Many madames have reminisced about the pleasures and pains of their work (Adler, 1953; Hollander, 1972; Kimball, 1972), as have some successful attorneys (Bailey and Aronson, 1971; Nizer, 1944). It is apparent that human beings enjoy or adjust to a variety of ways of making a living.

This is not to say that all jobs are equally wonderful. It is, rather, a

---

[2]The reports of participant-observers of the job scene should be qualified by the role of the reporter in the work. I have no data to prove this, but it seems plausible that one gets a different impression of work when the job taken is *temporary*, to find out what it is like, from that which one gets when the work is one's *livelihood*. In the former case, one is slumming, with the knowledge that the "dirty work" is not permanent and that it will be escaped on schedule. This is as true of college presidents who take their sabbaticals doing lower-echelon jobs (Coleman, 1974) as it was of George Orwell, who told of his experiences as a menial worker in his famous essay entitled *Down and Out in Paris and London* (1933). To be "really" down and out is to be there *without* an ace in the hole—without the college office to return to or relatives in England to bail one out.

My impression does not deny the honesty of such part-time participants; it only suggests a difference in attitude between doing a job "for real" and doing it for the experience.

comment on the variability in human interests and in the ability to accommodate to different living conditions. It is a comment, too, on the possible "ethnocentrism" of the academic observer looking out upon the world of work. The Rutgers psychiatrists put it well:

> To impute boredom, alienation, anomie, or the seeds of mental illness to another man's work or existence is a hazardous thing. To some blue collar workers, the social scientist's preoccupation with books, dry articles, tables of statistics, and obsessive academic discourse must seem more boring, more alienating, more fraught with anomie, than his own existence [Siassi et al., 1974, p. 164].

A personal advice follows: Never knock the other person's pleasure in his work. Quite apart from our condemnation of criminal careers, and however absurd a job may seem "in the cosmic scheme of things," work is our occupation and a prime source of the meaning of our lives.

SOURCES OF JOB SATISFACTION

Industrial psychologists have attempted to discover why some persons find their work laborious and others find their jobs pleasant. The research is voluminous. It is difficult to interpret, not merely because of its volume but also because it looks at the sources of satisfaction one at a time or in small packages of "causes." This kind of piecemeal investigation requires the constant qualification of findings with the deadening phrase, "other things being equal." One has to add this qualification because the student is examining factors one or two at a time when they never operate that way in reality. The fact that variables do not function one at a time is a justification for speaking of patterned variables, of *contexts,* as central to the understanding of our satisfactions and disaffections. However, it is a custom of Western thinking to attend to the kinds of things that make jobs more or less agreeable. In the consideration of our social concerns, this style of thought is congenial to the reformer's assumption that if he knows causes, he can treat them and cure "social diseases." To treat causes requires their isolation, and it has been such a desire that has energized much of the research on the pleasures and displeasures of work. In attending to the sources of worker contentment, however, it is well to view each source not as "its own thing" with strongly independent effects, but as one among a shifting complex of factors that influences our attitude toward work.

Is Happiness at Work Related to Happiness in General?

Yes. There are good reasons for believing that there is a general theme of contentment or of discontent running through a person's life. Some people seem disgruntled wherever they are and whatever happens to them. One may say of them, ironically, that they do not enjoy happiness when they have it. Other persons are happy warriors even under adverse circumstances.

The research addressed to this question is thin, but such as we have lends substance to our hypothesis. Studies show moderate to high correlations between job satisfaction and life satisfaction. The Rutgers research referred to yields a high association between pleasure in life and pleasure at work. Weitz (1952) reports a coefficient of .39 between measures of general satisfaction among life insurance agents and satisfaction with specific aspects of their work. For male workers, Brayfield et al. (1957) found comparable correlations ranging between .32 and .68 between measures of morale (general satisfaction) and two indicators of attitude toward office jobs. In this study, the female office workers revealed such an association (.43) on only one of the job-attitude measures. A similar degree of relationship between general contentment and job satisfaction is reported by Brophy (1959), who found a correlation of .50 between these attitudes among a sample of female nurses.

These associations do not tell us, of course, whether it is a miserable life that makes a person miserable at work, whether it is a miserable job that makes for a miserable life, or whether a miserable temperament produces both kinds of discontent. All we know is that job satisfaction and life satisfaction *tend* to go together.

Specific Sources

After recognizing the possibility that contentment may be a general disposition underwriting attitudes toward work, play, friends, and self, research attention has been turned to specific aspects of jobs that might contribute to their pleasantness. It seems inadvisable to try to rank these factors in importance because their meaning fluctuates as the bundle varies. The meaning of these factors seems to differ, too, between male and female workers and among personalities. The variation among personalities should be no surprise, since we do not have similar interests and needs.

Interests   A much investigated contributor to job satisfaction is interest. There are remarkable variations in the patterns of things we prefer doing. Some of us are outdoor types while others are parlor persons. Some of us need physical exercise; others hate it. Some people like to play with words and numbers while others prefer to manipulate things. Some individuals like to work with people; others wish to work alone. Some like to command; others prefer to be told what to do.

There are a number of standard tests of occupational interest. These have been applied to a variety of workers to ascertain the degree to which their satisfaction at work is related to the fit of the job to their interests. The findings are what we should expect—that a discrepancy between what the job requires and what the worker likes to do produces unhappiness. Sarbin and Anderson (1942), for example, found that 82 percent of a group of male workers who applied for vocational counseling because of discontent with their employment did *not* have the patterns of interest suitable for their jobs. Similarly, Jacobs and Traxler (1954) found that accountants who enjoyed their work had higher measured interest in clerical and computational tasks than did those accountants who were less satisfied. Additional research generally supports this association of interest with satisfaction. However, the associations are frequently modest. What is more important is that the degree of association between interest and contentment varies with the kind of work being done. There is a selective process at work. At one end of the job spectrum are vocations that require a narrowed attention, commitment to a line of study, and a long apprenticeship. People who end up following such callings tend to have been screened by the goodness of fit between their interests and the training procedures leading to the vocation. The result of this winnowing is that such vocations are intrinsically satisfying to their practitioners. The work suits their interests and is, hence, less laborious. At the other end of the job spectrum is work that may be important to the economy but that requires no diligence in its learning. The practitioners of such work are apt, then, to be motivated not by the intrinsic value of the work but by the paycheck, and such work is more likely to become labor.

Between these extremes lie innumerable jobs where the meshing of interests and work requirements is modest—neither close nor loose—because the process by which people fall into such work is less disciplining, less selective, than among the vocations. For example, Nettler's data (1964) on Canadian police officials show that about one-third of his sample of career policemen did *not* have profiles of occupational interest best suited to their work. Probing after the sources of this fact revealed that such men took their jobs during the Depression, when they had little choice of occupation. A job was a job. Once in the work, with families to support, it became difficult for these officers to find careers better suited to their interests.

Interests Are Not Abilities   Another factor that pushes people into work that is less than satisfactory is the gap between their interests and their abilities. Interest is what one *likes* to do. Ability is what one *can* do. A person may be interested in being an actor or a tennis pro yet lack what it takes. Where talent does not support interest in the job market, work becomes a second-best mode of survival.

A Counseling Advice   In vocational counseling, one sees young people, and some not so young, who are in quandaries about what to do with themselves. Testing their vocational interests sometimes uncovers possibilities for happy work about which the inquirers may have been uninformed. However, in order for the counselor to find these possibilities, the inquirer must have *some* interest. The person must have some pattern of preference, some things he likes to do better than others that can be channeled into economic activity. When there are peaks and dips in the profile of interests, the counselor can suggest a variety of satisfying jobs. One does meet seekers, alas, whose map of interests is flat. Nothing particularly intrigues such people and they are sad to counsel. Thus far, no one has discovered how to give the uninterested an injection of interest, and it is futile to ask the counselor for such treatment. Developing interests is something we do for ourselves.

Aspiration   It has already been remarked that satisfaction depends upon expectations and that happiness requires proportioning wants to possibilities. It seems to be a definition of satisfaction that a worker is contented if his position places him where he wants to be or where he thinks he ought to be, and, conversely, that dissatisfaction means being where one would rather not be.

Although the thesis seems circular, social scientists have nevertheless tested it. The testing has been guided by *reference group* theory, by the proposition that aspiration is generated and achievement evaluated in terms of those others with whom one compares oneself. For example, this is an interpretation given the interesting data unearthed by Centers and Cantril (1946) in their survey of a representative sample of adult Americans. Respondents were asked how much more money they would need to make their families happier or more comfortable. The investigators found, not surprisingly, that the higher a person's income, the more likely he was to be satisfied with it. Further, there was a tendency for people to specify *smaller proportions* of their present income as the increase needed to make them happier with movement up the income ladder from the bottom through the middle rungs. However, respondents in the *top* income brackets said that they required *larger proportions* of their present incomes to fulfil their aspirations. In brief, at the top of the income pyramid, workers' sights were *disproportionately elevated.* The explanation seems to be that the dissatisfied respondents in these upper income levels were principally professionals—lawyers, physicians, professors—who were comparing their needs against the much higher incomes of such workers as corporation executives.

With affluence, there is a further possibility that criteria *other than money* come to play a part in determining with whom one compares the satisfactions of his work. For example, Raddock (1973) comments that "doctors and professors of my acquaintance have increasingly of late confided not only severe dissatisfaction with their meaningless lot, but expressed preference, nay, yearning, towards careers as pop singers, film stars, or on occasion, as political activists of consequence."

Schooling Effects   Additional evidence of the influence of shifting expectations upon work satisfaction is seen in schooling effects. Mann's research (1953) is but one of many reporting the shift of expectation with education. Mann studied the job attitudes of blue-collar workers. When he held constant their length of service, skill level, sex, and kind of work, he found a *negative* association between job satisfaction and amount of schooling. "Too much" schooling spoiled personnel for the job. As the amount of schooling increased, so did the tendency among male blue-collar workers to complain about their companies, their jobs, their promotion opportunities, and their responsibilities.

Believing versus Being Where You Are   The lesson that is being extracted from these many investigations of job satisfaction is that contentment is a function of expectation. The status one *conceives* himself to have is more important than the status one really has. As an illustration, Rettig, Jacobson, and Pasamanick examined the interplay of objective measures of professional status with workers' own estimates of their status and their expressed job satisfaction. The subjects of this research were psychiatrists, psychologists, and social workers in mental health organizations (Jacobson et al., 1959; Rettig et al., 1958). The investigators found that those workers whose objective status was low but who *felt* their status to be higher were as satisfied with their jobs as were professionals of higher status whose self-estimates were more objective. Furthermore, among workers at the same professional level, those who believed they had a higher status than they actually had expressed greater job satisfaction. Apparently, an aspiration can be satisfied in the mind as well as in the bank account.

IN SUMMARY

A definition, then, of the disgruntled worker is that he is one who senses a gap between where he thinks he is and where he believes he ought to be. Moreover, the degree of his dissatisfaction seems to increase directly with the size of the perceived discrepancy between his position and his aspiration (Super, 1939).

On Relative Deprivation

Findings such as we have discussed point to a sense of relative deprivation as a source of discontent. In our assessment of happiness, pages 29–31, we noted the significance of a *balance* between expectation and realization as underwriting self-satisfaction. The mechanics of relative deprivation also explain some of the facts of the pleasures and displeasures of work and some of the motives for our killing each other (Chap. 13).

Relative deprivation is a construct introduced by social psychologists who were studying the sources of morale among the American military during World War II (Stouffer et al., 1949). This concept makes formal what has long been common observation: that how we feel about ourselves—our lot in life, our fate—depends on whom we use for comparison. It is not only real circumstances that affect our satisfactions; it is also our frames of comparison that tell us whether we are well off or not. The jazz singer Les McCann shouts the point when he asks, "Real, compared to what?"

The observers who coined the concept of relative deprivation did so to explain the fact that real conditions were not directly linked to contentment. Between our objective circumstances and our morale, interpretation intrudes. Interpretation, in turn, varies with where we have been compared with where we are, with where we *think* we are, and where we *believe* we *should* be. Where we should be varies, again, with whom we compare ourselves. It is a happy fact for our peace of mind that most of us compare ourselves with people like ourselves rather than with people in markedly different circumstances. After interviewing 1,415 adults in England and Wales about their status, Runciman (1966, p. 285) concludes that:

> Most people's lives are governed more by the resentment of *narrow* inequalities, the cultivation of *modest* ambitions, and the preservation of *small* differentials than by attitudes to public policy or the social structure as such [emphasis added].

What Is the Advice? The moving tension between reality, expectation, and aspiration entangles us in moral and political questions. The questions are tied together by a central one: In a given context, is it wiser to seek contentment by aspiring toward "better things" or by tailoring expectation?

The advice on this matter cannot be definitive. On the one hand, if there is no aspiration, there is no effort to improve oneself. On the other hand, aspiration can always outrun possibility.

Between these horns lies another devil. It is the truth—or truths—of the old maxim, "Never ask for what you want, lest you get it." There are three meanings buried in this conundrum. One meaning is that the grass in the other field really is no greener than that on our home ground. Another meaning is that traveling is better than arriving, and that it is better to have something to achieve than nothing to work for. A third meaning is that there is no end to aspiration. Once we are "there," we will want to be elsewhere.

School for Discontent It is the hazards that lie at the *extremes* of ambition and apathy that urge the classic advice to balance expectation against possibility. This advice has been ignored in Western countries by the common assumption that if the education of a nation is correlated with its wealth and if the income of its citizens is associated with their schooling, then more schooling for more people for longer periods of their lives will improve their economic condition. This assumption will be examined in the next chapter. For the moment it is enough to note that every wealthy land runs to a limit in the number of neurosurgeons, lawyers, and engineers it needs. Insofar as schooling elevates expectations, as it seems to do, and insofar as the great mass of middle work and dirty work needs to be done, the 1970s may experience greater worker discontent, as has been promised us (Sheppard and Herrick, 1972). A special task force study of work conducted for the U.S. Department of Health, Education and Welfare (O'Toole et al., 1972) puts it this way: "Traditionally lower-level white-collar jobs in both government and industry were held by high school graduates. Today, an increasing number of these jobs go to those who have attended college. But the demand for higher academic credentials has not increased the prestige, status, pay, or difficulty of the job. . . . It is not surprising, then, that [the Labor Department's] Survey of Working Conditions found much of the greatest work dissatisfaction in the country among young, well-educated workers who were in low-paying, dull, routine, and fractionated clerical positions" (p. 39).

Other Sources of Satisfaction

Fortunately for the running of an economy, there are sources of satisfaction in work other than the intrinsic interest of the job or its income and status gains. These additional factors affecting contentment at work are not ranked in order of their importance because their importance varies with the person and the job.

Security is a major consideration to many workers, and it probably becomes a more important factor among those workers who have suffered insecurity in their employment.

Companionship, working with agreeable colleagues and under appreciative supervision, is another source of job satisfaction. Again, the value of colleagueship may mean more after a worker has experienced disagreeable job situations.

What Veblen called the "instinct of workmanship" is another source of job satisfaction. This refers to the pleasures of *exercising a skill.* The ability to exercise a skill goes hand in hand with the satisfaction that comes from having *individual responsibility* for doing a piece of work. The rewards of using a skill and of being independently responsible for one's work vary, of course, with personal interests.

Yet another source of satisfaction stems from the feeling that one's work is *appreciated* and, more, that it is needed. The damage to self-esteem that sometimes accompanies routine, unskilled labor is part of an awareness that any other laborer could serve as well and that one is not needed for his distinctive contribution. Laborers in this condition become what Ellison (1952) has called "invisible" persons.

Ways Out

It has been seen that a first prescription in the remedy of discontent is its prevention. This calls for training oneself for that kind of work that meets one's interests. For young persons who would maximize the use of their talents, the additional advice is to find out what one likes to do that can be mated with a skill that others will pay for and that is in relatively short supply.

For those who prefer to work or must work at relatively routine and modestly skilled jobs, there are sources of satisfaction in the "community benefits" provided by many large industries. These include incorporating social life and recreational and educational activities with work. In varying styles Western companies have done this; however, the Japanese seem to have had a cultural advantage in effecting this blend of work with community involvement (Abegglen, 1958; Kahn, 1970).

Another remedy for the boredom of the assembly line is team assembly, such as the Saab Corporation and others have been trying in Sweden. In such a manufacturing process a group of workers does different jobs, rather than just one operation, and fabricates products from start to finish (Björk, 1975).

The task force report on work previously cited presents thirty-four "case studies in the humanization of work" from industries in Europe and North America. The principle on which such efforts rest is to organize the required work so that a greater variety of tasks is available to workers, who may set their own pace in accomplishing them. Where work teams are involved, this procedure allows for some movement of the team across work areas in the factory. Most of the cases analyzed in the task force report involve small experimental units functioning within the larger corporation. However, there are instances of total work forces planning and organizing their own work. All

400 employees of the American Velvet Company, for example, operate in this manner. Their sense of responsibility and their motivation are augmented by a profit-sharing plan. Some 6,000 employees of the Monsanto Textiles Company and almost 20,000 employees of the Imperial Chemical Industries have their work organized in similar fashion.

IN SUMMARY

These are some suggestions for improving the quality of our lives and for meeting one facet of our economic concerns. These suggested remedies are not, however, patent cures. There is none such. The reason for this has already been remarked: expectations can always exceed possibilities and there is no necessary end to discontent.

Our economic concerns are not limited, of course, to finding happy work. They also include an interest in raising the material level of living.

Chapter 10

Getting Ahead

There are two aspects of concern with raising the economic levels of our lives. One side of this concern attends to what has been called "making it" (Podhoretz, 1967), that is, with climbing the class ladder. The other facet of this concern is with raising the material standard of living of an entire population.

There is an association, but an imperfect one, between these two aspects of our economic concern. Within a particular society, we are interested in how wealth is distributed and with the procedures for getting ahead. We want to know why some people succeed and some fail in the competition for society's material rewards. The answer to this concern is not necessarily the same as the reply given to the issue of economic development, and the people who ask the first question may or may not be concerned with the second.

MAKING WEALTH AND DISTRIBUTING IT

These two, different concerns may be phrased this way:

A first question is: "How does an individual improve his economic lot within his society?"

A second question is: "How does a society as a whole improve its economic condition?"

In principle, we assume that there is a connection between the answer to the first question and the response to the second. We assume that there is some relationship between the way in which a society distributes its wealth and the increase or decrease of that wealth. While this assumption is acknowledged, economists continue to debate how the assumption is to be used. Does equalizing the distribution of wealth within a society foster its increase or its decrease? Is income inequality required as a means of increasing national productivity?

These questions are posed here not to receive definitive answers but to demonstrate two things: The first is that *both capitalist and socialist economists agree that an unequal distribution of a society's wealth is justified by a presumed relation between individual reward and productivity.*

Economists quarrel about how much inequality is thus justified and about how the inequality should be decided. The capitalist would let the market decide. The socialist prefers that his government decide.

These quarrels notwithstanding, some inequality remains rationalized by both "bourgeois" and "revolutionary" economists. For example, the Russian economist Petrov (1968, pp. 210–211) describes "the principles governing the distribution of the national income in the U.S.S.R." in this way:

> The part of the income equivalent to necessary labour is distributed among individual producers engaged in manual and mental activities in material production, the distribution being made in accordance with the quality and quantity of labour contributed by each producer. It is obvious, therefore, that producers do not receive equal shares, as the amount of compensation given to a producer is related to his contribution to social production or other socially useful activity. V. I. Lenin repeatedly emphasized the paramount importance of material incentives for efficient production under socialism and for stepping up labour productivity.

The second point to be demonstrated is that *the questions about personal advancement and economic development constitute separable concerns.*

It is apparent, for example, that when these concerns are taken into the political arena, the political combatants do *not* frequently make a connection between allowing or encouraging individuals to improve their economic condition and raising the material level of their society. It is possible, and often politically advisable, to attend to the conditions that foster economic growth without attending simultaneously to the manner in which the increased wealth of a country is distributed. Conversely, it is possible to attend to the distribution of wealth within a state without concern for the sources of national wealth. In short, politicians and others who want to *redistribute* the wealth of their nations do not necessarily know how to *produce* it.[1]

---

[1]There are many illustrations of economic ignorance to be found in the works and deeds of politicians in both advanced and underdeveloped countries. A sad but honest confession is given by the late Cuban revolutionary Ché Guevara (1963), who said, "We began to acquire factories, but we did not think of the raw materials for them that we would have to import. [So two years were lost] installing factories for a series of articles which could be bought at almost the same price as the raw materials that we needed to produce them."

These two categories of concern, personal advancement and economic development, will be discussed separately simply as a matter of convenience. We shall attend here to how people get ahead in relatively uncontrolled economies, while the following chapter will address the question of societal wealth. This separation of issues is arbitrary, however, and we are reminded that there *is* a connection between the wealth of a state and the rules of reward it follows. Rewarding individual *effort* rather than individual *need* does have different consequences for the economic development and political organization of a society. Of this, more later.

RULES OF THE GAME: A CONTEST OF PRINCIPLES

All "mass societies" distribute material rewards unequally. The differential privileges may be allocated through a market system, such as the Western world approximates, or through a politically controlled rationing system, as in the communist countries. The fact that many modern states exhibit mixtures of political and marketing principles in the distribution of their wealth does not mean that the differences in principle are nonexistent. Rather, this fact attests to the running battle between these principles, a contest that is worldwide.

The *marketing principle* proposes that individuals be allowed to charge for their work "what the market will bear." It operates by permitting each worker to sell his services or his products at whatever price someone is willing to pay for them. In opposition to this, the *political principle,* in its communist version, would allocate rewards as indicated by the motto: "From each according to his abilities, to each according to his needs."

In practice, neither principle is seen in its pure form. There is no society that allows people to make whatever they can from their work without restriction. The criminal law is there to say what is improper as a means of making money, and taxes are there to take away "too much" of legal income. Unions bargain collectively for a larger share of wealth, and legislation establishes minimum wages and transfer payments from one segment of society to another.

Similarly, there are few if any societies that allocate their resources equally according to the needs of their people. Indeed, as we have seen, "need" is a vague term and subject to political negotiation. The vagueness of this concept allows people to "need" different amounts of the wealth of their nations in a fashion reminiscent of George Orwell's *Animal Farm* (1946), on which "all are equal, but some are more equal than others." Approximations to a communist principle in which wealth is distributed equally among all subjects is presently found among poor societies like Cuba and the People's Republic of China. With an increase in affluence, this principle is more frequently violated, as in the case of the Soviet Union.

If the marketing and political principles are seldom fully realized in practice, they are yet exhibited *by degree.* Modern states are more and less open to the sale of individual talent. The degree of their openness makes a difference. It makes a difference to how one gets ahead, to how far one can go, and, hence, to the quality of one's freedom. For example, there is more marketability of individual effort in Canada, the United States, and Mexico than in Poland, the People's Republic of China, or the U.S.S.R. So, too, the market principle operates more strongly in West Germany than in East Germany, in the Ivory Coast than in Ghana, in Spain than in Greece. The fact of such differences in the rules of reward poses such questions as these:

> What kinds of people receive more and less of the wealth of their countries under the different principles?
> What are the relative costs and benefits of following one principle rather than another?
> Which principle is more just?

Of these questions, only the first need be addressed here in the context of concern with getting ahead. Because of the availability of data, the answer will be restricted to the recent experience of noncommunist states.

WHO MAKES IT?

The answer to this question depends, of course, on one's measure of "making it." Unfortunately for those who expect a simple answer, there is no single standard of success.

Criteria of Success

Industrial psychologists who have attempted to measure success and to study its sources have found it impossible to decide upon a single best criterion. All of us use some mixture of standards, and a different mixture, in judging whether we have succeeded. Furthermore, the blend of criteria used to evaluate success changes in time and from one occupation to another. For example, the dollar value of sales is the measure of success among salesmen (Rush, 1953). This standard may be refined into such dimensions as "percent of quota achieved" or "closing ability," but *income* remains the salesman's objective standard. This criterion contrasts with success as it is gauged among medical specialists. Here recognition of *competence* and *achievement* become a hallmark of success (Richards et al., 1965; Taylor et al., 1964). This standard, in turn, differs from that principally employed in the evaluation of the success of supervisors, foremen, and managers, for whom a *social relations effectiveness* criterion becomes important (Creager and Harding, 1958; Grant, 1955; Wrigley et al., 1957).

Five Common Meanings of "Making It"

In the context of our economic hopes and fears, five principal signs have been used to judge the quality of our material lives: wealth, security, reputation, skill, and contentment.

1   Having wealth is a prime meaning of being successful.

Wealth, it should be noted, is not the same as money. As people who live in inflationary times should know, money can have more or less value and it can purchase more or less wealth. Money is only a medium of exchange, but wealth is that which has value; it is the object of desire. The value of wealth may be convertible to money, or it may be exchanged for other things of value. Some wealth, however, is nontransferable. Health is the principal example of nonexchangeable wealth, although in the age of blood and organ transplants some portion of one's health may be sold for money.

Ordinarily, the term "wealth" is used in its exchange sense to refer to those values that can be given a price in money, time, things, or services.

Money Is Not Wealth   This distinction sounds academic, but it deserves emphasis because there is a popular tendency to talk about money as though it were a direct measure of wealth. It is not. The material quality of our lives is only in some part a reflection of the money we make. It is more adequately represented by the wealth we have. People who are concerned about their economic condition are more rightly attentive to wealth than to money.

A second reason for emphasizing the distinction between wealth and money is that noting this difference alerts us to the limits of creating wealth by manufacturing money. There is a widespread belief that if governments are only big enough, they can produce wealth by making money. There is a truth in this, but there is a limit to this truth that becomes significant when we try to relieve poverty or make economies grow. The point will be amplified on pages 266–269.

The Variable Value of Wealth   In economies in which most people live well above bare survival—in economies such as those in North America, Europe, and English-speaking Africa and Oceania—the importance of wealth as a measure of success varies with the vocational game one is playing.

For those who are working in commerce, and this includes the large entertainment industry, wealth and its signs are important markers of success. The value of wealth as a measure of achievement declines as the worker gets beyond the subsistence level and as other vocationally oriented objectives come into play.

2   The security of one's wealth is a second measure of economic well-being.

Security is recognizable as freedom from worry about survival. It is a measure that also declines in importance with the degree of security an individual has experienced. As with other human wants, security increases in value when it has been scarce. Those who have been in economic straits are more likely to prize the assurance of wealth in addition to its amount.

3   A third measure of success is reputation.

A good repute may have been individually earned, as through exceptional performance, or it may be attributed to a class of occupation. Some individuals get ahead by moving into work that is considered "better" whether or not the individual earns more money or exhibits greater competence. The division of work into manual and nonmanual is a classification that is meaningful largely as a matter of prestige rather than as a division by earnings or skills.

4   Performance is a fourth sign of success.

As with other indicators of getting ahead, the importance attached to being able to do a job well is a matter of the reference group from which one selects his standards and of some distance above subsistence. It is difficult to maintain performance as a sign of success if the performance does not pay.

5   A fifth criterion of success is contentment.

"Contentment" may be defined as "the attainment of a self-chosen goal" (Stott, 1950, p. 112). By this standard, being successful is fulfilling one's aspirations. Again, depending upon one's ambitions, this criterion raises or lowers the importance of wealth.

In sum, these five criteria vary in their importance with each person's experience, with the kind of work he does, with individual ambition, and with elevation above mere subsistence. Given the possible combinations among these determinants of success, some students have come to regard the concept as useless. For example, Thorndike (1963, p. 186) writes that "beyond survival in an occupation, 'success' is a meaningless concept, which we might as well abandon."

Thorndike believes that success is a meaningless notion, not merely because of the different ways in which one can be judged to have "made it" but also because so much of an individual's fate in industrialized societies is "institutionalized," that is, built into the operation of large organizations, like unions or governments, of which the worker is a part. In such settings, security and earnings become less a matter of the individual's competence and more a matter of his membership.

While psychologists like Thorndike may devalue the idea of success, getting ahead remains a social concern. It remains a concern of individuals who wish to improve their economic lot or that of their children and it is a moral concern of individuals who are offended by disparities in the lives of poor people and rich ones. Both concerns deserve our attention.

STUDIES OF "VERTICAL MOBILITY"

A sociological way of assessing who gets ahead studies the movement between those broad bands of people called social classes. Social classes, of course, do not really exist. The term is a concept with which sociologists interpret experience. The concept has a *basis* in reality, however, and derives from the common observation that individuals within a society do not have equal life chances—for health and survival—and that individuals do not associate completely freely with each other. There are patterns of preferred association that correlate with styles of life.

The styles of life are recognizable in speech, manners, and aesthetic taste. They are associated somewhat, but not perfectly, with the amount of schooling and the quality of education received, with the amount of wealth one has, and with the kind of work one does. When such clusters of conditions are acknowledged by the members of a society and when differential prestige is accorded these differences, sociologists speak of such broad categories of people as constituting social strata. If one's position in a stratum is not fixed at birth or by legal or religious prescriptions—if, that is, there is some possibility of movement between the strata—then such a pattern of stratification is called a class system and the strata are spoken of as social classes.[2]

Two public issues have sparked a host of studies of vertical mobility among social classes. One issue is that of *opportunity*—of how much there is, who has it, and who uses it. A second issue is that of *inequality*—its degree and its justification.

A Conclusion The research generated by these issues is voluminous. It leads to the conclusion that if one looks at large societies over long periods of time, *inequality and opportunity are persistent features of social organization.*

Movement up and down the ladder of prestige and wealth is continuous. There is a circulation among the social classes that has been recorded for widely different societies at different historical periods.

For example, Fahlbeck (1953) studied the histories of 1,547 noble families in seventeenth-century Sweden and found that 84 percent of them had been reduced from their high station by the third generation. In similar vein, Hsu (1949) studied the biographies of eminent persons recorded in the district histories of classical China. He found considerable movement between prestige levels in the population, with some 35 to 80 percent of the distinguished persons in the different districts being "new men." The Chinese bureaucracy allowed merit to move up. This is also illustrated by Kracke's (1947) research on Chinese vertical mobility during the twelfth and thirteenth centuries and by Chang's (1955) research on nineteenth-century China. Kracke estimates that between 35 and 45 percent of the staffs of Chinese bureaucracies were "new men."

---

[2]Class systems of stratification are often contrasted with caste and estate systems. The differences among these systems are the amount of movement they allow between strata and the justifications given for opening and closing the gates. A caste system, as it has been known in India, is based on religious beliefs that enforce endogamy—marriage within the caste only—and a relatively fixed pyramid of occupations. An estate system, as it was known in Europe until recent times, is based on man-made laws justified by the authority of a ruler who is believed to be divinely legitimized. The man-made regulation of estate systems allowed more movement between strata than the religious rules of a caste system. By contrast, a class system has neither man-made nor god-given laws against moving between strata.

In more recent times, it has been shown that the industrial countries of the West tend to have similar amounts of social mobility and that, contrary to a popular opinion, North America is no more the land of opportunity, in this sense, than western Europe (Lipset and Bendix, 1960; Sorokin, 1959).

Our conclusion is well stated by the economist Schumpeter (1951, p. 164) in his survey of European history. "There is a constant turnover," he writes. "The process always goes on, though at times extremely slowly and almost imperceptibly . . . each class resembles a hotel or an omnibus, always full, but always of different people."

Recent Research: Occupational Mobility Is Not Necessarily Class Mobility

Research on vertical mobility in modern times is better described as investigation of occupational change than of class mobility. What has been studied, for the most part, is shifts in occupation between generations and within a generation where the changes in occupation may or may not coincide with a change in social class as we have defined it. This is simply to say that people who move up or down a notch in income or occupational prestige may not do so in those correlated aspects of living that constitute "class." With high vertical mobility, for example, some middle-income people may not be middle-class any more than the *nouveaux riches* are "high class." The sociologist's *indicators* of class—such as income, schooling, and occupation—are not always accurate *descriptions* of class. With rapid mobility the style of life that defines a class becomes only loosely connected to such more easily counted correlates of stratification as money and work. In illustration of this, the hit motion picture *The Graduate* depicts people of high income who are neither middle or upper class in their manners, their morals, or their tastes.

So What?

The fact that people who move up the money ladder may not move up the class ladder does not bother most people who are concerned principally with "making it." It does bother hopeful reformers, however, who want people to behave differently as well as to have more. A promise of the economic determinist is that, as a population becomes more wealthy, its behavior changes. It may, but the quality of that change is not always what the materialist had prophesied. The failure of his prophecy is assured by the optimist's neglect of the fact that *how* one "makes it" makes a difference. Finding wealth, stealing it, or being given it are different processes. They do not have the same consequences for behavior as do earning money or producing wealth. Furthermore, having more or less wealth is only one of the determinants of our conduct.

The point is illustrated in the changing relation between the signs of stratification and the way one lives. Midway in the twentieth century, the hopeful promise had been that rising affluence would mean "the maintenance of high standards of diversified excellence among the keepers of high culture combined with a gradual improvement of mass tastes" (Wilensky, 1964a, p.

173). Studies of how people of different income levels now use their leisure show this promise to be largely unfulfilled. Wilensky, for example, studied the recreational activities of a sample of American men who ranged from skid row denizens through the "middle mass" and self-employed merchants to prominent professionals. His research reveals the fragility of exacting standards of aesthetic preference, at least. Abrams (1958) reports a similar effect in England.

By implication, what is true of the uses of leisure may also be true of standards of morality, so that it cannot be readily concluded that rising affluence necessarily means better conduct. Thus when an economist predicts that more money means less crime, we are skeptical. Fleisher (1966), for example, claims that "the combined effects of a $500.00 increase in income would probably be a reduction of about 5.2 arrests per 1,000 population. In areas of high tendencies toward crime, a 10 percent rise in incomes might well result in a 20 percent decline in delinquency" (p. 117).

This promise is viewed skeptically because it confuses one of the fluctuating correlates of social class—income—with the changing styles of life associated with more and less money. In view of the American debacle of Watergate and the evidence of both amorality and immorality among some of the economically advantaged leaders of the United States (Dirks and Gross, 1974), it ought to be easy to recognize, by now, that money does not automatically produce morality and that no one style of life is inextricably linked to an income level.

How Much Mobility Occurs?

Despite our cautions against assuming too much about the meaning of social mobility, getting ahead remains a major concern. A first set of questions asks how much mobility there is, which countries have more and less of it, and whether the opportunities to rise and fall have been increasing or decreasing.

A summary answer, derived from a host of studies in Western societies and some Asian ones, is, as we have noted, that movement up and down the status ladder is continuous. Furthermore, there seems to be a rough consistency in the amount of vertical mobility among modern industrialized countries (Lipset and Bendix, 1960; Lipset and Rogoff, 1954; Lipset and Zetterberg, 1955). The United States does not seem distinctive from other industrial countries in the amount of change from manual to nonmanual occupations, but it does seem to have "a higher rate of movement into the elite strata from the manual strata . . ." (Miller, 1960, p. 58). Finally, and in contradiction of a widely believed story, the volume of status change in developed lands has remained the same or increased somewhat over the past thirty to fifty years (Rogoff, 1953).

Whether this mobility is considered great or little depends, of course, upon one's expectations. The majority of a population remains at the same status level as its parents, but a minority moves. The bulk of such occupational shift in the work of fathers and sons is between adjacent status levels, although the great movements from low to high status do occur and remain a possibility.

The Evidence

There is much evidence to support these generalizations. For example, Rogoff (1953) studied the occupational origins and changes in two generations of white men in Indiana. Using marriage license applications as a source of her data, Rogoff compared the occupations of a sample of fathers and sons in 1905–1912 with a sample drawn in 1938–1941. She found that the most probable occupational destination of a son was in the work of his father. Where there was a change between generations, it was for the most part to an occupation not greatly different in status from that held by the father. Last, Rogoff reports that "the likelihood of a son being in an occupational class different from that of his father was *about the same in 1910 and in 1940*" (p. 106, emphasis hers). Rogoff makes this evaluation *after* having corrected for changes in the occupational structure of American society between the two periods of her study. Since there were more jobs at higher status levels in 1940 than in 1910, it seems fair to reinterpret these data to show more "opportunity" in 1940 than in 1910.

Similar results were obtained by Davidson and Anderson (1937), who analyzed occupational changes in a sample of men in California. They report that about two-thirds of the sons were at the same status position as their fathers or at an adjoining rank. Centers (1948) also found that most (71 percent) American sons tend to work at jobs at the same or adjacent status levels as their fathers. Centers adds, however, that the chances of a son climbing the status ladder are greater than the chances of his descending it. Similarly, McGuire (1950) calculated the mobility of men and women in a midwestern American town between 1920 and 1940 and found about 72 percent to have remained in the same status as their fathers. Of the balance, 23.3 percent improved their status while 4.6 percent declined.

Climbing High   Numerous other studies repeat these findings and reveal a similar pattern among western European countries during this century. Since such research describes the more common, small steps in movement among social strata, it is interesting, by contrast, to look at the proportions of people at the *top* of the "money mountain" to see who was born there and who climbed there.

Mills (1956) compiled data on "the very rich" in the United States where, by his definition, to be very rich was to have possessed at one time or another at least $30 million. Mills compared the origins of these "big rich" people at three periods—1900, 1925, and 1950—with results as indicated in Table 10-1. It seems that "making it" in the United States has become more difficult for those who are not born rich, yet almost one-third of Mills's sample that became very rich in 1950 started life poor or middling.

A rather different picture of changes in opportunity is given if we look, not at the extreme of wealth, but at another measure of success—becoming a president or chairman of America's largest corporations. Newcomer (1955) did this for the same years as Mills's study and found no decline in the possibility

Table 10-1   The Social Class Origins of "The Very Rich" 1900, 1925, 1950, United States (Percent)*

	Lower class	Middle class	Upper class
1900	39	22	39
1925	12	32	56
1950	9	23	68

*Data taken from C. Wright Mills, *The Power Elite.* © 1956 by Oxford University Press, Inc. Reprinted by permission.

of moving from humble origins to business leadership. Table 10-2 tells the story. About one-eighth of the corporation executives in 1950 had started life poor, as had a similar proportion in 1910. Meanwhile, the proportion of executives who started at the top *declined* from 1900 to 1950, while the proportion of middle-income people who had become commercially prominent *increased.* In the Western world, at least, lamentations about closed doors to opportunity seem premature.

The Rungs of the Ladder

Sociologists and psychologists have been interested in describing the rungs of the status ladder, that is, in describing how one moves up or down it. Two sets of factors have been examined for their possible impact upon getting ahead— the structure of the social environment and the personality of the individual.

Assessing the influence of the environmental variables is like estimating where people start in the status climb and the paths they use. Assessing the impact of personality variables is like estimating the differing qualities of the climbers.

The first factors, the environmental ones, are usually what is meant by "opportunities," although, as we shall see, this term is inexactly used. The second set of determinants refers to abilities. Common sense says that there must be some relationship between where one starts a career, how one uses his talents, and where one finishes. The difficult problem is how to measure the relative impact of ability and opportunity upon getting ahead. This evaluation is made difficult because the rungs of the ladder vary in their height as a career is run. In a changing society with a moving technology, a fluctuating occupational demand, and an increasingly schooled population, the importance of specific environmental and personal determinants changes as our lives unfold. Furthermore, there is an interaction between where one starts the climb, the kind of person one is, and the obstacles one does or does not meet in getting ahead.

Behavioral scientists have developed sophisticated techniques for measuring some of these variables and for plotting their causal influence. Despite such efforts, much of our status fate is left unexplained. *We do not know, beyond some modest relationships, why some people "make it" and others do not.* We do not know this even after we allow for differences in opportunities and abilities. We cover our ignorance with the word "luck." There are "breaks of the game," fair and foul calls by its referees, and players who are "hot" or "off their games."

A major reason why we know some things, but not everything, about getting ahead is that the causal variables studied, such as family background, peer influence, and intelligence, are broad categories crudely measured. Our measuring net is coarse, suitable for trapping the two or three or four big variables that make a difference but unsuitable for capturing the many small events that affect us. Moreover, this coarse measurement net is not well equipped for gauging the interplay of the large, sociopsychological variables among themselves and with the multifold conditioners that constitute our luck. Attempts to measure what helps us "make it" are so crude that the economist Machlup (1973, p. 360) rightly argues that these efforts be given the titles they deserve—estimates and valuations rather than measurements.

Bearing in mind this qualification of the adequacy of research, what do we know about who moves on the class ladder and how? The investigations to be reviewed represent a sample of large-scale studies of careers.

The Stanford Studies

The late Lewis Terman and his colleagues at Stanford University began a long-term study in the early 1920s of the fate of California schoolchildren who were highly intelligent. The original subjects were selected by one criterion: that they achieved IQs of 140 or higher in the Stanford-Binet mental test. The more than 1,000 children thus chosen for follow-up represented the upper 1.5 percent of American youngsters on such a standardized mental test. The careers of these individuals are under continuing study, with data being gathered on their children and grandchildren.

The importance of this longitudinal study lies in its control of a major determinant of our destinies: intelligence. There is, of course, more than one kind of intelligence, and it can be claimed that a mental test measures only one facet of those behaviors called bright or stupid. This claim is true, but it is also true that whatever mental tests test constitutes a significant factor in our getting ahead, and *more so* as one chooses to get ahead by the educational avenue (McNemar, 1964). There are other roads to success, but schooling has been an important path in democratic societies.

Table 10-2 Economic Status of Fathers of Corporation Executives: 1900, 1925, and 1950*

Economic status of father	Percent of executives		
	1900	1925	1950
Wealthy	45.6	36.3	36.1
Medium	42.1	47.8	51.8
Poor	12.3	15.8	12.1

*Adapted from M. Newcomer, *The Big Business Executive: The Factors That Made Him, 1900–1950.* © 1955 by Columbia University Press. Reproduced by permission.

In controlling for IQ, the Stanford studies have also homogenized their sample in terms of socioeconomic background. While both poor and rich children are represented in the original sample, the majority of this cohort was born to middle-class parents (Terman, 1925).

The major interest of Terman's research was to ascertain whether such gifted children fulfilled their promise. Generally they did. However, some of these individuals "failed," and it is in the contrast between those who "made it" and those who did not that we can find part of the answer to our question about who gets ahead and how.

Since the females among Terman's intelligent children tend to have careers as wives, the analysis of success and failure has been limited to males. At the time of a twenty-five-year follow-up of this group, the Stanford investigators classified the men into those "most successful" (the A group), those "normally or moderately successful" (the B group), and those "least successful" (the C group). This division was made in an effort to identify some of the nonintellectual factors that affect our careers. These factors come into sharper focus as those who have "really made it" (the A's) are compared with those who have not (the C's). The contrast between these groups shows that *an important determinant of getting ahead is a bundle of personality features.*

In comparison with the less successful men of like IQ, the successful ones were more emotionally stable and better adjusted socially. Furthermore, these differences were apparent in judgments made of these persons by their parents and teachers *when they were first studied as children in 1922* (Terman and Oden, 1947, p. 336). Early on, those who were later to become successful were more popular, more sensitive to others' opinions, more frequently leaders, and more free from feelings of either vanity or inferiority.

In addition, the successful men completed more years of schooling and earned disproportionately more degrees. The A's compared with the C's approached their vocational goals more directly and *persisted* toward their objectives with fewer deviations. Within twenty-five years the A's were making on the average more than 2 1/2 times as much as the C's, although income was *not* used as a criterion for classifying these men as successful or not.

As we should expect, the A's liked their work better than did the C's, and they more frequently felt that they had chosen their careers rather than that they had drifted into them (Terman and Oden, 1947, p. 326; 1959, pp. 148–149). In keeping with our earlier discussion of *interest* as a determinant of the difference between working and laboring, the successful men had more definite vocational interests than the unsuccessful, and they also showed more avocational interests.

Reading the five volumes in the *Genetic Studies of Genius* published by the Stanford psychologists leaves one with the conclusion that a major part of our economic destiny can be assigned to those personal characteristics that have been called, contrastingly, "being full of life" or "being run over by it" (Nettler, 1965). A theme that separates the two kinds of person is direction, involvement, persistence, and emotional orderliness.

Fortunately, there are other roads to success than this scholastic-vocational one. There is an openness in Western economic structures, and the school-to-vocation career is not the only way of "making it." However, the Stanford studies illuminate how—and hence why—those who use this channel do so with greater or lesser effectiveness.

The Duncans and Featherman Study

A different procedure for analyzing movement up and down the status ladder has been employed by O. D. and Beverly Duncan and D. L. Featherman (1972). These investigators used a body of interview data taken from samples of the adult male population twenty-five to sixty-four years old in the United States as of 1964. The data pool consisted of material gathered by seven different surveys that accumulated information on a man's present occupation and income, his marital status and fertility, his socioeconomic background, and some personality variables.

A statistical technique known as path analysis was applied to these data to ascertain the relative weights and the causal sequence of factors contributing to occupational achievement. The principal findings can be summarized as follows:

1 How much money a man earned in the United States a decade ago depended upon (varied with) the prestige of his principal occupation, the amount of schooling he had obtained, and three characteristics of the family in which he was reared—his father's educational attainment, his father's occupation, and the number of brothers and sisters he had. Coming from a large family is not helpful, nor is coming from an uneducated and poor one.

2 *Occupational status* depends, in turn, upon educational attainment and the three family background characteristics.

3 *How far one goes in school* depends upon the size of his nurturing family and his father's work and schooling. The greater the number of siblings and the lower the father's educational and occupational achievement, the lower the level of schooling a man obtains.

4 *The influence of schooling upon income* is more indirect than direct. That is, schooling affects income in the way most of us expect it to—by qualifying one for higher-paying and more prestigious work.

5 *The direct impact of the three family background* variables upon earnings is slight. The family environment has its greatest effect in determining the level of schooling completed, the least impact on income, and an intermediate influence in determining occupational status. In short, the family in which one was reared has most effect upon those events, like going to school, that are closer in time to the nurturing experience. *With the passage of time, our family backgrounds become less important in affecting our careers.*

6 *Intelligence, as measured, makes a difference.* IQ and family background are positively correlated, of course—the association running in favor of children from smaller families of higher educational and occupational status. However, intelligence has an effect upon occupational status, educational achievement, and income that is *independent* of family background. Much of the influence of IQ upon occupational level works through the greater tendency of brighter sons to stay in school and to do well there. Nevertheless, even when school and occupational levels are held constant, *intelligent men make more money.* The investigators write, "intelligence affects income directly to nearly the same extent as it influences differential earnings indirectly through schooling and occupational attainment." (p. 104).

   7   *Race makes a difference.* Black men did not earn as much as white men in America ten years ago even when their family backgrounds, years in school, and IQs were roughly the same. The investigators interpret this differential "as a handicap, or cost, to some men for being black" (p. 105).

   It is popular to attribute this cost, as do the authors (pp. 60–61, 67–68), to a process called discrimination. However, "discrimination" is an emotionally loaded term—not often defined—and easier to assume from results than to prove as a process. As noted earlier (p. 136), to assess discrimination in the sense of unjust treatment requires that a standard of fair treatment be specified and that a distortion in applying this standard be demonstrated. These requirements are seldom met by studies of discrimination (Hagan, 1975). Such studies tend to substitute *unequal result* for a measure of discrimination. This substitution has political utility, but it is poor research methodology. At this juncture of our science, it is more accurate to say of these "residual differences" in black and white achievement that their causes are not known.

   8   *"The occupational level at which a man begins his career is substantially predictive of the level at which he will be found at any age between 25 and 64"* (p. 252). A first job is sometimes a job taken before the completion of one's schooling. Men who interrupt their schooling to go to work have less favorable family environments than those who do not break their education even when they ultimately complete the same number of years in school. This unfavorable environmental factor helps explain why the level at which a man first goes to work is more highly correlated with the level at which he ends up for those whose education is interrupted.

   9   *Nonfarm migrants have an advantage in occupational mobility* when compared with either the "natives" or with migrants from farms. There is some evidence that this effect results from the "superior" backgrounds of nonfarm migrant families.

   10   *Men whose marriages break up do not climb the status ladder as well* as do those whose marriages remain intact.

   11   *Men who are fertile[3] have less success in the status climb.* Having many children is not helpful to a man's career, and having children soon after marriage increases the disadvantage.

Converting Research Results into Social Policy

Findings such as these suggest that where we start our careers—as indicated by family background, race, and schooling—helps determine where we end our

---

[3]Dictionaries today are not always discriminating guides (Macdonald, 1962), and many of them make no distinction between "fertility" and "fecundity." While the terms are frequently used interchangeably, demographers distinguish between them. To be *fertile* means here to *reproduce.* To be *fecund* is to be *capable* of reproduction. One can be fecund, of course, without being fertile.

careers. Such findings also suggest that what we bring to our efforts to "make it"—in the form of abilities, interests, and other features of our personalities—also plays a part in shaping our occupational careers.

In converting these research results into social policy, the personal factors have been ignored in favor of the background factors which, it is felt, can be more easily manipulated. In turn, the policy emphasis in Western countries has looked to *one* of these background factors—schooling—as the key to changing career patterns. This emphasis is embedded in a set of assumptions that deserve the title *ideology*.

THE IDEOLOGY OF OPPORTUNITY

The individual concern with getting ahead has been translated into a moral and political issue. The issue, in democracies, has been defined as a matter of giving everyone an equal chance. This definition has been strongly influenced by a sociology that stresses cultural determinism, or *the force of circumstance*. It is part of the professional role of the student of society to study the impact of social conditions upon our destinies, just as it is the professional task of a geneticist to study how a heredity is transmitted and how it affects a career.

It is not necessary to debate here how much of our lives, including our economic careers, is a result of circumstance or of what we bring to those circumstances. The point is that our democratic sense of justice calls for a chance for everyone to play the game and for keeping its rules fair. This is a different sense of justice from believing that everyone should win the game or that no one should. The first ethic fights for *equality of opportunity;* the second sense of justice demands *equality of result.*

Until recently at least, democrats (small "d") have preferred the "equal opportunity" ethic to the fully egalitarian ethic out of an awareness that *equality can be achieved, if ever, only by being imposed.* The imposition would require force and high cost. It seems, then, less harmful and yet fair to work for equality of opportunities rather than for equality of results.

The Trouble with the Idea   Opportunity, however, is difficult to measure. The very concept of an opportunity is slippery. We mean by it a time or a situation favorable to the attainment of a goal. It is "a chance." The perception of a chance, nevertheless, always depends upon the actor. For us to assess another's opportunities requires some notion, usually unstated, of what a person could have done if he had *had* "the chance," or if he had seen it and used it. Real opportunities may not be used ones. There is always a gap between the opportunities that were there and the opportunities that were perceived and acted upon. Opportunities, unfortunately, are much easier to recognize after they have passed than before they are grasped.

The vagueness of the concept of opportunity leads to difficulty in recognizing its presence or absence. It may be impossible to measure the presence of opportunities in advance of actions except in the crudest way. Certainly we can say that fifty years ago, a Greenland Eskimo had no opportunity to learn to surf. Similarly, the Fiji islander had no opportunity to ski. However, as we move from such extremes toward assessing the opportunities that affect economic careers within an affluent society, it becomes less certain what we mean by "opportunities" and what we should count when we estimate them.

The vagueness of the idea of opportunity and the difficulty in measuring it leads to a translation in which equality of *result* becomes the indicator of equality of *opportunity*. This translation does two questionable things: "(1) it assumes that all or most of the causes of a career are encompassed in something called 'the chances' or 'the breaks,' and (2) it performs a semantic cheat by substituting *how one is* for *the chances he had*. This translation trick is illegitimate because it first poses a cause of conduct called 'opportunity' and then uses as a measure of that 'opportunity,' its alleged effects. It is as if one were to argue that C causes E, and then prove the causal connection by using E as the measure of C" (Nettler, 1974a, p. 161).

The End of an Ideology

The difficulties with the opportunity structure thesis are not merely conceptual and logical. There are also factual reasons for doubting it. During the past decade the strongest version of the opportunity ethic—the equality of education theme—has been submerged under an avalanche of data. This is significant because, in the Western world, to equalize opportunity has meant principally to equalize the chance to go to school. Having schools available is obviously only one kind of opportunity, yet it has been stressed as a major avenue by which individuals might proceed to a higher level of material life. Public opinion polls show that citizens regard education as a right and as an economic elevator (Terrien, 1954).

The public is correct in its perception of the economic advantages of an education. The advice that follows for an individual may not constitute good advice, however, when translated without qualification into social policy. The defects of such a translation can be described by outlining the argument of the ideology of education. In shorthand form, the reasoning goes like this:

1 There is a correlation between years of schooling and earnings (Table 10-3).
2 The correlation describes a causal connection. It means that going to school qualifies one for better-paying work.
3 If some individuals, or some segments of a society, go to school longer than others, it is mainly because they have the opportunity to do so. "Opportunity" here includes the belief that some schools are better than others and that the goodness of one's educational chances refers also to the quality of education available.
4 Extending educational opportunities will equalize results. It is assumed that all people will use schools in the same way to climb the class ladder.

Table 10-3   Median Income of Families with Heads Twenty-five Years Old and Over by Race of Head and Years of School Completed: 1961 and 1970*

	Median income
1961	
White families	$ 6,100
Elementary school	4,419
Four years of high school	6,548
Four or more years of college	9,503
Negro and other families	3,340
Elementary school	2,593
Four years of high school	4,773
Four or more years of college	6,593†
1970	
White families	10,545
Elementary school	6,933
Four years of high school	11,054
Four or more years of college	15,841
Negro and other families	6,692
Elementary school	4,930
Four years of high school	8,239
Four or more years of college	14,470

*Adapted from U.S. Bureau of the Census, *Current Population Reports*, Series P-60, Table No. 531, 1972.
†Estimated, Base = less than 200,000.

This set of beliefs has been called an ideology because it is a mixture of some true statements and some false ones blended with some preferences and defended with the emotional fervor of a faith.

For industrialized countries, statement 1 is true. Statement 2 is partly true, which means, of course, that it is partly untrue. Statements 3 and 4 are more false than true.

During the late 1960s and early 1970s a series of American studies provided data that challenge the belief that we go to school in direct relation to the opportunity to do so and that equalizing educational opportunity will equalize educational results and our economic destinies. The findings of this research can best be summarized as answers to the questions that concern us.

Do children equally use the educational opportunities available to them? No.

As schools are presently constituted, their offerings obviously have more appeal to some individuals than to others. To say this is not to blame anyone. It is to describe a fact.

The evidence of this fact is abundant. In addition to those children who enjoy school, there are masses of young ones who find their schools merely boring. These children adjust with indifference. They play the game and do a minimum of studying. Beyond the delighted and the bored, however, are many children who actively hate their educational opportunities. They hate school-work and they hate their teachers. They express their hatred by destroying buildings and equipment, by vandalizing their teachers' desks and automobiles, and, on occasion, by raping their teachers (*L.A. Times,* 1973).

These angry youngsters do poorly in academic work, of course. They are characteristically retarded in grade and they score low on tests of mental performance. They are perceived by both their teachers and their classmates as troublemakers and they are, in general, disliked by both. The dislike is reciprocated. A partial roster of the evidence for this description is to be found in studies by Cooper (1960), Glueck (1964), Paranjape (1970), Peterson et al. (1959), Rivera and Short (1967), and Teele et al. (1966).

A Recommendation Facts such as these have led many educators to consider ways of reconstituting the schools. Coleman (1972), for example, has suggested that schools become productive communities that apprentice youth toward the fulfillment of responsible adult roles. Such schools would deem-phasize the child's acquisition of facts and cognitive skills and stress "working with others under the discipline imposed by a common task and purpose" (p. 75).

Since there would still be need for informed persons with specialized cognitive skills, such a recommendation in practice would probably revert to another form of "streaming." This may be practical, but it will not satisfy the egalitarian's objective.

In the United States, do children of poorer families or of minority ethnic status go to inferior schools? No.

A popular assumption has claimed that if children from economically poor homes do less well in school than children from families that are better off, the cause of their poorer performance lies in the inferiority of their schools. Similarly, it has been believed that those ethnic minorities that do less well in school than other minorities or than the average child are also disadvantaged by inadequate educational opportunity. Neither assumption is supported by fact.

The sociologist Coleman and his colleagues (1966) conducted one of the largest social science projects ever conceived to answer the question, among others, about the quality of schooling available to children of diverse ethnicity in the United States. Particular attention was paid to a comparison of the schooling given blacks and whites, Orientals, Amerindians, Chicanos, and Puerto Ricans. When quality of schools is measured by expenditure per pupil, teacher-student ratio, class size, type of curriculum, library and laboratory facilities, and teachers' salaries and degrees, no consistent advantage is found for any one ethnic group. If, *by these standards,* there are educationally deprived groups, they are *not* racial or ethnic minorities but children living in the South and in the nonmetropolitan North.

Critics who cannot believe these findings argue that the measures of school quality used are poor ones, although they are the indicators commonly mentioned in discussions of the relative goodness of schools. Such critics would like to see more sensitive measures of quality employed, such as teacher devotion, peer-group influence, and classroom environment. Except for the relative peace or turmoil of classrooms, these more sensitive measures would be difficult to standardize. There is always room for additional research, of course, but at present the negative conclusion to this question is justified.

Do children learn more in "good" schools than in "poor" ones? Not much.

In one sense the question answers itself. A "good" school is one in which a child learns more. There is another sense to the question, however. It asks whether putting more money into the schools, buying better equipment, reducing the student-teacher ratio, and employing more highly credentialed teachers results in better reading, writing, and arithmetic skills among the children.

The Coleman study found that such "school effects" were slight. The differences in school quality that were observed had little influence upon educational achievement. *Varying the educational input has only the slightest effect upon the scholastic output.*

The finding of the Coleman study is not singular. It has been replicated by the Plowden survey in England (Acland, 1973; Peaker, 1971) and by the Project Talent in the United States (Flanagan and Cooley, 1966; Folger et al., 1970). It is a finding that should be expected when we study the factors that make for excellence in "school product." These factors are not so much the ones that can be remedied by doses of money, as when governments try to reduce pupil-teacher ratios or increase budgets for gymnasiums and audiovisual aids. More frequently, school excellence is a result of the self-selection of motivated students backed by parents, teachers, and administrators who, in the words of one analyst, know "just what kind of education they [want] and how to produce it" (Sowell, 1974, p. 15).

The fact that many North American schools do not make much difference today in what a child learns is not to say that they cannot make a difference. It does not mean, moreover, that schools teach nothing. Children do learn more by going to school, particularly elementary school, than they would without schools. It is not some *absolute* effect of schooling that is challenged by these investigations but the *relative* effect when schools of varying quality are compared.

Given the tremendous expenditure on schools and the load of hope placed upon them, this is a stunning finding. Nichols (1966), in reviewing the Coleman report, emphasizes the importance of this point as follows:

> [We] may find it hard to believe that the 28-billion-dollar-a-year public education industry has not produced abundant evidence to show differential effects of different kinds of schools, but it has not. That students learn more in "good"

schools than in "poor" schools has long been accepted as a self-evident fact not requiring verification. Thus, the finding that schools with widely varying characteristics differ very little in their effects is literally of revolutionary significance.

Until these findings are clarified by further research they stand like a spear pointed at the heart of the cherished American belief that equality of educational opportunity will increase the equality of intellectual achievement (p. 1314).

Is economic inequality caused principally by the lack of educational opportunity? No.

Jencks and a Harvard University research team (1972) have further weakened the ideology of educational opportunity. Using the Coleman data and enlarging upon it, these investigators applied techniques of correlational analysis in an attempt to find the causes of differences in individual income. Their shocking findings, shocking at least to those who had pinned high hopes upon the schools as economic elevators and levellers, are these:

1   Currently at least, schools seem unable significantly to reduce inequalities among students in reading, arithmetic, and verbal skills. In general, the investigators say, "the character of a school's output depends largely on a single input, namely, the characteristics of its entering children. Everything else—the school budget, its policies, the characteristics of the teachers—is either secondary or completely irrelevant" (p. 256).

2   "Family background" is the single most important determinant of the number of years a person goes to school.

3   "Cognitive skill" is second only to family background in determining how long a person remains in school.

4   Going to school, getting the credentials, leads to better jobs, as the public believes. It is, however, the *amount* of schooling, rather than its *quality*, that affects where one ends up occupationally. In short, family background and scholarly talent make school more congenial (less painful) for some individuals than for others. Those who stay in school longer move into better positions.

5   *Income* is another matter, however. While occupational status and income do vary with cognitive skills and years of schooling, education does *not* account for the differences in earnings received by persons working within the same occupation. Since Jencks and his colleagues are unable to isolate any bundle of characteristics that explains these differences, they attribute the variation to luck. It has already been noted that "luck" is a word employed to cover our ignorance. We are left with the commonsensical assumption that there are differences in talent, in effort, and in personality that affect how much money people make.

This is not only true of individuals working within the same occupation; it is true even within a family. "There is nearly as much economic inequality among brothers raised in the same homes," Jencks writes, "as in the general population. This means that inequality is recreated anew in each generation, even among people who start life in essentially identical circumstances" (pp. 7–8).

6   Whatever these unmeasured characteristics are that affect income, they seem *not* to be qualities bred by schools. North American schools do not function as a principal agency of indoctrination, discipline, or character molding.

Do the higher earnings of the more highly schooled result from a work-oriented competence produced by the schools, or is the correlation between income, occupation, and schooling due to other factors? It depends.

The answer to this question will vary somewhat with the kind of work. It is apparent that some schooling yields information which, when mixed with talent, produces a highly paid skill. Becoming an electrical engineer or a neurosurgeon are cases in point. However, if the job scene is viewed *in general,* it then appears that schools have been *oversold* as instruments for increasing the productivity—the value, that is—of workers.

This does not deny the soundness of the popular advice that says "If you want to get a good job, get a good education." Our question raises a different issue. It asks whether the higher education was really necessary for the better job. It asks whether, in qualifying for the higher position, it is the educational *credential* that counts or some *skill* that is distinctively signified by that credential.

A continuing series of studies addressed to this and related issues has been conducted at Columbia University under its Conservation of Human Resources Project. In this series the sociologist Ivar Berg (1970) has produced a study entitled *Education and Jobs* that answers our question. His answer is summarized by his subtitle, *The Great Training Robbery.*

Berg used data gathered by the U.S. Department of Labor, by the armed services, and by the federal civil service to ascertain to what extent the educational prerequisites for jobs were relevant to the performance required by the work. He concludes that Americans have been suffering from an "education craze." Over time there has been a tendency for more and more people to be in jobs that require *less* schooling than they have. In some types of work, there is evidence that higher education is a hindrance. For example, in the selling of insurance, salesmen with *less* schooling are more successful than the highly certificated (Ginzberg, 1970, p. xiii).

With the increased schooling of a population, employers have shown a tendency to elevate their educational demands without regard to the significance of the school credential to the work to be done. At the same time there are numbers of *schooled* persons who are not well enough *educated* to be satisfactorily employed (pp. 214–216). In short, *there is now only a loose and uncertain relation between what diplomas are believed to signify, what their holders can and cannot do, and what jobs require.*

Berg's data demonstrate that beyond some minimum of schooling, the crucial factors determining one's job performance are personality and environmental conditions, *not* educational qualifications. This finding accords with that of the Stanford studies.

What an *optimum* level of education might be for each job is not specified. What is clear from Berg's research, however, is that employers, economists, and educators have helped spread the ideology of education, with all the risks attendant upon the production of a surplus of overly schooled workers. The United States, for example, confronts a possible oversupply of certificated manpower (Ehrich, 1974; Ginzberg, 1972).

If schooling, occupational status, and income are correlated, not directly and causally, but by reason of factors *other* than the particular skills produced by the schools, then additional questions are suggested—questions whose answers are subversive of the ideology of education. For example: To what extent does a diploma signify a competence? How much education results from going to school? Do less able students learn more from going to school with more able students?

Does going to school give one an education? Yes and no.

An adequate answer to this question is unavailable, but there are enough data to indicate that going to school, particularly in the United States, need not yield much of an education. The United States is singled out because, despite its tremendous expenditure on schools and the increase over the past decades in the certification of its teachers, this country does poorly in comparison with other modern lands in teaching its children how to use their language and how to calculate.

For example, Buswell (1958) reports the results of a graded arithmetic test given a cross-section of 3,191 eleven-year-olds in England and 3,179 children of like age in California. Of the seventy test problems, 428 students in England solved fifty-three or more correctly. *Not one child* in California achieved as high a score.

Similarly, Husén (1967) and his associates tested the mathematics skills of 132,775 students, age thirteen, in 5,348 schools in twelve countries: Australia, Belgium, England, Finland, France, Israel, Japan, the Netherlands, Scotland, Sweden, the United States, and West Germany. Japan had the best record and Sweden the worst, with the United States next to last. Thirty-one percent of the Japanese sample scored among the upper 10 percent of all students, while only 4 percent of the Americans achieved this level. It is notable that many sons of unskilled workers in Japan were better at mathematics than many sons of college-trained professionals in the United States. The authors of this study believe that neither American students nor their teachers are interested in mathematics.

The philosopher Arendt (1958) attributes "the crisis" in American education to three disastrous educational assumptions:

1 That "the child's world or the society that children form among themselves is independent by nature and must . . . be left to them to govern" (p. 500).
2 That a teacher is a person "who can simply teach anything; his training is in teaching—not in the mastery of any particular subject" (p. 501).

3 That "you can only know and understand what you have done yourself. . . . [The application] to education is as primitive as it is obvious: to substitute . . . doing for learning . . . and to obliterate . . . the distinction between play and work—in favor of the former" (p. 501–502).

Whatever the sources of this American weakness, the results are shocking. *A sample of the loose connection between getting a diploma and having a skill* illustrates the point:

1 "According to the Economic Development Council of New York, there are at least 10,000 clerical jobs unfilled in the city because firms cannot find enough high school graduates who can read and write" (Editorial, Television Station WNBC, New York, cited by Council for Basic Education, 1971a, p. 14).

2 *"The Detroit News* reports that councilmen in that city were shocked last month to find that some high school graduates can't read well enough to decipher their diplomas. The facts came to light in a discussion of . . . an anti-poverty effort to retrain 2,200 out-of-school, unemployed youths. The project director told the city council that 84 percent of the group were *high school graduates,* but that many could not read at the *second-grade* level and many could not pass seventh-grade arithmetic tests" (Council for Basic Education, 1965, p. 7, emphasis added).

3 The U.S. Defense Department's compensatory education effort, "Project 100,000," has been given to men among whom "45 percent [were] *high school graduates,* but only 20 percent [of whom] tested at eighth grade or above in reading, and only seven percent . . . at eighth grade or above in arithmetic" (Council for Basic Education, 1970, p. 8, emphasis added).

4 "Jerome W. Hull, president of Pacific Telephone Company, California's largest employer, is unhappy with the product of our schools who apply for jobs. Four out of every ten high school graduates interviewed for jobs by PT&T, or 120,000 individuals a year, cannot measure up to the company's reading and writing standards, which are about at eighth-grade level" (Council for Basic Education, 1971b, p. 15).

Given such sorry facts, it is no surprise to read that some students are suing teachers for malpractice. The press carries a report (UPI,1973c) of an eighteen-year-old California youth who is suing teachers and school officials for $1 million because he was graduated from high school with B-minus grades although he is able to read at only a fifth-grade level. School systems are now being charged with fraud (Educational Policy Research Corporation, 1973).

A roster such as this angers. It angers teachers who feel insulted, taxpayers who feel cheated, and students who feel deprived. It angers others who believe that reading, writing, and arithmetic are no longer "relevant" capabilities. As one Canadian minister of education put it in a conversation, "Reading requirements are reactionary." His opinion is seconded by an American linguist who claims that the ability to read "is not a necessary part of being civilized or uncivilized, useful or useless" (O'Neil, 1970, p. 260). These views are given implicit support by the United States Supreme Court, which has recently held (Oregon v. Mitchell, 1971) that the ability to read and write is not a necessary qualification for voters in federal elections.

Whatever one's emotional response to the uncertain connection between schooling and education, the fact of a gap remains. The looseness of this connection further challenges the necessity of years of schooling as the only way of getting ahead.

It bears repeating that this conclusion says nothing about the *minimum* educational requirements essential for getting ahead or desirable for citizens of a democracy. What has been challenged is the alleged *necessary* relationship between years of schooling, educated skills, and the requirements of many jobs.

If poorer academic performers go to school with better performers, does it improve the academic achievement of the less able children? Probably not.

Educators continue to quarrel about teaching strategies—in particular, whether it benefits or harms children to attend classes with pupils of similar or different academic ability. It was once believed to have been a kindness, and a sign of progress, that retarded children were placed in separate classes so that differential attention could be given the "special child." It was believed to be an advantage for both the slow and rapid learners for them to be in separate "streams" in the schools so that they need not hamper each other's work or provide invidious comparisons within the classroom.

Recently, however, the separation of children by academic ability or interest has come under attack for many reasons, a chief one being the fact that ability "streaming" results in a clustering of children along social class lines and, in some places, by ethnic membership. It has been argued that such separation reduces the educational opportunities of the disadvantaged classes or minorities without enhancing the opportunities of the advantaged.

This argument takes on a terrible importance in the United States, where a history of enforced racial segregation is in the process of being overcome. The United States Supreme Court, in its famous decision *Brown v. Board of Education,* 1954, ruled that it was unconstitutional to use local laws to compel the racial separation of children in public schools. Social scientists played a significant role in this decision by testifying that such segregation was damaging to the self-conceptions of the minority children (Clark, 1954). This social science testimony has itself been challenged (Van den Haag, 1960); but regardless of the validity of the social science employed, the enforced segregation of persons by reason of race is a dying practice. There is now no industrialized state outside the Republic of South Africa that legally compels the segregation of schoolchildren by ethnicity.

Since the legally enforced segregation of children has been deemed harmful to their confidence and to their opportunity to learn, it has been inferred that *any* separation of children by categories of social class, ethnicity, or sex may be equally unjust. The United States, alone among modern states, has moved vigorously to force an ethnic balancing of children in its schools. Where the normal processes of voluntary association and residence have resulted in local schools that are preponderantly black, white, Chicano, Oriental, or Indian, the United States government has used the power of the courts and federal funds to compel a more representative ethnic mixing of students. The avowed objectives are integration and the provision of equal opportunity to learn.

A Note on "Integration"   Before examining the results of this federal policy, it will be helpful to clarify our language. The verb "to segregate" means to set apart from the group. It comes from the Latin meaning "to part from the flock." In the context of this public issue, the verb popularly used as its opposite is "to integrate." This usage is inexact.

"To integrate" means to make whole. It connotes the restoration of a unity, a oneness. More accurately, the opposite of segregation is congregation. "To congregate" is to gather with the flock. Our language tells us, then, that *it is possible for people to congregate without integrating.*

This distinction is noted because the enforced association of persons of diverse cultures produces their congregation without necessarily effecting their integration. Those who advocate compulsory congregation hope, of course, that such enforced mixing will result in integration. Realization of this hope depends upon the *similarities* of the cultures brought together and the *proportions* of their carriers who congregate. The more similar the cultures and the smaller the minority, the more readily does congregation lead to integration (Berelson and Steiner, 1964, p. 515).

What Are the Academic Results of Enforced Congregation?   *If* the sign of equal educational opportunity is equal academic productivity, then, to date, the enforced mixing of cultures in the American schools has not achieved its objective.

The Coleman study found what smaller investigations have noted for decades—that there is an ethnic gradient in academic performance. In American schools the children of Chinese, Japanese, and Jewish parents consistently do well on standardized tests of academic achievement, verbal and nonverbal. The children of Amerindian, Latin, and black parents do less well on the same tests. Compared with the latter three minorities, white children in general have better records of academic achievement.

The continuing question is, "What causes this?" As we have seen, it is part of the ideology of education to assume that such differences reflect principally differences in educational opportunity. The finding of the Coleman study that, at least as objectively measured, ethnic minorities were *not* attending inferior schools presents a challenge to this assumption. However, another finding of the Coleman research bolstered the hope that balancing the ethnic mixture in schools might reduce the gap in academic performance. The Coleman study found that black children in schools with *high proportions* of whites did better on achievement tests than did black children in more segregated schools. A conclusion *erroneously drawn* from this finding was that this correlation indicated a causation, and that, as the U.S. Commissioner of Education, Howe, then inferred, if the "right" congregation of black and white students were effected, the performance of the minority would improve.

The trouble with this reasoning is that correlations by themselves do not prove a causal connection. One cannot conclude that it was the seating of black students with white ones that produced the observed difference in the performance of black children without first having controlled for the informal selection of black children by their preschool abilities for attendance in the predominantly white schools of higher socioeconomic constituency.

The error in attempting to draw a causal inference from this correlation was immediately apparent to some black leaders. For example, Floyd McKissick (1966), then head of the Congress for Racial Equality, angrily noted that such a causal conclusion from a mere association is tantamount to saying, "mix Negroes with Negroes and you get stupidity." McKissick's criticism of the too easy assumption of causation from a correlation is strengthened by observation of black excellence in particular black schools (Sowell, 1974).

More academically, the psychologist Dyer (1968) has pointed out that the student body correlates of educational achievement cannot be interpreted as supporting "the flat assertion in the summary of the Coleman Report that 'if a minority pupil from a home without much educational strength is put with schoolmates with strong educational backgrounds, his achievement is likely to increase.' Quite the contrary. There is nothing whatever in the Coleman analysis that can justify such an inference. The Coleman study contains no data at all on the effects that might accrue from 'putting' minority pupils with different kinds of schoolmates" (p. 53).

Despite such warnings, the enforced congregation of pupils of diverse ethnicity has become American governmental policy. Policy measures can be evaluated on moral grounds, of course, as good or bad in themselves. In the context of the concern with getting ahead, however, the *morality* of a policy of enforced congregation is not at issue. Sociologists, this one included, have no greater competence than any other observers for making a *moral* evaluation of this policy. What social scientists can assess are some of the consequences of the policy and, in particular, whether it has achieved one of its objectives, the improvement of the academic work of certain minorities.

A number of studies have been conducted in American cities in an attempt to evaluate the effects of enforced school congregation. There have been projects, for example, in New York City, Evanston, Berkeley, Boston, Hartford, New Haven, Philadelphia, and Buffalo. These investigations do *not* confirm the promise that compulsory ethnic congregation of schoolchildren will reduce differences in their academic performance (Jencks et al., 1972, p. 259).

On Testing Social Policy with Social Science

In giving counsel to governments, a social science proceeds best when it tests specific programs designed to produce a result against the "null hypothesis." The null hypothesis assumes that no difference has been produced by a particular intervention. Scientists can then examine the results of a policy change to ascertain whether it has made a sufficient difference to justify rejecting the hypothesis of no difference. In debater's language, "the burden of proof is on the affirmative." Those who claim that their program has produced some desired change must prove it. The scientist need not *disprove* it. He only observes results to see whether there have been changes consequent upon an experiment and whether the changes are sufficiently great to warrant rejecting the assumption that the program has done nothing.

From the data at hand, the most reasonable inference is that the American experiment in reducing academic differentials through ethnic balancing has not worked.

This conclusion is still disputed. The interested student can sample this debate in a concentrated form in the exchange between Pettigrew and colleagues and Armor (1973). The debate illustrates Wilson's "two laws" (1973) of evaluation research:

> *First Law:* All policy interventions in social problems produce the intended effect—*if* the research is carried out by those implementing the policy or their friends.
> *Second law:* No policy intervention in social problems produces the intended effect—*if* the research is carried out by independent third parties, especially those skeptical of the policy.

Wilson's "laws" become valid because the debate on the results of school congregation is energized by more than scientific motives. Moral preferences are at stake. Those who dislike the negative conclusion are fearful that its publicity will be used to fight continuing efforts to integrate a nation through the congregation of its people. This moral objective must stand on its own merits. The *morality* of busing, or any other form of compulsory congregation, ought not to be confused, however, with its *practical* effects. These effects are more than one. Our discussion has been limited to one concern only—whether academic achievement, and the occupational careers dependent upon it, are equalized through an ethnic balancing of school attendance. The negative answer weakens the ideology of education.

WHAT DOES IT ALL MEAN?

The conclusions to be pulled from this mass of data can be used to take personal advice and to inform social policy.

The Personal Advice

In personal matters it is far from certain that we act upon advice and it is even debatable whether we *can* do so, but we continue to seek guidance.

For those who would get ahead, the research on vertical mobility suggests the following cautions—apart from the counsel to "choose" to have talent, the "correct" parents, the "right" temperament, and a lively pattern of interests:

1 Do *not* leave school early for a low-paying job.
2 There is more than one way to get ahead. Find out early where your vocational interests lie, ascertain how to develop the skills that will satisfy those interests, and get "on track."
3 Be ready to *move* to improve your educational and vocational chances.
4 Do *not* beget children soon after marriage (or before marriage, for that matter), and do *not* produce "too many" of them.

On Social Policy

If, as a citizen:

1 You want equality of *educational achievement,* equal schools are not enough.
2 You want equality of *economic condition,* neither equal schools nor equal education is enough. Political coercion will be required (Jencks et al., 1972, pp. 264–265).

There *is* an association between years of school attendance and income within a population. It is to be noted, however, that this is only a correlation which, from our studies, does not indicate a necessary connection. We are cautioned against leaping from correlations to causes, particularly when we are seeking simple answers to our hearts' questions.

It should be recognized, too, that this association is found when data are plotted for large numbers of people. Since the correlation is less than perfect, there are many exceptions to the tendency for incomes to increase with schooling. In short, there is more than one path to success and, for any society, there is an unknown optimum of schooling beyond which no job-related skills are acquired.

The concern with improving the economic lives of individuals within rich societies is linked to a concern with elevating the material standard of living among the poor majority of mankind. While the global issue is not of such immediately personal import to most citizens in developed countries, the facts of world poverty and population increase will, nonetheless, affect our future.

Chapter 11

Poverty and Population

Our world has undergone a threatening transformation during the past thirty years. Good intentions have employed medical science to reduce death rates dramatically. This change has unleashed the human potential to reproduce, and our species, unconstrained by the classic population checks of famine, disease, war, or what Malthus (1803) called "moral restraint," is blooming.

THE FACTS OF LIFE

The facts of world population increase are straightforward and well publicized. The implications of these facts remain in dispute. However, insofar as we can count people and make estimates of their numbers, it is appropriate to call the recent increase in population an explosion.

The awesome nature of this revolution in reproduction has been estimated by the biologist Hardin (1972, p. 169). His calculations are listed in Table 11-1. These tabulations are, of course, crude approximations to the actual numbers of human beings on earth since accurate counting of people is difficult and far from universal. Although the ancient Romans and Jews counted their numbers, much of the world has not done so and at least thirty modern countries still do not do so (*Newsweek,* 1974b). Furthermore, even governments that do take censuses make errors in their tallies. However, if we consider Hardin's figures

Table 11-1 Population Growth in Times Past World Population Estimates from Deevey (1960), Carr-Saunders (1936), and United Nations: Time Reckoned with Reference to Year A.D. 1970*

Years in past	Date	World population in millions	Average growth rate In interval, percent per year	Doubling time in years
1,000,000		0.125	0.000297	233,333
300,000		1.00	0.000439	158,060
25,000		3.34	0.00310	22,335
10,000		5.32	0.0697	994
6,000		86.5	0.0108	6,445
2,000		133.00	0.0840	826
320	1650	545.00	0.290	239
220	1750	728.00	0.438	158
170	1800	906.00	0.514	135
120	1850	1,171.00	0.636	109
70	1900	1,608.00	0.660	105
50	1920	1,834.00	0.911	76
40	1930	2,008.00	0.991	70
30	1940	2,216.00	0.826	84
20	1950	2,406.00	2.14	33
10	1960	2,972.00	2.03	35
0	1970	3,632.00	2.00†	35†

*From Garrett Hardin, *Exploring New Ethics for Survival* © 1968, 1972 by Garrett Hardin. Reprinted by permission of The Viking Press.
†Figures supplied from Freedman and Berelson (1974).

as estimates of magnitude rather than as precise tabulations, we see a picture of our globe on which there may have been no more than 125,000 humans a million years ago. Since then, the rate of human increase has probably *averaged* about one-thousandth of 1 percent per year. At such an average growth rate, it requires 67,447 years for a population to double.

By contrast, the current rate of population increase throughout the world is estimated to be about *2 percent per year,* a rate that doubles the population in *thirty-five years.* Starting at the present, Hardin calculates that, if human beings were to continue to reproduce at the rate at which they did during the 1960s, "there would be literally 'standing room only' on all the land areas of the world in only 615 years" (p. 172).

This unpleasant possibility is made more awkward by the fact that the worldwide average rate of growth is unequally distributed among countries. The sad fact of life is that it is the poorer lands, rather than the richer ones, that are increasing at rates higher than the average. The population of India, for example, is now growing at a rate that will double the numbers of its poor people in about twenty-eight years. It is estimated that all of Latin America is increasing at about 2.6 percent per year, a rate that will double its population in twenty-seven years (Fraser, 1971, p. 198). Particular areas have even *higher* rates of increase. Colombia, for example, is increasing at a rate that will double its size in about twenty-three years and, in some rural areas, its present rate of increase approaches a *doubling in sixteen years* (Lyle, 1967).

FEEDING PEOPLE

When populations increase at such high rates, their need for food increases at a faster rate. This is simply a result of the fact that the amount of food required by a developing human being increases steadily from birth into the late teens. Poor countries whose people double every generation have populations about half of whom are under fifteen years of age. Thus Bennett (1970) estimates that just "to maintain the Indian population at its present level of nutrition would require 20 percent more food in 1975 than in 1965 *if no new children were added during this ten-year period"* (p. 91, emphasis his).

Facts such as these should be interpreted against the present condition of undernourishment (insufficient calories) and malnutrition (inadequate diet) in the world. The citizens of Canada, the United States, some western European states, Australia, New Zealand, Argentina, and Uruguay consume on the average more than 3,000 calories a day (Fraser, 1971, p. 43). A recommended minimum energy intake is 2,100 calories for the average woman and 2,800 for the average man. *It is estimated that half, or slightly more than half, of the human race consumes less than this recommended minimum.*

Malnutrition is experienced in rich lands as well as in poor ones, but there remains a strong tendency for the quality of a diet to drop as the amount of food decreases. Thus in addition to the approximately half of the world that does not get enough food today, probably another one-fourth does not get an adequate diet. For example, Fraser (1971, p. 43) tells us that, while a typical North American diet is only about one-quarter carbohydrate, the average Asian diet is about three-quarters carbohydrate and deficient, of course, in protein.

In brief, most of the world is poorly fed *now*. In 1972 it was estimated that between 10 and 20 million people were dying of starvation each year[1] (Ehrlich and Ehrlich, 1972, p. 319). By 1974 climatic changes had produced droughts in Africa and Asia that have helped cause what may be the greatest famine in history, with between 30 and 100 million people estimated to be slowly starving (Dickinson, 1974).

Two programs have been suggested in the relief of hunger—one is to increase the production of food, the other is to reduce the growth of population. Both programs will have to be implemented if hunger is to be relieved, but the first program will not work without the second. Indeed, the second policy is more important than the first. Efforts to control population

---

[1]People who die of "starvation" usually die of disease, tuberculosis in particular. However, in hungry countries, both the citizens and their physicians recognize the connection between famine and vulnerability to disease and attribute the deaths of the undernourished to lack of food rather than to a bacillus.

growth are more important than efforts to increase food supplies because the earth is finite and because it is easier to create babies than it is to produce food.

ARTICLES OF FAITH

People who can remain unconvinced of the dangers of such facts of life are indeed fortified by faith. Two major faiths deny the urgency of controlling the world's population growth—Roman Catholic Christianity and Marxism. These religions make strange bedfellows, but they are powerfully organized and the instruments of their propaganda combine to make difficult any rational attention to the reduction of misery. Both organizations—the Church and the communist parties—claim special knowledge of "the working of things"— God's law in the first case and the laws of history in the second. God's law is said to condemn "artificial" birth control as a form of murder. The Marxian laws of history reveal birth control to be unnecessary because communism will allegedly increase production so that more people will have more to eat.

The Catholic position has been in flux and continues to receive varying interpretation. Some spokesmen are firmly opposed to birth control, apparently by whatever means and whatever the circumstances. For example, the Jesuit Hanley (1946) told a Harvard conference on "Tomorrow's Children" that "no social power and no conceivable set of circumstances can justify birth control." Another speaker, Taylor (1952), is reported to have said that "no stress of poverty, no health reason, no prediction of a doctor, no economic struggle—in a word no reason whatsoever, can render it [artificial birth control] allowable."

For centuries the official attitude of the Church condemned contraception as a form of homicide (Noonan, 1965, pp. 168–169). However, in 1930 a section of the papal encyclical *Casti connubii* was interpreted to allow a "natural" form of birth control *if* there was a "serious motive" for limiting reproduction. "The means permitted by the Catholic Church are based upon what Pope Pius XI referred to . . . as 'the circumstance of time' known as the Safe Period method," write the editors of *Fortune* (1938). This so-called "rhythm method" of birth control involves abstaining from sexual intercourse during the woman's fecund period in her menstrual cycle. It is, of course, among the least efficient procedures of spacing pregnancy and it cannot be counted on to reduce the disastrous effects of an exponentially increasing population in a finite world. Nevertheless, the rhythm method remains the one religiously lawful method of birth control according to Catholic doctrine *if* the procedure is adopted for "just motives." This position was reaffirmed in the encyclical *Humanae vitae* (1968) of Pope Paul VI, which reiterated that

> Each and every marriage act must remain open to the transmission of life. . . .
> Abortion, even if for therapeutic reasons [is] absolutely excluded . . . [so also is]
> sterilization, whether perpetual or temporary, whether of the man or of the woman.
> Similarly excluded is every action which, either in anticipation of the conjugal act,
> or in its accomplishment, or in the development of the natural consequences,
> proposes, whether as an end or as a means, to render procreation impossible.

Catholic doctrine is being contested from within the faith. Although the large family remains a Catholic ideal, there is evidence that Catholic couples do not conform completely to the religious restrictions against birth control. Surveys in the United States indicate that more than half of Catholic spouses use contraceptive methods that are condemned by their church (Birmingham, 1964; Freedman et al., 1959, pp. 182–186; Petersen, 1969; pp. 190, 537–539). American studies of attitudes toward fertility control and of the practice of such control both reveal an increasing endorsement of "artificial" contraception by Catholic women (Westoff and Ryder, 1967, 1969).

In addition, the Catholic clergy is now divided on the dogma of contraception and abortion (Moore, 1974). A survey of opinion among 1,640 priests in the state of New York reports that "nearly four in ten priests . . . say that they disagree with or have doubts about the 'traditional Church teaching regarding direct abortion'" (Traina, 1974, p. 152).

The communist faith has its own texts in the works of Marx, Engels, and Lenin to justify optimism in the face of poverty and fertility. Engels (1844), for example, believed that

> . . . the productive power at the disposal of mankind is immeasurable. The productivity of land can be infinitely increased by the application of capital, labor and science. . . . Capital increases daily; labor power grows together with population; and science masters natural forces for mankind to a greater extent every day. This immeasurable productivity, administered consciously and in the interests of all, would soon reduce to a minimum the labor falling to the lot of mankind.

We can excuse Engels his ignorant optimism by noting that he wrote over a hundred years ago. It is more difficult, however, to pardon his vague and hopeful language about productive power being "immeasurable" and the productivity of land being "infinite." *Neither land nor its productivity is infinite.*

Communist writers continue to use such passionate language nevertheless, and their emotionally laden terms serve to cloud our thinking. For example, the former Soviet Party Secretary Nikita Khrushchev (1954) told a communist youth organization that "the theory of overpopulation [is a] cannibalistic theory [invented by] bourgeois ideologists." Just as some Christians call demographers' proposals for reducing the rate of population increase murder, advocates of the New Left call these policies "genocide" (Weissman, 1971, pp. xviii–xx). Dictionaries tell us that "genocide" means "the deliberate and systematic extermination of a national or racial group," a policy that no ecologist has recommended. The "hot word" has its propaganda value, however, which is to say, its anti-intellectual uses.

The United Nations and Facts of Life   The United Nations declared 1974 to be "World Population Year." In an attempt to sponsor global cooperation in meeting the population problem, the UN sponsored an international conference in Bucharest to which 141 countries sent delegates. At this congress communist and Catholic spokesmen and some other religionists repeated their articles of faith. They refused to accept rapid population increase as an obstacle to economic well-being and held that the attainment of "social justice" and the wider use of science would *improve* the lives of even the *doubled* population that is expected on earth by the year 2000.

China's representative Yu Wang said that "predictions that the world's population will double every thirty-five years were only 'meant to frighten people'" (Reuter, 1974).

Another Chinese representative, Hsu Shou-yen, assured his UN audience that "pessimistic views are groundless. The future of mankind is infinitely bright."

India's Karan Singh argued that "They shout and scream about 'standing room only,' but we believe in reincarnation, my friend, so don't worry. You'll be back."

And Nigeria's representative, Dr. Dora Obi Chizea, added this bit of logic: "You cannot scare us by saying that we will die of hunger, because we die of hunger every day" (*Newsweek,* 1974b).

Such faithful refusal to face facts guarantees pain. Famine is now daily news (Kann, 1974a, 1974b; *U.S. News & World Report,* 1974d; Vicker, 1974).

For those of us to whom the facts of population increase and hunger are real, neither the emotional language nor the promises of faithful protagonists is convincing. Biologists repeatedly advise us that we live in a "web of life" and that we are dependent on the resources of a limited sphere. "We live on a spaceship," Hardin (1972) reminds us. "*Men* can escape from it, but *mankind* cannot" (p. 175, emphasis his).

The biological message is clear: If human beings do not consciously adapt to their increasing numbers and curtail them, other processes will force the adjustment. The other processes run a range from riot and revolution to famine and war. They are at work now, and they all spell death.

Two connected questions arise: Why has population increased so rapidly and what can be done about it?

WHY HAS WORLD POPULATION INCREASED SO RAPIDLY?

Three broad factors account for the recent surge in the number of people on earth: (1) the application of medical science and sanitary engineering to reduce death rates, particularly infant mortality; (2) the fact that people like to have children; and (3) the pleasures of sex and the ignorance of and indifference to contraceptive techniques. All three factors are bolstered, in varying degree, by political and religious preferences.

1 Declining Death Rates

The development of medical science and surgical technology produced a drop in mortality among western Europeans during the latter half of the nineteenth century. As an illustration, in England and Wales in the 1840s the chance of surviving to age *fifteen* was about 6.7 in 100 for a male and about 7.0 for a female. In a hundred years life expectancy had so changed that roughly similar chances obtained in the 1940s that people would live to age *sixty* (Stolnitz, 1955, 1956).

Immediately after World War II, the techniques of modern death prevention were transferred from Europe and North America to Latin America, Asia, Africa, and Oceania with the consequent increase in survival rates and in numbers of people.

2 The Desire for Children

A second cause of the rapid growth of population is the fact that people *like* having children. Surveys around the world show that, on the average, couples want to have four children (Petersen, 1969, pp. 613, 623). In the United States the average number of children desired ranges from 4.0 among Catholic couples whose breadwinner is a professional to 3.4 among Catholic families in which the husband is an unskilled worker. Among eight Protestant denominations, the average number of children desired varies between 2.8 and 3.1, while among Jewish couples, the average considered ideal is 2.7 (Westoff et al., 1961, 1963). At present mortality rates, these numbers of children exceed the number required for generational replacement, and the ideal itself becomes part of the population problem.

People like having children for many reasons in addition to the mixed pleasures of parenthood. In both the West and the East, religions place a sacred value upon procreation. In many cultures family pride requires heirs and masculine pride is appeased by the signs of virility in numerous offspring. Moreover, some status systems accord prestige to the parents of large families, and many governments, including those in North America, reward procreation through tax benefits and child allowances.

In poor lands, children continue to constitute a form of social security and old-age insurance. Last, of course, children in agricultural societies are a form of cheap labor. They are not seen by poor farmers as a *cause* of their poverty but rather as a means of working more land and possibly escaping from poverty (Mamdani, 1973).

These many motives for having children are frequently misunderstood by Western researchers and family planning advocates. Such concerned citizens tend to work with what Benedict (1973) has called "a technological view of birth control." It is the view expressed by a physician Benedict cited as saying:

> Solving the population problem in India is not really all that difficult. One simply needs to distribute the pill to the women, packaged in long strips . . . with instructions to take them daily. They could be delivered to the villages in lorries. Eventually the women's menstrual cycles would be governed by the pills (p. 1045).

This technological view of the reasons for procreation—or, better, for the failure to contraconceive—ignores the multiple motives that sponsor human indifference and hostility to contraception. A review of recent research on family planning concludes that "birth control depends on many more factors than the availability of easily used contraceptives. . . . Birth control succeeds or fails insofar as people see their own individual life chances in terms of more or fewer children" (Benedict, 1973, p. 1046).

Birth control of a magnitude sufficient to reduce the threat of overbreeding requires more than informing people and making contraceptives available. How the contraceptives that are available are used comes down to a matter of motives—a matter of how people want to live and of the consequences that they foresee, or fail to foresee, when they use their sexuality, in or out of marriage. These attitudes are difficult to change. Meanwhile, poverty is ensured in both rich and poor lands by the production of children by parents who cannot and often do not care for them. This is not the *only* cause of poverty; it is, however, one of its guarantees.

3 Inadequate Contraception

The application of science to save lives, especially infant lives, has not been accompanied by as successful a use of science to prevent reproduction, particularly unwanted reproduction. There is, of course, a scientific technology available to reduce unwanted conception, but there is widespread ignorance of these techniques and resistance to the employment of the most efficient contraceptive procedures. The ignorance and the resistance are not limited to so-called underdeveloped countries. Ignorance, indifference, and hostility toward contraception are also apparent in the richer lands. Combining these attitudes with the greater sexual permissiveness experienced in western Europe and North America in recent decades assures an increase in unwanted pregnancy (Blake, 1973).

The Contraceptive Knowledge and Practice of American Teen-age Women

The point is illustrated in the results of interviews conducted in 1971 with a national sample of American female teen-agers (Kantner and Zelnik, 1973; Zelnik and Kantner, 1972). Women fifteen to nineteen years of age, 4,611 in number, were asked about their sexual lives. Eight percent of this sample were or had been married. Of the 92 percent who had never been married, about 28 percent reported having had sexual intercourse. This proportion increases with age, of course. While 14 percent of the fifteen-year-olds said they had had heterosexual experience, the proportion rises to 46 percent by age nineteen.

What is significant for present purposes is the ignorance and the carelessness associated with the sex act. For example:

1 "Of the sexually active 15–19-year olds," Kantner and Zelnik write, "*53 percent failed to use any kind of contraception* the last time they had intercourse; and *among the youngest group—those aged fifteen—the figure reaches 71 percent.* The picture for *consistent* use is even worse. *Less than 20 percent* of sexually experienced fifteen-to-nineteen-year-olds report that they

'always' use some method to prevent conception during intercourse. A partial explanation of the low level of current use is the fact that a substantial number of those who have failed to use contraception believe that they cannot become pregnant . . ." (1973, pp. 21–22, emphasis added).

2 Although most teen-agers who did not use a contraceptive at last intercourse believed that they could not become pregnant, a considerable proportion of these women either did not care whether they became pregnant or were trying to have a baby. About one-eighth of the white girls gave these as their reasons for not taking precautions, while about one-fourth of the black girls so responded (1972, p. 370, table 15).

3 Concerning the likelihood of conception at different times during the menstrual cycle, "only about two-fifths of the teenagers had a generally correct idea of the period of greatest risk" (1973, p. 21).

The dominant tendency among these teen-agers is to believe that the time of the menses is the time of greatest risk of pregnancy. This erroneous belief is also widespread among older women (1972, p. 361). Black girls differ from white girls in one significant way with respect to beliefs about times of greatest fecundity: Among black girls who do not believe that the menses are associated with risk of pregnancy, the tendency is to accept another erroneous belief— that the risk of pregnancy is the same throughout the menstrual cycle.

In short, what most young women and many older ones believe about the times of greatest risk of pregnancy is false.

4 "One-fifth of all never-married black females between the ages of 15 and 19 have experienced a pregnancy, a figure almost 10 times the proportion of whites who have ever been pregnant. Differential pregnancy between the sexually active of the two racial groups is considerably smaller but still substantial, with 40.8 percent of these blacks having been pregnant in contrast to 10.0 percent of the whites. The bulk of the ever-pregnant black females, 76.3 percent, have had a child; the remainder either are currently pregnant for the first time or have failed to deliver a live birth because of a miscarriage, stillbirth, or abortion. In contrast, 37.8 percent of the whites who have been pregnant and have remained unmarried have had a child" (1972, p. 371).

5 "More than seven in 10 sexually experienced teen-agers specify that the pill, condom or withdrawal was the method used most recently" (1973, p. 35).

On this point, it should be noted that contraceptive measures vary greatly in their effectiveness. The most effective method is surgical sterilization. In the female this involves a cutting or tying of the fallopian tubes (salpingectomy), so that ova cannot travel from the ovaries to the uterus. This is a major operation, although it can be performed expeditiously during childbirth. In the male, the surgery involves a cutting and tying of the vas deferens (vasectomy), so that sperm are not emitted during ejaculation. This operation is a minor and safe procedure, performed with only a local anesthetic. Surgical sterilization tends to be irreversible, of course.

Second to surgical sterilization, the safest contraceptives are "the pill," a progestin-estrogen tablet taken orally to prevent ovulation, and intrauterine devices. These procedures have an estimated accidental pregnancy risk of between 0.1 and 1.0 percent for the pill and about 1.0 percent for the intrauterine devices (Pincus, 1965, pp. 297–299). By contrast, other contraceptive methods carry a significantly higher pregnancy risk. Diaphragm and spermicide combined have an estimated risk of about 1 in 8; the condom about 1 in 7; coitus interruptus (withdrawal), between 1 in 5 and 1 in 6; spermicide alone, 1 in 5; the rhythm method, between 1 in 2.5 and 1 in 4; and the douche alone, between 1 in 2.5 and 1 in 3 (Pincus, op. cit.).

The Zelnik and Kantner research shows that the pill and the condom are more popular among American blacks than among whites, while withdrawal is more common among white teen-agers. Among white teenage women, the most popular and recently used contraceptives were withdrawal (33.0 percent), pills (25.0 percent), and the condom (21.8 percent). Among black teenage women, the most popular and recently used contraceptives were the condom (32.5 percent), pills (26.5 percent), and douche (12.1 percent; 1972, p. 369, table 14).

In summary, a considerable proportion of American teen-agers engage in sexual intercourse without adequate contraceptive caution. They run high risks of pregnancy and they, their offspring, and society at large pay a high price for their ignorance and their indifference. One reason many people remain poor in industrial societies is that they have children they are not equipped to care for.

And the Poor Get Children

The contribution of fertility to poverty is not limited to teen-agers, of course. Poor people of whatever age, and throughout the world, have more children than they can adequately rear and, frequently, more than they want. As in the case of American teen-agers, this excess fertility is sponsored in part by the desire to have children, but it is also maintained by ignorance, indifference, and fatalism.

The operation of these lazy, fatalistic, and uninformed attitudes is illuminated by a study of working class families in Chicago and Cincinnati. Rainwater and colleagues (1960) interviewed in depth ninety-six persons of diverse religion and ethnicity in a pilot study of the lives of relatively poor people.

The majority of these individuals do not know how the male and female reproductive systems work. Slightly more than one-fourth of these respondents of both sexes believe that getting pregnant is largely the work of the man who "lays the egg" in the woman during intercourse. Rainwater describes this belief as "the father plants it, the mother grows it" (p. 145).

About half of these working class men and women cannot explain pregnancy beyond saying that it results from sexual intercourse. There are, of course, superstitions associated with this ignorance, such as the false beliefs that loving or female orgasm are necessary for pregnancy.

The fatalism is illustratively expressed by the husband in one of Rainwater's families, a family that in five years has had five children, one of them illegitimate. The husband says:

It doesn't make any difference to me how many we have. I like large families. I believe you always manage somehow even if you have a lot of children and they enjoy each other more. . . . I think a couple will have just what they should have. Maybe that's crazy but it is the way I feel. If you aren't supposed to have them, you won't; if you are, you will. . . .

When we talk about this, she says I'm crazy and I should do something to keep from getting her pregnant. She says we have enough now and should not have any more children. I just laugh at her and tell her if she isn't supposed to have them she won't get that way (p. 11).

WHAT IS TO BE DONE?

Students and others who do not believe the facts about human reproduction or who do not recognize the dangers to the good life inherent in rapid population growth do not ask the question, "What is to be done?" If there is no concern, there is no question.

Such less concerned persons believe, with other fatalists, that "things will work out," that technology will provide food and shelter for however many people inhabit the earth, and that no one has a right to deny reproduction to parents or birth to unborn souls. This point of view sees no threat to the quality of life that comes from crowding. It ignores or denies the aesthetic values of space and quiet, along with the engineering problems of disposing of human and industrial waste. It denies, as well, the production difficulties of providing increasing quantities of food, clothing, and shelter to a hungry and yet expectant world.

This unconcerned attitude is supported by each person's immediate interest in his daily life, by the teachings of some powerful ideologies, and by political interests. It is an attitude condoned by an ethic that we shall call suicidal. It receives support, too, from such august bodies as the United Nations. According to its then Secretary General U Thant, the United Nations' *Universal Declaration of Human Rights* (1967) describes "the family as the natural and fundamental unit of society. It follows that any choice and decision with regard to the size of the family must irrevocably rest with the family itself, and cannot be made by anyone else."

On Working Things Out Naturally

It is true that, if we do nothing, "things will work out." Populations that exceed their economic base provoke natural responses that reduce them. Among both human and infrahuman species, these mechanisms have been famine, disease, and killing.[2] As we have noted, these processes are at work *now*. They are not mere threats; they are actualities.

The concern with the good life seeks to avoid these natural responses to overbreeding. It seeks, then, to take thought, to do something rational, to plan. However, every plan of population control thus far conceived is either ineffective or contrary to someone's interest. We have here a fine illustration of

---

[2]The fact that fighting and killing are associated with famine should not be interpreted to mean that overpopulation and hunger are the only causes of war. As we shall see (Chaps. 13–14), there are many occasions and other justifications for our killing each other.

the difference between social problems and social concerns. "Problems," by definition, have solutions, by which is meant relatively cost-free and conflict-free ways out. Concerns, however, confront difficulties. Every rational response to the conditions of poverty and excessive fertility runs into difficulty. The difficulties are costs. These costs mean that there are no solutions to our concerns, but only greater or lesser penalties, of an uncertain gravity and distribution, for every action or inaction. "Inaction" is a misleading term, of course. *Doing nothing does something.* This is to say that there will be undesirable consequences whichever way we turn. This is one sense in which the human situation is tragic.

The Tragedy of the Commons

In an important essay, Hardin (1968) has described the burden of population upon resources as involving "the tragedy of the commons." The tragedy lies in "the remorseless working of things." It lies in the fact that there are foreseeable and unpleasant consequences of our actions that are not transformed by good intention, hope, and promise.

"The commons" is public ground; in the present sense it is our finite globe, on which every human born places a demand for a share of limited resources. According to Hardin, the tragedy of the commons develops in this way:

> Picture a pasture open to all. It is to be expected that each herdsman will try to keep as many cattle as possible on the commons. Such an arrangement may work reasonably satisfactorily for centuries because tribal wars, poaching, and disease keep the numbers of both man and beast well below the carrying capacity of the land. Finally, however, comes the day of reckoning, that is, the day when the long-desired goal of social stability becomes a reality. At this point, the inherent logic of the commons remorselessly generates tragedy.
>
> As a rational being, each herdsman seeks to maximize his gain. Explicitly or implicitly, more or less consciously, he asks, "What is the utility *to me* of adding one more animal to my herd?" This utility has one negative and one positive component.
>
> 1. The positive component is a function of the increment of one animal. Since the herdsman receives all the proceeds from the sale of the additional animal, the positive utility is nearly +1.
>
> 2. The negative component is a function of the additional overgrazing created by one more animal. Since, however, the effects of overgrazing are shared by all the herdsmen, the negative utility for any particular decision-making herdsman is only a fraction of −1.
>
> Adding together the component partial utilities, the rational herdsman concludes that the only sensible course for him to pursue is to add another animal to his herd. And another. . . . But this is the conclusion reached by each and every rational herdsman sharing a commons. Therein is the tragedy. Each man is locked into a system that compels him to increase his herd without limit—in a world that is limited. Ruin is the destination toward which all men rush, each pursuing his own best interest in a society that believes in the freedom of the commons. Freedom in a commons brings ruin to all [p. 12, emphasis Hardin's. © 1968 by The American Association for the Advancement of Science].

The tragedy of the commons is that *there is no merely technical solution* to the miseries being produced by the rapid rise in the numbers of people. Any rational response to this plight involves a challenge to someone's morality. A rational response—one that does not leave human lives subject to the "remorseless workings" of starvation, disease, and warfare—will require a change in morality. The necessity of such a change can be demonstrated and the kind of change can be described, but neither of these expositions will necessarily affect our sense of right and wrong (Nettler, 1973).

Confronting the tragedy, most governments temporize while some governments experiment with campaigns of birth planning. Meanwhile, the historical processes of population reduction—famine, morbidity, infanticide, and abortion—are at work.

Modernization and Birth Control

It has been a working assumption of many demographers that the most effective impulse toward birth reduction is economic development. The reasoning derives from one epoch and from the experience in social structures of a particular sort. In western Europe, and particularly in England, the development of capitalist economies from the nineteenth century onward was associated with the rise of a middle class whose economic aspirations made family limitation sensible. In such "open societies," numerous children were seen as an impediment to class climbing and birth control became rational. The French demographer Dumont (1890) put the rationale bluntly:

> For one who starts at the bottom to arrive at the top, it is necessary to run fast and not to be encumbered with baggage. Thus, while an ambitious man can be served by a good marriage, either because of the wealth or the contracts it brings him, his own children, particularly if they are numerous, almost inevitably slow him down [p. 110].

The Assumption of Demographic Transition   From the differences in the observed reproductive patterns of agricultural and industrial societies, students of population have devised the hypothesis of demographic transition. According to this hypothesis, preindustrial societies are, or were, characterized by high fertility and high mortality, so that the rate of population increase was negligible. Industrial societies were supposed to have fairly stable populations characterized by relatively low fertility and mortality. Societies in transition, changing from agricultural to industrial bases, are characterized as having high birth rates but declining death rates, and, consequently, a high rate of natural increase.

The assumption has been that once the economic transition is made, the usual middle-class aspirations arise that make family limitation rational. The assumption is usually applied with the qualification that it works in the long run, but there is no assurance that this is a causal law of population growth and "the long run" presently is apt to be too long for comfort. The disquieting fact is that during the transition there are forces operating to *increase* reproduction.

Petersen (1969, pp. 608–609) suggests several such factors. Economic development usually means improved health care, and improved health means higher fecundity. In addition, the decline of a traditional society under the impact of industrialization often means a change from later to earlier marriage, the abandonment of old-fashioned modes of population control such as infanticide, and the breakdown of religious practices that once limited natural increase. The movement from polygamy to monogamy in Muslim lands is an example of an institutional change that may increase the fertility of each woman. Last, when economies grow, there is a tendency for marriage rates to increase, and this, in turn, affects reproduction rates.

The fact that fertility declined in Western industrialized countries as their economies developed ought to be interpreted against the background of their particular institutions and social structures. There is no guarantee from this limited experience that the passage of a demographic transition will spare us the pains of population increase in the next decades.

Government Programs of Fertility Reduction

Some states have been aware that they could not wait for a demographic transition to carry them from excessive growth of their populations toward stability. Furthermore, even in those countries that had allegedly undergone the transition, some intellectual leaders urged the need for government action to provide information and clinical services in the reduction of unwanted pregnancy. The concern that motivates the family planning movement in both rich and poor lands is a concern with reducing poverty, dependency, and the harmful effects of being reared as an unwanted child.

The struggle to move governments to action has not been an easy one, however. In the United States as recently as 1971, a federal statute classified contraceptives as "obscene or pornographic materials" and several jurisdictions in Canada and the United States had laws forbidding the sale of contraceptives and even the dissemination of information about them. Reviewing the history of this struggle, Jaffe (1973) notes that

> In 1959, after a Presidential committee had recommended that the U.S. Government provide assistance on population programs to other nations requesting it, discussion of public policy on family planning became linked with discussion of the population problem. The ensuing debate was marked by the opposition of the Catholic bishops of the U.S. to the use of any public funds for birth-control programs at home or abroad and President Eisenhower's statement of opposition to a Government program (he reversed his position four years later) [p. 18].

Jaffe also points out that it was not public monies but private resources which, during the 1960s, developed the two most revolutionary contraceptives—the oral contraceptive and the intrauterine device.

As a result of effort of the planned parenthood movement, the American government has reversed its policy over the past decade. This reversal was also encouraged by the fact that the introduction of family planning services in maternity clinics showed a demand for assistance in family limitation and a physical health benefit from the return of women to these clinics for other kinds of postpartum care.

Japan has a longer record of success in reducing its rate of population increase since World War II. Japan and a few other countries have used a broad and mixed repertoire of family planning projects toward this objective. Propaganda, counseling, and clinical services have been combined to induce changes in attitudes toward birth control. These programs seek to convince people of the advantages of smaller families, to inform them of contraceptive techniques, to reduce the shame associated with the discussion of sexual matters, and to make contraceptives readily available. In addition to these educational measures, some countries have included in their fertility reduction programs projects for the sterilization of volunteers and the provision of legal abortion.

Government programs in the less developed parts of the world have had a checkered career. Where small, stable countries with efficient governments have pressed these programs, they seem to have contributed to lower birth rates. Jamaica, Taiwan, Singapore, South Korea, and Puerto Rico are reported to have been able to reduce the rate of population growth through combinations of propaganda, education, and clinical services. However, the people who have most frequently taken advantage of these programs have been persons with higher standards of living and women who have completed their families, often with four or more children. Extending the limited success of such projects to younger and poorer parents and to the vast masses of Asia, Africa, and Latin America is quite another matter. Many of the rapidly growing countries in these areas have not even started family planning projects. The effort required to bring these populations within the carrying capacity of their economies is tremendous, and it may be beyond the political determination of most impoverished lands.

The magnitude of the effort required is illustrated by the results of fertility reduction programs in several rapidly growing areas. The consistent finding of research on the subject is that people *say* they want fewer children, particularly after they have had three or four, but they do not use the contraceptive methods available to them. They do not use contraceptive techniques for all the well-worn reasons: They are "too much trouble," or one of the spouses does not like the method, or the woman thinks she is "safe," or there are beliefs about the harmful effects of the contraceptive and superstitions about "going against nature."

Experiments show that poor people do not use contraceptive devices efficiently if no more is done than to make them available. For example, Hill and his colleagues (1959) found that, while more than half of a sample of Puerto Rican women had used some method of family limitation, less than one-third had done so regularly. Sterilization seems an easier solution for these women than diligent contraception. About one-fourth indicated that they had been sterilized, another one-fourth said they would like to be, and an additional 14 percent said they planned to be sterilized.

The indifferent use of available contraceptives is also reported in studies of Indian programs. Rao (1959), for example, found that in a sample of 200 couples that had accepted contraceptive suppositories, only 69 ever used the technique and only 25 used the contraceptive regularly. Chandrasekhar (1959) also reports that the same contraceptive, given in another area of India, still allowed more than one-third of the women to become pregnant within two years.

In Japan experiments combining counseling, medical advice, and free contraceptives were able to reduce birthrates significantly (Ozawa, 1955). However, this reduction required regular visits by the studies' physicians and social workers, sympathetic listening, and constant encouragement. In short, changing the *contraceptive habits* of people is a difficult and expensive chore.

Several Indian states have gone beyond educational campaigns for contraception to subsidized sterilization. The laws permitting payment to women and men for their sterilization vary among the jurisdictions and are, at best, half-hearted. The laws require the written consent of both spouses, a minimum age of the petitioner, and a minimum number of living children. It is not surprising that a study of the vasectomy program in one section of India showed that the men receiving this operation were on the average forty years old and had an average of 5.3 children (Dandekar, 1963). Results of this nature are of little help in relieving the pressure of India's population on the land.

Reducing reproduction rates requires governmental will (consensus), massive propaganda, and the neighborhood organization and provision of family planning services. The People's Republic of China, for example, does not rely upon a demographic transition to reduce its rate of population growth. The demographer Stycos (1974) reports that the Chinese

> . . . have put more resources into direct family planning education and services than any other nation. Indeed, . . . Pi-Chao Chen speaks glowingly of the fact that "China has not subscribed to a laissez faire attitude of merely providing contraceptive services, while leaving the decision on family size to individuals. Instead, the Chinese program has stressed the importance of inculcating an ideal family size norm since the early 1960s," and in addition has adopted a "population planning strategy" of encouraging late marriage and "persuading married couples to space births at five-year intervals."

Stycos concludes that "if the Chinese ever believed in 'take care of the people and the population will take care of itself,' they clearly do not believe it now" (p. 163).

Appealing to Conscience

Some years before Hardin described the tragedy of the commons, India's Registrar General recognized it (Gopalaswami, 1951). He defined having more than three children as "improvident maternity," and his response to his recognition was the common one—an appeal to conscience. In reporting the Indian census, Gopalaswami wrote:

> The task before the nation is first of all to bring about such a change in the climate of public opinion that every married couple will accept it as their duty (to themselves, to their family, and to that larger family—the nation) that they should avoid improvident maternity. The occurrence of improvident maternity should evoke social disapproval, as any other form of anti-social self-indulgence [pp. 218–219].

Thirty years later, the UN Population Conference concluded with a similar appeal to people to be "responsible." Summarizing the work of this congress, the noted anthropologist Margaret Mead (1974) writes that "to the human right of individuals and couples to decide on the number and spacing of their children, there is now [added] the responsibility for the well-being of future children and the community."

This sounds as though something new had been added to plans to relieve poverty. However, Mead's statement predicates nothing. It sermonizes. Such appeals to conscience seldom stimulate motives. Appeals to conscience affect those who already have the requisite morals, but they are ineffective with those who do not agree with the message. The appeal to conscience is, in Hardin's phrase, "self-eliminating."

> People vary. Confronted with appeals to limit breeding, some people will undoubtedly respond to the plea more than others. Those who have more children will produce a larger fraction of the next generation than those with more susceptible consciences. The differences will be accentuated, generation by generation. . . .
> The argument has here been stated in the context of the population problem, but it applies equally to an individual exploiting a commons to restrain himself for the general good—by means of his conscience. To make such an appeal is to set up a selective system that works toward the elimination of conscience from the race [p. 1246.]

Hardin's argument does not propose that conscience is inherited. His logic operates whether conscience is transmitted genetically or whether it is, as we believe, learned. The appeal to conscience to bridle self-interest is not only largely futile but the effects it has are apt to be harmful.

Challenge and Response

Our concern with survival and with improving the quality of our lives is challenged by the global increase in population. This rapid growth makes it improbable that the next decades will witness an improvement in the material standard of living of the majority of mankind.

When faced with a threat to the goodness of our present lives and to our aspirations for better lives, there are three policies we can adopt, none of which assures happy results. We can try to run away from the trouble; we can deny its gravity and sit back and see what happens; or we can confront the threat and try to control it.

In the case of the world increase in population, there is, finally, nowhere to run. For the present there are state boundaries that separate rich and poor lands, but the earth remains finite as it shrinks, and the consequences of overbreeding in one part of the globe affect other parts.

There is a strong inclination to follow the second policy, to discount the facts of life and to believe that "something will happen" to save us from our increasing numbers.

This inertia is motivated in part by the uncertainty of every future. If the future is less than clear, then the demographer's projections may be disputed. The dispute is fatiguing, and one way we respond to the fatigue is with apathy. There are daily lives to be lived, and it is more comfortable to attend to these immediacies than to plan for emergencies that may not occur.

This wait-and-see attitude is supported by yet another interest, our interest in freedom. *Our freedom to do as we want, including to breed as we wish, is threatened by any rational plan to reduce birthrates.*

When the commons is threatened, the only rational response is to invent controls that limit the self-interested action of everyone. The subject of social control always raises the question of justice, that is, of the fairness of the rules and the legitimacy of those delegated to enforce them. We become concerned with the ancient question: "Who controls the custodians?"

There is no perfect answer to this question. A republican (small-r) answer is to divide power among the custodians we have elected and to define the divisions of power by a contract. The contract, often called a constitution, permits "mutual coercion, mutually agreed upon" (Hardin, 1968, pp. 1246). The mutual agreement represents an exchange, an abandoning of freedom in return for a similar restriction upon others so that the commons will not be overrun. Such a social contract is not engaged until a majority of people who would live together perceives its necessity. On our globe, this majority perception of the population explosion does not yet prevail.

Being Rational versus Being Moral

This is the trap we are in. We are in this predicament because our appetites are at war with the conditions of our lives. What we want—in this case, the freedom to reproduce—will defeat other desires, such as the possibility of more people being well fed, well housed, and happy. When we try to use our heads to get out of this predicament, we run into another conflict—that between rationality and morality.

There is a difference between being rational and being moral. For some, the difference is difficult to comprehend because both words are "good" words. We claim a preference for being rational *and* for being moral. However, what is rational in a particular context may not be moral. The terms deserve definition because *the threat of global population pressure will not be met rationally until there has been a change in morality.*

To be rational is to employ one's reason to select the most appropriate means for the attainment of an empirical goal (Cousineau, 1967). This definition says several things. It says, first, that a rational act is a purposive act. It is consciously engaged in in order to obtain an objective. Purely expressive behavior, like dancing for joy, is its own end. It is, thereby, nonrational without being irrational.

Second, this definition limits the objectives of a rational act to those that can be tested in experience. When one is behaving rationally, it is possible to ascertain whether his goals have been achieved. Did doing this get you that? Objectives that can never be *experienced*—such as getting to heaven or achieving "the greatest good for the greatest number"—such objectives may be good goals, but they are not rational ones. One can never know whether they have been realized.

Last, we call an act rational not when it has led to success accidentally, but only when there has been an informed choice of the most economical means.

To be moral, however, is something else. To be moral may or may not be rational. Efficiency is not the same as morality, and neither the objective of a rational act nor the means used to attain it need be moral. In contrast, a moral act is one that conforms to a social rule that is considered by our group to be superior and legitimate (Ladd, 1957, pp. 101–107). The "superiority" of a moral prescription lies in its *priority* and in its *autonomy.*

The priority of a moral commandment is its demand that it precede other considerations. Morality requires that its prescribed conduct be placed before efficiency.

The autonomy of a moral code is its ultimacy. While moral feelings may be given justification, they are not justified and cannot be justified nonmorally. A moral statement is the end of argument. One either has the moral sense of his tribe or he does not. Every appeal to reason in defense of a moral prescription rests upon moral grounds, not empirical ones. The sign that someone has touched our morality is that we believe certain actions to be right or wrong regardless of their consequences.

When our morality and that of another tribe conflict, there is no objective way to resolve the issue. The conflict is never decided by reference to facts. It is decided by living apart and ignoring and despising the persons of barbarian morality or by killing each other. As we shall see (Chaps. 13–14), human beings have long killed each other for moral reasons, and we continue to do so.

The conflict between some present moralities and efficiency in meeting our concern with poverty and overpopulation will not be resolved in any textbook. It will be worked out historically. That means painfully. The conflict can be illustrated, however, in one debate: that about abortion.

The Abortion Issue

People who do not adequately restrict *conception* will restrict their *reproduction.* This statement is not a recommendation; it is a fact. Infanticide, the killing of a child after its birth, and abortion, the killing of the embryo or fetus,[3] are practices as old as history.

Infanticide is now condemned in all developed countries, although it has been a common practice in hunting and agricultural societies. The moral attitude toward abortion is less clear, however. In fact, even its definition is vague. The roots of the word "abortion" mean to prevent from coming into being. In the physician's vocabulary, to abort means to miscarry, to give bith prematurely, or to cause a premature delivery. In the lawyer's language, on the other hand, the word usually refers to illegal actions taken to prevent the development of an embryo or fetus. The vagueness of the term has moved the World Health Organization to avoid using it in its vital statistics (United Nations, 1954, p. 4).

In the public debate about abortion, what is at issue is the morality and the legality of the *intentional* destruction of the fertilized human egg. It can only be guessed how much abortion, in this sense, occurs. Freedman (1965) believes that abortion "may be the most widely used single method in the world today." The anthropologist Devereux (1955) examined reports on 400 preliterate societies and could find only one in which induced abortion did not occur.

When one tries to count the number of illegal abortions, his figures become guesses. An American conference devoted to this and related questions (Calderone, 1958) placed the range of illegal abortions from at least 5 percent of all conceptions to as high as 23 percent. For a working figure, Hardin (1973b, p. 13) compromises this range and estimates that about 10 percent of all conceptions in the United States are terminated by illegal abortion. Other guesses run as high as one in five pregnancies ended by illegal abortion (Bates and Zawadzki, 1964, p. 3; Lader, 1966). Even in a nominally Catholic country such as Chile, a recent survey of urban women reports that 27 percent of them admit to having had an induced abortion (Hardin, 1973b, p. 14). Similar estimates are made for Catholics in Hungary, Brazil, and Poland (Population Council, 1968; Tietze and Dawson, 1973).

The United States Supreme Court has decreed that it is a woman's constitutional right to have an unwanted pregnancy terminated by a physician *(Doe et al. v. Bolton,* 1973; *Roe et al. v. Wade,* 1973). With the removal of legal restrictions against abortion, it is possible to accumulate data on the number of legal operations and their consequences. In a recent year, the Center for Disease Control (1972) counted a half million *legal* abortions in the United States and estimated that there may have been twice that number of *illegal* operations. Tietze (1973a) calculates that New York City's liberalized abortion law resulted in the substitution of 100,000 legal operations for this number of illegal and more dangerous procedures in the first two years after the reformed law was passed.

---

[3]In viviparous animals, the fertilized egg is called an embryo or a fetus at different stages in its development. In the human being, one speaks of an *embryo* up to the last part of the third month of pregnancy and of a *fetus* after that. In the fetus the bodily structures of the species are recognizable.

Public Opinion about Abortion

Whatever we believe about the ethics of abortion, it is a widespread practice. The extent of its practice and changing public opinion about it illuminate a conflict of moralities and the boundary that morality draws around rationality.

The conflict is apparent, for example, in citizens' responses to public opinion polls. A Harris survey taken in April 1973 found that 52 percent of Americans favored "the U.S. Supreme Court decision making abortions up to three months of pregnancy legal." Forty-one percent opposed this legalization and 7 percent were uncertain of their opinion. Young people favored legalization by a 2-to-1 margin while people over fifty years of age opposed the Supreme Court decision by 49 to 44 percent.

Over three-fourths of Americans agreed that "unless abortions are legalized, many women will die from having illegal and badly done abortions" and 68 percent believed that "so long as a doctor has to be consulted, the matter of an abortion is only a question of a woman's decision with her doctor's professional advice." In addition 57 percent of these respondents felt that "many mothers have unwanted babies, and it is better to have abortions that are safe and legal."

Despite these beliefs about consequences and preferences, two-thirds of this same sample of citizens agreed that "it is against God's will to destroy any human life, especially that of an unborn baby," and more than half (55 percent) believed that "no one's life should be taken without permission of the individual, and an unborn infant obviously cannot give his permission."

It is apparent that some Americans hold conflicting opinions about abortion. Being divided within ourselves about moral issues is nothing unusual, of course. While each of us likes to think that his own opinions are coherent, logical consistency is not a dominant characteristic of our beliefs (Harding, 1948; Winthrop, 1946). Some of the inconsistencies of our moral beliefs are apparent in the arguments advanced for and against induced abortion.

The Arguments Pro and Con

The arguments for and against legalized, induced abortion are *practical and moral*. In principle at least, the practical arguments are soluble in facts. That is, facts can help us decide the validity of statements about the physical and social consequences of abortion. The moral arguments, however, are *not* soluble in facts. Moral arguments rest on definitions and on sentiments. They are not answered by facts, and they can only be met by other definitions and other feelings.

A difficulty in thinking about this as well as other moral concerns is that the practical and the moral arguments are entangled. They are entangled because the *interpretation* of facts depends upon moral values. The facts do not speak for themselves when they are addressed to moral issues.

This confounding of practical and moral claims leads people to argue as if a fact will change, or ought to change, a moral preference—usually, of course, that of the other person. This entanglement also encourages the denial of facts if they conflict with our morals and it supports the assumption that our morals are better grounded in facts than our opponent's.

In the political arena the practical and moral arguments are characteristically blurred. Here we shall try to keep them separate, although every policy conclusion that is allegedly derived from facts is colored by morals.

The Practical Arguments

The practical arguments *against* abortion include these contentions: (1) that abortion is a dangerous procedure—hazardous to the physical and psychic health of the pregnant woman; (2) that abortion deprives society of potentially valuable persons (the "lost Beethoven" argument); and (3) that the practice of abortion leads to genocide (the "slippery slope" argument).

The practical arguments *in favor of* legal abortion are (1) that abortion is a necessary part of programs of population control and (2) that both society at large and the individuals involved suffer high costs in the birth of unwanted children.

The Practical Arguments against Abortion

1   *The hazards of abortion*

If abortion is alleged to be dangerous, the question that follows is, "Compared with what?"

The fairest comparison of mortality ratios associated with abortion would be with a population of women of like age and health who are also pregnant but who do not have abortions. No exact comparisons, controlling for the age and health of pregnant women, are available, but the measured differences between abortion and maternal mortality ratios do not justify the argument about the hazards of abortion. This argument is particularly challenged when maternal morbidity statistics are compared with mortality ratios for lawful abortions performed during the first three months of pregnancy.

For example, maternal mortality in Canada and the United States today runs about 12 deaths per 100,000 live births (*Demographic Yearbook,* 1972, Table 26). By contrast, in New York City, the legal abortions performed during the first two years after passage of the state's liberalized abortion law resulted in 3 deaths associated with 111,200 first trimester abortions and 8 deaths associated with 31,300 second trimester abortions, or mortality ratios of 2.7 and 26, respectively, per 100,000 abortions (Tietze et al., 1973).

Where elective abortion is limited to the first three months of pregnancy, as in Hungary and Czechoslovakia, the mortality ratios are even lower: 1.2 and 2.6 respectively, per 100,000 abortions (*Family Planning Digest,* 1973, p. 8).

The risk of death from childbirth is considerably higher than the risk of death from abortion, particularly when abortion is performed during the first trimester of pregnancy. Analysis of reports from several countries and different localities within those countries indicates that the hazards of abortion vary with the duration of the pregnancy, the surgical technique used, and the experience of the medical facility and the individual practitioners (Branch, 1972, p. 195; Tietze, 1973b). It is expected that the increasing availability of legal abortion will result in a steady decline in abortion-related morbidity and mortality (Tyler, 1972).

2   The "Lost Beethoven" argument

An emotional argument against abortion that is yet a practical argument is that abortion may deprive the world of valuable persons.

In its personal form, the argument appears as it was posed to Hardin: "If your mother had had an abortion, where would *you* be today?" (1973b, p. 38, emphasis his).

In its impersonal form, the argument is phrased as "the lost Beethoven riddle." Again, Hardin reports the riddle this way:

> Two physicians are talking shop. "Doctor," says one, "I'd like your professional opinion. The question is, should the pregnancy have been terminated or not? The father was syphilitic. The mother was tuberculous. They had already had four children: the first was blind, the second died, the third was deaf and dumb, and the fourth was tuberculous. The woman was pregnant for the fifth time. As the attending physician, what would you have done?"
> "I would have terminated the pregnancy."
> "Then you would have murdered Beethoven" (ibid., p. 39).

The argument is ridiculous, of course. There is no way to predict these "might have been's." The absurdity of the argument becomes apparent if, as Hardin suggests, one substitutes for a valuable person like Beethoven some monster such as Hitler, Caligula, or Genghis Khan.

The absurdity becomes more patent as one considers that nature *is* wasteful. Hardin notes:

> Beethoven's mother, like all women no doubt, started life with about 30,000 immature eggs in her ovaries. She produced only seven children. Therefore 29,993 eggs, all potential human beings, must have perished. Should we weep for this "loss"? And what about the 100,000,000 sperm his father produced every day of his mature years—say, some 1,000,000,000,000 in all? If certain technical problems had been solved, Mr. Beethoven senior could have populated the world 1,200 times over all by himself. Does the fact that his million, million sperm did not meet and fertilize an equal number of eggs constitute a loss in any meaningful sense? Considering our population problem it would be hard to defend this thesis [p. 39].

3   The "slippery slope" assumption

A third practical argument against abortion holds that legalizing such a practice paves the way to genocide. This argument claims that the right to life is not only an ethical absolute but that any definition that denies humanness to the fertilized human egg will deny humanity to other categories of life—to old people, sick people, and to people otherwise "inferior." According to Thimmesch (1973), "the abortion culture" leads to the gas chamber. The moral path, it is said, runs down the slippery slope from advocacy of abortion to the advocacy of "mercy killing" (euthanasia) and hence to the approval of mass extermination.

The evidence for this moral career is thin. The argument rests on its emotional appeal and on the uncertain observation that, as Thimmesch puts it, "pro-abortionists now also serve on pro-euthanasia organizations."

The allegation that the approval of abortion is correlated with the approval of euthanasia and therefore with the approval of genocide is just that—an allegation. Its logic is similar to the conclusion that, since those who *disapprove* of contraception and birth control—presumably including abortion—tend to approve of capital punishment (Comrey and Newmeyer, 1965), there must therefore be a causal connection between opposing abortion and prescribing other kinds of killing.

Defining Life and Death   There are no facts with which to resolve this issue. It is pertinent to note, however, that all societies define life and death, and that people set boundaries to their actions by these definitions. Being "alive" or "dead" is more than a matter of passing some physiological test. It is also a matter of social definition.

For example, Sudnow (1966) reports for an American hospital that:

An expelled fetus is either considered "human" or not . . . the dividing line is 550 grams, 20 centimeters, and 20 weeks of gestation. Any creature having smaller dimensions or of lesser embryonic "age" is considered non-human . . . and if "born" without signs of life, is properly flushed down the toilet, or otherwise simply disposed of. . . . Any creature having larger dimensions or of greater embryonic "age" is considered human, and if "born" without signs of life, or if born with signs of life which cease to be noticeable at some later point, cannot be permissibly flushed down the toilet, but must be accorded a proper ritual departure from the human race [pp. 176–177].

A difficulty in defining important concepts like "life" and "death," "human being" and "creature," is that there are always lexical borderlands where the definitions are in dispute. This holds, too, for the verb, "to kill," and it is a reason why we have different words for different styles of ending life—words like "murder," "suicide," and "war."

We do not often notice that we have *defined* life and death. Our daily definitions are conventional and the habitual meanings are part of us. However, as others point out to us that we are operating with a definition, we become morally aroused. Furthermore, as others urge a *different* definition from ours, we become morally offended. When we are morally affronted, we wonder, rightly, "Where will it all lead?"

Unfortunately, we have no science of moral movements with which to answer such a question. Some sociologists who have tried to measure these things, as Sorokin (1937) has, tell us that morals swing between extremes, like a pendulum. Whether or not this is so, it does not follow that moving a moral boundary from A to B (from illegal to legal abortion) necessarily promotes moving the ethical border brom B to Z (from legal abortion to genocide). Our moral connections are less predictable than this linear argument suggests (Nettler, 1973).

The Practical Arguments in Favor of Abortion

1   *Abortion as part of family planning*

A practical argument in favor of abortion holds that family planning cannot be successful without the backup possibility of abortion. This argument includes the assumptions that both "responsible parenthood" and the reduction of poverty require the rational limitation of reproduction (Chandrasekhar, 1974; David, 1973).

Since, as we have seen, men and women in both rich countries and poor ones do not use contraceptives efficiently, the right to abortion is claimed as necessary for the improvement of our material and psychic lives (Enke, 1973; Pohlman, 1967; Sanders, 1970).

2   *Abortion and adequate child-rearing*

A second practical argument carries moral overtones. It is the argument that bringing unwanted children into the world is not healthful for the children, their parents, and, hence, for society at large. This argument rests upon an abundance of evidence, which need not be reviewed here, demonstrating what common sense tells us: that it is not good for children to be reared without love (Bowlby, 1952).

This practical argument also claims rights for the parents, particularly for the women who bear the children. In the form presented by advocates of "women's liberation," the claim is for the right to control what happens within one's own body. In this context, the argument is given moral and political significance by women who argue that the antiabortion laws are written by *men* who are not held responsible for the unwanted children, for the unhappy mothers, and or for the hazardous illegal abortions that their laws produce. In short, the moral aspect of this practical argument accuses male lawmakers of evading the consequences of their legislation.

The practical arguments pro and con abortion cannot be balanced. They cannot be weighed because any scale used to assess the practical effects of legal abortion will find a moral weight added to the assessment. Consequences are not evaluated as good or bad in themselves, but as gauged by some moral standard.

The Moral Argument

In the debate about abortion the practical arguments are not decisive. *The issue is moral.*

The moral argument against abortion calls it murder. It is held that human life begins upon fertilization of the female egg and that every human life, so defined, is equally valuable. It is, therefore, a moral absolute, a rule without exception, that abortion be condemned and punished.

The moral argument in favor of abortion claims that life never "begins" except as we *define* a beginning. To the biologist, life is not "begun"; "it is just passed on from one living cell to another" (Hardin, 1973b, p. 17).

The moral argument in favor of abortion also contends that, just as "life" is *defined,* so is "murder." Removing tissue from the uterus of a woman during the first three months of a pregnancy represents a destruction of that tissue, but it does not, according to this argument, represent murder.

In this vein, it is further contended that the death of embryos is a normal occurrence and that, when this fact is appreciated, induced abortion loses some of its emotional coloration. Hardin (1973b, p. 18) puts the argument this way:

> Instinct does not tell us what our attitude toward a fertilized egg should be. We can adopt whatever attitude we wish. As a matter of principle, I submit that facts should influence us in our choice of attitude. The fact is—and this is not generally known—about 30 percent of all children conceived are spontaneously aborted. Only about 10 percent are lost at a late enough age for the mother to know it. The other 20 percent are lost so early, so painlessly, so quietly, that it has taken painstaking research to reveal the fact of their death. In other words, the four million babies born each year in our country represent only the remainder of an initial six million or so. About two million little embryos die naturally each year and disappear. This is normal.

On Evaluating Moralities

There are all kinds of moralities. Different people at different times have felt different moral urgencies and have responded to different taboos. Moral commandments are emotionally buttressed and difficult, if not impossible, to quarrel with. As our previous discussion of morals suggests (pp. 238–239), it is one of the characteristics of a morality that it is resistant to reason, and a prime signal that we have touched a moral sensibility is that there is nothing more to say. Saying something will not change anything.

It is possible, nevertheless, to assess the *results* of acting with one morality rather than another. This assessment will not influence many "moral" people—those who already know what they believe—but it may influence those who are marginal to a particular moral issue.

A Conflict of Principles   A traditional Western morality says that it does not matter what the consequences are when one behaves morally. To attend to consequences is "utilitarian," and this is being something less than moral. What matters, according to this ethic, is that a particular principle be obeyed, the principle of refusing to destroy life.

A difficulty with this principle is that, while it purports to be rigid, it is not. It moves. It moves by defining and redefining "life" and "murder." Those who oppose abortion, for example, do not necessarily oppose capital punishment, "justifiable" homicide, or war.

In this debate, the reverence-for-life morality conflicts with another code that advances a principle of responsibility. This morality says that each person should bear the full consequences of what he does, although "full" consequences can never be discerned.

The "responsibility" ethic calls it unjust for the costs of my actions to fall on you, and vice versa. It holds that, if you and I make babies, the babies are ours, which means that it is up to us to care for them. Whatever price babies cost, according to this code of responsibility, the price is ours to pay, and it is irresponsible—that is, immoral—to expect others to pay for our sexual and philoprogenitive pleasures.

Now whichever of these moralities we prefer, there are consequences peculiar to each. If we reject the ethic of parental responsibility, then we are pushed back, once again, into the tragedy of the commons. Why should you and I desist from our pleasures if anonymous others pay their costs? If we demand, morally, the right to reproduce, how can others resist our claim for the support of that reproduction?

An Opinion

In the context of the present growth of population, the consequence of denying the morality of responsibility in favor of an absolute morality of the right to life is disaster. If we reject the ethic of responsibility by calling it inhumane or antilife, we shall, by this rejection, produce death in another dress.

Labeling consequences disastrous evaluates these results, but it does so with a popular standard. There is widespread agreement about the value of survival and hence of the meaning of "disaster."

IN SUMMARY

From the heights of our affluence, most of the world lives in poverty. A reduction in rates of reproduction is a necessary step toward the reduction of that poverty. It is but one of the required steps, however. Chapter 12 discusses some of the other remedies for a low material standard of living.

Increasing the Wealth of Nations

A major concern, we have seen, is economic. It is a concern with attaining some level of material comfort and a concern with securing that level against loss. Chapter 10 discussed some of the ways by which individuals get ahead within modern societies. Chapter 11 dealt with a major obstacle to the economic advancement of both individuals and societies. Our present attention is to the question, "Assuming that the obstacle of excessive reproduction is managed, how does a society as a whole improve its economic condition?"

Almost every person who enters the political arena claims to have the answer to this question. The political answers come out as slogans, as simple formulas prescribing cures for what ails us economically. We take sides in favor of or against these prescriptions. Taking sides means engaging in conflict, and conflict stimulates emotion. The emotion generated by the concern and by its ideological presentation obscures such facts as might allow an intelligent answer to the economic question. The facts are obscured, too, by the tendency of political answers to economic questions to contain moral preferences. The moral coloration of political answers to economic questions means that policies that are politically and morally palatable are frequently substituted for courses of action that are economically rational. We are returned, again, to the difference between moral conduct and rational action. *Economic decisions that are made for political reasons are likely to have poor economic consequences.*

An Example   A clear illustration is provided by the United States government's attempts during the early 1970s to control the inflation of prices and the
devaluation of its dollar. In mid-1973, a price freeze was imposed on certain
finished industrial and food products in response to general public concern and
housewives' boycotts. Trying to control the prices of finished products without
controlling the prices of the materials entering those products and without the
ability to control demand is, of course, like King Canute trying to stem the tide
by his words. The effect of the American attempt to regulate prices was to
reduce production and hence to aggravate the inflation which the controls were
supposed to cure (Friedman, 1973). A price freeze that seemed to make some
sense politically made no sense economically.

The Lesson Learned   The lesson to be learned from this and similar
instances of political "rationality" favors citizen skepticism. In the political
forum, as in the domestic sanctuary, promises are not performances.
    The American example given is but one of many that illustrate an
important point, namely, that governmental action, like individual behavior,
can produce the opposite of what it intends. We do not like to believe this. We
prefer positive thinking.[1] We like to believe that "our side," when it acts,
produces what it promises or, at worst, that it does no harm. The point to be
considered here is that some portion of intentional action—and in particular of
political action—gets the opposite of what is desired.

WHY THE ECONOMIC QUESTION IS DIFFICULT TO ANSWER

After centuries of study of the "dismal science" of economics, it would seem
that there should be indisputable laws of economic growth that could inform
public policy. Unfortunately, there are no such unchallenged rules for increasing the wealth of nations. There are, however, some general principles that
allow us to improve our judgment of economic affairs, but these principles
remain in dispute and are not frequently followed. They are not often followed
for two major reasons. One is that the factors that produce wealth are plural
and intertwined. The second reason is that we want other things *along with* the
economic development.

The Intertwined, Plural Sources of Wealth

The production of wealth depends upon the availability of material resources
and of people with the skills adequate to exploit these resources. It depends
upon tools which, in turn, require capital, a saving from the past production of

---

[1]Experimental studies of how we think demonstrate that we think less well than a computer because,
among other reasons, we have trouble comprehending what it means when "things are *not*." We accentuate the
positive and devalue the negative. In laboratory problem-solving situations, there is a strong tendency for people
to ignore and deny *negative* evidence. This built-in tendency in laboratory settings is probably exaggerated when
we think about our emotional concerns in public. Research on this cognitive bias can be read in Peterson and
Beach (1967) and Wason and Johnson-Laird (1972).

wealth applied to its future creation. Last, the production of wealth depends upon the organization of people, tools, and capital in some disciplined fashion.

"People with skills" means more than just individuals with minds and muscles and the training to use them. It means also people who are willing to work together in some organized way. Working when one feels like it does not produce the same quantity of wealth as does teamwork with specialization of function.

Organizing people with skills to apply a technology in the fabrication of wealth requires a social structure, including a governing authority, to ensure that wealth will not be stolen. There are many modes of theft, as we have seen (Chap. 7) but as used here, "theft" refers to some ill-defined gap between what one contributes to the production of wealth and what one receives. This gap is subjective. It varies with how a people define value. Therefore it cannot be accurately measured; it can only be judged. It cannot be absolutely decided; it can only be subjected to some agreed-upon rules of the game.

Because what each of us contributes to the production of wealth cannot be accurately calculated, defining the difference between what we do and what we get is a matter of contention in modern states. Any move to narrow or widen this subjective gap leads to conflict. This conflict is destructive of the production of wealth if it becomes a fight without rules. That is, if it becomes simply a power play, where having power is not the same thing as making a productive contribution. On the other hand, the conflict about who deserves how much of total national product need not be an obstacle to increasing the wealth of a population insofar as some rules do not "kill the goose that lays the golden egg." To kill the gold-producing goose means to make it uneconomical for wealth producers to work, which is to say to divorce reward from productive contribution. A tension to separate reward from productive contribution is a constant feature of all societies above the level of tribes and even among some smaller bands (Schoeck, 1966). It is a tension generated by our moral conceptions about the consequences of wealth production. These moral conceptions refer to a second difficulty in answering the economic question.

Wanting Wealth Along With Freedom, Justice, and Happiness

Every idea about how to increase the wealth of a people is challenged on moral grounds. We do not want economic development alone. We want a better life, and freedom, and a more just society *along with* the material comforts. Furthermore, we are not clear as to which we want first or most. The demagogue characteristically steps into this confusion of appetites with the promise that his program will "bring it all," so that we need not choose among our values or compromise them.

"Getting It All Together" Herein lies the source of the human tragedy— that we want to maximize several values simultaneously. That is, we want the best of everything all at once and all together. A "package deal." It is mathematically impossible, however, to maximize two or more values simultaneously (von Neumann and Morgenstern, 1947, p. 11). This is one way of saying that there are prices for our pleasures. Economic growth has its own price.

A reason why the ideological answers to our economic question are false is that they deny the prices of particular political actions, and they obscure these prices by mixing together a variety of objectives (promises) to be gained through a political program. The popular ideologies entangle the question of how economies grow with other questions about the just distribution of income, about the fair ownership of property, about the contentment of workers, "exploitation," "alienation," and the control of our personal destinies. In short, the economic concern and the economic question become enmeshed with other concerns involving ethics and envy.

Politics as Drama   Denying the costs of action, mixing moral questions with economic ones, and wanting all good things at once—these are the ingredients of political drama. Instead of analyzing the grave question of how the bulk of humankind can be lifted out of poverty, the battles for political and ideological power convert the explanation of economic misery into a scenario that Richard LaPiere (1938) has called "the dramatic triad." The forces with which we contend are dramatized as the three major characters of every romance: the hero, the heroine, and the villain.

In this politicoeconomic play, some vaguely defined portion of a population, usually called "the people," is depicted as the heroine, the innocent character to be saved, sometimes even from itself. The hero is, of course, our side, embodied in our leader, our party, or in a particular "class" supporting our ideology. The villain is that other portion of our society, usually described as a powerful minority, that, temporarily, prevents the hero from rescuing the heroine.

The Point of the Story   The point of describing this typical scenario is that this political drama conceals issues. It hides the dull economic facts of life in a more interesting morality play in which goodness struggles with evil to defend "the people." The persistence of this political drama can be tested by a content analysis of political speeches. Our hypothesis is that politicians who speak to their publics on economic issues seldom discuss *how wealth is produced.* They address themselves, instead, to specific items of discontent that their constituents feel, such as taxes, prices, profits, wages, and the justice or injustice of all of these. The central question—"How is wealth created?" or "How can we improve the material life of our people?"—this question is ignored. It is a question, however, that underwrites a major concern.

SUMMARY

If we are to think about how groups of people who live together under one political power can raise the levels of their material lives, we had better attend to that question alone. If we try to answer the economic question with arguments about correlated issues such as justice, freedom, and happiness, we shall lose sight of the economic issue.

Now saying this does not reduce the importance of our concern with justice and liberty. The point is simply that it is difficult to discuss the conditions of economic well-being without becoming waylaid by all these other questions about who has power, who owns, who gets, and whether it is all fair or unfair.

REVOLUTION AS "THE ANSWER"

This point has to be made, repeatedly and laboriously, because a popular promise of improvement in the material lives of people around the world is given by those who advocate revolution following the teachings of Marx-Engels, Lenin, and, more recently, Mao. The advocacy of revolution illustrates the point about the entanglement of moral issues with the economic concern, for it is of the essence of a revolution that it reorder society, including its economic arrangements, and that it produce a new kind of "human nature." The thoroughgoingness of a revolution—its overturning institutions and people—is what distinguishes a revolution from reform.

The mixture of objectives that distinguishes a revolution makes it difficult to analyze the economic consequences of overthrowing present and recent societies. Quarrels with communists about the material standards of living in their totalitarian states as compared with the material quality of life in less state-controlled economies are characteristically sidetracked into discussions about the less objective questions of who is more "oppressed" or "alienated."

Let us be clear, then, about which concern occupies our attention. For the moment we are asking if there are more and less efficient routes to higher planes of material life. In addressing this question, let us be clear, too, that this issue is of universal and perennial interest and that communists as well as capitalists call the question crucial. Socialists and communists are "materialists" and they tell us that economic growth is the principal measure of the success of their system. "Material production is the decisive sphere of human endeavor," Nikita Khrushchev said in a 1959 speech. In this he was seconding Lenin, who also claimed that "We exert our main influence on the international revolution by our economic policy" (1960).

To repeat, attending to the economic concern does not in the least deny that "men do not live by bread alone" and that other concerns have their urgency. Men do *not* live by bread alone, it is true, and many well-fed, well-housed people are ungrateful and unhappy with their materially secure lives. This, however, is not the present issue. The issue is: "What seems to assist or obstruct economic development?"

PLANNING ECONOMIC GROWTH VERSUS ENCOURAGING IT—WITH OR WITHOUT REVOLUTION

Historically there have been two roads by which nations have moved toward a richer life: by stealing wealth and by producing it. Since stealing the wealth of other countries is likely to meet with devastating military resistance today, the option is to increase the productivity of nations.

The economic question then becomes one of how best to *produce* wealth. The question is answered today from two sides. One side urges that economic development be planned through state ownership of the instruments of production and through the use of state power to determine what shall be produced and how the product shall be distributed. Another side urges that economic development be subject to a minimum of state regulation, or none, and that what shall be produced and how it shall be distributed should be left to private choice in a market.

Those who advocate economic planning differ among themselves in the formulas they favor. Where governments are *strong,* these advocates favor a *socialist* solution—that is, a constitutional takeover of "natural monopolies" and selected industries. Where governments are *weak,* the planners favor a revolutionary solution, usually under a *communist* banner, although a socialist solution may be accepted as a halfway house on the road to complete communism.

Polls of North American social scientists (Lipset, 1970) indicate that these thinkers, when compared with professors of other studies, tend to favor the "rationality" of economic planning to the "anarchy" of the marketplace. This preference is usually but not necessarily justified by reference to the ideas of Marx-Engels and, more currently, Mao Tse-tung.

Marx as Economic Adviser

Marxists, like other thinkers before them, have been concerned with the production of wealth, with the conditions of its distribution among a people, and with the material and nonmaterial consequences of different systems of production and distribution.

A Marxian reason for thinking about these matters is to aid men in improving their lives. This reason is an intellectual one. It seeks *to know what one is doing.* It finds support among all practical persons, whether or not they are Marxists. Theory is to be a guide to action. It is to be developed and tested in action. Theory, if it is to be more than an aesthetic play with ideas, is to be used to get results. If, in acting upon a theory, one does not get the predicted results, the theory itself is to be questioned.

Followers of the Marxian conception of history have bet their lives, and those of uninvolved others, on the accuracy of their theory. Given the continuing popularity of Marxism and its recommendations as the cure for the troubles of economically backward countries, it is important to ask, "How good a guide has the Marxian formula been?"

The answer will not come easily. It will vary with the availability of evidence, with the evidence one trusts, with the time span considered, and—most important—with the comparisons one makes. The question is always: "Compared with what?"

Two kinds of comparison have been made in testing the validity of state planning of economies: (1) a comparison of a present Marxist economy with what-might-have-been-if . . . and (2) a comparison of a controlled economy with a free one.

As illustrations of these comparative approaches, (1) theoreticians have imagined what Russia might be like today if the Kerensky (pre-Bolshevik) government had not been overthrown and (2) economists have compared changes in the material wealth of roughly similar states with relatively planned and unplanned economies—states like Ghana and the Ivory Coast; East and West Germany; Chile and Argentina; Great Britain and Japan; and, of course, those colossi: the U.S.S.R. and the United States.

Arguments will persist as to the standards to be applied under both types of comparison, yet these kinds of comparison always seem to be involved when we quarrel about the best way to make an economy grow.

When we make these comparisons, the market economies appear more successful than the planned ones. The Marxian promise of a unique road to improved material well-being is *not* fulfilled when state-regulated economies are compared with relatively free markets. Comparing countries with comparable resources and technologies, the Ivory Coast is richer than Ghana; West Germany has a higher material standard of living than East Germany; Japan is economically more successful than Great Britain; and the difference between the material standard of living in the United States and the Soviet Union is astronomical.

In comparison with the relatively free-trading economies, the planned prescriptions for economic growth do not work well. This negative conclusion says nothing about the ability of Marxists or any other revolutionaries to redistribute power and privilege. This is not at issue. This conclusion is silent also about the *psychic* satisfactions of revolutions, whatever their economic consequences may be. This, too, is not at issue, for it is granted that there is heroic gratification in fighting quite apart from any economic goals attained (see Chaps. 13 and 14).

A Contrary Thesis

In opposition to the idea that economic development is best encouraged through state ownership of the means of production and distribution, it will be argued that

1 In the short run, revolutions destroy economies. (What revolutions do "in the long run" cannot be discovered since one person's "long run" is too long for the impatient and too short for the hopeful.)

2 Nationwide economic planning has no such record of success as might lend reasoned confidence to its procedures as a chart for improving the economic life of a people.

3 There are two strong reasons why central planning of an economy has not proved as productive as a market economy. These reasons can be

summarized as *(a)* ignorance and *(b)* the organization paradox. These reasons overlap, and a "psychology of ignorance" will be outlined that explains why governments are *less* likely to know what they are doing than are individuals.

   4   Some of the conditions necessary for economic growth can be specified, as can some of the obstacles to improved economic well-being. Neither the conditions required for growth nor the obstacles impeding growth are those emphasized by Marxian theory.

   5   After the quarreling is over, there remains a democratic test of the goodness of life, particularly of the goodness of *material* conditions. This test is "how people vote with their feet when they can." The results of this test, thus far, have not favored the state control of economies as the best means of increasing wealth.

   Each of these points will be amplified.

The Revolutionary Disruption of Economies

The internal warring that is a revolution damages the productive and distributive capacity of a society. Revolutionaries know this as well as do others. The revolutionary justification of the present pain, however, is the promise of future gain. The promise has proved illusory in most modern countries. Such promise is called misleading, not because gains in the material standard of living are forever denied revolutionary states ("long runs" get stretched beyond our test) but because the gains promised do not come readily from "land reform," nor economically from the nationalization of industry, nor assuredly from the destruction of the price system.

   Revolutionary situations do not carry a guarantee that allows one to calculate likely gains against probable pains. Contrary to what revolutionaries and some of their enemies may *believe,* no one *knows* how to transform unjust societies into just ones or poorly productive societies into rich ones.

   The word "knows" is emphasized because *to have knowledge* about how to move a society from poverty to affluence would mean that there were verified empirical laws which, if followed, would change social organizations according to intention. That is, to *know* how to improve a society's economy would require a science of economic engineering. There is none such, however. The best we have are some empirical principles. Rules of thumb. Common-sense guidelines. For example, it seems obvious that where an impoverished population has been living on a subsistence level and where this low standard of life has been produced by years of political disorganization, civil war, banditry, and foreign invasion—then, in such a situation, the imposition of *rule* will improve the material quality of life. The building of the People's Republic of China illustrates the point, a case in which a revolution followed by a tyranny brought order to chaos and an improvement in the economy (Myrdal and Kessle, 1971; Richman, 1969; Scalapino, 1963).

    This is not to say that the improvement is cheaply achieved[2] or that it brings material standards of life up to those taken for granted in industrialized countries. The applicable metaphor is that, with totalitarian rule and some managerial efficiency, a poor and chaotic society like China of the 1940s may have had nowhere to go but up. The "up" is not very high according to standards in the developed lands, East and West. Hard labor and meager rations are still the lot of China's one-fifth of the world's population.[3] However, Chinese agricultural production has improved in recent years and may at least keep up with its population growth of some 18 million people a year (*Newsweek,* 1974c).

    By contrast with the effects of revolution upon the economies of subsistence-level societies, the overthrow of states that have relatively well-organized economies producing in excess of a bare livelihood for their people characteristically results in economic regression. Two recent examples are Allende's Chile and Castro's Cuba.

    The economic loss is clear for the immediate years after the revolution. How persistent the decline appears to be is a matter of debate, where the debate varies with the country at issue, the length of time considered, and the expectations involved. For example, how rich *should* East Germany or Poland be today to justify their economic doctrines? *How long after* the Bolsheviks' accession to power should one have to wait before expecting economic well-being in the Soviet Union to be comparable to that in France or Canada?

The Soviet Example

The example of the Soviet Union is important if only because it has been a revolutionary state whose program most excited modern intellectuals. In 1959 the Soviet leader Khrushchev announced the *complete victory* of socialism and the entering upon a new state of development that would build communism within the next twenty years. In 1961, at the twenty-second Party Congress in Moscow, Khrushchev publicized a timetable for the achievement of communism that included catching up with the United States in industrial production by 1970 and, after that, "the satisfaction of all economic needs and desires." (Greenslade, 1968, p. 422). Speaking about the same time, the Soviet economist

---

[2]Estimates of the human costs vary. The numbers of deaths attributed to the Maoist revolution range in the *millions.* Some of the discrepancy in the tallies is a result of trying to count direct victims, those killed outright as "enemies of the people," and indirect victims, those deaths above normal expectation that seem assignable to the exigencies of the power struggle (Petersen, 1969, Chap. 17).

    Allowing for such variations, Walker (1955) reports estimates of the human casualties of the Communist revolution in China from the first Civil War (1927–1936) to the present that run from a low of *34 million* deaths to a high of *64 million.*

    Similarly high figures are given as the human cost of building Soviet Communism. Conquest (1968) puts the estimates at between *35 and 45 million* lives lost in the Soviet enterprise. Petersen's population estimates (1969, p. 664) are in accord with Conquest's.

[3]Scalapino (1963, p. 131) estimates an average Chinese diet in 1962 to have been "no more than 1,700 calories a day, with some regions unable to achieve even that average. Generally, a minimum of 2,000 calories per day has been considered necessary over a protracted period to maintain good health."

    As we have seen, the average daily intake of Western Europeans and North Americans has been estimated to be in excess of 3,000 calories (United Nations, 1970, pp. 478–482).

Petrov (1968, pp. 218–219) promised a "programme of gigantic economic expansion which envisages a five-fold increase of the country's national income in the twenty years from 1961 to 1980. . . . In total," Petrov said, "in ten years (i.e., by 1970) the *per capita* real income in the U.S.S.R. will double. By the end of the twenty-year period, these incomes will grow over 3.5 times and will exceed the present level of incomes of the workers in the United States by 75 per cent" (italics in the original).

Against these promises, the disappointing economic facts of Soviet life have been of this order:

1 "From 1928 [the peak year of the 1920s] to 1938 [the peak year of the 1930s], real weekly earnings of wage and salary earners *declined about 20 per cent* in terms of purchasing power, while average hours worked were slightly reduced. By 1948 real weekly earnings . . . dropped about 40 per cent as against 1938, while the number of hours increased substantially. As compared to 1928, *the total decline in real wages in 20 years amounts to about 50 per cent*" (Schwarz, 1948, italics added).

2 Agricultural production has continued poor. Jasny's careful study (1949) estimates that United States farm labor was then 4 1/2 times as productive as Soviet labor, that urban consumers' standards of food consumption *had continually declined since the revolution,* and that the vast police and office staffs of the collectives constituted a new village plutocracy.

Jasny's later study (1961) reports improvements in Soviet industry and construction from 1928 to 1950, but "farm output appears to have practically stagnated over the same period" (p. 6). Further, Jasny comments, "the figures . . . indicate a worsening of the incomes of the peasants relative to those of wage and salary earners, although they were already particularly low before the start of the Great Industrialization Drive. Small as the total personal incomes were, there was an immense stratification among wage and salary earners and, to a smaller extent, among peasants. The lower strata of the working people, very broad strata at that, were reduced to the position of paupers" (p. 10).

3 During 1961–1965, the growth rate of agricultural production declined to about 2 percent per year, urban housing continued scarce, and Soviet gross national product may actually have declined (Greenslade, 1968, pp. 422–423).

4 Becker's detailed study (1969) entitled *Soviet National Income, 1958–1964,* offers the only published national income and product accounts for that country in recent years. In terms of the Communists' own objective of "overtaking and surpassing" the advanced capitalist states, the "plan to shake the world" (Becker, p. 288) has proved disappointing.

"Important goals of the Seven-Year Plan were not met; some others were, or the shortfalls were small," Becker writes. "Output in several noncommunist states picked up while USSR agriculture stagnated, and Soviet per capita consumption grew at a pace a quarter to a third slower than planned. . . . Although the rate of investment remained high, capital-output ratios rose more rapidly but aggregate growth rates less rapidly than anticipated. Soviet planners too, like their less experienced brethren in developing countries, 'often mistake the shadow of investment for the substance of production'" (p. 288).

5   The Soviet Union constitutes *one-sixth* of the earth's land mass, and it is so fertile and so rich in minerals that its mathematician-economist Kantorovich believed (1959) that efficient management could raise productivity from 30 to 50 percent. Despite this potential, the journalist Anatol Shub (1969), himself the son of David Shub, a Russian revolutionary and biographer of Lenin, has suggested that living standards in the Soviet states may now be *lower* than in the Russia of 1913.

For example, Shub notes that "a pint can of cooked pears that had to be recooked to be edible, cost 1.05 rubles. The average Soviet wage is less than 30 rubles a week—worth $33. at the official rate of exchange, but closer to $7. judging . . . from currency speculators" (p. 70). On the average, families in the Soviet Union spend about half of their incomes for food. In the United States, on the average, families spend less than one-fifth of their incomes on food (Gass, 1967b, p. 44). In the Soviet Union about 55 percent of the calories ingested are from bread and potatoes; in the United States, only about 23 percent of caloric intake is from these foods (ibid.). It follows that meat, dairy products, fruit, and vegetables are relatively scarce in the Soviet Union and command premium prices.

"In no other advanced industrial nation is living-space so meager [as in the Soviet Union]; West Germany has, per capita, more than twice as much" (Gass, 1967b, p. 45). "On the most optimistic projection of Soviet plans," Shub reports, "the housing space per person in 1990 will still be less than that available to the Imperial subject of 1909. It should be added that Soviet housing plans have not been fulfilled for fourteen consecutive years" (p. 73).

In sum, *more than half a century after* the Russian Revolution, the Soviet Union, with a population about one-fifth greater than that of the United States and with a minerally rich land more than *twice* the size of the United States, has a total national product about *half* that of the Americans (Gass, 1967a, p. 65). The discrepancy in the material standard of living of the people of these two large countries is so great that one student of Soviet and American societies concludes that "paradoxically poverty is seen as a social problem in the United States, but not in the Soviet Union. It is an American social problem to a large extent *because* the standard of living is high and consequently expectations are also higher. In the Soviet Union, against the background of generally low living standards, poverty is not a social problem, but rather a normal state of affairs" (Hollander, 1973, p. 334, emphasis his).

Similar records of comparatively poor performance can be cited for the other communist countries of Eastern Europe when contrasted with the freer economies of Western European nations, Japan, Taiwan, or North America (Gass, 1967b; Goldstücker, 1971). When compared with the performances of market economies, *the promises of the planned economies have not been fulfilled.*

The Cuban Example

In the Western hemisphere, the Cuban revolution also promised the end of exploitation, the birth of freedom, and an improved material standard of living. Cuba was, in its pre-Castro days, the richest of the Caribbean islands and among the economically most advanced of Latin American countries (Thomas, 1971). After more than ten years of revolutionary government, Cuba is an impoverished land with a faltering economy.

As of the early 1970s, journalists reported that in Cuba "people who used to eat well now eat badly, and people who used to eat badly still eat badly. There is no starvation, however" (*U.S. News & World Report,* 1970, p. 38). A year later the same news source reported that "Many people are avoiding work [in Cuba]. A tough law against 'vagrancy' is planned. . . . Some 300,000 to 400,000 children under 16 have dropped out of school. . . . Production of tobacco, a traditional foreign-currency earner for Cuba, suffered last year from the diversion of labor and fertilizer to the canefields. . . . The country failed to meet its 1970 sugar goal. . . . Rationing is stricter than ever" (*U.S. News & World Report,* 1971).

The Cuban agricultural failures have been matched by its industrial fiascos, as noted by Ché Guevara's admission (p. 193, n. 1). A decade after its revolution the Cuban economy provides *a monthly ration per family* of "one roll of toilet paper, 2.5 cakes of soap, and one package of detergent," despite its receipt during the 1960s of "more economic aid per capita than any nation on earth" (Gall, 1971, p. 56). The individual ration of meat for Cubans is now three-fourths of a pound every nine days and child labor is impressed into agriculture and light industry (*U.S. News & World Report,* 1974c). A consequence of the failed economy has been the militarization of production and the death of liberty.

In comparison with more free economies, the controlled systems of revolutionary states have *not* provided a more efficient way of improving the material lives of their citizens. In some recent cases, as in Chile and Cuba, thriving economies have been destroyed. While the failures are apparent, they are not readily admitted by the planners, of course. It is as one Cuban refugee, Illuminado, said of his former leader, "If *El Caballo* (Fidel) tried to help us, then he failed. He failed because his ideas didn't work out; but he couldn't admit it and kept the idea all the same" (cited by Colebrook, 1973, p. 52).

A similar conclusion can be drawn from the record of nonrevolutionary states that have attempted, in varying degree, to socialize their economies.

National Economic Planning Has a Poor Performance Record

A parallel history of persistent faith in a failed idea can be observed in the developed countries, where some politicians and some intellectuals continue to believe that they can improve economic matters through state ownership of land and industry and through state planning of production and distribution.

In evaluating this idea, it must be kept in mind that there are *degrees* of central planning of economies and *contexts* in which the plans are implemented. That is, industrialized states have "nationalized" industries in differing amounts and under different material and structural circumstances. This fact of *variety* in economic planning allows for continuing argument about the success or failure of plans and about the reasons for fluctuating results.

Counting Results   There are data, however, that permit reasoned conclusions about the success of state-planned economies. The data do not validate a faith in centralized planning of a country's production and distribution as the most efficient way to increase wealth.

This conclusion continues to be disputed because attempts to count the results of state-controlled economies run into two difficulties. A first difficulty is the lack of adequate tallies of production and, in totalitarian countries, the distortion of records by officials who are under pressure to make their performance appear satisfactory. A second difficulty is that many government programs do not have clear objectives, so that one cannot evaluate their achievements against their promises. There are, of course, good reasons for being vague when one makes political promises, for if one is vague it is difficult to be proved wrong. It is the "empty abstractions," Simone Weil tells us (1946, p. 72), "which, throughout history, have inspired the combined spirit of sacrifice and cruelty."

The political trick is to stimulate enthusiasm by promising programs that *mean* something without *specifying* much. For example, here is the repeated punch line of a popular politician as reported by one of the journalists with his campaign:

> 'As George Bernard Shaw said,' he continued, and there is a rustle in the crowd. This is his windup line and the reporters all begin to run back to the train. 'You see things; and you say, Why? But I dream things that never were; and I say, Why not?' Unsure of its meaning but certain that the line calls for response, the crowd cheers him, and the bright stranger . . . fades away into the growing dusk [Wainwright, 1968].

A Personal Recommendation   In listening to political candidates, every thinking citizen ought to ask himself how he would know if the political promises did or did not come true. Asking this question is illuminating. One discovers that many programs, economic as well as more generally social, have *no clear goals.* Reading official statements of government policies in search of their concrete objectives is a disillusioning exercise. For example, Biderman (1966) did this with the United States President's commission report on "national goals," 1960. Biderman could find mention of what might count as a sign of goal attainment in only 59 percent of the statements of objective. This means that more than 40 percent of government programs were so phrased that no one could find out whether or not they had worked.

Tallies   However, when governments *do* specify economic objectives to be reached through bureaucratic control of production and distribution, their performance is not encouraging. The literature on this subject is extensive, and only a sample of the data-counting results can be summarized here.

We can begin a résumé of the fate of economic plans in developed countries by looking at government efforts to cure the Great Depression of the

1930s. Statesmen in Europe and the Americas consulted with their economists and received, of course, conflicting advice. As one wit said after listening to this babel of economic counsel "If you laid all the economists in the world end to end, you still would not reach a conclusion." Nevertheless, the Great Depression called for action and "things" were done. Years after this economic debacle, the American economist Moulton (1949) summarized these varied efforts by saying that "the most striking fact revealed by the study of the 1929–1933 depression is that recovery eventually began everywhere (throughout the world), *regardless of the type of government policy being pursued*" (p. 85, italics supplied).

More recently, Cohen (1970) analyzed the results of the four major economic programs initiated by the French government since 1945. *Not one* of these economic plans attained its stated objectives. How much success or failure one attributes to these economic shortfalls depends, of course, on one's faith. That is, faith will accommodate some failure, excuse it, and call the plan less of a failure than the skeptic sees it.

A similar analysis of governmental attempts to control economies according to plan has been written by Devons (1950), with particular attention to the British experience. Devons's research and that of other economists concerned with the rationality of economic planning have been brought together by Cairncross (1970) with findings that do *not* justify confidence in the ability of governments to manage economies in a more efficient fashion than the market.

There are reasons, of course, why planned economies are less productive than market economies, and some of these will be outlined below (pp. 262–266). However, before listing the sources of economic growth and the obstacles to it, a summary of the extensive research on the efficiency of state-run economies deserves quotation. Wildavsky (1971), reviewing the records of totalitarian economies, was led to conclude:

> Is there a single example of successful national economic planning? The Soviet Union has had central planning and has experienced economic growth. But the growth has not been exceptional and has not been according to the plan. Is there a single country whose economic life, over a period of years, has been guided by an economic plan, so that targets set out in the plan bear a modest resemblance to events as they actually occur? No doubt each reader will be tempted to furnish the one case he has heard about. The last two suggested to me were Ceylon and Pakistan. Yet the very fact . . . that it is so difficult to think of an example suggests that the record of planning has hardly been brilliant. For all we know, the few apparent successes (if there are any) constitute no more than random occurrences. Despite the absence of evidence on behalf of its positive accomplishments, planning has retained its status as a universal nostrum. Hardly a day goes by in some part of the world without a call for more planning as a solution to whatever problems ail the society in question. Doubts as to the efficacy of national economic planning are occasionally voiced, casually discussed, and rarely answered. Advocates of plans and planning, naturally enough, do not spend their time demonstrating that it has been successful. Rather they explain why planning is wonderful

despite the fact that, as it happens, things have not worked out that way. Planning is defended not in terms of results but as a valuable process. It is not so much where you go that counts, but how you did not get there [pp. 95–96].

Why State-controlled Economies Are Less Productive Than Market Economies

There are two major reasons why economies managed according to government plan are less efficient than economies that are responsive to a market-place. The first reason can be stated simply—we are ignorant. Economic planning assumes more knowledge than we have. The second reason has been called "the organization paradox," the idea that organizations get in the way of their own objectives. The bureaucracies required to manage economies constitute impediments to the achievement of their own economic goals.

On Economic Ignorance   There is a difference between having information and having knowledge. Much that we "know" in the social studies is information. Little that we "know" in the social studies is knowledge. However, state management of a large economy according to plan would require knowledge, not just information. The difference between having knowledge and having information deserves attention.

To have information is to be able to state a fact (Nettler, 1972). We are full of facts in economics and sociology. Facts are the building blocks of knowledge, but they do not in themselves constitute knowledge or, much less, wisdom.

To have knowledge is to be able to state a nontautological empirical rule (Nettler, 1972). People who have knowledge can specify regularities in nature, regularities for which there is good evidence. "Good evidence" is *empirical* evidence, data based upon reliable observations rather than upon inferences from coincidences such as justify, let us say, faith in astrology.

In the realm of economic affairs, there are some well-proved rules, some of which will be mentioned when we discuss how economies grow. However, there are two things wrong with our knowledge of economics.

The first difficulty is that what economic knowledge we have is not good enough. There are holes in it and uncertainties, and these uncertainties mean that government officials who would use economic knowledge to improve our material lives make errors. The uncertainties are apparent when we ask economists to make predictions and then count their hits. Astrophysical knowledge allows us to hit the moon on schedule; economic knowledge does not allow us to forecast economic events accurately or to make people richer on plan (Heilbroner, 1966; Morgenstern, 1963; Postan, 1968; Schoeffler, 1955; Zarnowitz, 1967).

The second thing wrong with our economic knowledge is that it does not fit our hopes. Economic knowledge, like much sociological knowledge, tells us more surely what we *cannot* do than what novel thing we can do (Popper,

1962). The sadness is that we do not approach the economist to have him tell us what we cannot have. We want him to tell us how we can get more of what we want. The social reformer and other altruists place the volume of human needs above the present supply of their satisfiers. The wish is that more satisfaction—more food, housing, clothing, health care—be provided than present economies produce. This wish is father to the uneconomic idea that governments can *produce* wealth by *distributing* it. There is a little truth in this idea, but it is not the whole truth. This ideal persists, nevertheless, and its persistence explains why few specialists in sociology and social work take courses in economics.[4]

There is, nevertheless, a real economic world out there and confusing wish with reality is always costly. Goethe was talking about this confusion in the domestic department, but his statement applies as well to the economic sphere. "Love," Goethe wrote, "is an ideal thing, marriage a real thing; a confusion of the real with the ideal never goes unpunished."

One can paraphrase Goethe and say that "Satisfying material needs justly is an ideal thing, producing wealth a real thing; those who confuse the ideal with the real pay a penalty."

There is a difference in magnitude, however, between the punishment exacted from confusing ideals with realities in the household and confusing these matters in politics. The domestic penalties are limited. Unfortunately, when persons who run governments confuse their economic ideals with reality, the penalty is paid by many innocent people.

On Knowing What One Is Doing   The present point about governmental inefficiency in the direction of economies is difficult for some young people to accept. Looking at the world with innocent eyes, some students ask how governments can be stupid.[5] The answer can be put in this logical form:

1   We often say of a person, "He does not know what he is doing."
2   Governments are composed of human beings.
3   Therefore. . . .

The situation is *worse* than this logic implies, however.

We speak of a person knowing what he is doing when his objectives are clear, when they are empirical (that is, testable), and when the individual's actions are appropriate to the achievement of his goals. Conversely, we say that a person does *not* know what he is doing when he does not know what he wants, or when he wants conflicting things, or when his actions are at war with his ends.

---

[4]This is offered as a personal opinion, and not as a fact. It is, however, an opinion that could be tested empirically.
[5]Since the American involvement in Vietnam and the Watergate fiasco, this question may be asked less frequently than formerly.

It is of the nature of government that it preside over conflict. This activity reduces rationality.

The Function of Government A principal function of government is to *rule.* In relatively free societies, this means to *referee* among competing interests. In relatively totalitarian societies, this means to *dominate* conflicting interests.

The necessity for governments to contend with conflict among their subjects means that compromise and vagueness of objective are built-in features of governance. These features do not make rationality in government impossible, but they make it difficult. These aspects of ruling assure that governments, as compared with individuals, will seek conflicting objectives and employ inappropriate means. They will less often know what they are doing.

A particular cause of this ignorance can be described by "the psychology of political stupidity."

The Psychology of Political Stupidity There is one fact of life, fortunately, that keeps most of us knowing what we are doing much of the time. This fact is *feedback.* Something happens when we act, and what happens tells us whether we are on the right track or not. There are imperfections in feedback, of course. Information is imperfect and it is also complex. There are mixed signals, and we sometimes do not know which lesson we ought to have learned from the things that happened when we did this or that. Despite these imperfections, however, we do learn something from the consequences of our actions. This is how we improve at tennis or skiing. It is also a way of learning what makes us happier, healthier, or wealthier.

All this becomes less true when we engage in politics. To be political is to try to make *others* happier, healthier, or richer. In this enterprise it is much more difficult to know what one is doing because feedback is faint. The statesman who would do good for thousands, and even millions, of anonymous others stands light-years away from the impact of his actions. The legislator, the jurist, the administrator often do *not* know what they are doing because there is no immediate report to them, and no certain report, of the consequences of their actions. In such positions of power we fall back upon the goodness of our intentions and the support of our friends, who also believe in our good intentions. The *cause* justifies. But the person in politics is always at some distance from the effects of his intentions, and however good they may be, the person with power to influence our economic lives has only the foggiest notion whether he is doing good, evil, something, or nothing.

In our individual lives, the consequences of our actions allow us to know what we are doing. *When we immunize actors from the effects of their actions, however, we make them stupid.*

This is the psychological reason why governments are *less* likely to know what they are doing than individuals. It is not that administrators never feel the effects of their decisions; it is only that they are so often removed from the consequences of their policies. This is one definition of being irresponsible, and it is a reason why individual producers and traders more frequently know what they are doing than do political managers of economies.

The psychology of political stupidity applies to the activities of organizations as it does to the activity of political persons.

The Organization Paradox   Individuals know what they are doing, we have said, inasmuch as they feel the effects of their actions. An organization is less likely to know what it is doing because each individual's action within it has only a remote connection with the objective of the organization. It becomes more difficult, therefore, for the "brains" of the organization to find out what is keeping the aggregate of individuals moving toward or away from target.

This fact underlies a second source of inefficiency in the centralized planning of large economies. This source of inefficiency has been called "the organization paradox." It is the paradox that, when large numbers of people are brought together to achieve an objective, the very fact of their being so organized gets in the way of attaining the goal.

It is not that large organizations never get anything done. They do. Armies win or lose wars; factories build airplanes; universities educate some people. However, there is always slippage between what the organization is supposed to do and what gets done when large numbers of people are brought together to perform diverse tasks in the service of some common end. The organization paradox is a name for *inefficiency.* It is not a description of total failure. Efficiency, like other marks of success, is a matter of degree, and the organization paradox also works "more and less."

The paradox cannot be dismissed, however. The risk of planning a large enterprise, and in particular the risk of trying to run an entire economy from a central office, is that the difficulty of coordinating the varied activities of thousands of people in the achievement of a clear objective always makes the achievement more costly than it had been estimated to be and always produces unanticipated consequences, some of which are bound to be penalties. Ludwig von Mises wrote a classic description of this process in his book *Bureaucracy* (1944), and his commentary has been brought up to date by Jackson Grayson's *Confessions of a Price Controller* (1974), a work that illustrates how a bureaucracy can produce the opposite of what is intended.

The only solution that has thus far been devised to reduce the inefficiency of large organizations is, somehow, to make each individual responsible for his actions. *To be responsible* means to feel the effects of one's acts; it is to suffer and enjoy the consequences of what one does.

Our thesis is that this occurs more readily when individuals act in their own economic interests than when distant politicians control the economic preferences of their anonymous constituents. Bureaucracies can and do fake information, and they can and do immunize their directors against information.

By contrast, the market provides relatively prompt feedback to producers, sellers, and consumers.

What Are the Conditions That Facilitate or Hinder Economic Growth?

Present purposes do not require a detailed recounting of the content of economics textbooks. It will be sufficient for our concern to abstract from these texts and from the history of modern economies some of the principles operative in economic development. Before listing these principles, however, a reminder is required: the reminder that our desires have costs, and that a benefit on one side of the ledger may be a cost on the other.

On Material and Moral Benefits This caution is required, again, because the economic objective is frequently obscured by moral objectives. For example, there is a tendency to talk about "the problems of poverty and equality" in the same breath, as though "solving" one problem removed the other. In particular, it is popular to speak as though promoting equality necessarily removed poverty. On the contrary, it is possible, of course, to promote a society in which all are equally poor.

Equality is not the central issue in our concern about economic matters, and certainly the concern is not to achieve an equality in misery. When people express their economic hopes and fears, their concerns are for security and for improvement in the material standard of their lives. Both security and material comfort require the production of wealth. The conditions of productivity deserve attention, then. As will be seen, the conditions that permit an increase in wealth are not always pleasant, nor are they readily available to poor countries. Assuming, again, that the population growth of a land can be brought into line with its productive potential, the interconnected conditions that produce wealth and contribute to its increase are *improved tools, capital, human resources, and stable, sensible rule.* Each of these factors can be looked at separately, although they are intertwined in operation.

1 Putting Better Tools to Work

Increasing the production of wealth requires putting better tools to work. The better tools today are derived from the application of a peculiar way of thinking called "scientific" to agriculture and industry. Science and scientists are therefore part of the wealth-generating resources of countries, and the better tools they have devised are themselves part of the wealth that makes wealth—*capital.*

On the basis of this fact, it is frequently argued that lending or giving poor countries better tools (machinery, for example) or allowing them to steal the tools (nationalizing industries without compensation) will automatically increase the wealth of a nation by increasing its capital. There is more to making wealth than this, however. Capital is both human and nonhuman, and improved technology is only a *necessary* element, but not a *sufficient* one, in the production of wealth.

2 Acquiring Capital—Human and Nonhuman

The capital stock of a country includes its natural endowment of land and resources plus every material thing human beings have made out of these natural resources. The *nonhuman capital* includes buildings, food, tools, and any other material object of value. The test of whether a material thing has value is whether it is *exchangeable.*

Capital stock also includes a human element—the skills, interests, motivation, ideas, and social organization of individuals—that is, those human qualities that affect productivity.

The growth of human and nonhuman capital is interrelated. To develop capital requires *saving,* and this is as true of the development of a human resource as it is of a nonhuman bit of capital. To save means to forgo consumption. It means to invest some energy in the future. The willingness and the ability to save are functions of the psychology of a people, but investment in the future also rests upon the stability and sensibility of governments. Saving, the accumulation of capital, requires confidence that one's government will not change the rules of the game or tax the reward to savings. Unstable governments encourage hasty hedonism, the attitude that it is wiser to spend what one has, now, lest someone take it away. It is this attitude, among others, that makes it difficult for Third World nations to develop the capital required to improve their lot (Johnson, 1971; Rodman, 1971).

3 Developing Human Resources

How people work and save, how they associate in order to produce and distribute, and the skills they have acquired are important factors in the manufacture of wealth. These human qualities probably are as important to the production of wealth as the presence of natural resources or even of tools. The economist Boulding (1965, p. 142) puts it this way:

> The process of economic growth . . . which all agree is one of the major goals of economic policy, is imperfectly understood. It is certainly *not* mere technology: physical inputs and outputs, dams and roads, even though these things must be part of the process. Neither is it mere economics: stabilization and trade, investment and consumption, money and budgets. It involves subtle things such as motivation and morale, conflict management and political legitimacy, family structure and religious belief, and so on almost indefinitely.

Both common sense and professional expertise recognize that the human variable affects productivity, but *it is not known how to improve the working psychology of a people.* Whether called social habits or the work ethic, the way in which a people applies itself to production, the incentives for working well, and the motivation to resist corruption or yield to it—all these human factors affect our economic lives and are acknowledged to do so by both capitalist and communist economists. There is, however, no science that teaches us how to implant productive habits in others.

Psychologists have attempted to promote "achievement motivation" among groups in less developed countries, but without any noticeable success (Atkinson, 1958; McClelland, 1953, 1955, 1961). A more favored route to the development of human resources has been through schooling. Certainly the educational level of a population influences its productivity. Skills are required to convert science to a technology applied to agriculture, industry, and health. Attending to education does *not* mean, however, that everyone should have a university degree in order to elevate the economy of a country. In fact, Myrdal's large-scale project (1969, 1970), directed toward an analysis of the sources of Asian poverty and its remedy, concluded that one factor that keeps such countries as India poor is an outmoded system of education that produces too many lawyers, civil servants, and academics and not enough engineers and workers.

4 Stable and Sensible Government

The good intentions of governments are no substitute for economically sound policies. Indeed, the mask of good intention often conceals the folly of our ways.

Governments affect the productivity of their people in many ways—most strikingly through taxation but also through their attitudes toward land reform, trade unions, and wage and price controls. The very *stability* of government affects the accumulation of capital and its use. Shaky governments, or those that change the rules of the economic game, are governments that *discourage* economic growth. For example, the economist Miller (1973, p. 697) tells us that "the threat of nationalization which hangs over most Latin American nations probably prevents a massive amount of foreign investment that might be necessary to allow these nations to become more developed." The threat of changed rules of ownership and the lack of local investment opportunity drives the needed domestic capital out of unstable, poor countries into more secure financial havens. This movement of money can be seen in the flight of Asian and "white" capital from Africa, of Latin capital from South America, and of Arab wealth from Asia Minor (U.S. News & World Report, 1974a).

"The only way to acquire wealth," economists tell us, "is to save. The more certain private property rights are, the more capital accumulation there will be" (Miller, 1973, pp. 592, 696). Governments that are unstable or that are hostile to the accumulation of private property are governments that stand in the way of a better material life for their people.

Government stability is not enough, therefore, and an additional requirement for economic growth is that the government be sensible. A list of governmental follies that have *reduced* the wealth of their countries is long and need only be sampled here. In this sample it will be seen that many economically unsound policies have a strong nationalistic flavor and they may, for this reason, have some popular support; but this kind of misplaced patriotism does not make the nationalistic policy productive. Among the *wealth-destroying* practices employed by many poor countries, and some not so poor, are:

1 The expulsion of enterprising ethnic minorities who are richer than the natives.

2 The neglect of a country's agricultural markets in favor of an attempted, imposed industrialization.

3 Reliance on increased taxation of traditional activities, such as agriculture, that reduces the reward for productivity (Johnson, 1971).

4 Discouragement of some industries, such as the tourist trade, because they use "menial" labor.

5 Investment in "national vanities," as McDowell (1973b) calls them, such as unprofitable state airlines and showy construction projects.

6 Populist "land reform," such as the *ejido* system in Mexico, that divides huge holdings into small parcels. Such parceling makes it difficult to capitalize agriculture and to convert farming into the industry that it must be if it is to be productive (Lipsey and Steiner, 1966, pp. 684–685).

7 The impulse to *autarky*. Autarky is the movement of a country to become economically independent, to produce everything that it needs. This impulse opposes specialization—doing what one can most profitably do—and it is an obstacle to trade. *The willingness to trade* is a major characteristic that distinguishes economically successful from unsuccessful lands. The trading idea means that attention is paid to what one can most economically produce with a willingness to exchange such production for those needs more cheaply met by other people. The willingness to specialize and to trade accounts for the wealth of such resource-poor countries as Denmark, Norway, Sweden, and Holland.

The urge to become economically independent has military significance and it is always a matter of patriotic pride, but the impulse to autarky is a desire that is expensively gratified.

A Democratic Test of "The Good Life"

Our exposition of the factors that create wealth or destroy it runs against the grain of some popular opinions about how to reduce economic misery. Our position takes the side of a market system against a centrally planned economy. It favors trade over autarky and the private accumulation of capital with the freedom to invest it over state monopoly of capital.

As we have seen (p. 253), there is another side in the debate about how best to meet the social concern for an improved standard of living. In this debate, our side submits a *democratic* test of the comparative goodness of life in countries of diverse economy. This test is *independent* of a student's bias. It rests on how people choose. It is the test of migration: *How do people vote with their feet when they can?*

The net movement of people is away from societies with centrally planned economies toward societies with more open, market economies. People in West Berlin do not hammer for entry at the gates of East Berlin but rather the reverse. People do not flee Hong Kong for the People's Republic of China but rather the reverse. Canadians do not seek residence in the Ukraine but rather the reverse. And Americans do not exchange citizenship of the United States for that of the Soviet Union as frequently as Soviet citizens seek to become Americans.

SUMMARY

The relief of economic deprivation throughout the world has been shown to require a reduction in the growth of population, particularly among the poorer countries, and the facilitation of wealth production. The obstacles to the improvement of our material lives are, in small part, our ignorance of any "laws" of economic development but, in greater part, a matter of our morals and of the changing realities of the world in which we live. These changing realities mean that what has enabled countries in the past to increase their wealth may not be options in the future. Physical and social changes are in process that force some scholars, against their wishes, to foresee a global movement toward "wars of redistribution" and " 'iron' governments . . . of a military-socialist cast" (Heilbroner, 1974).

The moral movements and physical facts that prompt such a dismal forecast are, in outline, these:

The increase in population.
The ethical objections to the control of human reproduction.
The ethical demand for equality of material condition (as contrasted with equality of "opportunity").
The pride of patriotism that fosters the impulse to autarky.
The morality that hates commerce and the private uses of capital.
The depletion of resources and the need to dispose of the garbage that economic development produces[6].
The necessity to control monopolies of labor and tools—in short, the need for strong governments to control conflicting interests.

Against such gloomy prophecy, we hope that science and its offspring, technology, will save us (Beckmann, 1973; Lundberg, 1961). Science may do so, and one would be foolish to shut the door now to the possibility of increases in knowledge and know-how (Popper, 1957). However, on the road to this

---

[6]There are conceivable limits to industrial growth forced not only by the demand for energy but also by the parallel need to dispose of waste. The waste is not just human and industrial garbage but also the heat generated by industrial processes and spilled into the atmosphere. Presently, "the amount of heat added to the natural flow of solar and planetary heat is estimated at about 1/15,000 of the latter—an insignificant amount. The emission of man-made heat is, however, growing exponentially, as both cause and consequence of industrial growth. This leads us to face the incompatibility of a fixed 'receptacle,' however large, and an exponentially growing body, however initially small" (Heilbroner, 1974, p. 51).

solution, we are assured of continuing difficulties, difficulties that flow from present deficiencies in our knowledge and from the conflict of our desires.

The conflict of our desires is a conflict *within* us, as individuals who want conflicting things, but it is also a battle *between* us. The battles between us are engaged by individuals and by groups. We engage in these fights because the other person or group threatens what we have or stands in the way of what we want. These fights often become deadly quarrels. The killing is another matter of concern to be addressed in the next chapter.

Chapter 13

Killing Each Other: Murder

Homo sapiens, "Man, the wise," is the most dangerous organism on earth. This upright mammal is a killer. Human beings are a danger to their own species and to others. Though not the only organism that kills its own kind, *Homo sapiens* is the only species that kills for so many reasons and that can simultaneously express anguish and pride about the homicide.

The concern with our killing each other flows from this recognition: that deadly conflict is a constant. Shortly after "it all began," we have been told, Cain killed his brother, Abel. The killing since then has been *continual,* but not, of course, *continuous. Mortal fighting is a perpetual, recurring characteristic of the human connection.*

Our concern is to remain connected without getting killed. This concern for peace, like the occasions for deadly battle, fluctuates. It is not a constant quantity. In fact, our varying concern with peace is also a reason given for our killing each other. Human beings fight in order to achieve peace.

Some people call this a moral contradiction, or a logical one. It yet remains a common justification. Human beings kill each other to stop the killing. At least they utter this reason for the homicide they recommend, whether or not we believe that this reason is a cause of conflict.[1] Human beings say that they fight

---

[1]Reasons need not be causes. Every student of human behavior should be alert to the difference. A reason is a statement given in explanation or justification of an act. A cause is that which produces the act.

Without becoming too philosophic here, it is apparent that reasons are sometimes causes, but sometimes they are not.

for peace, and they prescribe it. Here are some "civilized" and "primitive" examples:

Fighting for Peace:

> We will have peace even if we have to fight for it [General Dwight Eisenhower, upon the conclusion of World War II, 1946].

> We are advocates of the abolition of war, we do not want war; but war can only be abolished through war, and in order to get rid of the gun it is necessary to take up the gun [Chairman Mao, 1967, p. 35].

> When one group of clans finally decides to invite its enemies for a *gaingar* (a ritualistic clan battle), the people always say that this is a spear fight to end spear fights, so that from that time on there will be peace for all the clans and tribes. This is sincerely believed at the time, since it is an effort to stop clan feuds [Thomas, 1937, p. 496, describing a "primitive" tribe].

> Peace Activists Defend Bombing [Headline in *The New York Times,* concerning the trial of a university building-bomber-killer. *National Review,* 1973].

Mortal Semantics

This sampling of justifications is but an introduction to the causes of our killing each other. This introduction suggests that the occasions for homicide are many. It is difficult, however, to classify these occasions because the names given to them do not merely *describe* the kinds of killing; they also *justify* or *deplore* the homicide. The titles of the homicides take sides. For example, "murder" is the name for unjustified, intentional homicide. The word has a *legal* meaning—homicide that the criminal law of our state calls crime—but it also has a *moral* meaning—homicide that is disapproved. Thus when terrorist bands kill their enemies or the symbols of their enemies in the form of innocent bystanders, the terrorists absolve themselves of murder by calling their killing an execution. Elevating homicide to execution makes a claim for its justice; reducing homicide to murder denies the fairness with which death is dealt.

The intrusion of *justification* upon *description* means that it is difficult to apply clear labels to the varied styles of homicide. Language, it has been noted, is strongly evaluative (Osgood et al., 1957). Words are saturated with preferences. Our wishes influence our interpretation of violence as we choose sides in the battles. The sides we choose affect, therefore, the names we call the killing. In turn, and to make matters worse, the titles we give the fights reflect the programs we prefer for peace. For example, if what the killers want seems just, the recommendation is for those social changes that will give them what they "need."[2] On the other hand, if the violence is deemed unjust or, at best, unfortunate, the prescription calls for control of the actors or treatment of their motives. The justifications given for people killing people determine

---

[2]We have already had occasion to remark on the vagueness of the concept of need (pp. 7; 104). The vagueness demonstrates the saturation of words with preferences. For example, the transformation of "what he wants" into "what he needs" is a moral translation.

recommendations. They do so as much as, or more so than, "the facts of the matter."

IN SUMMARY

Our excursion into the semantics of homicide illustrates these points:

1 That human beings simultaneously deplore and praise their homicide.
2 That the different titles given the homicide indicate approval or disapproval of the killing.
3 That the policies proposed to reduce the killing take sides and that the sides can be known by the names given the homicide.
4 That mixing description of the killing with its condemnation or approval means that a "mere" scientific explanation of humanity's homicidal proclivity will not satisfy most inquirers. A scientific explanation does not satisfy because we are asking for more than a description of "the facts of the matter" or a statement about the regularities that seem to determine these facts. We are also concerned with remedies. The two motives—the scientific one and the prescriptive one—are not necessarily congenial and are themselves often at war.

THE KILLING OCCASIONS

If we ask, "Why do newborn ladybugs eat their brothers?" (Hagen, 1970) or "Why does the female praying mantis sometimes eat her mate?" as in the photograph from Roeder (1967), we are usually satisfied with a *dispositional* explanation.

A male praying mantis about to be eaten head first by the female he is trying to court. (*From Nerve Cells and Insect Behavior by K. D. Roeder, 1967, p. 163, Harvard University Press. © 1963, 1967 by the President and Fellows of Harvard College. Reproduced by permission.*)

"Well," we say, "that's the way they are."

If scientists wish to go further, they ask what *makes* these creatures the way they are, and the search for causes proceeds from *conditions* in the environment and *occasions* for the cannibalism to *mechanisms* within the organisms. All these kinds of causes can be found, and are found. They are found for humanity as they are for the mantis.

However, when we ask ourselves, "Why do human beings kill each other at so great a rate?" a dispositional explanation does not comfort us. We do not wish to hear that human beings kill each other because "that's the way they are." So we look for circumstances that seem to trigger the homicide. But the killing occasions are numerous and varied—so much so that, at the end of our inquiry, we seem forced back to a dispositional explanation.

All classifications of our deadly quarrels are unsatisfactory because they *mix* considerations of

The *numbers* of people involved.
The *relations* between killers and their victims.
The *personal characteristics* of both.
The *degree of impulse or plan* in the homicide.
The *reasons* given by the actors in the drama.
Our *approval or disapproval* of the attack and its "reasons." This also affects

A *shifting location of the "causes"* of the homicide. We move the causes about among killers, their victims, their histories, and their circumstances as we approve or disapprove of the combatants.

Moving Causes

Sociopsychological research reveals a tendency to locate the causes of behavior in different places when we explain "good" people doing "good" acts or "bad" ones, and "bad" people doing "good" deeds or "evil" ones.

The tendency is to attribute the good deeds of good people to their character or their purposes, and similarly for bad people doing wicked things. Our conception of a moral consistency between the actor and his acts puts the causes of his behavior "in him." However, where people behave inconsistently with our approval or disapproval of them and their behavior, we shift the location of the causes from inside the actor to outside, and we tend to attribute the sources of his behavior to luck, accident, or circumstance (Leifer, 1964; Regan et al., 1974; Schiffman and Wynne, 1963).

We can diagram this peculiar tendency in causal attribution as in Table 13-1.

The moral tendency to move the location of causes so as to balance our evaluation of acts and actors makes a classification of the styles of homicide difficult. However, one way of giving order to the varied modes of deadly fighting is to consider the killing as falling along a continuum of impulse and intent.

Homicide on an Expressive-Instrumental Continuum

The innumerable combinations of causes, reasons, and circumstances of homicide may be regarded as occurring along an expressive-instrumental continuum. An advantage of studying the killing this way is that it relieves us of the belief that we shall find *the* cause of our mortal combat. A disadvantage of this arrangement of the killing occasions is that it does not tell us much about where to draw the line between killing that is accidental and that which is intended. Much killing is, of course, a mixture of accident and intent.

Omitting for the moment those homicides that might be called accidental, killing can be conceived as varying from that which is highly *expressive* (impulsive) to that which is purely *instrumental* (rational). Between these poles, there are homicides which, in varying degree, represent blends of expressive and instrumental causes. For example:

Expressive Homicide

Much of the killing of one person by another is impulsive. It is an outburst that is purely expressive, such as results from a barroom brawl or a domestic fracas. This kind of killing is not planned, but it is provoked. Frequently it is mutually provoked—by both the killer and his victim. In many such cases, the roles of killer and victim are only accidentally decided.

In industrialized countries it is a rule of thumb that at least half of all murders, as legally defined, are of this passionate nature. Loved ones and other acquaintances are the single most frequent source of murder (Gillin, 1946; Koestler, 1956, pp. 145–146; McClintock, 1963; Morris, 1955; Wolfgang, 1958). Impassioned killing among intimates is so frequent as to have earned it the title of "*'normal'* passionate homicide" (Wolfgang and Ferracuti, 1967, p. 365, emphasis added).

Instrumental Homicide

Human beings also kill each other because it is useful to do so. The uses vary, of course. There is, for example, the utility of killing the other person in order

Table 13-1 Evaluating Actors and Acts and Locating Their Causes

| | Location of the cause of behavior ||
Approval/disapproval of person/behavior	In person (character; intention)	In circumstance (luck; accident; "pressure")
Good person, good deed	+	
Bad person, bad act	+	
Good person, bad act		+
Bad person, good act		+

to take his money. There is also the rationality of murder as a profession, of being a "hired gun" in the service of gangs or states, and there is the classic utility of killing as an instrument of conquest. The most common cause, or reason, for large-scale killing—planned and organized—is the achievement of some ideal.

In brief, people resort to violence because it is a way of getting what one wants. This is as true of muggings, student riots, civil rights demonstrations, and labor-management fights as it is of terrorist attacks and war (Gamson, 1974). *Violence works.* How much it *costs* is another matter.

For centuries philosophers have called attention to the rationality of battle while simultaneously noting its emotional satisfactions. In modern times the Prussian general Karl von Clausewitz (1780–1831) emphasized the rationality of organized homicide by calling war "a continuation of diplomacy by other means."

Political power rests on the ability to use and justify homicide. Power that is legitimate—that is supported by its subjects—need not resort to killing. Political power that would maintain itself against challenge or that would extend itself will kill. Political power that has not yet been achieved but that is desired will also resort to homicide. This reminder is given by Chairman Mao (1967, p. 33), who is echoing von Clausewitz. "Every Communist must grasp the truth," Mao said in 1938, "[that] political power grows out of the barrel of a gun."

Instrumental killing, for whatever purpose, is not always *intended* as part of the show of force, but the resort to armed force as an instrument for getting what one wants is an occasion and a provocation of homicide.

Mixed Motives: Expressive-Purposive Homicide

Much killing, perhaps most, is stimulated by a moving mixture of emotion and purpose. It is *both* expressive and rational, an end in itself and a means to an end.

People kill people for rational reasons—to achieve their objectives—but at the same time they kill as an expression of their emotions, emotions that range from hatred to joy and that include pride as well as shame.

The popular association of killing with hating should not obscure the pleasures of homicide. In fact, for some people, hating is its own pleasure.

The mixtures of rationality and emotionality that mark most intended and recommended homicide can best be sampled by allowing the participants to speak for themselves:

1 *Violence is sexy* (as Sigmund Freud told us):

Dotson Rader: Personally, I would welcome a violent revolution, because there's something in me personally that finds violence . . .

William Buckley: You find it sexy?
Dotson Rader: I find it sexy, yes [1973].

2 *Shooting is living*

Cin knew that to live was to shoot straight [Patty Hearst, speaking of her leader, Cinque, 1974].

3 *But kill the right people (no. 1):*

There's nothing wrong with killing people as long as they're the right people [Dirty Harry, speaking in *Magnum Force,* 1974].

4 *But kill the right people (no. 2):*

I do not really see anything wrong with burning university professors. Some of them are criminals [the philosopher Jean-Paul Sartre, 1973].

5 *But kill the right people (no. 3):*

It is not necessary for a black man to hate a white man, or to have any particular feelings about him at all, in order to realize that he must kill him [the novelist James Baldwin, 1972, p. 191].

6 *Achieve dignity through brutality (no. 1):*

. . . for the colonised people this violence, because it constitutes their only work, invests their characters with positive and creative qualities. The practice of violence binds them together as a whole, since each individual forms a violent link in the great chain, a part of the great organism of violence which has surged upwards in reaction to the settler's violence in the beginning . . . the building up of the nation . . . is helped on by the existence of this cement which has been mixed with blood and anger. . . . At the level of individuals, violence is a cleansing force. It frees the native from his inferiority complex and from his despair and inaction; it makes him fearless and restores his self-respect [the psychiatrist Franz Fanon, 1963, p. 73].

7 *Achieve dignity through brutality (no. 2):*

Haven't you ever seen a crowd collecting to watch a street brawl? *Brutality is respected.* Brutality and physical strength. Why babble about brutality and be indignant about tortures? The masses want that. Terror is the most effective political instrument [Adolf Hitler, as reported by Rauschning, 1939, pp. 89–90, emphasis in the original].

8   *Achieve dignity through brutality (no. 3):*

One of the best guarantees to make a man a man is a gun in his hand [Saul Landau, 1972].

9   *Violence is edifying:*

Violence alone, violence committed by the people, violence organized and educated by its leaders, makes it possible for the masses to understand social truths and gives the key to them [Fanon, 1963, p. 117].

10   *Liberation requires killing (no. 1):*

There is only one means of shortening, simplifying, concentrating the murderous death-pangs of the old society and the bloody birth-pangs of the new, only one means—revolutionary terror [Karl Marx, 1848].

11   *Liberation requires killing (no. 2):*

Until you people are prepared to kill your parents you aren't ready for the revolution [Jerry Rubin, 1970].

12   *Happiness is justified hatred:*

The great moment had come. The curtain of fire lifted from the front trenches. We stood up.

With a mixture of feelings, evoked by bloodthirstiness, rage, and intoxication, we moved in step, ponderously but irresistibly, toward the enemy lines. I was well ahead of the company, followed by Vinke and a one-year veteran named Haake. My right hand embraced the shaft of my pistol, my left a riding stick of bamboo cane. I was boiling with a mad rage, which had taken hold of me and all the others in an incomprehensible fashion. The overwhelming wish to kill gave wings to my feet. Rage pressed bitter tears from my eyes.

The monstrous desire for annihilation, which hovered over the battlefield, thickened the brains of the men and submerged them in a red fog. We called to each other in sobs and stammered disconnected sentences. A neutral observer might have perhaps believed that we were seized by an excess of happiness [Ernst Juenger, from his World War I diary, as cited by Gray, 1959, p. 52].

13   *Justice requires killing* (as Hammurabi told us about 1760 B.C.):

To the question most commonly asked about the Eichmann trial: What good does it do? there is but one possible answer: It will do justice [the philosopher Hannah Arendt, 1964, p. 254, justifying the trial and hanging of the Nazi Eichmann].

What It All Means

This sample of citations takes no sides with any of the justifications given for homicide. It is provided at this length, and still inadequately, to disabuse us of the wishful belief that homicide is only an accident, a mistake, a misunderstanding, or an inhuman aberration which, upon some knowledge or some therapy, will no longer mark our history. On the contrary, killing is a constant.

Incidental Points The statements of the protagonists above illustrate points incidental to this principal conclusion:

1   That people advocate killing for "good" reasons as well as "bad" ones.
2   That there is no end to the possibility of justification.
3   That there is pleasure and pride as well as pain and shame in the recommendations for homicide.

We struggle against ourselves. It is as Pogo said, "We have met the enemy, and he is us." Nevertheless, we strive to understand some of the homicide in the hope that we can reduce it. This effort can be examined for two of the many styles of deadly quarrel: *murder and war.*

MURDER: ILLEGAL HOMICIDE

"Homicide" is a general term for taking human life. Within English-speaking states, homicide becomes the crime called murder if it is not excusable or justifiable and if it is committed "with malice aforethought" or in the commission of a felony (indictable offense).

Homicide is *excusable* if it is the result of an accident that is *not* defined as "culpable negligence." This is like saying that the law does not regard all "accidents" as accidental. It holds us responsible for unintended deaths inflicted as a result of carelessness, as in the case of a drunken driver killing a pedestrian.

Homicide is *justifiable* when it is an intentional killing done in accordance with legal obligation or in circumstances where the criminal law recognizes no wrong. Examples of justifiable homicide, varying in their definition by jurisdiction, are the execution of criminals by the state and the killing necessary to prevent a major crime (felony) or to arrest a suspected felon. Killing in self-defense or in the protection of one's home is also regarded in some states as justifiable homicide.

The criminal homicide called murder is itself graded by degree. Murders that are deliberately committed or that occur as part of the attempt to commit an indictable offense such as arson, rape, burglary, robbery, or kidnapping, are "murders in the first degree." In states that allow the death penalty for such homicides, they are also "capital murders."

Second-degree murder, or manslaughter, is culpable homicide committed without premeditation.

These styles of homicide indicate that there is some discretion in the definition of murder, manslaughter, and even suicide or self-inflicted death. Therefore, attempts to count and compare murder rates are qualified by the possibility that different countries and different jurisdictions within countries define homicide somewhat differently. It is best, then, to consider the statistics of deadly crime as estimates of the magnitude of such fatal quarrels rather than as exact figures. If this qualification is kept in mind, some aspects of the murder record can be reported.

Some Murder Records

Police statistics indicate that the "open" industrialized countries of North America are more murderous than the older industrialized countries of Europe. Japan, the industrial giant of the East, seems a little more homicidal than Western Europe but less so than the violent United States. Table 13-2 tells something of the recent story.

Among the less industrialized countries, Latin lands and some African states have notably high homicide rates, running in the order of 20 to 34 murders reported for every 100,000 people (Wolfgang and Ferracuti, 1967, pp. 274–275). However, in all large countries, there are pockets of violence. Some areas are more dangerous than others. For example, the Caserta district near Naples, Italy, has a persisting record of murder, probably the highest rate of personal attack in Europe. Similarly, the state of Morelos in Mexico succeeds in more than doubling the high murder rate of the rest of that country (Wolfgang and Ferracuti, 1967, pp. 279–281).

In the United States, the risk of murder also varies with place, race, and

Table 13-2 Homicides in Selected Countries: 1957, 1967, and 1968 (Rate per 100,000 Inhabitants)*

Country	Male			Female		
	1957	1967	1968	1957	1967	1968
United States	7.6	11.3	13.4	2.4	3.4	3.4
White	3.5	5.4	6.6	1.4	2.0	2.0
Black and other	43.4	58.8	68.6	10.8	13.2	13.6
Canada	1.5	1.9	2.2	0.9	1.2	1.3
Scandinavia and the Netherlands	0.6	0.7	0.6	0.5	0.5	0.5
Western Europe†	1.4	1.1	NA	0.6	0.8	NA
Japan	2.8	1.9	1.8	1.4	1.0	1.0

*Source: Statistical Abstract of the United States, 1973, Table No. 236.
†Includes the United Kingdom, France, Ireland, Belgium, Switzerland, and the Federal Republic of Germany.

class. Thus the southern region has long had a more murderous record than other sections of the country, and the violent difference persists, as Table 13-3 shows. Furthermore, large cities have higher murder rates than rural areas which, in turn, have higher rates than the suburbs (Table 13-3).

Race, too, makes a difference. Within the United States, blacks have much higher murder rates than whites (Table 13-2). These differences are largely a matter of *intraracial* homicide, that is, these differences mean that blacks kill blacks at a greater rate than whites kill whites. For example, Graham (1970) estimates that blacks accounted for almost two-thirds of the arrests for murder during the 1960s, and Wolfgang (1958) found young black men to be convicted of criminal homicide at a rate more than twenty-five times that of white men of similar age. The dissimilarity in racial murder rates is sufficiently great that black *women* produce murder rates that run two to four times higher than that of white *men* (Table 13-2; Wolfgang and Ferracuti, 1967, p. 154).

Social class differences are also associated with variations in homicide, as they are with many other kinds of crime (Chapter 7). Poor people kill each other more frequently than do more affluent people (Henry and Short, 1954; Lalli and Turner, 1968). These class differences in murder rates persist when race is held constant, and the race differences persist when social status is held constant. For the United States, at least, race and class have independent significance for murder rates.

Changing Rates   These variations within countries by class, place, and race are observed against a background of changing rates of homicide in different lands. Thus, while murder in England and Wales has remained at a fairly constant, low level from the mid-1960s into the 1970s (Central Statistical Office, 1973), murder rates in Canada have progressed from lows of about 1 per 100,000 population in the 1950s to about 1.5 per 100,000 during the early 1960s and steadily upward since then to levels around 2.5 per 100,000 during the early 1970s (Statistics Canada, 1974). In recent years the United States has shown greater increases in the amount of recorded violent crime. Its murder rate of 9.3 per 100,000 inhabitants in 1973 represents an 86 percent increase over its rate for 1960. The interval between these years was marked by a steady climb in

Table 13-3   Murder Rates by Region and by Urbanity, United States, 1973 (Rate per 100,000 Inhabitants)*

North-eastern states	North central states	Southern states	Western states	Cities over 250,000	Rural	Suburban	Total U.S.
7.6	7.6	12.9	7.8	20.7	7.5	5.1	9.3

*Source: Uniform Crime Reports for the United States, 1973, p. 2.

murder rates accompanied by an increase in other violent attacks such as forcible rape, robbery, and aggravated assault (*Uniform Crime Reports,* 1973).

It has been popular to attribute much of this increase in American violence to changes in the age composition of the population. The most murderous people are young men, and it has been assumed that the postwar "baby boom" might account for the increase in homicide. However, a careful analysis of changes in murder rates between 1963–1965 and 1971–1972 in the fifty largest cities in the United States demonstrates that "less than one-tenth of the actual rise in the national homicide rate since the 1960s can be explained by demographic changes" (Barnett et al., 1974, p. 23). These investigators show that homicide rates increased in every one of the fifty cities during the late 1960s and early 1970s. When these rates are adjusted to take account of variations in the age and ethnic composition of the cities—differences that make a difference in murder rates—it is found that the greatest increase in homicide has been in Detroit, Buffalo, and Honolulu. Detroit has been given the title of "murder capital of the world" because of this dramatic increase in its homicide rate and because its 1971–1972 rate is the highest among American cities. Its killing rate of 38.93 murders for ever 100,000 residents is probably the highest in the world.

Barnett and his colleagues conclude that murder rates in American cities are higher than many people believe and that "at current . . . levels, a randomly-chosen baby born in a large American city has almost a two percent chance of dying by homicide; among males, the figure is three percent. Thus, an American boy born in 1974 is more likely to die by murder than an American soldier in World War II was to die in combat. With the reduction in auto fatalities because of lower speed limits and new safety devices, it is plausible that murder might soon surpass auto accidents as a cause of death in America" (p. 35).

Explaining the Variations

Students have offered some morally and politically satisfying interpretations of such group differences and changes in murder rates, but the scientific foundation for their explanations is thin.

Groups are said to differ in their proclivity to kill each other for the same reasons they are said to cheat and steal at different rates (see, again pp. 140–145). Some investigators emphasize the *subcultural* patterns of violence. Others call attention to the *social structures* in which different people live and which make murder "understandable" and sometimes rational. Still other researchers emphasize the differences in values—in aspirations, ideals, and beliefs about the world—that stimulate some people to kill each other at higher rates. And other students emphasize the *modes of training* and the *models of behavior* that constrain or promote homicide. Since there are different occasions of our deadly quarrels, each of these explanations points to something true some of the time.

There *are* people who are reared in social settings where violence is encouraged, where weapons are carried as part of one's costume, and where beliefs, teachings, and models of behavior encourage taking offense quickly and settling the argument by force (Gastil, 1971; Wolfgang and Ferracuti, 1967). The trouble with this subcultural style of explanation is that it often reduces to a dispositional explanation or a tautology. It comes down to saying, "People kill each other at a high rate because they are violent." The advantage of this style of explanation is that, if the subculture is described in sufficient detail, the killing becomes "understandable" and our curiosity rests.

Structural explanations try to break out of the apparent circularity of subcultural explanations by noting aspects of the social environment that pressure people into murder or that make murder rational. For example, some situations are seen as frustrating and therefore deserving of attack. Frustration occurs, of course, but, as we shall see (pp. 285–287), it is not uniformly related to aggression.

The trouble with structural explanations of our mortal battles parallels the difficulty with the subcultural theory. Both theories tell plausible stories and both appeal to making things "understandable" as evidence for their interpretation. However, a peculiar risk of the structural theory is that it is often used as a *justification* of the events explained, where the justification adds little to our ability to predict or control those events.

One sign that a structural explanation is used to justify, rather than to explain scientifically, is that it is used inconsistently. That is, the structure—the situation the group is in—"explains" the violence of people we like but not that of those we dislike. It "explains" the violence of student protesters, for example, but not that of the National Guard; it "explains" the violence of our favorite guerrillas, but not that of Hitler's storm troopers.

A second sign that structural explanations may serve better as justifications than as scientific hypotheses appears in the weakness of a popular version of the situational explanation: *the frustration-aggression hypothesis.*

Does Frustration Produce Aggression?

A favorite form taken by structural explanations of homicide is that of the frustration-aggression hypothesis. This idea is the common-sense one that being frustrated makes people angry and that anger is the fuel for violence—individual and collective. It is then argued that this or that kind of social structure provides more and less frustration.

It is obvious that some kinds of frustration make some kinds of persons angry and aggressive. Our own emotions tell us so. However, raising this plausible notion to the status of a scientific hypothesis provokes important questions, the answers to which qualify the easy application of the frustration-aggression hypothesis. At least five questions have been asked of the scientific use of this idea:

1 Is frustration a *matter of circumstance,* a *state of mind,* or *some combination* of the two? In short, what does "frustration" mean?
2 *What* frustrates *whom?*
3 *How much* frustration is required, for *which* persons, before they respond violently?
4 Does frustration *necessarily* lead to aggression?
5 Does aggression occur *without* frustration?

The answers are, briefly, that "frustration" means more than one thing, that people are not frustrated to the same degree by similar circumstances, and that people who seem equally frustrated are not equally violent. Finally, much aggression occurs without much frustration. These points will be amplified.

"Frustration$_1$" (Objective Meaning) Is Not "Frustration$_2$" (Subjective Meaning)

"Frustration" is a fuzzy word. Sometimes it refers to a blocking, a thwarting, an obstacle that prevents a person from getting what he wants. At other times it refers to emotions, to feelings of despair and anger, or to a free-floating discontent.

The first meaning is *objective.* Observers can watch animals strive for goals and can agree about their success or failure: whether the monkey gets the banana or the runner wins the race. The second meaning is *subjective.* It refers to feelings attributed to the striver who fails. The objective failure that is sometimes called frustration is not the same set of events as the angry feelings called frustration. One can *be* frustrated without *feeling* frustrated, and vice versa.

The relation between the two meanings of "frustration" is far from perfect, and it is presumptive to infer one from the other. No one has yet mapped the coordinates of frustration. No one knows which persons under which circumstances feel more or less frustrated by which failure. In fact, the very ideas of success and failure have not been adequately diagrammed for people of diverse ways of life.

What Frustrates Whom, and How Much Frustration Is Required to Produce Violence?

If we attend solely to the *objective* definition of "frustration," it is apparent that frustration is a condition of social life. Living with others means that one cannot have everything he wants when he wants it in the manner he would like it. To say, then, that a thwarting of wants and needs is what causes us to kill each other is at the same time commonplace and only partly true. The truism ends by pointing everywhere to frustrating circumstances that make us hostile.

The frustration-aggression hypothesis is vulnerable to stretching so that any and all facts fit it. An illustration is provided by the British publisher John Calder (1970, p. 86) in his attempt to explain violence. Violence, Calder contends

> is always the direct result of frustration, whether it is the frustration of a political or social minority that feels it is suppressed or discriminated against . . . or a social class that feels it is exploited . . . or a play-group (as for instance a gang of youths whose frustration consists in there being no outlet for their natural energy, because the local authorities provide them with nothing to do and nowhere to go). In the latter case, gang warfare develops out of boredom, or else the violence of individuals whose frustration could be financial, or sexual, or lack of opportunity which finally vents itself in some direct or indirect violence.
>
> The most difficult age for a child is when he is not yet able to communicate through words, having something to communicate, but not knowing how; and the child's frustration comes out in various forms of naughtiness if not in direct violence. The teen-agers have problems arising from emotional and sexual frustration which again leads them into irrational behavior that often takes violent forms. . . . Poverty is most frustrating when it co-exists with riches, and it is in those rich societies today where poverty survives for substantial minorities that we can find the highest crime rate. Crime is a form of violence that arises directly out of frustration. . . .

The construction of such an encyclopedia of frustration describes so wide a range of the human predicament as to explain nothing. Abused in this manner, "frustration" becomes an empty category that may be filled to suit convenience. The hypothesis becomes a promiscuous apology for homicidal behavior by claiming that all unsatisfied wants lead to frustration and by seeing frustration everywhere. The important question is left unanswered: *"Which individuals, with what kinds of pasts, are apt to experience which kinds of obstacle as how frustrating?"*

Our ignorance on this matter is met by proposing some "mediators" that filter the interpretation of our failures into anger or away from it. These mediators are attitudes that define the frustration as justified or not. It is "unjust failure" that is angering. This formulation places a variable, *belief,* between the *circumstance* of being thwarted, the *feeling* of frustration, and *acts* of violence.

Captives of Fate, and Masters   Following the work of Julian Rotter (1966), psychologists have studied the effects of a personality variable designated as "belief in the control of one's own destiny" as a factor filtering the interpretation of failure.

Rotter and other students (De Charms, 1968) have shown that "generalized expectancies for internal versus external control" of one's fate are differentially distributed among individuals. Some people see themselves as masters of their own fates (as having internal control) while others see more of their lives as subject to forces beyond their powers (as being under external control).

As might be expected, differences on the internal-external (I-E) variable are associated with differences in effort, achievement, and the way information is used (Davis and Phares, 1967; Feather, 1967; Lefcourt et al., 1968; Lessing, 1969; Phares, 1968). There is evidence, for example, that persons with a stronger sense of *internal* control are better able to stop smoking (James et al., 1965), have a longer time perspective (Tolor et al., 1970), and have a greater commitment to social action (Gore and Rotter, 1963). For the United States, at least, racial and sexual differences are also reported on the I-E dimension, with white persons and men scoring higher on internal control (Lefcourt and Ladwig, 1965; Lessing, 1969; Platt et al., 1970).

What is most relevant to our present concern is the fact that a sense of personal control is related to a *willingness to defer gratification,* a variable that is associated with *immunity* to violent response (Lessing, 1969).

A Hypothesis   Given this kind of evidence, it seems plausible to propose psychological mediators that interpret our circumstances and that qualify any simple structural explanation of homicide. It is likely that individuals who have a stronger belief in their ability to control their own lives are less apt to blame their failures upon others or upon "the odds." If one could hold constant the objective opportunities for achievement and the intensity of ambition, it would seem a safe bet that the same amount of objective frustration would produce more violence among "externals" than among "internals."

SUMMARY

We have not been able to draw an accurate map describing which juncture of circumstance with which belief produces how much sense of being frustrated. Our ignorance allows consumers of the frustration-aggression hypothesis to defend their idea by fluctuating between the two meanings of the key term. Sometimes "frustration" is defined objectively—as in the conditions; sometimes it is defined subjectively—as in the interpretations.

However, most of us regard frustration as produced by a mixture of objective and subjective factors, although we cannot specify the proportions for different individuals in varying circumstances. Our recommendations for social action will vary, then, with our moral definitions, and these will call either for reform of the frustrating conditions or reform of the frustrated people.

Does Frustration Necessarily Lead to Aggression?

If we restrict the term "frustration" to objectively discernible goal blocking, it is clear that human beings and other organisms may be frustrated without becoming violent (Morlan, 1949).

It has been demonstrated, for example, that some kinds of frustration lead to *regression*—to more childlike behavior—rather than to attack (Barker et al., 1947; Himmelweit, 1950). Repeated frustration of children during their nurturing has also been reported to produce an *accommodation,* an acceptance of frustration, rather than violence (Bateson, 1941). The anthropologist Whiting (1944) reports that he was able to distinguish at least four patterns of response to frustration among a New Guinea tribe. Among the Kwoma, Whiting says, frustration sometimes produces *submission,* sometimes *dependence,* and, on other occasions, *avoidance,* as well as *aggression.* Similarly, Maier (1949) found that frustrated animals sometimes respond aggressively, but that they also exhibit regressive, apathetic, and fixated (stereotyped) behaviors.

If long-term unemployment may be considered to be frustrating, then there is additional evidence that apathy may be one of the effects of frustration (Jahoda et al., 1960).

Since we respond to goal blocking with such a variety of reactions, the original proponents of the frustration-aggression hypothesis were led to a revision of their thesis (Miller et al., 1941). Their revised thesis says that frustration leads to *several* patterns of response, *one* of which is aggression. This modified proposal holds that if frustration is not sufficiently relieved through other outlets, an aggressive response becomes more probable.

Does Aggression Occur Without Frustration?

Of course it does. There are many roads to homicide, and frustration is not the only path. Describing some of these many paths challenges the notion that only frustrated people attack.

Rational Killing   Killing is sometimes a rational tactic, as we have seen (pp. 276–277). It can be used as an instrument in the service of some objective, where the objective need *not* have been constructed out of frustration. Such instrumental violence is produced without its agents first having been thwarted or angered. We recognize this possibility by calling such rational killing cold-blooded, as when it is enacted by Mafiosi or revolutionary terrorists.

Normative Killing   Violence is also normative; that is, it is a widely advocated, group-supported way of "being a person." The Latin code of *machismo* and the clan code of *vendetta* are representations of the human definition of fighting and killing as requisite to honor. To attack when insulted is part of the meaning of dignity in such codes, a dignity that distinguishes "men from the worms."

Therapeutic Killing   The psychiatrist Fanon (1963) concurs with the normative idea when he tells us that killing is therapeutic for the aggrieved aggressor. Similarly, the sociologist Coser (1956; 1967) notes that being violent represents an achievement for deprived segments of society.

These interpretations may be placed within the frustration-aggression framework, but they need not be. They need not be because being dominant—exercising the power to damage—is its own pleasure. It has long been accorded such status in folklore and literature, and it continues to receive the applause of sports spectators.

Killing for Community   Being violent under appropriate circumstances is not only recommended as therapeutic and dignifying for individuals but is also regarded as a symbol of communal solidarity and a way of building it. Conflict reinforces community sentiment (Coser, 1956). For example, among North American Indians, Sumner observes (1911, p. 15), "those had the intensest feeling of unity who were the most warlike." Students of comparative animal behavior agree. The ethologist Lorenz (1966c, p. 36) concludes that "personal friendship is always coupled with aggression. We do not know of a single animal which is capable of personal friendship and which lacks aggression."

Killing Difference   The community spirit that is reinforced by conflict feeds on difference. The perception that others are unlike us is a common motive for disliking them and attacking them, whether or not they have frustrated us. Among many social animals, difference in itself provokes aggression (Allee, 1931; Lorenz, 1966b; Tinbergen, 1953; Wallis, 1965). Man, struggling with his own contrary morality, exhibits similar hostility toward the strange and foreign. For example, modern states that attempt to govern unequal nationalities are experiencing a stepped up pace of ethnic warfare. Catholic and Protestant have long killed each other in Northern Ireland, and they continue to do so. Fleming and Walloon dislike each other in Belgium. French- and English-speaking Canadians contend for power, and other Canadian minorities—Indians, Ukrainians, West Indians—are entering the fray. Catalans and Basques would like to rid themselves of Spain, and some Scots would like to be free of England. Hausa and Yoruba contend with Ibo in Nigeria, and both the U.S.S.R. and the United States struggle to maintain order among competing nationalities within their borders. The rising "fever of ethnicity" in modern states does not promise an early end to differences that kill (Alpert, 1972; Glazer and Moynihan, 1974).

Mortal Envy   One quality of dislike of the different that is readily converted to attack is envy. Envy is resentment of the other person's perceived superiority—of his or her beauty, happiness, or success. Envy is ill will. It wishes the other person did not have the envied qualities, despite the fact that no advantage is to be gained by depriving the envied person of these things. In

English, "envy" and "jealousy" are often used interchangeably. They ought to be kept separate, however, since envy is *disinterested resentment* while jealousy is *interested*. That is, the jealous person fears a loss of something he or she values because of the competition of another. If, for example, "she" dances too long with "him" and nibbles his ear, I may feel jealous—afraid of losing her to him. Envy, however, has nothing to lose by what the other enjoys, and it has nothing to gain except psychic satisfaction when the envied person is brought down.

Envy is its own emotion, an independent motive that has been universally recognized in myth, literature, and religion as requiring social control lest it become disruptive. The frustration-aggression hypothesis denies the autonomy of envy and, by so doing, obscures an important motive for mortal combat. Helmut Schoeck (1966), one of the few students of envy, documents the impulse to "crimes of envy," from vandalism to murder, that seem motivated by "the consuming desire that no one should have anything [that we do not, and by] the destruction of pleasure in and for others, without deriving any sort of advantage from this" (p. 115).

Pleasurable Homicide   Being violent is not only useful at times, symbolic of our "dignity," and expressive of our envy, it is also fun. Such sporting fighting has been called *agonistic,* from the ancient Greek idea of athletic combat. Human beings and other animals engage in aggression that is playful and ritualistic. According to ethologists, such struggle has a function: it helps "the young members discover, learn, and communicate their place in an ordered set of relationships" (Nieburg, 1970, p. 58). Human beings differ from their mammalian cousins, however, in that they seem to have less control over their aggression, so that fighting that starts as ritualistic play among people often gets out of hand and ends in death (Lorenz, 1966a).

Part of the pleasure in fighting derives from the relief of boredom. Fighting among humans is associated with feelings of joy and fraternity, and many warriors have commented on "the comradeship in danger and delight in destruction" (Gray, 1959, p. 29; 1970, p. 1).

Contagious Killing   There are still other paths to violence. Aggression is readily learned and the lesson easily communicated. Violent responses can be attached to neutral stimuli through conditioning, and the conditioned violent habit persists (Creer et al., 1966; Vernon and Ulrich, 1966; Willis et al., 1966). Furthermore, watching fighting models makes people want to fight, and they do (Bandura and Walters, 1959; Bandura et al., 1963; Soares and Soares, 1969). Violent news stimulates some people to imitate what they hear on the radio and see in newspaper and television. Suicide rates go up after famous people end their lives, and the increase is directly linked to the amount of publicity provided (Phillips, 1974). Not all violence is imitated, of course, just as not everyone catches the flu when it goes around. But killing is contagious (Berkowitz and Macaulay, 1971; Wheeler et al., 1966).

SUMMARY

This incomplete map of the various routes to homicide has been drawn to indicate that "frustrating social structures," in any objective sense of that phrase, are not the only sources of deadly struggle. We seem pushed back to some nonspecific dispositional explanation of our killing each other, such as "that's the way we are." Some students add to this explanation the notion that human belligerence is bound to come out with any disruption of the rituals and institutions that control us. So Scott reminds us (1966, p. 637) that "one of the most important newer findings arising from the study of animal behavior [is] that a major cause of destructive fighting in animal societies is social disorganization."

Other scholars refuse to see a continuity between the lessons learned from studying other animals and how humanity behaves. These investigators believe that *Homo sapiens* is markedly distinguished from lesser animals by the ability to think and to symbolize. It is, then, that product of thought and symbol, *ideas,* that are held crucial for promoting or reducing our violence. This assumption is applied particularly toward efforts to reduce that mass killing called war.

Chapter 14

Killing Each Other:
War

"Wars begin in the minds of men." So a framer of the United Nations Charter assured us. His statement sounds as though it says something, but it does not. Nothing is predicated; no information is given. "The minds of men" *are what we are.* Our "minds" are all that we consciously think, feel, will, and do.[1] The statement draws a circle.

UN authorities make such statements because they would like to dissolve conflict in talk and because they confuse what we say with everything that is "in our minds."

UN officials believe such circular sentiments for another reason. They, like the rest of us, are torn between recommending death and condemning it. The meaningless statement flows from this suppressed conflict. Justice and peace require killing, "one more time." But we wish, too, that there be an end to the

---

[1]When philosophers attempt to define "the mind," they are led to describe a mixture of feeling, willing, sensing, thinking, and conscious doing. Thus Susanne Langer (1967) titles her study *Mind: An Essay on Human Feeling,* and Gilbert Ryle (1949, p. 199) claims that "to talk of a person's mind . . . is to talk of the person's abilities, liabilities and inclinations to do and undergo certain sorts of things and of the doing and undergoing of these things in the ordinary world."

killing. The wish is parent to the idea that if "some significant variable" can be isolated as the germ of homicide, then we may be able to control it. The germ, however, as it is described by such good men as those who devised the UN charter—that germ is no more than how we behave. It is not independent of us—something out there that "bugs" us. It *is* us.

This conclusion derives from our attempts to count our big battles, their occasions and their consequences. The study of war, like the study of murder, reveals the many causes for which we take up arms.

STUDIES OF WAR

A war is a collective fight in which elimination of the enemy is the objective if he will not otherwise submit to our wishes. It is an organized struggle among groups of individuals who regard themselves as *politically independent* and *morally justified* in asserting their will violently.

Our vocabularies give special titles to the different occasions for war. We recognize, for example, that some wars occur *within* states where a government claiming a monopoly of power is challenged, as in civil or revolutionary combat. The internal fighting itself runs a range of planfulness from riots and "governmental crises" through political assassination, terrorism, and guerrilla warfare to outright rebellion. This kind of killing within a state need not have the same causes as struggles *between* states. A first fact culled from our study of war is that domestic and international wars do have different occasions.

Dimensions of Mass Conflict

Scholars who have counted mass conflict within and between states have isolated dimensions of the mortal battles. A dimension represents a number of antagonistic acts that are highly correlated with each other. Statistical techniques, such as factor analysis, permit the identification of dimensions among a large number of variables and allow one to ascertain how such variables are clustered.

Factors in Fighting   Rummel (1969) summarized research on the dimensions of mass combat for modern states through 1964. His survey indicates that domestic and international warring are *separate* dimensions of struggle. *"There are no common conditions or causes of domestic- and foreign-conflict behavior,"* Rummel concludes (p. 226, emphasis his).

This means that some states experience much internal conflict but little foreign fighting while other states have little domestic turmoil but much external conflict. This conclusion means, also, that still other political bodies suffer relatively high amounts of both internal and external violence, while a fourth group of states has little of either kind of conflict.

Not only are internal and external conflicts different dimensions of warring but the internal type of struggle itself reveals styles of fighting that range from relatively unplanned and spontaneous rioting (the "turmoil" dimension) to organized assassination and guerrilla war (the "internal war" dimension). The fact that there are such clusters of combat means that states that experience much internal turmoil need *not* suffer revolution and that those states that have much guerrilla fighting need *not* experience "turmoil."

Studies of Interstate Wars

Wars between states have fascinated their historians as they have their participants for as long as we have records of human activity. In the twentieth century three major investigations and some minor ones have told us of the continuity of war and of its varied occasions.

The three large-scale studies were conducted by a sociologist (Sorokin, 1937), by a professor of international law (Wright, 1942), and by a physicist-mathematician (Richardson, in two works, 1960a, 1960b).

Sorokin counted "all recorded, major interstate wars" from 500 B.C. to A.D. 1925 in the histories of Greece, Rome, Austria, Germany, England, France, the Netherlands, Spain, Italy, Russia, Poland, and Lithuania. He arrived at a total of 967 such conflicts or *an average of one war every two or three years.* The proportions of years during which each nation was, for any part of a year, at war vary from a *low* of 28 percent for Germany to a *high* of 67 percent for Spain. It cannot be said from such a record that war has been an abnormality among civilized countries.

Wright took all of history and the traces of prehistory for his scope. His work reports on the fragmentary evidence of organized fighting among preliterate people and on the more detailed records since the fifteenth century. Table 14-1 gives his tally of the number of battles in which "important states" engaged from 1480 to 1941. Formal fighting appears, again, to be a common experience rather than some kind of deviance.

Richardson's works are attempts to fit mathematical models to the data of deadly quarrels. His research assumes that "an essential characteristic of a war may be said to be casualties" (Richardson, 1960b, p. 5). Furthermore, since wounds vary from the slight to the severe, it makes sense to Richardson to tabulate only *mortalities* since, in his words, "deaths are more alike, and therefore more reliable as statistical evidence" (ibid.).

Richardson then classifies his object of interest—intentionally induced deaths—by their *magnitude.* That is, he groups wars by the size of the killing, as "the logarithm to the base ten of the number of people who died because of that quarrel" (1960b, p. 6).

The advantage of such a logarithmic scale is that it groups deaths by their numbers in large categories. It allows, thereby, for a range of error in the results. One can "give or take" some differences in reported fatalities for a particular conflict without disturbing the *rank order* of such battles.

The range of Richardson's scale runs "from 0 for a murder involving only one death . . . to 7.4 for World War II" (ibid.). A search of criminal statistics and histories for the entire world between 1820 and 1949 yielded the following tally of mortal quarrels by grouped numbers of deaths:

    I. *Magnitudes in the range 7 ± 1/2*
       (from over 3,000,000 deaths to more than 31,000,000 deaths)
       Two Conflicts: World Wars I and II.
   II. *Magnitudes in the range of 6 ± 1/2*
       (from over 300,000 to more than 3,000,000 deaths)
       Seven Conflicts
  III. *Magnitudes in the range 5 ± 1/2*
       (from over 30,000 deaths to more than 300,000 deaths)
       36 Conflicts
  IV. *Magnitudes in the range 4 ± 1/2*
       (from over 3,000 deaths to more than 31,000 deaths)
       70 Conflicts

Below the fourth rank of fatal conflicts enumeration fades into estimates based on questionable counting. Richardson's list of deadly quarrels in the range 3 ± 1/2 and less is offered only as tentative and as a stimulus to inquiry. However, *the smaller the scope of mortal fighting, the more numerous the battles.*

For example, Richardson counts some of these "small-sized wars of the past 500 years—those with more than 300 fatalities but less than 3,200—and finds "over 170 military campaigns by the United States; over 100 international, and 300 domestic, conflicts [of this size] in Latin America; and *in the twentieth century before* World War II, over 70 campaigns by Great Britain and over 500 by all countries" (emphasis added).

What the Studies Reveal

It is no news in the twentieth century to be told that there has been much war. We have been living, says Sorokin (1937, p. 487), in one of the "bloodiest . . . and most turbulent periods in the history of Western civilization and perhaps in the history of mankind." Sorokin wrote this in the mid-1930s, but he would have no reason to correct his judgment today.

We are concerned, then, to find out what seems to be associated with war in the hope that we might change those conditions. Unfortunately for these hopes, our studies of war tell us more surely what is *not* so than what is. They more readily disprove assumptions about the occasions of war than they illuminate the path to peace. The *negations* may be outlined as follows:

1 There is no sign that human beings are growing more pacific.

This negation puts it mildly. Actually, the historical record points to a tendency for wars to be more frequent in recent times (Richardson, 1960b, p. 142), for a larger proportion of the resources and the populations of belligerent states to be involved, and, in Wright's words, for warring now to be "more intense, more extended, more costly . . . [and] less functional, less intentional, less directable, and less legal" (p. 248).

2 There is no sign that wars are more readily controlled now than formerly.

Both Richardson and Wright demonstrate that it is increasingly difficult for

Table 14-1   Number of Battles Engaged in by Principal European Powers, by Decades, 1480–1940*†

Decade	Great Britain	France	Spain	Austria	Prussia	Russia	Turkey	Netherlands	Denmark	Sweden	Participations by these states‡	Battles within modern civilization
1480–89	2	1	4	0			2				9	5
1490–99	1	2	2	2			1				8	4
Total	3	3	6	2			3				17	9
1500–09	0	3	3	0		0	0	0	0	0	6	3
1510–19	4	4	0	0		1	3	0	0	0	12	8
1520–29	0	2	2	4		0	3	0	2	2	15	10
1530–39	0	1	5	0		0	1	0	0	0	7	8
1540–49	8	1	1	2		0	0	0	0	0	12	10
1550–59	3	3	1	1		0	1	0	0	0	9	7
1560–69	2	5	5	0		1	4	4	0	0	21	14
1570–79	1	1	13	0		0	1	12	0	0	28	16
1580–89	4	2	5	0		0	0	2	0	0	13	7
1590–99	1	1	1	1		0	1	2	0	1	8	4
Total	23	23	36	8		2	14	20	2	3	131	87
1600–09	2	0	1	0		0	0	1	0	0	4	3
1610–19	0	0	0	0		1	0	0	3	4	8	4
1620–29	1	1	8	12		0	1	2	4	2	31	19
1630–39	0	18	16	27		0	0	1	0	22	84	39
1640–49	4	25	17	14		0	0	1	2	11	74	36
1650–59	10	5	4	1		1	8	10	2	4	45	27
1660–69	4	3	4	5		0	30	4	0	0	30	19
1670–79	5	27	13	9		0	2	16	4	4	80	35
1680–89	2	4	2	23		0	21	0	0	0	52	27
1690–99	10	20	10	11		1	10	13	0	0	75	30
Total	38	103	75	108		3	52	48	15	47	483	239

Decade												
1700–09	38	76	38	57		17	0	36	1	24	287	113
1710–19	10	18	15	34		5	10	15	4	7	118	49
1720–29	0	0	0	0		0	0	0	0	0	0	0
1730–39	0	10	7	28		7	18	0	0	0	70	35
1740–49	17	47	14	52	15	2	0	16	0	2	165	77
1750–59	29	32	0	31	38	4	0	0	0	2	136	71
1760–69	15	16	0	19	27	8	2	0	0	2	89	43
1770–79	11	3	0	2	2	14	14	0	0	0	46	27
1780–89	20	15	4	5	0	8	7	1	0	3	63	30
1790–99	46	284	24	179	32	36	11	42	0	5	659	336
Total	186	501	102	407	114	101	62	110	5	45	1,633	781
1800–09	26	177	32	88	31	26	10	0	1	3	394	188
1810–19	35	178	42	34	64	93	11	2	0	3	462	189
1820–29	1	1	0	0	0	14	17	0	0	0	33	17
1830–39	0	0	0	0	0	6	5	0	0	0	11	12
1840–49	1	1	0	27	3	10	1	0	3	0	46	37
1850–59	6	12	0	5	0	12	10	0	3	0	48	17
1860–69	0	0	0	17	21	0	0	0	4	0	42	79
1870–79	0	53	0	0	53	26	26	0	0	0	158	92
1880–89	0	0	0	0	0	0	0	0	0	0	0	2
1890–99	10	0	4	0	0	0	1	0	0	0	15	18
Total	79	422	78	171	172	187	81	2	11	6	1,209	651
1900–09	8	0	0	0	0	18	0	0	0	0	26	18
1910–19	218	81	7	117	310	213	137	0	0	0	1,083	662
1920–29	0	0	0	0	0	11	5	0	0	0	16	17
1930–40	3	3	100	0	20	2	0	1	1	0	129	195
Total	229	84	107	117	330	244	142	1	0	0	1,254	892
Grand total	558	1,136	404	807	616	537	354	181	33	101	4,727	2,659

*Reprinted from Q. Wright, A Study of War, vol. I, table 22. © 1942 by The University of Chicago Press. Reproduced by permission.

†Participation in battles by one of these states prior to its active relationship to the modern family of nations is not counted in this table.

‡The figures in this column are usually greater than the corresponding ones in the last column because in most cases at least two of these powers participated in a single battle, although, in case of civil wars, only one participation by the state is counted. Where the figures in the last column are greater, it is because states in the modern family of nations other than the European states here listed were the participants in a considerable number of battles of the decade.

states to remain neutral in wartime and that, as the number of combatants increases, more neutrals are drawn into the conflict. Fighting is infectious.

3 It cannot be assumed that some nations are characteristically more belligerent than others.

4 It cannot be assumed that any one religion, even one that preaches peace, practices pacifism more than another. Christians are no more pacific than infidels.

5 There is no evidence that democracies and republics are more peaceful than autocracies and monarchies.

6 There is no evidence that prosperous societies are more peaceful than poor ones or that periods of prosperity reduce the fighting.

On this economic ground, there is also no evidence that the relative wealth and poverty of neighbors explains much of the warring. Richardson, for example, finds little of the killing to have been occasioned by "class conflict." For large-scale homicide of a magnitude greater than 3.5 on Richardson's scale, economic issues represent an estimated 29 percent of the "direct causes" of war (1960b, p. 210).

7 It cannot be assumed, from these studies, that a shared religion or a common language or a bond of citizenship reduces the deadly quarrels.

Religious similarities have little relevance for war or peace, Richardson finds, but religious differences, particularly those between Christians and Muslims, have stimulated our killing each other.

8 It cannot be assumed that being "neighbors" makes for peace.

On the contrary, warring increases in proportion to the number of states with which a country shares frontiers. Fights over territory loom large as a condition of combat.

9 The data of these extensive studies of war do not support the hope that "enlightenment" produces peace.

A widespread assumption claims that "education" or "understanding," variously and vaguely defined, pacifies humanity. This assumption fails when it meets facts. Cattell (1950) looked at the clusters of characteristics of states that waged more and less war between 1837 and 1937. He found that countries that frequently go to war engage in a high number of political disputes with other countries, thus lending support to von Clausewitz's dictum. In addition, the more warring states write a disproportionately large number of treaties. They also have a high ratio of tertiary to primary occupations; that is, they are bureaucratized, industrialized countries. These fighting states are territorially expansive. They have big governments, and they win a disproportionate number of Nobel prizes in science, literature, and (supreme irony!) peace.[2] In short, they are "civilized."

An Affirmation

These many negations do not support a faith in progress toward peace nor do they point to any remedy for war in aspects of social life that are readily manipulable.

---

[2]This irony begins with the fact that Alfred Nobel (1833–1896), the patron of the prizes that bear his name, was a Swedish chemist who made much of his fortune from his invention of dynamite. Since citizens of warring states have so often won his prize for peace, some wits have interpreted the award as a grant for need rather than a recognition of achievement. The 1974 awards for peace confirm the cynicism (*Newsweek,* 1974d).

The one thing correlated with peacefulness, as revealed by Richardson's study, is the length of time people have shared a common government. The longer men have been united under one rule, the less likely they are to have engaged in fatal battles.

Richardson considered this last finding to carry a promise of peace, if anything does. It must be noted, however, that this correlation does *not* allow the causal conclusion that *creating* a government produces peace. All that this association says is that, when people have lived together under one authority—however that living together may have *evolved*—there has been a tendency for them to kill each other less frequently and less extensively.

A Conclusion

What remains from our consideration of the many negations and the one affirmation is the unsurprising information that government controls belligerence. This is its first reason for being—*to rule*, that is, to serve as umpire applying the code of the game we have agreed to play.

This fact does not tell us how to achieve peace, however, since it does not specify the conditions under which individuals agree to play this game rather than that one. Against the hope that *creating* a government will produce peace, we are reminded that the consensus that makes governing possible *evolves* and that its *evolution* includes the possibility of its *dissolution.* No government is permanent and neither is any peace.

PROPOSALS FOR PEACE

Our concern for survival looks to prescriptions for peace. The proposals can be grouped as recommending:

1 Individual action
2 Peace through play
3 Peace through evolution or revolution
4 Peace through plans such as
   a Disarmament
   b Education
   c World government
5 Peace through power

Individual Action for Peace

This prescription includes a range of ideas from the recommendation of apathy through the Yoga path of self-improvement to the advocacy of "conscientious objection."

When conscientious objection involves organization and the public demonstration of one's attitude toward a war, it becomes a variety of collective plan for peace. In its more popular variety, however, conscientious objection means the resistance of *individuals* to the call to arms. The slogan is, "What if they gave a war and no one came?" Or, "If no one fought, there would be no war." Such truisms are not helpful. For on the road to this conflict-free end, some who lay down their arms will be conquered by others not burdened by a similar ethic.

It is then argued that being conquered, and even "dying for peace," is better justified than war. However, under conditions of alien conquest, this justification loses its appeal and, again, people fight to be free.

We are reminded that some 3 million British youths solemnly subscribed to the "Oxford Oath" during the late 1920s. They swore on the Bible that they would never engage in that killing called war. As with many another resolution, changed conditions altered the resolve.

Individual resistance to war does not promise peace, but it does provide one solution for some individuals who find themselves in belligerent situations.

Peace through Play

Play has been advanced as a therapy for violent emotion. Pacifying propositions of this sort assume that aggression is part of human nature and that the cure for war is to allow the aggression to be expressed in some substitute form. The American psychologist William James (1917) called such less deadly forms of aggression "the moral equivalent of war." The idea is to provide contests that allow humanity, that belligerent species, to blow off steam. The assumption is that *expressing* one's belligerence *reduces* it. This assumption, known as the catharsis hypothesis, holds that Olympic Games and similar international sporting struggles will drain off warlike impulses while educating people in fraternity.

We did not need the debacle of the Munich games (1972) to teach us that the catharsis hypothesis is a weak one. The evidence from the psychological laboratory as well as the playing field indicates that, contrary to the catharsis hypothesis, the expression of aggression often promotes it (Mallick and McCandless, 1966). Furthermore, even *observing* the aggressive game, much less playing in it, stimulates the fighting urge (Bandura et al., 1963; Baron and Kepner, 1970; Berkowitz and Geen, 1966; De Charms and Wilkins, 1963).

The record of brawling among the players and fans of soccer, football, and hockey—to name only the more stimulating of body-contact games—hardly builds confidence in sport as the path to peace. For example:

El Salvador, Honduras Sever Relations Over Soccer Riots [*International Herald-Tribune*, 1969].

Vanishing Sport
    There has been a deep, disturbing, and almost unnoticed change in the pattern of big-city high school athletics. . . . Not since 1965 have Detroit public schools been allowed to enter Michigan's high school basketball tournament. On the last occasion two city teams met on a neutral court, at night, and when the game was over nine youths had been stabbed [*Sports Illustrated*, 1968].

Peace through Evolution or Revolution

Since war is waged through organizations that institutionalize their practices, it has been assumed that specific institutions *cause* war and that removing these institutions or drastically changing them will produce peace. According to this doctrine, these changes may occur through "natural evolution" or they may be planned through a revolution.

The institutional argument is strongly voiced by the sociologist Sorokin (1944, p. 442), who claims that "the basic institutions of contemporary society are permeated by . . . militarism and are incessantly generating interindividual, civil, and international conflicts." The institutions Sorokin nominates for militarism are "private property," "the state," "political parties," "occupational unions," "the family," and our popular heroes who are "invariably fighting persons who successfully crush their rivals, whether on the football field, in cut-throat business rivalry, on a battle field, in political machinations, or in class war."

One trouble with the institutional argument is that every theorist who proposes changing social arrangements as a means of producing peace *selects* his preferred blameworthy institutions and exonerates "innocent" institutions. Thus Sorokin does not mention religious institutions as militant and, in a personal communication (1945), excused his omission on the ground that religious institutions were not distinctively generative of conflict. However, as we have seen, Sorokin's excuse is challenged by some statisticians of deadly quarrels (Richardson, 1960b, Chap. 9).

Nevertheless, Sorokin has distinguished company among philosophers who believed that social arrangements would evolve, or could be made to change through revolution, toward institutions that would guarantee peace. For example, Auguste Comte (1798–1857) and Herbert Spencer (1820–1903) believed that war was produced by the agricultural-feudal stage of development and that the evolution to industrialism would pacify nations. Karl Marx (1818–1883) and Thorstein Veblen (1857–1929) saw war as motivated by plutocracy and remedied by a proletarian revolution. Similarly, Richard Cobden (1804–1865) and Woodrow Wilson (1856–1924) blamed war on "despotic elites" and put their hope for peace in "the power of the people."

History has not been kind to these hopeful prophecies. History *does* warrant the assumption that thoughtful persons will continue to advocate changing some hated arrangement of public affairs as a guarantee of peace. The advocacy will itself generate conflict and run the risk of urging men to kill each other for "the last great cause."

Plans for Peace

Innumerable plans for peace have been advanced. Only a few need be discussed here. However, all proposals for international peace assume that human beings can establish a pacific world if they want to do so. This assumption is probably a tautology.

   A tautology is a statement in which whatever is said to be true of a subject is contained *within* the subject. That is, a tautology predicates nothing that can be observed *independent* of the subject; it is part of it, as when one says, "You won't get bald if you don't lose your hair," or, as a former President of the United States once remarked, "When many men are out of work, you have a lot of unemployment."

   Thus, if people are observed at peace, it can be assumed that they must have "willed" it, and, if they continue to fight, it is assumed that they do so because they have not yet "willed" peace hard enough.

   Quite apart from the difficulties of knowing how to test the assumption that peace can be achieved if people want it badly enough, there are philosophers who doubt that human beings desire a world without conflict. William James, for example, felt that "the plain truth is that people *want* war."

   The plans for peace would reeducate that want or change the conditions that allegedly sponsor it. By contrast, the diplomatic response to this desire, through a balance of power, seeks to control its expression.

   The more popular forms of plans for peace are disarmament, education, and world government.

   Disarmament   Reducing the weaponry is recommended to states not only out of a desire for peace but also out of moral concern over the expenditure of labor and resources in such an unproductive manner. These issues are separate. Here, attention is directed only to disarmament as a cure for war.

   Disarmament is advocated as a pacifying plan on the grounds that armaments constitute a threat to neighbors who in turn arm to defend themselves and thus set off an escalating spiral. Advocates of disarmament assume that the hostile atmosphere of an arms race leads to an ignition point at which one of the antagonists, sensing an advantage, takes it. The period 1909–1913 in Europe is cited as a classical arms race leading inevitably to war, and some students interpret the events of the 1930s as additional evidence that preparing for war produces it.

   Belief in disarmament as a program for peace depends, of course, on assumptions about the causes of war. Advocates of disarmament often find themselves arguing for a simple and singular cause of war—weapons—where otherwise they would know better. Increasing the weaponry can be seen as having an *independent* effect upon the promotion of war or it can be seen as an *accompaniment* of whatever else is causing people to arm. In short, the question is, "Are armaments symptoms or causes?"

   Studies of arms races, such as Richardson conducted (1960a), cannot resolve the issue. The data are unclear and do not allow an assignment or a denial of an independent causal impact of military might as a stimulus to war. For example, expenditures on arms, one index of the race, are concealed by totalitarian countries and difficult to assess. Where estimates *are* made of military preparedness among possible combatants, it becomes clear that arms races run varied courses. They may *stabilize* for a time, in which case the condition appears peaceful. They may *escalate without igniting* into open warfare, as in the rivalry of the U.S.S.R. and the United States since 1945. They may *deescalate,* as in the behavior of the United States following World War I; or arms races may, as in the 1910s model, *move into war.*

Does fear, then, cause war or control it? The crux of the argument in favor of disarmament is that the increasing military strength of a neighbor provokes fear, fear generates hostility, and hostility underwrites war. This argument is, however, a two-edged blade since fear, whatever its impact upon hatred, may also *control* belligerence. "The bomb" may be a deterrent to war rather than a cause of it. There may be substance to Sir Winston Churchill's comment that he "looked forward with great confidence to the potentiality of universal destruction" as a guarantor of peace.

Is disarmament possible? However one answers the question about the deterrent or inflammatory role of fear, the plan for peace through disarmament appears weak when we ask whether it is *possible* to disarm. Quite apart from the difficulties of enforcing agreements to limit arms, every condition of disarming is partial and unstable. If countries agree to abandon nuclear bombs and bacterial sprays, rifles remain, and, when these are removed, there are yet knives, clubs, rocks, and fists. The industrial country that disarms today can arm itself tomorrow. Disarmament, then, is a kind of band-aid against the eruption of war rather than a guarantor of peace.

Education for Peace   A popular prescription to cure war calls for education. One of the satisfactions in using the word "education" is that it is difficult to disapprove of it. Since education is advocated as a means of healing many social ills, its content remains vague. However, "education for peace" would teach two things: understanding of foreigners and the horrors of war. For example:

> Education Can Build Peace [runs a newspaper headline].
>   A suitable education will implant the desire for peace, says a . . . professor.
> . . . Dr. . . . was explaining a new organization called the International Association of Educators for World Peace. . . . The group feels that if the idea of peace is taught to the very young the world will eventually benefit.
>   [This group] will study defects of the local education system that might forbid understanding of other peoples and their cultures . . . [*Edmonton Journal,* 1970].

Education for peace assumes that countries engage in war out of ignorance of war's costs or out of prejudice against misunderstood enemies. Such an assumption emphasizes incorrect belief as the cause of war, and it ignores the fact of conflict of interest. Conflicts of interest are, however, real. Human beings fight because some want what others have, and, despite the horrors of war, people "find themselves in situations" in which fighting seems more tolerable, if not actually more desirable, than submission. Each of us can think of his own examples—whether they be rebellious or defensive, treasonous or patriotic.

In this plan for peace, "education" is frequently propaganda; that is, it substitutes desire for fact. Propaganda for peace, like that for war, is not new. It changes with the social climate, as does all education. Its record in preventing war is either unreadable or negligible.

World Government Since much warfare appears to be the result as well as the accompaniment of chaos, the best program for peace would seem to be one that calls for government. As we have seen, studies of war point to common rule as a pacifying agent, although it is neither absolutely nor permanently so. For world peace, then, the "solution" is world government.

The idea is not novel. Dante argued for a "universal empire" in 1313. About 300 years later, Émeric Crucé proposed that a "new kingdom" be created with a permanent international assembly in Venice to which all international disputes would be submitted and which would assure free trade, peace, and economic progress. In the early seventeenth century the Duc de Sully imagined a federation of Europe to be presided over by France. His vision was seconded more seriously by William Penn, who, later in that century, proposed a European parliament and a league of nations.

These ideas received renewed encouragement following the world wars of the twentieth century. The reasoning in favor of world federation is expressed this way by one of its advocates:

> No plans are going to save us unless they are enforced, and force is a function of government. That means world government, and, if we are to forestall another war, it means world government now . . . [Turner, as cited by Pelcovits, 1946, p. 397].

To achieve world government, model world constitutions have been drawn and global parliaments designed. In the context of concern for peace, there are two major questions about world federation:

> Will nations now subscribe to a world government?
> Would such a union guarantee peace?

The answers to both questions appear negative. Given the diversity of interests, ideologies, and standards of living throughout the world, the voluntary waiver of values and advantages does not seem likely. Furthermore, world federation does not promise peace. At least three defects are apparent in world union as a plan for peace. These defects have been well defined by Pelcovits (1946), whose arguments are summarized here:

The error of assuming that constitutions create governments. The first flaw in world federalism as a plan for peace is that it puts the cart before the horse. In logic, this is known as the fallacy of *hysteron proteron,* or "inverting the natural order of reason." This poor logic assumes that, if constitutions occur where there are communities, then making a constitution will create a community.

On the contrary, constitutions and their supporting laws operate pacifically *when* there is community. They do not create this consensus. Effective law represents the *end* of a process in which community has developed. Constitutions formalize agreements among men. In themselves, they are powerless to produce the concord upon which the force of law functions with a minimal resort to violence.

This point should be apparent to Westerners who live under governments that are constitutionally established and that are, nevertheless, challenged. "Law and order," concord and liberty, require more than documents, more, even, than those ratified documents called constitutions.

The weak assumption that wars are misunderstandings. If wars were disputes, then courts might adjudicate them. Asking for world courts to prevent fights assumes that wars are, in Pelcovits's words, "lawsuits fought with bombs instead of briefs."

If wars are ever the result of misunderstanding, they are not *only* that. They are conflicts, not debates. The contenders do not and have not appealed to what is lawful in pressing for their interests, and they are not apt to be pacified by the application of a world law that rules against their wants.

Again, the point should be clear to those who watch the fighting within their own states, where the rule of law is supposedly established. If fighting groups *within* a state can argue that their courts are corrupt, if intellectuals *within* a country can hold that its established laws cannot do justice,[3] then there is all the more reason to expect that world courts will be similarly challenged.

The weak assumption that national sovereignties are the sole cause of war. Programs for peace through world government view wars as the result of "clashing national sovereignties." Accordingly, it is assumed that if sovereign countries were absorbed into a world federation, then peace would be assured.

Such reasoning, however, forgets the facts of civil and revolutionary wars. It overlooks the cases of enduring peace, or at least nonwar, between neighboring nations (the United States and Canada, for example), just as it slights the many cases of governments overthrown regardless of the status of their laws and constitutions.

IN SUMMARY

The weakness of these and other plans for peace is their denial of the *reality of conflict.* These plans suppose that the issues over which people kill each other can be reduced in importance or happily compromised. Unfortunately for such plans, human beings continue to behave as if some things they value cannot be compromised. The way out of war requires a dissolution of these conflicts of "ultimate interest." But we do not know today how to achieve this any more than did Mo-ti, the Chinese sage, who centuries ago asked: "Where standards differ, there will be opposition. But how can the standards in the world be unified?"

---

[3]Many examples of this contention can be given. Kingman Brewster, Jr., the president of Yale University, provides a recent example when he is reported to have said, "I am skeptical of the ability of black revolutionaries to achieve a fair trial anywhere in the United States" (*Time,* 1970).

If human beings persist as they have in the past, "the standards in the world" will be unified, if ever, with fighting. This is not to say that fighting will *produce* the unity. It is to say that movement in the direction of "one world" will be characterized by battle.

Meanwhile, the moments of peace seem best guaranteed, as they long have, through some balance of power. A "best guarantee" is not an absolute one; it is only a better warranty than others.

Peace through Power

It has been seen that prescriptions for peace are less informed by knowledge than generated by concern and maintained by hope. Wars wax and wane less as a result of the plans of societal engineers and more in response to the fumbling measures of diplomacy. To call these antique measures fumbling is not to label them unthinking; it is only to call attention to their operation under conditions of uncertainty and imperfect knowledge.

These diplomatic measures fill the void between nations and persons that is always present this side of love. Love means identification, a fusion of interests, so that what harms the loved one injures the lover. Love, however, is as unstable a condition as is a balance of power. The relations described by both ideas are never still. They change. To borrow a metaphor, they grow and die.

As social arrangements move from a harmony of interest through polite attention and the exchange of gratifications to a conflict of interest, peace remains possible only under constraint. In everyday social life, the constraint is called manners. In civil strife, the duress is law and its police arm. In international and revolutionary conflict, the pacifier is military power.

This view of peace maintained by power is uncomfortable. It runs counter to the yearning, in a nuclear age, for a time of perpetual peace, of peace guaranteed once and for all. No truthful reading of history, however, can answer this longing. Regardless of our wishes, people contend. The threat of thermonuclear war has not brought contention to an end. In fact, as William James reminded us and as we have seen (pp. 278–280), it is not at all clear that human beings *wish* strife to cease. There are thinking persons today who continue to recommend killing for their "good causes."

Peace through balanced power has been a common-sense maxim since classic times. The philosopher David Hume (1804) demonstrated its exercise, for example, in his study of the Peloponnesian War. However, despite its *practice,* its *advocacy* fluctuates. There is a moral compunction, felt by some Western statesmen at least, against admitting that states operate to ensure their security by balancing powers. Working toward peace through the application of force, or its threat, is criticized, therefore, on two grounds: *(a)* that it is immoral and *(b)* that it does not work.

Is a Balance of Power Immoral?   The charge of immorality is always made from a position that claims the injustice done by the power applied. Some contender's idea of justice is bound to be offended by any application of force that prevents him from getting his way.

To resolve the unpleasant fact of conflict, some moralists have conceived of an abstract justice and its international court to which people should appeal when their interests clash. This notion seems to underwrite both the hopes for perpetual peace and the disapproval of power as a pacifying instrument. It is a faith that people are, or will be, reasonable, that all quarrels can be compromised, and all conflicts dissolved in understanding.

The world is not made that way, however. "One of the hardest things for people to realize—to believe—is that there are people in the world who don't *want* an agreement." This, with his emphasis, is the comment of a lawyer-economist-professor who had worked in the U.S. Department of State during the late 1960s (Rostow, as cited by Whitworth, 1970, p. 46). Professor Rostow continues:

> Our politics are politics of compromise, of accommodation, and it's very difficult for us to imagine that the Egyptians or the North Koreans or Hanoi or the Russians don't *want* to make an agreement. I was talking to some students the other day, and one of them said very earnestly, "Well, why don't people try to reach an understanding with the Russians?" I answered, "What on earth do you think we've been trying to do?" And I told him about some of our efforts in this direction— troop reductions in Europe, compromise in the Middle East, a solution in Vietnam, and so on. And he said, "If I believe what you say, then I don't know what I believe about the world" [emphasis in the original].

The morality of power—even when it guarantees peace—is, as usual, a function of whose side one is on and who has the power.

Does a Balance of Power Work? Whether something works depends, again, on what it is compared with. The criticism that a balance of power does not work reduces to the complaint that life is not as one might wish it to be.

"To live is to struggle," Zorba tells us, and our concern for peace wishes it weren't so. "Life *is*, in fact, a battle," Henry James reiterates, and we accept or deny this, depending, largely, on whether our own lives have been hazardous or secure. The repetitive irony is that, armed with a concern for peace, people impose their wills upon each other.

Every peaceful equilibrium is unstable. In this sense, no plan for peace nor any balance of power works. The application of power remains, however, the best means yet evolved or designed for controlling the intraspecific killing to which humanity is prone.

WHAT SHALL WE CONCLUDE?

The facts of our killing each other are unpleasant. The hopes that would change these facts seem unsupported. What attitude shall we adopt, then?

Every prescription is personal, and what is comfortable for one of us may not be so for another. Here, however, are some suggestions:

1 Forget the assumption that conflicts are nothing but misunderstandings that can be resolved by communication, education, or empathy. There are misunderstandings that generate conflict, but they are minor causes of collective violence. Conflicts that promote wars are, for the most part, real and not merely a result of incorrect perception.

2 Abandon the idea that permanent world peace can be achieved. In particular, resist the notion that one last deadly struggle against this society or that will usher in an age of peace.

3 Remain skeptical of all promises of peace, grateful for any present peace, and stoical in the face of conflict.

Epilogue

What have we learned? We wish to have learned more than just facts because facts are often dull and, besides, facts change. Our attention to social concerns may have taught us some principles—attitudes, if you like—with which to judge our worlds. These themes can be given titles for their easy recognition. They may be called *the principles of moral selectivity, incompleteness, pragmatism, limits, and webs.*

1 *The principle of moral selectivity* says that our hopes and fears sift facts for the *right* answer, which may or may not be the *correct* one.

We never answer a question about a social concern with information alone. We are never concerned solely with efficiency. We seek, instead, our right answer, justified, if possible, by some comforting facts. Even as social theorists, we are tempted to fudge against life and have knowledge prove our desires factually correct as well as morally sound.

The impotence of facts in the face of our desires is not merely a result of the strength of our moral urges; it is also a result of the frailty of knowledge.

2 *The principle of incompleteness* acknowledges that we can never know enough. All answers are less than complete. It follows, then, that there are many windows through which to look upon the social scene and that each vista is partial. There are, however, clearer and cloudier views provided by different perspectives, particularly as different issues are brought into focus. The test of clear vision is pragmatic: *What works?*

   3   *The pragmatic principle* is a bundle of assumptions. It assumes, first, that the answers one gets depend on the questions one asks. It recognizes the difference between a silly question and an answerable one and between the different styles of answerable question.
   A silly question is one that can have no empirical answer or one that can take any empirical answer. *Nothing* that happens or *everything* that happens can satisfy a foolish question. When a person asks, "What color is justice?" or "Why did this have to happen to my child?" we know better than to look for an empirical answer. Such a question can have psychological significance, of course, and we can assuage the discomfort of the person who asks such unanswerable questions by massaging him with the right words. Words can allay anxiety without giving information.
   The pragmatist not only can distinguish between empirical and nonempirical questions, but he also recognizes that there are different styles of answerable questions. For example, asking *why* does not necessarily ask *how*. Similarly, asking for a *prediction* of a behavior need not ask for its *explanation.* Furthermore, asking whether people define an action as *good* does not ask whether it is *efficient.*
   The pragmatic principle attends, then, to the question that is being asked, but it also assumes that the best test of an answer to an empirical question is what it tells one to do and how well the prescription works. An answer works when, in comparison with other descriptions of reality, it suggests a *distinctive* course of action that proves *economic.* "Economic" means that the answer gets us more of what we want at lower cost, which is to say, with fewer mistakes.
   The idea that we strive for knowledge in order to reduce our errors implies that all action carries its price and that, in this world, "there is no free lunch." There are limits to possibilities even though we strain against them.

   4   *The limiting principle* says that not all things are possible. It is a keystone of scientific thought.
   The human organism has built-in boundaries to its possibility. The earth is finite as a system within which social concerns are addressed. If one thinks as a scientist—and there are other ways to think—then one is impressed with the limits to action. On the other hand, if one thinks as an engineer—physical or societal—he is apt to adopt the engineering slogan: "The difficult we do now; the impossible takes a little longer."
   The limiting principle rests, in turn, upon the assumption that the causes that affect us operate in a web of influence.

   5   *The webbing principle* reinforces the limiting principle. The idea of social relations as occurring in a web suggests that social behavior is better interpreted as *interaction* than as *serial linkage.* Interaction means that causes generate effects that "feed back" upon the causes to alter them. This conception differs from the image of social relations as a chain of events, such as is perceived in the fall of dominoes.
   When we look for what causes what in addressing our social concerns, it

appears that causes ebb and flow, intersect, and change in their powers. The notion of *causal webs,* in contrast with *causal chains,* means that organisms struggle in an ecological net. The ecologist draws two strong implications from the fact of life in a causal web with boundaries: "We can never do merely one thing. We can never do nothing" (Hardin, 1973a, p. 10).

Acting to achieve target one also hits nontargets two, and three, and four someplace. Social action ramifies, and there are unforeseen consequences as well as achieved objectives. Furthermore, not acting is also action with consequences, foreseen and unforeseen. For any particular social concern in any particular predicament, it is foolish to *prejudge* the greater rationality of action versus inaction. In the Western world as opposed to the traditional Eastern sphere, the popular assumption is that every concern calls for its program of collective work. However, some animals know when lying still is safer than moving.

SUMMARY

These principles are tools in the service of judgment. They do not guarantee wisdom, but they may protect us from some major follies. These attitudes do not produce a singular theory that explains all the conditions or behaviors of social concern. It is doubtful that there can be such a singular, grand theory, not just because social issues differ in content but also because the questions asked about our concerns vary.

The summary advice is to be clear about the questions one is asking, to use clean concepts in answering these questions, and to recognize that our best answers are informed inferences rather than certainties.

REFERENCES
INDEX

Numbers in brackets [ ] at the end of each entry refer to pages in the text on which the reference is cited.

Abegglen, J. C. 1958. *The Japanese Factory: Aspects of Its Social Organization.* Glencoe, Ill.: The Free Press [190].

Abrams, M. 1958. "The mass media and social class in Great Britain." Paper read at the Fourth World Congress of Sociology. Stresa, Italy [200].

Acland, H. 1973. Review of "The Plowden Children Four Years Later." *Harvard Educational Review,* **43:**296–298 (May) [211].

Adams, J. R. 1974. "Shut up, professor!" *The Wall Street Journal,* **90:**8 (June 24) [138].

Adcock, C. J. 1970. Review of the Thematic Apperception Test. In O. K. Buros (ed.), *Personality Tests and Reviews.* Highland Park, N.J.: The Gryphon Press [105*n.*].

Adler, P. 1953. *A House Is Not a Home.* New York: Rinehart & Company, Inc. [183].

Allee, W. C. 1931. *Animal Aggregations.* Chicago: The University of Chicago Press [289].

Allen, K. E., and F. R. Harris. 1966. "Elimination of a child's excessive scratching by training the mother in reinforcement procedures." *Behaviour Research and Therapy,* **4:**79–84 (May) [83].

——— et al. 1965. "Effects of social reinforcement on isolate behavior of a nursery school child." In L. P. Ullmann and L. Krasner (eds.), *Case Studies in Behavior Modification.* New York: Holt, Rinehart, and Winston [83].

Alpert, R. 1972. "A fever of ethnicity." *Commentary*, **53**:68–73 (June) [19*n*., 93, 289].

American Institute of Public Opinion. 1939. Poll on "Happiness" (March 8) [20].

———. 1949. Poll on "Marital Happiness" (February 26) [112].

———. 1950. Poll on "Marital Happiness" (March 25) [112].

American Psychiatric Association. 1968. *Diagnostic and Statistical Manual of Mental Disorders*. Washington, D.C.: American Psychiatric Association [34, 41, 67*n*.].

American Social Health Association. 1968. *Today's VD Control Problem*. Washington, D.C.: A joint statement by the American Public Health Association, the American Social Health Association, and the American V.D. Association [107].

Anderson, N. 1923. *The Hobo*. Chicago: The University of Chicago Press [183].

Anderson, R. T. 1958. "The Danish and Dutch settlement on Amager Island: Four hundred years of sociocultural interaction." *American Anthropologist*, **60**:683–701 (August) [102].

Angrist, S. et al. 1968. *Women After Treatment*. New York: Appleton-Century-Crofts [70].

Arendt, H. 1958. "The crisis in education." *Partisan Review*, **25**:493–513 (Fall) [214–215].

———. 1964. *Eichmann in Jerusalem: A Report on the Banality of Evil*. New York: The Viking Press, Inc. [279].

Argyris, C. 1964. "T-groups for organizational effectiveness." *Harvard Business Review*, **42**:60–74 (No. 2) [85].

Armitage, A. K. et al. 1968. "Pharmacological basis for the tobacco smoking habit." *Nature*, **217**:331–334 (No. 5126) [151].

Armor, D. J. 1973. "The double standard: A reply." *The Public Interest*, **30**:119–131 (Winter) [219].

Aronfreed, J. 1961. "The nature, variety, and social patterning of moral responses to transgression." *Journal of Abnormal and Social Psychology*, **63**:223–240 (October) [127–128].

Atkinson, J. W. (ed.). 1958. *Motives in Fantasy, Action, and Society*. Princeton: D. Van Nostrand Company, Inc. [268].

Auerbach, L. (ed.). 1944. *The Babylonian Talmud*. New York: Philosophical Library, Inc. [29].

Avison, W. R. 1973. *The Prediction of Social Events: An Investigation of Some of the Correlates*. Edmonton, Canada: The University of Alberta, Department of Sociology, M.A. thesis [176].

———, and G. Nettler. 1975. "World views and crystal balls." Paper in submission [37*n*.].

Axelbank, J. 1974. "The goldbrick society." *Newsweek*, **84**:52 (July 29) [176].

Babchuk, N. et al. 1967. "Change in religious affiliation and family stability." *Social Forces*, **45**:551–555 (June) [102].

Bailey, F. L., and H. Aronson. 1971. *The Defense Never Rests*. New York: Stein and Day Incorporated [183].

Bain, R. 1958. "Our schizoid culture and sociopathy." *Sociology and Social Research*, **42**:263–268 (No. 4) [64].

Baldwin, J. 1972. *No Name in the Street*. New York: The Dial Press, Inc. [278].

Ball, J. C. 1957. "Delinquent and non-delinquent attitudes towards the prevalence of stealing." *Journal of Criminal Law, Criminology, and Police Science*, **48**:259–274 (September–October) [130].

———et al. 1968. "The association of marihuana smoking with opiate addiction in the United States." *Journal of Criminal Law, Criminology, and Police Science*, **59**:171–182 (June) [164].

Bandura, A., and R. H. Walters. 1959. *Adolescent Aggression.* New York: Ronald Press Company [290].

———et al. 1963. "Imitation of film-mediated aggressive models." *Journal of Abnormal and Social Psychology,* **66:**3–11 (February) [290, 300].

———et al. 1967. "Vicarious extinction of avoidance behavior." *Journal of Personality and Social Psychology,* **5:**16–23 (January) [83].

Banfield, E. C. 1958. *The Moral Basis of a Backward Society.* New York: The Free Press [124].

Barclay, A. M., and R. N. Haber. 1965. "The relation of aggressive to sexual motivation." *Journal of Personality,* **33:**462–475 (September) [106].

Barker, R. G. 1968. *Ecological Psychology.* Stanford: Stanford University Press [57].

———. 1969. "Wanted: An eco-behavioral science." In E. P. Willems and H. L. Raush (eds.), *Naturalistic Viewpoints in Psychological Research.* New York: Holt, Rinehart, and Winston, Inc. [57].

———et al. 1947. "Experimental studies of frustration in young children." In T. M. Newcomb and E. Hartley (eds.), *Readings in Social Psychology.* New York: Holt, Rinehart and Winston, Inc. [288].

Barnett, A., et al. 1974. *On Urban Homicide: A Statistical Analysis.* Cambridge, Mass.: Massachusetts Institute of Technology, Operations Research Center [283].

Baron, R. A., and C. R. Kepner, 1970. "Model's behavior and attraction toward the model as determinants of adult aggressive behavior." *Journal of Personality and Social Psychology,* **14:**335–344 (April) [300].

Baron, S. W. 1952. *A Social and Religious History of the Jews.* Vol. IV. 2d ed. New York: Columbia University Press [178*n.*].

Barron, F. 1955. *Toward a Positive Definition of Psychological Health.* Unpublished manuscript. Berkeley: University of California, Institute of Personality Assessment and Research [132].

Barron, M. L. 1951. "Research on intermarriage: A survey of accomplishments and prospects." *American Journal of Sociology,* **57:**249–255 (November) [102–103].

Barschak, E. 1951. "A study of happiness and unhappiness in the childhood and adolescence of girls in different cultures." *Journal of Psychology,* **32:**173–215 (October) [20].

Bates, J. E., and E. S. Zawadzki. 1964. *Criminal Abortion: A Study in Medical Sociology.* Springfield, Ill.: Charles C Thomas, Publishers [240].

Bateson, G. 1941. "The frustration-aggression hypothesis and culture." *Psychological Review,* **48:**350–355 (January) [288].

———et al. 1956. "Toward a theory of schizophrenia." *Behavioral Science,* **1:**251–264 (October) [76].

Baughman, E. E., and W. G. Dahlstrom. 1968. *Negro and White Children: A Psychological Study in the Rural South.* New York: Academic Press, Inc. [22, 30].

Becker, A. S. 1969. *Soviet National Income, 1958–1964.* Berkeley: University of California Press [257].

Becker, H. 1940. "Constructive typology in the social sciences." In H. E. Barnes, H. Becker, and F. B. Becker (eds.), *Contemporary Social Theory.* New York: Appleton-Century Company [178*n.*].

Becker, H. S. 1963. *Outsiders: Studies in the Sociology of Deviance.* Glencoe, Ill.: The Free Press [144].

Beckmann, P. 1973. *Eco-Hysterics and the Technophobes.* Boulder, Colo.: Golem Press [270].

Belson, W. A. 1968. *The Extent of Stealing in London Boys and Some of Its Origins.*

London: London School of Economics and Political Science, The Survey Research Center. Report No. 39 (December) [130].

Benabud, A. 1957. "Psychological aspects of the cannabis situation in Morocco: Statistical data for 1956." *Bulletin of Narcotics,* **9**:1–16 [157].

Benedict, B. 1973. "Other people's family planning:" *Science,* **180**:1045–1046 (June 8) [227–228].

Bennett, I., Jr. 1970. "People and food." In M. Hamilton (ed.), *This Little Planet.* New York: Charles Scribner's Sons [223].

Bensman, J., and I. Gerver. 1963. "Crime and punishment in the factory: The function of deviancy in maintaining the social system." *American Sociological Review,* **28**:588–598 (August) [142].

Berelson, B., and G. A. Steiner. 1964. *Human Behavior: An Inventory of Scientific Findings.* New York: Harcourt, Brace & World, Inc. [217].

Berg, I. 1970. *Education and Jobs: The Great Training Robbery.* New York: Frederick A. Praeger, Inc. [213].

Berger, B., et al. 1971. "Child-rearing practices of the communal family." In A. Skolnick and J. Skolnick (eds.), *Family in Transition.* Boston: Little, Brown and Company [116].

Bergin, A. E. 1966. "Some implications of psychotherapy research for therapeutic practice." In G. E. Stollak et al., (eds.), *Psychotherapy Research.* Chicago: Rand McNally & Company [88].

Berkowitz, L., and R. G. Geen, 1966. "Film violence and the cue properties of available targets." *Journal of Personality and Social Psychology,* **3**:525–530 (May) [300].

———, and R. E. Goranson. 1964. "Motivational and judgmental determinants of social perception." *Journal of Abnormal and Social Psychology,* **69**:296–302 (September) [99].

———, and J. Macaulay. 1971. "The contagion of criminal violence." *Sociometry,* **34**:239–260 (June) [290].

Berkson, J. 1955. "Smoking and lung cancer, some observations on two recent reports." *Journal of the American Statistical Association,* **53**:28 [165n.].

Berliner, J. S. 1961. "The situation of the plant manager." In A. Inkeles and K. Geiger (eds.), *Soviet Society: A Book of Readings.* Boston: Houghton Mifflin Company [142].

Bernard, J. 1956. *Remarriage: A Study of Marriage.* New York: The Dryden Press, Inc. [26].

Berne, E. 1964. *Games People Play: The Psychology of Human Relationships.* New York: Grove Press, Inc. [79].

Best, E. W. R., et al. 1961. "A Canadian study of mortality in relation to smoking habits, a preliminary report." *Canadian Journal of Public Health,* **52**:99–106 (March) [149n.].

Bettelheim, B. 1943. "Individual and mass behavior in extreme situations." *Journal of Abnormal and Social Psychology,* **38**:417–452 (October) [28].

Biderman, A. D. 1966. "Social indicators and goals." In R. A. Bauer (ed.), *Social Indicators.* Cambridge, Mass.: The M.I.T. Press [260].

Bierce, A. 1958. *The Devil's Dictionary.* New York: Dover Publications, Inc. [98].

Birmingham, W. 1964. *What Modern Catholics Think About Birth Control.* New York: New American Library [225].

Björk, L. E. 1975. "An experiment in work satisfaction." *Scientific American,* **232**:17–23 (March) [190].

Blake, J. 1973. "The teenage birth control dilemma and public opinion." *Science,* **180:**708–712 (May 18) [228].

Blakeslee, A. F., and T. N. Salmon. 1935. "Genetics of sensory thresholds: Individual taste reactions for different substances." *Proceedings of the National Academy of Science,* **21:**84–90 (No. 2) [165*n*.].

Blauner, R. 1960. "Work satisfaction and industrial trends in modern society." In W. Galenson and S. M. Lipset (eds.), *Labor and Trade Unionism: An Interdisciplinary Reader.* New York: John Wiley & Sons, Inc. [177, 179].

Block, J. 1961. *The Q-Sort Method in Personality Assessment and Psychiatric Research.* Springfield, Ill.: Charles C Thomas, Publisher [28].

Blum, R. H. 1971. "To wear a Nostradamus hat: Drugs of the future." *The Journal of Social Issues,* **27:**89–106 (No. 3) [149].

—— et al. 1969. *Students and Drugs.* San Francisco: Jossey-Bass [149].

Boehm, L. 1957. "The development of independence: A comparative study." *Child Development,* **28:**85–92 (March) [127].

Bogg, R. A. et al. 1969. "Some sociological and social psychological correlates of marihuana and alcohol use by Michigan high school students." Unpublished paper presented at the Midwest Sociological Society meeting. Indianapolis (May 2) [162–163].

Bossard, J. H. S. 1932–1933. "Residential propinquity as a factor in marriage selection." *American Journal of Sociology,* **38:**219–224 (September) [100].

Bottomore, T. B., and M. Rubel. 1956. *Karl Marx: Selected Writings in Sociology and Social Philosophy.* London: C. A. Watts & Co. [175].

Boulding, K. E. 1965. Review of A. Löwe, "On economic knowledge: Toward a science of political economics." *Scientific American,* **212:**139–142 (May) [267].

Bowden, K. M., et al. 1958. "A survey of blood alcohol testing in Victoria (1951–1956)." *The Medical Journal of Australia,* **2:**13–15 (July 5) [160].

Bowen, M. 1973. Research cited in E. D. Macklin (ed.), *Cohabitation Research Newsletter,* **2:**4 (April) [117].

Bowlby, J. 1952. *Maternal Care and Mental Health.* Geneva: World Health Organization [74, 245].

Bradburn, N. M. 1969. *The Structure of Psychological Well-Being.* Chicago: Aldine Publishing Company [25].

——, and D. Caplovitz. 1965. *Reports on Happiness.* Chicago: Aldine Publishing Company [16–19, 23–25].

Braginsky, B. M. et al. 1969. *Methods of Madness: The Mental Hospital as a Last Resort.* New York: Holt, Rinehart, and Winston [66].

Brain, W. R. 1965. *Drug Addiction: The Second Report of the Interdepartmental Committee.* London: HMSO [172].

Branch, B. N. 1972. "Out-patient termination of pregnancy." In M. Potts and C. Wood (eds.), *New Concepts in Contraception.* Baltimore: University Park Press [243].

Brayfield, A. H., et al. 1957. "Interrelationships among measures of job satisfaction and general satisfaction." *Journal of Applied Psychology,* **41:**201–205 (August) [185].

Brecher, E. M., et al. 1972. *Licit and Illicit Drugs.* Boston: Little, Brown [172].

Bridge, P., et al. 1974. "Why some Scout leaders padded troop rolls." *The National Observer,* **13:**6 (June 22) [128].

Brill, N. Q., and H. A. Storrow. 1960. "Social class and psychiatric treatment." *Archives of General Psychiatry,* **3:**340–344 (October) [37].

———et al. 1970. "The marihuana problem." *Annals of Internal Medicine,* **73**:449–465 (September) [166].

Brinton, C. 1938. *The Anatomy of Revolution.* New York: W. W. Norton & Company, Inc. [30].

Brock, D. 1960. "The innocent mind: Or, my days as a juvenile delinquent." *Canadian Journal of Corrections,* **2**:25–35 [148*n*.].

Brogden, H. E. 1940. "A factor analysis of 40 character traits." Psychological Monographs, **52**:39–55 (Whole No. 234) [127].

Bronfenbreener, U. 1962. "The role of age, sex, class, and culture in studies of moral development." *Research Supplement to Religious Education* (July–August). New York: The Religious Education Association [127].

Broom, L. 1956. "Intermarriage and mobility in Hawaii." *Transactions of the Third World Congress of Sociology,* Vol. 3. London: International Sociological Association [103].

Brophy, A. L. 1959. "Self, role, and satisfaction." *Genetic Phychology Monographs,* **59**:263–308 (May) [185].

Bruce, G. 1969. *The Stranglers: The Cult of Thuggee and Its Overthrow in British India.* New York: Harcourt, Brace & World [48].

Buckley, W. F., Jr. 1973. "On the right." *National Review,* **25**:166–167 (February 2) [19*n*.].

Bukovsky, V. 1972. "The Bukovsky papers: Notes from Soviet asylums." *National Review,* **24**:633–636 (June 9) [70*n*.].

Bullock, H. A. 1955. "Urban homicide in theory and fact." *Journal of Criminal Law and Criminology,* **45**:565–575 (February) [160].

Burgess, A. 1962. *A Clockwork Orange.* London: Heinemann [83–84].

Burgess, E. W., and L. S. Cottrell, Jr. 1939. *Predicting Success or Failure in Marriage.* New York: Prentice-Hall, Inc. [27, 109, 112].

———, and P. Wallin. 1944. "Homogamy in personality characteristics." *Journal of Abnormal and Social Psychology,* **39**:475–481 (October) [100].

———, and ———. 1953. *Engagement and Marriage.* Philadelphia: J. B. Lippincott [100, 109].

Burma, J. H. 1949. "The present status of the Spanish-Americans of New Mexico." *Social Forces,* **28**:133–138 (December) [100].

———. 1963. "Interethnic marriage in Los Angeles, 1948–1959." *Social Forces,* **42**:156–165 (December) [103].

Burt, C. 1938. "The analysis of temperament." *British Journal of Medical Psychology,* **17**:158–188 (January) [104].

Burton, R. V. 1963. "Generality of honesty reconsidered." *Psychological Review,* **70**:481–499 (November) [126].

Buswell, G. T. 1958. "A comparison of achievement in arithmetic in England and Central California." *The Arithmetic Teacher,* **5**:1–9 (February) [214].

Byrne, D., and W. Griffitt. 1966. "A developmental investigation of the law of attraction." *Journal of Personality and Social Psychology,* **4**:699–702 (December) [99].

Cahalan, D. 1970. *Problem Drinkers: A National Survey.* San Francisco: Jossey-Bass [153, 159].

——— et al. 1969. *American Drinking Practices: A National Study of Drinking Behavior and Attitudes.* New Brunswick, N.J.: Rutgers Center of Alcohol Studies [158, 159].

Cairncross, A. (ed.), 1970. *Planning and Economic Management.* Manchester, Eng.: Manchester University Press [261].

Calder, J. 1970. "A reply to Pamela Hansford Johnson on 'The Pornography of Violence.'" *Encounter,* **34**:85–90 (April) [286].

Calderone, M. S. (ed.). 1958. *Abortion in the United States.* New York: Harper & Brothers [240].

Campbell, A. et al. 1975. *The Perceived Quality of Life.* New York: Russell Sage Foundation [112, 181].

Campbell, A. M. G. et al. 1971. "Cerebral atrophy in young cannabis smokers." *Lancet,* **2**:1219–1224 (December 4) [157].

Campbell, J. P., and M. D. Dunnette. 1968. "Effectiveness of T-group experiences in managerial training and development." *Psychological Bulletin,* **70**:73–104 (August) [85].

Cantril, H. 1965. *The Pattern of Human Concerns.* New Brunswick, N.J.: Rutgers University Press [9–12].

Carr-Saunders, A. M. 1936. *World Population: Past Growth and Present Trends.* Oxford: Clarendon Press [222].

Carter, H., and P. C. Glick. 1970. *Marriage and Divorce: A Social and Economic Study.* Cambridge, Mass.: Harvard University Press [108, 118].

Cassell, E. J. 1973. "Disease as a way of life." *Commentary,* **55**:80–82 (February) [31].

Cattell, R. B. 1950. "The principal culture patterns discoverable in the syntal dimensions of existing nations." *Journal of Social Psychology,* **32**:215–253 (November) [298].

———, and J. R. Nesselroade. 1967. "Likeness and completeness theories examined by 16 PF measures on stably and unstably married couples." *Journal of Personality and Social Psychology,* **7**:351–361 (December) [100].

Catton, W. R., and R. J. Smircich. 1964. "A comparison of mathematical models for the effect of residential propinquity on mate-selection." *American Sociological Review,* **29**:522–529 (August) [100].

Center for Disease Control, Health Services, and Mental Health Administration. 1972. *Abortion Surveillance Report: Legal Abortions, United States Annual Summary, 1971.* Atlanta: U.S. Department of Health, Education and Welfare. Publication No. 73-8205 [240].

Centers, R. 1948. "Occupational mobility of urban occupational strata." *American Sociological Review,* **13**:197–203 (April) [201].

———. 1949. "Marital selection and occupational strata." *American Journal of Sociology,* **53**:530–535 (May) [100].

———, and H. Cantril. 1946. "Income satisfaction and income aspiration." *Journal of Abnormal and Social Psychology,* **41**:64–69 (January) [187].

Central Statistical Office. 1973. *Annual Abstract of Statistics, 1973.* London: H.M.S.O. [282].

Chambliss, W. 1972. *Box-Man: A Professional Thief's Journey.* New York: Harper and Row, Publishers, Incorporated [183].

Chancellor, L. E., and L. G. Burchinal. 1962. "Relations among inter-religious marriages, migratory marriages, and civil weddings in Iowa." *Eugenics Quarterly,* **9**:75–83 (June 1) [103].

Chandrasekhar, S. 1959. "Family planning in an Indian village: Motivation and methods." Paper read at the Sixth International Conference on Planned Parenthood. New Delhi; India. (February 14–20) [236].

————. 1974. *Abortion in a Crowded World: The Problem of Abortion with Special Reference to India.* Seattle: University of Washington Press [245].

Chang, Cung-li. 1955. *The Chinese Gentry: Studies on Their Role in Nineteenth-Century Chinese Society.* Seattle: University of Washington Press [198].

Chapel, J. L. 1967. "Treatment of a case of school phobia by reciprocal inhibition." *Canadian Psychiatric Association Journal,* 12:25–28 (February) [83].

Chopra, R. N., and G. S. Chopra. 1965. "Studies of 300 Indian drug addicts with special reference to psycho-sociological aspects, etiology, and treatment." *Bulletin of Narcotics,* 17:1–9 (April) [165].

————et al. 1942. "Cannabis sativa in relation to mental diseases and crime in India." *Indian Journal of Medical Research,* 30:155–171 [165].

Christozov, C. 1965. "L'aspect marocain de l'intoxication cannabique d'ápres des études sur maldes mentaux chroniques: lere partie et 2eme partie." *Marocain Médecin,* 44:630–642, 866–899 [165].

Church, G., and C. D. Carnes. 1973. *The Pit.* New York: Outerbridge & Lazard [85–86].

Clague, A. J., and S. J. Ventura. 1968. *Trends in Illegitimacy, U.S. 1940–1965.* Washington, D.C.: U.S. Department of Health, Education and Welfare, Public Health Service Series 21, **No. 15** [107].

Claridge, G. et al. 1973. *Personality Differences and Biological Variations: A Study of Twins.* Toronto: Pergamon of Canada [104].

Clark, E. L. 1963. Unpublished study cited by R. F. Winch, *The Modern Family,* p. 345, n. 49. New York: Holt, Rinehart, & Winston [100].

Clark, K. B. 1954. Testimony in *Bolling v. Sharpe,* 347 U.S. 497; testimony in *Brown v. Board of Education,* 347 U.S. 483 [216].

Cleaver, E. 1968. *Soul on Ice.* New York: McGraw-Hill Book Company [138].

Cleckley, H. M. 1964. *The Mask of Sanity.* 4th ed. St. Louis: C. V. Mosby [44].

Cleveland, F. P. 1955. "Problems in homicide investigation IV: The relationship of alcohol to homicide." *Cincinnati Journal of Medicine,* 36: 28–30 [160].

Cloward, R. A., and L. E. Ohlin. 1960. *Delinquency and Opportunity: A Theory of Delinquent Gangs.* New York: The Free Press [142].

Cohen, S. S. 1970. *Modern Capitalist Planning: The French Experience.* Cambridge, Mass.: Harvard University Press [261].

Colebrook, J. 1973. "Key West, with Cubans." *Commentary,* 56:50–60 (July) [259].

Coleman, J. R. 1974. *Blue-Collar Journal: A College President's Sabbatical.* Philadelphia: J. B. Lippincott Company [183n.].

Coleman, J. S. 1972. "The children have outgrown the schools." *Psychology Today,* 5:72–75, 82 (February) [210].

———— et al. 1966. *Equality of Educational Opportunity.* Washington, D.C.: U.S. Government Printing Office [210–212, 217–218].

Coles, R. 1967. "Is prejudice against Negroes overrated?" *Trans-Action,* 4:44–45 (October) [63–64].

Comrey, A. L., and J. A. Newmeyer. 1965. "The measurement of radicalism-conservatism." *Journal of Social Psychology,* 67:357–369 (December) [244].

Connor, W. D. 1972. *Deviance in Soviet Society: Crime, Delinquency, and Alcoholism.* New York: Columbia University Press [142, 149, 172n.].

Conquest, R. 1968. *The Great Terror.* New York: Macmillan [256n.].

Cooley, C. H. 1902. *Human Nature and the Social Order.* New York: Scribner's [31].

Cooper, C. C. 1960. *A Comparative Study of Delinquents and Non-Delinquents.* Portsmouth, Ohio: The Psychological Service Center Press [210].

Corso, G. 1959. "On marriage." *The Evergreen Review*. 3:160–163 (Summer) [122].

Cortes, J. B., and F. M. Gatti. 1965. "Physique and self-description of temperament." *Journal of Consulting Psychology*, 29:432–439 (September) [104].

—— and ——. 1966. "Physique and motivation." *Journal of Consulting Psychology*, 30:408–414 (September) [104].

Coser, L. A. 1956. *The Functions of Social Conflict*. Glencoe, Ill.: The Free Press [289].

——. 1967. *Continuities in the Study of Social Conflict*. New York: The Free Press [289].

Council for Basic Education. 1965. *Bulletin*, 9 (April). [215].

——. 1970. *Bulletin*, 14 (January). [215].

——. 1971a. *Bulletin*, 15 (January). [215].

——. 1971b. *Bulletin*, 16 (September). [215].

Cousineau, D. F. 1967. *Some Current Conceptions of Rationality and the Policy Sciences*. Edmonton, Canada: The University of Alberta, Department of Sociology, M.A. thesis [239].

Creager, J. A., and F. D. Harding, Jr. 1958. "A hierarchical factor analysis of foreman behavior." *Journal of Applied Psychology*, 42:197–203 (June) [195].

Creer, T. L., et al. 1966. "Classical conditioning of reflexive fighting." *Psychonomic Science*, 4:89–90 [290].

Crites, J. O. 1969. *Vocational Psychology: The Study of Vocational Behavior and Development*. New York: McGraw-Hill Book Company [176].

Crocetti, G., et al. 1972. "Multiple models and mental illnesses: A rejoinder to 'Failure of a moral enterprise: Attitudes of the public toward mental illness' by T. R. Sarbin and J. C. Mancuso." *Journal of Consulting and Clinical Psychology*, 39:1–5 (August) [69].

Cross, H. J. 1964. "The outcome of psychotherapy: A selected analysis of research findings." *Journal of Consulting Psychology*, 28:413–417 [88].

Cruz, C. J. 1943. "Sexual criminogenesis and other medicolegal considerations." *Revista Méxicana de Psiquiatría, Neurología y Medicina Legal*. 1:3–14 [160].

CTV Broadcast. 1974. "Eye-to-eye: On public apathy." (January 28) [137].

Dandekar, K. 1963. "Vasectomy camps in Maharashtra." *Population Studies*, 17:147–154 (November) [236].

David, H. P. 1973. "Psychological studies in abortion." In J. T. Fawcett (ed.), *Psychological Perspectives on Population*. New York: Basic Books, Inc., Publishers [245].

Davidson, P. E., and H. D. Anderson. 1937. *Occupational Mobility in an American Community*. Stanford: Stanford University Press [201].

Davie, M. R., and R. J. Reeves. 1938–1939. "Propinquity of residence before marriage." *American Journal of Sociology*, 44:510–517 (January) [100].

Davie, W. E. 1973. "Being prudent and acting prudently." *American Philosophical Quarterly*, 10:57–60 (January) [45].

Davies, J. C. 1962. "Toward a theory of revolution." *American Sociological Review*, 27:5–19 (February) [30].

Davis, A. 1970. "Her revolutionary voice cries damnation on the system," *Life*, 69:26–27 (September 11) [139].

Davis, M. S. 1971. "That's interesting!: Towards a phenomenology of sociology and a sociology of phenomenology." *Philosophy of the Social Sciences*, 1:309–344 (December) [70].

Davis, W., and E. Phares. 1967. "Internal-external control as a determinant of information-seeking in a social influence situation." *Journal of Personality,* **35:**547–561 (December) [287].

De Charms, R. 1968. *Personal Causation: The Internal Affective Determinants of Behavior.* New York: Academic Press, Inc. [287].

———, and E. J. Wilkins. 1963. "Some effects of verbal expression of hostility." *Journal of Abnormal and Social Psychology,* **66:**462–470 (December) [300].

Deevey, E. 1960. "Human population." *Scientific American,* **203:**195–204 (September) [222].

De Leon, G., and W. Mandell. 1966. "A comparison of conditioning and psychotherapy in the treatment of functional enuresis." *Journal of Clinical Psychology,* **22:**326–330 (July) [83].

Dement, W. C. 1972. "But still I cannot sleep at night." *The Stanford Alumni Almanac* (December):5–6. [87].

Demerath, N. J. 1942. "Schizophrenia among primitives." *American Journal of Psychiatry,* **98:**703–707 (March) [65].

Demographic Yearbook. 1972. New York: United Nations Publishing Service. [242].

Dencker, P. G. 1947. "Results of treatment of psychoneurosis by the general practitioners: A follow-up study of 500 cases." *New York State Journal of Medicine,* **46:**2164–2166 (October 1) [89].

Deutsch, A. 1950. *The Trouble with Cops.* Boston: Little, Brown and Company [131].

Devereux, G. 1955. *A Study of Abortion in Primitive Societies: A Typological, Distributional, and Dynamic Analysis of Birth in 400 Preindustrial Societies.* New York: The Julian Press [240].

Devons, E. 1950. *Planning in Practice.* Cambridge, Eng.: Cambridge University Press [261].

Dickinson, R. L., and L. Beam. 1931. *A Thousand Marriages: A Medical Study of Sex Adjustment.* Baltimore, Md.: Williams & Wilkins [106].

Dickinson, T. 1974. "Death trapped in a tree." *Harper's Magazine,* **248:**15–16 (June) [223].

Dinitz, S., et al. 1960. "Mate selection and social class: Changes during the past quarter century." *Marriage and Family Living,* **22:**348–351 (November) [100].

Dirks, R. L., and L. Gross. 1974. *The Great Wall Street Scandal.* New York: McGraw-Hill Book Company [125, 200].

Doe et al. v. Bolton. 1973. 410 *U.S.* 179 [240].

Dohrenwend, B. P., and E. Chin-Shong. 1967. "Social status and attitudes toward psychological disorder: The problem of tolerance of deviance." *American Sociological Review,* **32:**417–433 (June) [69].

——— et al. 1962. "The orientation of leaders in an urban area toward problems of mental illness." *American Journal of Psychiatry,* **118:**683–691 (February) [69].

Doll, R., and A. B. Hill. 1964. "Mortality in relation to smoking: Ten years' observations of British doctors." *British Medical Journal,* **1:**1399, 1460 [149*n.*].

Doorenbos, N. J., et al. 1971. "Cultivation, extraction, and analysis of *Cannabis sativa L.*" *Annals of the New York Academy of Science,* **191:**3–12 [157].

Dorcus, R. M. 1925. "Effect of suggestion and tobacco on pulse rate and blood pressure." *Journal of Experimental Psychology,* **8:**297–309 (August) [151].

Dorn, H. F. 1958. "The mortality of smokers and non-smokers." *Proceedings* of the Social Statistics Section, American Statistical Association, 34 [149*n.*].

Downing, J. J. 1970. "The tribal family and the society of awakening." In H. A. Otto (ed.), *The Family in Search of a Future.* New York: Appleton-Century-Crofts, Inc. [116].

Dubin, R. 1958. *The World of Work.* Englewood Cliffs, N.J.: Prentice-Hall, Inc. [178].

Dublin, L. I. 1951. *The Facts of Life: From Birth to Death.* New York: The Macmillan Company [108].

——— et al. 1949. *Length of Life: A Study of the Life Taable.* New York: Ronald Press [26].

Dumont, A. 1890. *Depopulation et Civilisation: Études Demographiques.* Paris: Lecrosnier et Babe. [233].

Duncan, O. D., et al. 1972. *Socioeconomic Background and Achievement.* New York: Seminar Press [205–206].

Dunn, W. L., Jr. (ed.). 1973. *Smoking Behavior.* New York: Halstead Press [156].

Durkheim, E. 1951. *Suicide: A Study in Sociology.* (G. Simpson, ed.). Glencoe, Ill.: The Free Press [141].

Dyer, H. S. 1968. "School factors and equal educational opportunity." *Harvard Educational Review,* **38**:38–56 (Winter) [218].

Easterlin, R. A. 1973. "Does money buy happiness?" *The Public Interest,* **30**:3–10 (Winter) [22].

Eaton, J. W., and R. J. Weil. 1953. "The mental health of the Hutterites." *Scientific American,* **189**:31–37 (December) [65].

———. 1954. *Culture and Mental Disorders.* Glencoe, Ill.: The Free Press [65].

———. 1955. "The mental health of the Hutterites." In E. M. Rose (ed.), *Mental Health and Mental Disorder: A Sociological Approach.* New York: W. W. Norton & Company, Inc. [65].

Edmonton Journal. 1970. "Education can build peace." 30 (August 6) [303].

Educational Policy Research Corporation. 1973. "Fraud in the schools: Court challenge to accountability." Syracuse, N.Y.: The Corporation [215].

Edwards, H. 1969. *The Revolt of the Black Athlete.* New York: The Free Press [183].

Edwards, J. H., et al. 1966. "Monozygotic twins of different sex." *Journal of Medical Genetics,* **3**:117–123 [51*n*.].

Ehrich, T. 1974. "Looking for work: As economy tightens far more applicants seek unskilled jobs." *The Wall Street Journal,* **90**:1, 10 (June 6) [214].

Ehrlich, P. R., and A. H. Ehrlich. 1972. "What can be done? In Q. H. Stanford (ed.), *The World's Population: Problems of Growth.* New York: Oxford University Press [223].

Eibl-Eibesfeldt, I. 1970. *Ethology: The Biology of Behavior.* New York: Holt, Rinehart and Winston, Inc. [129*n*.].

Eliot, T. S. 1948. *Notes Towards a Definition of Culture.* London: Faber and Faber [91].

Elliott, K. (ed.). 1970. *The Family and Its Future.* London: J. and A. Churchill [27].

Ellis, A. 1962. *Reason and Emotion in Psychotherapy.* New York: Lyle Stuart [80].

———. 1964. *The Theory and Practice of Rational-Emotive Psychotherapy.* New York: Lyle Stuart [80].

Ellison, R. 1952. *The Invisible Man.* New York: Random House, Inc. [190].

Engels, F. 1844. "The myth of overpopulation." Excerpt from his *Outlines of a Critique of Political Economy.* In R. L. Meek (ed.), *Marx and Engels on the Population Bomb.* 1971. Berkeley, Calif. The Ramparts Press [225].

English, J. P., et al. 1940. "Tobacco and coronary disease." *Journal of the American Medical Association,* **115**:1327 (October) [155].

Enke, S. 1973. "Population growth and economic growth." *The Public Interest*, 32:86–96 (Summer) [245].

Epictetus. 1925. *Discourses*. Transl. by G. Long. New York: U.S. Book Company [148].

Erskine, H. G. 1974. "The polls: Fear of violence and crime." *Public Opinion Quarterly*, 39:131–145 (Spring) [140].

Esquire. 1974. "The last time we had dinner at Melvin Laird's we thought the silver pattern looked familiar." 81:90 (January) [130].

Essen-Möller, E. 1955. "The calculation of morbid risk in parents of index cases, as applied to a family sample of schizophrenics." *Acta Genetica*, 5:334–342 [51].

———. 1956. "Individual traits and morbidity in a Swedish rural population." *Acta Psychiatrica et Neurologica Scandinavica*. Supplementum No. 100 [65].

Etzioni, A. 1968a. *The Active Society: A Theory of Societal and Political Processes*. London: Collier-Macmillan [7].

Etzioni, A. 1968b. "Toward a critical and objective sociology." et al., 1:11 (Summer) [7].

Evans, K. M. 1962. *Sociometry and Education*. London: Routledge & Kegan Paul [99].

Evans-Pritchard, E. E. 1965. *Witchcraft, Oracles, and Magic among the Azande*. Oxford: Clarendon Press. [5].

Eysenck, H. J. 1963. "Smoking, personality, and psychosomatic disorders." *Journal of Psychosomatic Research*, 7:107–130 [151].

———. 1966. *The Effects of Psychotherapy*. New York: International Science Press [37].

———. 1967. "New ways in psychotherapy." *Psychology Today*, 1:39–47 (June) [89].

———, and D. B. Prell. 1951. "The inheritance of neuroticism: An experimental study." *Journal of Mental Science*, 97:441–467 [51].

———et al. 1960. "Smoking and personality." *British Medical Journal*, 1:1456–1460 (May 14) [165n.].

Fahlbeck, P. E. 1953. "La noblesse de Suede: Etude demographique." *Bulletin de l'Institute International de Statistique*. Rome: The Institute [198].

Fairchild, H. P. 1944. *Dictionary of Sociology*. New York: Philosophical Library [4n.].

Fairchild, M. 1930a. "Skill and specialization: A study in the metal trade. Part I—The nature and measurement of skill." *Personnel Journal*, 9:28–71 (April–June) [183].

———. 1930b. "Skill and specialization: The significance of skill." *Personnel Journal*, 9:128–175 (August) [183].

Family Planning Digest. 1973. "Abortion statistics: Mortality, morbidity in legal abortions drop as women learn early procedures safer." 2:8–9 (May) [242].

Fancher, R. E., Jr. 1966. "Explicit personality theories and accuracy in person perception." *Journal of Personality*, 34:252–261 (June) [48].

———. 1967. "Accuracy vs. validity in person perception." *Journal of Consulting Psychology*, 31:264–269 (June) [48].

Fanon, F. 1963. *The Wretched of the Earth*. New York: Grove Press, Inc. [278, 279, 289].

Farber, S. M., and R. H. L. Wilson. 1963. *The Potential of Women*. New York: McGraw-Hill Book Company [128].

Faris, R. E. L., and H. W. Dunham. 1939. *Mental Disorders in Urban Areas*. Chicago: University of Chicago Press [57].

Feather, N. T. 1967. "Some personality correlates of external control." *Australian Journal of Psychology*, 19:253–260 (December) [287].

Felix, R. H., and M. Kramer. 1953. "Extent of the problem of mental disorders." *Annals of the American Academy of Political and Social Sciences*, 286:5–14 (March) [46].

Feuer, L. 1963. "What is alienation? The career of a concept." In M. Stein and A. Vidich (eds.), *Sociology on Trial*. Englewood Cliffs, N.J.: Prentice-Hall, Inc. [180].

————. 1969. *The Conflict of Generations: The Character and Significance of Student Movements.* New York: Basic Books, Inc. [134].

Fiedler, F. E., et al. 1952. "Unconscious attitudes as correlates of sociometric choice in social groups," *Journal of Abnormal and Social Psychology,* **47**:790–796 (October) [99].

Fisher, R. S. 1951. "Symposium on the compulsory use of chemical tests for alcohol intoxication." *Maryland Medical Journal,* **3**:291–292 [160].

Flanagan, J. C., and W. W. Cooley. 1966. *Project Talent One-Year Follow-Up Studies.* Pittsburgh: University of Pittsburgh Press [211].

Fleisher, B. M. 1966. *The Economics of Delinquency.* Chicago: Quadrangle Books, Inc. [200].

Folger, J. K., et al. 1970. *Human Resources and Higher Education.* New York: Russell Sage Foundation [211].

Form, W. H. 1972. "Technology and social behavior of workers in four countries: A sociotechnical perspective." *American Sociological Review,* **37**:727–738 (December) [180–181].

Fort, J. 1973. *Alcohol: Our Biggest Drug Problem.* New York: McGraw-Hill Book Company [158].

Fortune editors. 1938. *The Accident of Birth.* New York: Farrar and Rinehart [224].

Frank, G. 1967. *The Boston Strangler.* New York: New American Library, Inc. [90].

Frank, L. K. 1949. *Society as the Patient.* New Brunswick, N.J.: Rutgers University Press [64].

Fraser, D. 1971. *The People Problem: What You Should Know About Growing Population and Vanishing Resources.* Bloomington, Ind.: University Press [223].

Freedman, R. 1965. "Family planning programs today: Major themes of the Geneva Conference." *Studies in Family Planning,* **8** (Supplement) [240].

————, and B. Berelson. 1974. "The human population." *Scientific American,* **231**:31–39 (September) [222].

———— et al. 1959. *Family Planning, Sterility, and Population Growth.* New York: McGraw-Hill Book Company [225].

Freeman, H., and O. Simmons. 1963. *The Mental Patient Comes Home.* New York: John Wiley & Sons [70].

Freeman, L. C. 1955. "Homogamy in inter-ethnic mate selection." *Sociology and Social Research,* **39**:369–377 (July–August) [100].

————. 1958. "Marriage without love: Mate-selection in non-Western societies." In R. F. Winch (ed.), *Mate-Selection.* New York: Harper & Row Publishers, Incorporated [100].

Freeman, V. J. 1960. "Beyond the germ theory: Human aspects of health and illness." *Journal of Health and Human Behavior,* **1**:8–13 (Spring) [56].

Freud, S. 1958. *Civilization and Its Discontents.* Garden City, N.Y.: Doubleday & Company, Inc. [65].

Friberg, L., et al. 1959. "Smoking habits of monozygotic and dizygotic twins." *British Medical Journal,* **1**:1090–1092 (April 25) [165*n*.].

Friedman, M. 1973. "What the president should have done." *Newsweek,* **82**:72 (July 16) [249].

Fromm, E. 1947. *Man for Himself.* New York: Rinehart & Company, Inc. [179].

————. 1955. *The Sane Society.* New York: Holt, Rinehart and Winston, Inc. [180].

————. 1956. *The Art of Loving.* New York: Harper & Row Incorporated [98].

Fuller, J. L. 1967. "Experiential deprivation and later behavior." *Science,* **158**:1645–1652 (December 29) [74].

Gall, N. 1971. "How Castro failed." *Commentary,* **52:**45–57 (November) [259].

Galle, O. R., et al. 1972. "Population density and pathology: What are the relations for man?" *Science,* **176:**23–30 (April 7) [57].

Gallup Poll. 1971. "Per cent who want to emigrate—and where." Princeton, N.J.: The Gallup Opinion Index, Report No. 71 (May):25 [17].

Gamson, W. A. 1974. "Violence and political power: The meek don't make it." *Psychology Today,* **8:**35–41 (July) [277].

Garfinkel, H. 1967. *Studies in Ethnomethodology.* Englewood Cliffs, N.J.: Prentice-Hall, Inc. [9].

Gass, O. 1967a. "China, Russia, and the U.S. I." *Commentary,* **43:**65–73 (March) [258].

———. 1967b. "China, Russia, and the U.S. II." *Commentary,* **43:**39–46 (April) [258].

Gastil, R. D. 1971. "Homicide and a regional culture of violence." *American Sociological Review,* **36:**412–427 (June) [284].

Gelfand, D. M., and D. P. Hartmann. 1968. "Behavior therapy with children: A review and evaluation of research methodology." *Psychological Bulletin,* **69:**204–215 (March) [89].

Ghiselli, E. E., and C. W. Brown. 1955. *Personnel and Industrial Psychology.* New York: McGraw-Hill Book Company [177].

Gibran, K. 1923. *The Prophet.* New York: Alfred A. Knopf, Inc. [99].

Gilbert, G. M. 1938. "The new status of experimental studies on the relationship of feeling to memory." *Psychological Bulletin,* **35:**26–35 (January) [21].

Gillin, J. L. 1946. *The Wisconsin Prisoner.* Madison: University of Wisconsin Press [276].

Ginzberg, E. 1970. "Foreword" to I. Berg, *Education and Jobs: The Great Training Robbery.* New York: Frederick A. Praeger, Inc. [213].

———. 1972. "The outlook for educated manpower." *The Public Interest,* **26:**100–111 (Winter) [214].

Glasscote, R. M., et al. 1967. *The Treatment of Alcoholism: A Study of Programs and Problems.* Washington, D.C.: American Psychiatric Association and the National Association for Mental Health [159].

Glasser, W. 1965. *Reality Therapy: A New Approach to Psychiatry.* New York: Harper & Row Publishers, Incorporated [80].

Glazer, N., and D. P. Moynihan. 1963. *Beyond the Melting Pot.* Cambridge, Mass.: M.I.T. Press and Harvard University Press [93].

———.1974. "Why ethnicity?" *Commentary,* **58:**33–39 (October) [289].

Glick, P. C. 1949. "First marriages and remarriages." *American Sociological Review,* **14:**726–734 (December) [108].

———. 1958. *American Families.* New York: John Wiley & Sons, Inc. [108].

———, and A. J. Norton. 1970. "Probabilities of marriage, divorce, widowhood, and remarriage." Paper presented at the annual meeting of the Population Association of America. Atlanta, Ga. (April 16–18) [108].

———. 1971. "Frequency, duration, and probability of marriage and divorce." *Journal of Marriage and the Family,* **33:**307–320 (May) [108, 119].

Glueck, S. 1964. "The home, the school, and delinquency." In S. and E. Glueck (eds.), *Ventures in Criminology: Selected Recent Papers.* London: Tavistock [210].

Goldfarb, W. 1955. "Emotional and intellectual consequences of psychological deprivation in infancy: A reevaluation." In P. Hoch and J. Zubin (eds.), *Psychopathology of Childhood.* New York: Grune and Stratton [74].

Goldhamer, H., and A. W. Marshall. 1949. *Psychosis and Civilization.* Glencoe, Ill.: The Free Press [46, 65].

Goldstein, I. B. 1964. "Role of muscle tension in personality theory." *Psychological Bulletin.* **61**:413–425 (June)[104].

Goldstein, S. G., and J. D. Linden. 1969. "Multivariate classification of the alcoholic by means of the MMPI." *Journal of Abnormal Psychology,* **74**:661–669 (December) [164n.].

Goldstücker, E. 1971. "Lessons of Prague." *Encounter,* **37**:75–82 (August) [258].

Goode, W. J. 1956. *After Divorce.* Glencoe, Ill.: The Free Press [26, 118].

———. 1962. "Marital satisfaction and instability: A cross-cultural analysis of divorce." *International Social Science Journal,* **14**:507–526 (No. 3) [118].

———. 1963. *World Revolution and Family Patterns.* Glencoe, Ill.: The Free Press [119].

———. 1964. *The Family.* Englewood Cliffs, N.J.: Prentice-Hall, Inc. [102, 107].

Goodman, P. 1956. *Growing Up Absurd.* New York: Random House, Inc. [142].

Gopalaswami, R. A. 1951. *Census of India.* Volume I, Part 1-A. New Delhi: Superintendent of Census Operations [236–237].

Gorbanevskaya, N. 1972. *Red Star at Noon.* New York: Holt, Rinehart and Winston, Inc. [70n.].

Gordon, T. J., and O. Helmer. 1964. *Report on a Long-Range Forecasting Study.* Santa Monica: The Rand Corporation [87].

Gore, P. M., and J. B. Rotter. 1963. "A personality correlate of social action." *Journal of Personality,* **31**:58–64 (March) [287].

Goss, A., and T. E. Morosko. 1969. "Alcoholism and clinical symptoms." *Journal of Abnormal Psychology,* **74**:682–684 (December) [164n.].

Gottesmann, I. I. 1963. "Heritability of personality: A demonstration." *Psychological Monographs,* **77** (Whole No. 572). [51, 104].

———, and J. Shields. 1972. *Schizophrenia and Genetics: A Twin Study Vantage Point.* New York: Academic Press [55].

Gough, H. G., and D. R. Peterson. 1952. "The identification and measurement of predispositional factors in crime and delinquency." *Journal of Consulting Psychology,* **16**:207–212 (June) [130].

Gould, L., et al. 1974. *Connections: Notes from the Heroin World.* New Haven: Yale University Press [164].

Gove, W. R. 1970a. "Who is hospitalized?: A critical review of some sociological studies of mental illness." *Journal of Health and Social Behavior,* **11**:294–303 (December) [70].

———. 1970b. "Societal reaction as an explanation of mental illness: An evaluation." *American Sociological Review,* **35**:873–884 (October) [70].

———. 1972. "Sex roles, marital roles, and mental illness." *Social Forces,* **51**:34–44 (November) [25].

———. 1973. "Sex, marital status, and mortality." *American Journal of Sociology,* **79**:45–67 (July) [25].

———, and B. J. Lester. 1974. "Social position and self-evaluation: A reanalysis of the Yancey, Ribsby, and McCarthy data." *American Journal of Sociology,* **79**:1308–1314 (March) [25, 26].

Graham, F. P. 1970. "Black crime: The lawless image." *Harper's Magazine,* **241**:64–78 (September) [282].

Grant, D. L. 1955. "A factor analysis of managers' ratings." *Journal of Applied Psychology,* **39**:283–286 (August) [195].

Gray, J. G. 1959. *The Warriors: Reflections of Men in Battle.* New York: Harper & Row Publishers, Incorporated [279, 290].

————. 1970. *On Understanding Violence Philosophically and Other Essays.* New York: Harper & Row Publishers, Incorporated [290].

Grayson, C. J., Jr. 1974. *Confessions of a Price Controller.* New York: Dow Jones-Irvin [265].

Green, A. W. 1946. "The middle-class male child and neurosis." *American Journal of Sociology,* **51**:523–530 (May) [63].

Green, H. W. 1939. *Persons Admitted to the Cleveland State Hospital.* Cleveland: Cleveland Health Council [57].

Greenslade, R. V. 1968. "The Soviet economic system in transition." In H. Kohler (ed.), *Readings in Economics.* New York: Holt, Rinehart and Winston, Inc. [256, 257].

Grinspoon, L. 1969. "Marihuana." *Scientific American,* **221**:17–25 (December) [152].

Guevara, Ché. 1963. Speech reported in *Revolución.* (August 21) [193*n*.].

Gurin, G., et al. 1960. *Americans View Their Mental Health.* New York: Basic Books, Inc., Publishers [19, 25, 26].

Haberman, P. W., and J. Sheinberg. 1966. "Education reported in interviews: An aspect of survey content error." *Public Opinion Quarterly,* **30**:295–301 (Summer) [132].

Haddon, W., et al. 1960. *Controlled Studies of the Characteristics of Adult Pedestrians Fatally Injured by Motor Vehicles in Manhattan: A Preliminary Report.* Ithaca: Department of Public Health and Preventive Medicine, Cornell University Medical College [161].

Hadley, E. E., et al. 1944. "Military psychiatry: An ecological note." *Psychiatry,* **7**:379–407 (November) [57].

Hagan, J. L. 1973. "Labeling and deviance: A case study in 'the sociology of the interesting.'" *Social Problems,* **20**:447–458 (Spring) [40, 70].

————. 1975. "Ending 'discrimination': Notes on the sociological utility of a moral concept." Paper in submission [136*n*.].

Hagen, K. S. 1970. "Following the ladybug home." *National Geographic,* **137**:543–553 (April) [274].

Hall, P., and H. W. Locke. 1938. *Incentives and Contentment: A Study Made in a British Factory.* London: Sir Isaac Pitman & Sons, Ltd. [183].

Halleck, S. 1967. "Sex and mental health on campus." *Journal of American Medical Association,* **200**:684–690 (No. 8) [117].

Hamilton, G. V. 1929. *A Research in Marriage.* New York: Boni [108].

Hamlin, R. M., and W. D. Ward. 1973. "Schizophrenic intelligence, symptoms, and release from hospital." *Journal of Abnormal Psychology,* **81**:11–16 (February) [35].

Hammond, E. C. 1958. "Smoking and death rates: A riddle in cause and effect." *American Scientist,* **46**:331–354 (December) [151].

————, and D. Horn. 1954. "The relationship between human smoking habits and death rates: A follow-up study of 187,766 men." *Journal of the American Medical Association,* **155**:1316–1328 (August 7) [149*n*., 151, 155].

Hampton, P. J. 1947a. "A descriptive portrait of the drinker: I. The normal drinker." *Journal of Social Psychology,* **25**:69–81 (February) [159, 160].

————. 1947b. "A descriptive portrait of the drinker: V. The compulsive drinker." *Journal of Social Psychology* **25**:151–170 (May) [153].

————. 1951. "Differences in personality traits between alcoholic and non-alcoholic subjects." *American Psychologist,* **6**:313 (August) [164*n*.].

Hanley, J. 1973. "Mental health care." *Science,* **179**:1182–1183 (March 23) [91].

Hanley, T. R. 1946. "Tomorrow's children." *Boston American,* (July 9) [224].

Hardin, E., and G. L. Hershey. 1960. "Accuracy of employee reports on changes in pay." *Journal of Applied Psychology,* **44**:269–275 (August) [132].

Hardin, G. 1968. "The tragedy of the commons." *Science*, **162**:1243–1248 (December 13) [232, 237, 238].

———. 1972. *Exploring New Ethics for Survival: The Voyage of the Spaceship Beagle.* New York: Viking [221–222, 226].

———. 1973a. "Ecology and growth—The tragic insight." *Research Management*, **16**:9–12 (No. 6) [311].

———. 1973b. *Stalking the Wild Taboo.* Los Altos, Calif.: William Kaufmann [240, 243, 246].

Harding, L. W. 1948. "Experimental comparisons between generalizations and problems as indices of values." *Journal of General Psychology*, **38**:31–50 (First Half) [241].

Harmsworth, H. C., and M. S. Minnis. 1955. "Non-statutory causes of divorce: The lawyer's point of view." *Marriage and Family Living*, **17**:316–321 (November) [119–120].

Harrison, G. A. 1964. "The modern Mr. Forster." *The New Republic*, **150**:15–16 (January 11) [98].

Hart, H. 1940. *Chart for Happiness.* New York: The Macmillan Company [17, 23].

Hartshorne, H., and M. A. May. 1928–1930. *Studies in the Nature of Character.* Three Volumes. New York: The Macmillan Company [126–129].

Hassan, A. 1972. In E. Pell (ed.), *Maximum Security: Letters from Prison.* New York: E. P. Dutton & Co., Inc. [138, 138*n*.].

Hathaway, S. R., and E. D. Monachesi. 1957. "The personalities of predelinquent boys." *Journal of Criminal Law, Criminology, and Police Science*, **48**:149–163 (July–August) [130].

Hawkins, R. P., et al. 1966. "Behavior therapy in the home: Amelioration of problem parent-child relations with the parent in a therapeutic role." *Journal of Experimental Child Psychology*, **4**:99–107 (September) [83].

Hearst, P. 1974. Citations from a tape-recording. *Newsweek*, **83**:35 (June 17) [278].

Heath, C. W. 1958. "Differences between smokers and nonsmokers." *A.M.A. Archives of Internal Medicine*, **101**:377–378 (February) [165*n*.].

Heer, D. M. 1962. "The trend of interfaith marriages in Canada, 1922–1957." *American Sociological Review*, **27**:245–250 (April) [102, 103].

Heilbroner, R. L. 1966. "Is economic theory possible?" *Social Research*, **33**:272–294 (Fall) [262].

———. 1974. *An Inquiry into the Human Prospect.* New York: W. W. Norton & Company, Inc. [270, 270*n*.].

Heiss, J. S. 1960. "Premarital characteristics of the religiously intermarried in an urban area." *American Sociological Review*, **25**:47–55 (February) [102].

Henry, A. F., and J. F. Short, Jr. 1954. *Suicide and Homicide: Some Economic, Sociological, and Psychological Aspects of Aggression.* Glencoe, Ill.: The Free Press [282].

Henry, A. F., and J. F. Short, Jr. 1954. *Suicide and Homicide: Some Economic, Sociological, and Psychological Aspects of Aggression.* Glencoe, Ill.: The Free Press [282].

Heston, L. L. 1966. "Psychiatric disorders in foster home reared children of schizophrenic mothers." *British Journal of Psychiatry*, **112**:819–825 (August) [53].

Hewett, F. M. 1965. "Teaching speech to an autistic child through operant conditioning." *American Journal of Orthopsychiatry*, **35**:927–936 (October) [83].

Heyndrickx, A. et al. 1970. "Toxicological study of a fatal intoxication in man due to cannabis smoking." *Journal de Pharmacie de Beligique.* **24**:371–376 [150].

Hilgard, E. R. 1962. *Introduction to Psychology.* 3d ed. New York: Harcourt, Brace & World, Inc. [81–84].

Hill, R. J. et al. 1959. *The Family and Population Control: A Puerto Rican Experiment in Social Change.* Chapel Hill: University of North Carolina Press [235].

Himmelfarb, G. 1974. *On Liberty and Liberalism: The Case of John Stuart Mill.* New York: Alfred A. Knopf, Inc. [168*n*.].

Himmelweit, H. T. 1950. "Frustration and aggression: A review of recent experimental work." In T. H. Pear (ed.), *Psychological Factors of Peace and War.* London: Hutchinson's University Library [288].

Hinsie, L. E., and R. J. Campbell (eds.), 1970. *Psychiatric Dictionary.* 4th ed. London: Oxford University Press [98].

Hirschfeld, M. 1956. *Sexual Anomalies: The Origins, Nature, and Treatment of Sexual Disorders.* New York: Emerson Books, Inc. [106].

Hirsh, J. 1949. *The Problem Drinker.* New York: Duell, Sloan & Pearce, Inc. [160].

Hobart, C. A. 1974. "Trial marriage among students: A study of attitudes and experience." In S. P. Wakil (ed.), *Marriage and the Family in Canada: A Reader.* Toronto: Copp Clark [116].

Hoch, P. H. 1972. In M. O. Strahl and N. D. C. Lewis (eds.), *Differential Diagnosis in Clinical Psychiatry: The Lectures of Paul H. Hoch, M.D.* New York: Science House [68].

Hollander. P. 1973. *Soviet and American Society: A Comparison.* London: Oxford University Press [258].

Hollander, X. 1972. *The Happy Hooker.* New York: Dell Publishing Co., Inc. [183].

Hollingshead, A. B., and F. C. Redlich. 1958. *Social Class and Mental Illness: A Community Study.* New York: John Wiley & Sons, Inc. [37, 58–61, 63].

Holmes, O. W., Jr. 1926. In *The Holmes-Laski Letters: The Correspondence of Mr. Justice Holmes and Harold J. Laski, 1916–1935.* Vol. II. (Edited by M. DeW. Howe) Cambridge, Mass.: Harvard University Press [94].

Honzik, M. P. 1966. "Prediction of behavior from birth to maturity." In J. Rosenblith and W. Allinsmith (eds.), *The Causes of Behavior.* Boston: Allyn and Bacon, Inc. [38].

Hoppock, R., and C. L. Odom. 1940. "Job satisfaction: Researches and opinions of 1938–1939." *Occupations,* **19:**24–28 (October) [176].

———, and H. A. Robinson. 1949. "Job satisfaction researches of 1948." *Occupations,* **28:**153–161 (December) [176].

———. 1950. "Job satisfaction researches of 1949." *Occupations,* **29:**13–18 (October) [176].

———. 1951. "Job satisfaction researches of 1950." *Occupations,* **29:**572–578 (May) [176].

———, and S. Spiegler. 1938. "Job satisfaction researches of 1935–1937." *Occupations,* **16:**636–643 (April) [176].

Hoult, T. F. 1969. *Dictionary of Modern Sociology.* Totowa, N.J.: Littlefield, Adams. [4*n*.].

Howard, J. 1970. *Please Touch: A Guided Tour of the Human Potential Movement.* New York: McGraw-Hill Book Company [85].

Hsu, E. H. 1951. "The neurotic score as a function of culture." *Journal of Social Psychology,* **34:**3–30 (August) [35].

Hsu, F. L. K. 1949. "Social mobility in China." *American Sociological Review,* **14:**764–771 (December) [198].

Hughes, E. C. 1958. *Men and Their Work.* Glencoe, Ill.: The Free Press [178].

Hume, D. 1758. *An Inquiry Concerning Human Understanding.* Reprinted 1957. New York: The Liberal Arts Press [130].

———. 1804. *Essays and Treatises on Several Subjects.* Edinburgh: Bell and Bradfute [306].

Hundziak, M., et al. 1965. "Operant conditioning in toilet training of severely mentally retarded boys." *American Journal of Mental Deficiency,* **70**:12–124 (July) [83].

Hunt, C. L., and R. W. Coller. 1957. "Intermarriage and cultural change: A study of Philippine-American marriages." *Social Forces,* **35**:223–230 (March) [102–103].

Husén, T., et al. (eds.). 1967. *International Study of Achievement in Mathematics: A Comparison of Twelve Countries.* New York: John Wiley & Sons, Inc. [214].

Hyman, H. 1944–1945. "Do they tell the truth?" *Public Opinion Quarterly,* **8**:557–559 (Winter) [132].

International Herald-Tribune. 1969. "El Salvador, Honduras sever relations over soccer riots." **2**:28–29 (June) [300].

Jacobs, R., and A. E. Traxler. 1954. "Use of the Kuder in counseling with regard to accounting as a career." *Journal of Counseling Psychology,* **1**:153–158 (Fall) [185].

Jacobson, F. N., et al. 1959. "Status, job satisfaction, and factors of job satisfaction of state institution and clinical psychologists." *American Psychologist.* **14**:144–150 (March) [188].

Jaffe, F. S. 1973. "Public policy on fertility control." *Scientific American,* **229**:17–23 (July) [234].

Jaffe, J. H. 1974. "Tobacco addiction." *Science,* **185**:1039–1040 (September 20) [156].

Jahoda, M., et al. 1960. *Die Arbeitslosen von Marienthal.* Allensbach und Bonn: Verlag für Demoskopie [288].

James, W. 1917. "The moral equivalent of war." *Memoirs and Studies.* London: Longmans [300, 306].

James, W. W., et al. 1965. "Effects of internal and external control upon changes in smoking behavior." *Journal of Consulting Psychology,* **29**:184–186 (April) [287].

Janov, A. 1970. *The Primal Scream: Primal Therapy, The Cure for Neurosis.* New York: G. P. Putnam's Sons [79].

———. 1972. *The Primal Revolution: Toward a Real World.* New York: Simon and Schuster [79].

Jasny, N. 1949. *Socialized Agriculture in the USSR.* Stanford: Stanford University Press [257].

———. 1961. Soviet Industrialization, 1928–1952. Chicago: University of Chicago Press [257].

Jaspers, K. 1948. *Allgemeine Psychopathologie.* Berlin: Springer-Verlag OHG [78].

Jencks, C., et al. 1972. *Inequality: A Reassessment of the Effect of Family and Schooling in America.* New York: Basic Books, Inc., Publishers [212, 213, 218, 220].

Johnson, C. D., and J. Gormly. 1972. "Academic cheating: The contribution of sex, personality, and situational variables." *Developmental Psychology,* **6**:320–325 (March) [128].

Johnson, H. 1971. "A word to the Third World." *Encounter,* **37**:3–10 (October) [267, 269].

Johnson, W. B., and L. M. Terman. 1935. "Personality characteristics of happily married, unhappily married, and divorced couples." *Character and Personality,* **3**:290–311 [109–110].

Jones, H. B. 1956. "Estimation of effect of radiation upon human health and life span." *Proceedings of the Health Physics Society.* 114–126 (June) [149*n.*].

Josephson, E., et al. 1972. "Adolescent marijuana use: Report on a national survey." In

S. Einstein and S. Allen (eds.), *Proceedings of the First International Conference on Student Drug Surveys*. Farmingdale, N.Y.: Baywood [163].

Jourard, S. M. 1958. "A study of self-disclosure." *Scientific American*, **198**:77–82 (May) [98].

Kael, P. 1973. "The current cinema: Out of tragedy, suds." *The New Yorker*, **48**:77–80 (February 3) [21].

Kahn, D. G. 1973. Cited in E. D. Macklin (ed.), *Cohabitation Research Newsletter*. **3**:10 (October) [117].

Kahn, H. 1970. *The Emerging Japanese Superstate: Challenge and Response*. Englewood Cliffs, N.J.: Prentice-Hall, Inc. [190].

———. 1973. "How peace will change life in America." *U.S. News & World Report*, **74**:42–48 (March 12) [19*n*.].

Kallmann, F. J. 1938. *The Genetics of Schizophrenia*. Locust Valley, N.Y.: J. J. Augustin Publisher [51].

Kann, P. R. 1974a. "Land of despair: In Bangladesh, hopes fade, spirits break, future seems bleak." *The Wall Street Journal*, **91**:1, 20 (November 26) [226].

———. 1974b. "Land of despair: Vignettes of life in Bangladesh add up to national tragedy." *The Wall Street Journal*, **91**:1, 15 (November 27) [226].

Kantner, J. F., and M. Zelnik. 1973. "Contraception and pregnancy: Experience of young unmarried women in the United States." *Family Planning Perspectives*, **5**:21–35 (Winter) [228–230].

Kantorovich, L. 1959. Cited by A. Shub, *The New Russian Tragedy*. New York: W.W. Norton & Company, Inc. [258].

Kapadia, K. M. 1958. *Marriage and Family in India*. 2d ed. London: Oxford University Press [100].

Katz, J. 1974. "Coeducational living: Effects upon male-female relationships." In D. A. DeCoster and P. L. Mable (eds.), *Student Development and Education in College Residence Halls*. Washington, D.C.: American College Personnel Association [117].

Katzenbach, N. de B. 1967. *Task Force Report: Drunkenness*. Prepared for the President's Commission on Law Enforcement and Administration of Justice. Washington, D.C.: U.S. Government Printing Office [160].

Kelly, E. L. 1937. "A preliminary report on psychological factors in assortative mating." *Psychological Bulletin*, **34**:749 (November) [100].

———. 1940. "Psychological factors in assortative mating." *Psychological Bulletin*, **37**:473 (July) [100].

———. 1952. "The prediction of success in clinical psychology." In P. Hoch and J. Zubin (eds.), *Relation of Psychological Tests to Psychiatry*. New York: Grune & Stratton, Inc. [48].

———. 1955. "Consistency of the adult personality." *American Psychologist*, **10**:659–681 (November) [38, 100].

Kelsen, H. 1957. *What Is Justice?: Justice, Law, and Politics in the Mirror of Science*. Berkeley: University of California Press [7].

Kempe, C. H. 1972. *Helping the Battered Child and His Family*. Philadelphia: J. B. Lippincott Company [72].

Kennedy, R. J. R. 1942–1943. "Premarital residential propinquity and ethnic endogamy." *American Journal of Sociology*, **48**:580–584 (March) [100].

———. 1952. "Single or triple melting pot?: Intermarriage in New Haven, 1870–1950." *American Journal of Sociology*, **58**:56–59 (July) [101].

Kennedy, W. A. 1965. "School phobia: Rapid treatment of fifty cases." *Journal of Abnormal Psychology*, **70:**285–289 (August) [83].

Kentucky Mental Health Planning Commission. 1964. *Kentuckians' Attitudes Toward Mental Illness*. Louisville, Ky.: The Commission [69].

Kephart, W. M. 1955. "Occupational level and marital disruption." *American Sociological Review*, **20:**456–465 (August) [118].

Kety, S. S., et al. 1968. "The types and prevalence of mental illness in the biological and adoptive families of adopted schizophrenics." In D. Rosenthal and S. S. Kety (eds.), *The Transmission of Schizophrenia*. London: Pergamon Press [54, 55].

Khrushchev, N. 1954. Public speech cited by K. Sax, *Standing Room Only: The World's Exploding Population*. 2d ed., 1960, p. 190. Boston: Beacon Press [225].

Kiev, A. 1968. *Psychiatry in the Communist World*. New York: Science House [80].

Kilpatrick, F. P., and H. Cantril. 1960. "Self-anchoring scale: A measure of individual's unique reality worlds." *Journal of Individual Psychology*, **16:**158–173 (November) [20].

Kimball, N. 1972. *Nell Kimball: Her Life as an American Madam*. (Edited by S. Longstreet.) New York: The Macmillan Company [183].

Kinkade, K. 1973. *A Walden II Experiment: The First Five Years of Twin Oaks Community*. New York: William Morrow & Company, Inc. [116].

Kinsey, A. C. et al. 1948. *Sexual Behavior in the Human Male*. Philadelphia: W. B. Saunders Company [106, 107].

———. 1953. *Sexual Behavior in the Human Female*. Philadelphia: W. B. Saunders Company [106, 107].

Klare, G. R. 1950. "Understandability and indefinite answers to public opinion questions." *International Journal of Opinion and Attitude Research*, **4:**91–96 (Spring) [132].

Koestler, A. 1956. *Reflections on Hanging*. London: Victor Gollancz [276].

Koller, M. R. 1948. "Residential propinquity of white mates at marriage in relation to age and occupation of males, Columbus, Ohio, 1938 and 1946." *American Sociological Review*, **13:**613–616 (October) [100].

Kornhauser, A. 1965. *Mental Health of the Industrial Worker: A Detroit Study*. New York: John Wiley & Sons, Inc. [177].

Kracke, E. A., Jr. 1947. "Family vs. merit in Chinese civil service examinations under the empire." *Harvard Journal of Asiatic Studies*, **10:**103–123 [198].

Krafft-Ebing, R. F. 1959. *Aberrations of Sexual Life*. (A reissue of *Psychopathia Sexualis*). New York: Capricorn Books [106].

Krebs, R. L. 1969. "Teacher perceptions of children's moral behavior." *Psychology in the Schools*, **6:**394–395 (October) [127, 128].

Kuzel, P., and P. Krishnan. 1972. "Changing patterns of remarriage in Canada, 1961–1966." Paper presented at the annual meeting of the Canadian Sociology and Anthropology Association. Montreal: May–June [108].

Ladd, J. 1957. *The Structure of a Moral Code*. Cambridge, Mass.: Harvard University Press [96–97, 239].

Lader. L. 1966. *Abortion*. Indianapolis: Bobbs-Merrill Company, Inc. [240].

Laing, R. D. 1967. *The Politics of Experience*. New York: Pantheon Books [66, 68, 70].

Lalli, M., and S. H. Turner. 1968. "Suicide and homicide: A comparative analysis by race and occupational levels." *Journal of Criminal Law, Criminology, and Police Science*, **59:**191–200 (June) [282].

Lampson, R. S. 1935. "A quantitative study of the vasoconstriction induced by smoking." *Journal of the American Medical Association,* **104:**1963 (June) [151].

Lang, R. O. 1932. *The Rating of Happiness in Marriage.* Chicago: The University of Chicago, Department of Sociology M.A. thesis [112].

Langer, S. K. 1967. *Mind: An Essay on Human Feeling.* Baltimore: The Johns Hopkins Press [292*n.*].

Langner, T. S. 1963. "Some problems of interpretation and method." In T. S. Langner and S. T. Michael, *Life Stress and Mental Health. Vol. II of the Midtown Manhattan Study.* Glencoe, Ill.: The Free Press [63].

LaPiere, R. T. 1938. *Collective Behavior.* New York: McGraw-Hill Book Company [251].

L.A. Times. 1973. "Principal describes violence, terror at school in L.A." (March 14) [210].

Laubscher, B. J. F. 1937. *Sex, Custom, and Psychopathology.* London: Routledge & Kegan Paul, Ltd. [65].

Lawton, M. P. 1962. "Psychosocial aspects of cigarette smoking." *Journal of Health and Human Behavior,* **3:**163–170 (Fall) [151].

Lefcourt, H. M., and G. W. Ladwig. 1965. "The American Negro: A problem in expectancies." *Journal of Personality and Social Psychology,* **1:**377–380 (April) [287].

——— et al. 1968. "Internal versus external control of reinforcement and attention in a decision-making task." *Journal of Personality,* **36:**663–682 (December) [287].

Lehner, G. F. J. 1952. "Defining psychotherapy." *American Psychologist,* **7:**547 (September) [79].

Leifer, R. 1964. "The psychiatrist and tests of criminal responsibility." *American Psychologist,* **19:**825–830 (November) [275].

Leighton, D. C. 1955. "The distribution of psychiatric symptoms in a small town." Paper read at the annual meeting of the American Psychiatric Association [46].

Lemert, E. M. 1951. *Social Pathology.* New York: McGraw-Hill Book Company [66].

———. 1962. "Paranoia and the dynamics of exclusion." *Sociometry,* **25:**2–20 (March) [66].

———. 1967. *Human Deviance, Social Problems, and Social Control.* Englewood Cliffs, N.J.: Prentice-Hall, Inc. [66].

Lemkau, M. 1962. "Professional and public attitudes regarding the care of mental patients in Carroll County, Maryland." Mimeographed. Westminster, Md.: Western Maryland College [69].

———, and G. M. Crocetti. 1962. "An urban population's opinions and knowledge about mental illness." *American Journal of Psychiatry,* **118:**692–700 (February) [69].

Lenin. V. I. 1960. *Collected Works. Vol. 32 (December, 1920–August, 1921).* Moscow: Foreign Languages Publishing House [252].

Lenneberg, E. H. 1967. *Biological Foundations of Language.* New York: John Wiley & Sons, Inc. [75].

Lessing, E. E. 1969. "Racial differences in indices of ego functioning relevant to academic achievement." *Journal of Genetic Psychology,* **115:**153–167 (December) [287].

Levinger, G. 1966. "Sources of marital dissatisfaction among applicants for divorce." *American Journal of Orthopsychiatry,* **36:**803–807 (October) [120].

Levitt, E. E. 1957. "The results of psychotherapy with children: An evaluation." *Journal of Consulting Psychology,* **21:**189–196 (June) [37].

Levy, R. et al. 1947. "Effect of smoking cigarettes on the heart." *Journal of the American Medical Association,* **135:**417 (October) [151].

Lewis, O. 1959. *Five Families: Mexican Case Studies in the Culture of Poverty.* New York: Basic Books, Inc., Publishers [16].

———. 1966. *La Vida.* New York: Random House, Inc. [16].

Life. 1971. "A flood of responses to our crime questionnaire." **71:**3 (December 10) [140].

Lilienfeld, A. M. 1959. "Emotional and other selected characteristics of cigarette smokers and non-smokers as related to epidemiological studies of lung cancer and other disease." *U.S. National Cancer Institute Journal,* **22:**259–282 (February) [151].

Lindner, R. M. 1944. *Rebel without a Cause: The Hypnoanalysis of a Criminal Psychopath.* New York: Grune & Stratton, Inc. [80].

Lipset, S. M. 1970. "The politics of academia." Mimeographed. Berkeley: The Carnegie Commission on Higher Education [253].

———, and R. Bendix. 1960. *Social Mobility in Industrial Society.* Berkeley and Los Angeles: The University of California Press [199, 200].

———, and N. Rogoff. 1954. "Class and opportunity in Europe and the U.S.: Some myths and what the statistics show." *Commentary,* **36:**562–568 (December) [200].

———, and H. L. Zetterberg. 1955. *A Theory of Social Mobility.* Publication A-185 of the Bureau of Applied Social Research. New York: Columbia University [200].

Lipsey, R. G., and P. O. Steiner. 1966. *Economics.* New York: Harper & Row Publishers, Incorporated [269].

Locke, H. J. 1951. *Predicting Adjustment in Marriage: A Comparison of a Divorced and a Happily Married Group.* New York: Holt, Rinehart and Winston, Inc. [109].

London, P. 1974. "The psychotherapy boom: From the long couch to the push-button for the bored." *Psychology Today,* **8:**63–68 (June) [77].

Lorber, J. 1967. "Deviance as performance: The case of illness." *Social Problems,* **14:**302–310 (Winter) [66].

Lorenz, K. 1966a. *On Aggression.* New York: Harcourt, Brace, & World, Inc. [290].

———. 1966b. "On aggression." *Encounter,* **27:**29–40 (August) [289].

———. 1966c. "Ecce Homo!" *Encounter,* **27:**25–39 (September) [289].

Lorr, M., et al. 1962. "Evidence of ten psychotic syndromes." *Journal of Consulting Psychology,* **26:**185–189 (April) [68].

Lott, A. J., and B. E. Lott. 1965. "Group cohesiveness as interpersonal attraction: A review of relationships with antecedent and consequent variables." *Psychological Bulletin,* **64:**259–309 (October) [99].

Lovaas, O. I., et al. 1965. "Experimental studies in childhood schizophrenia: Analysis of self-destructive behavior." *Journal of Experimental Child Psychology,* **2:**67–84 (March) [83].

Lovibond, S. H. 1963. "The mechanism of conditioning treatment of enuresis." *Behaviour Research and Therapy,* **1:**17–21 (May) [83].

Ludwig, A. M. 1965. *The Importance of Lying.* Springfield, Ill.: Charles C Thomas, Publisher [124].

Lundberg, G. A. 1961. *Can Science Save Us?* New York: Longmans, Green [270].

———, and L. Dickson. 1952. "Inter-ethnic relations in a high-school population." *American Journal of Sociology,* **58:**1–10 (July) [99, 103].

Lundy, R. M. 1956. "Self-perceptions and descriptions of opposite sex sociometric choices." *Sociometry,* **19:**272–277 (December) [99].

Lyle, D. 1967. "The human race has, maybe, 35 years left." *Esquire,* **68:**116–118, passim (September) [223].

Maccoby, M. 1964. "Love and authority." *The Atlantic Monthly,* **213:**121–126 (March) [97].

Macdonald, D. 1962. "The string untuned: A review of the third edition of Webster's New International Dictionary." *The New Yorker,* **38:**130–160 (March 10) [206*n.*].

Machlup, F. 1973. "Perspectives on the benefits of postsecondary education." In L. C. Solmon, and P. J. Taubman (eds.), *Does College Matter?: Some Evidence on the Impacts of Higher Education.* New York: Academic Press, Inc. [203].

Mackie, M. 1969. *The Accuracy of Folk Knowledge Concerning Alberta Hutterites and North American Indians: An Available Data Stereotype Validation Technique.* Edmonton: The University of Alberta, Department of Sociology. Ph.D. dissertation [39].

———. 1973. "Arriving at 'truth' by definition: The case of stereotype inaccuracy." *Social Problems,* **20:**431–447 (Spring) [39].

MacKinnon, D. W. 1938. "Violation of prohibition." In H. A. Murray (ed.), *Explorations in Personality: A Clinical and Experimental Study of Fifty Men of College Age.* New York: Oxford University Press [125].

Macmillan, B. 1964. "Personality and tobacco addiction." Mimeographed. Edmonton: The University of Alberta, Department of Sociology [165*n*].

Magus, R. D., and L. S. Harris. 1971. "Carcinogenic potential of marijuana smoke condensate." *Federal Proceedings,* **30:**279 [157].

Maier, N. R. F. 1949. *Frustration: The Study of Behavior without a Goal.* New York: McGraw-Hill Book Company [288].

Mallick, S. K., and B. R. McCandless, 1966. "A study of catharsis of aggression." *Journal of Personality and Social Psychology,* **4:**591–596 (December) [300].

Malthus, T. R. 1803. *An Essay on the Principle of Population.* 2d ed. Edited by G. Himmelfarb, *On Population,* 1960. New York: Modern Library, Inc. [221].

Mamdani, M. 1973. *The Myth of Population Control.* New York: Monthly Review Press [227].

Mann, F. C. 1953. *A Study of Work Satisfaction as a Function of the Discrepancy between Inferred Aspirations and Achievement.* Ann Arbor, Mich.: University of Michigan. Ph.D. dissertation [187].

Manson, M. P. 1949. "A psychometric analysis of psychoneurotic and psychosomatic characteristics of alcoholics." *Journal of Clinical Psychology,* **5:**77–83 (January) [165*n.*].

Mao, Tse-tung. 1967. *Quotations from Chairman Mao Tse-tung.* New York: Bantam Books, Inc. [150, 273, 277].

Marcuse, H. 1955. *Eros and Civilization: A Philosophical Inquiry into Freud.* Boston: Beacon Press [180].

Marshall, H. 1947. "A study of the personality of alcoholic males." *American Psychologist,* **2:**289 (August) [165*n.*].

Marvin, D. M. 1918–1919. "Occupational propinquity as a factor in marriage selection." *Journal of the American Statistical Association,* **16:**131–150 [100].

Marx, K. 1844. *Economic and Philosophic Manuscripts of 1844.* Edited by the Institute of Marxism-Leninism of the Central Committee of the CPSU, 1956. Moscow: Foreign Languages Publishing House [180].

———. 1926. "On the Jewish Question." In *Selected Essays.* Translated by H. J. Stenning. (Re-issued, 1968). Freeport, N.Y.: Books for Libraries Press [178*n.*].

Masters, W. H., and V. E. Johnson. 1966. *Human Sexual Response.* Boston: Little, Brown and Company [106].

Matarazzo, J. D., and G. Saslow. 1960. "Psychological and related characteristics of smokers and non-smokers." *Psychological Bulletin,* **57:**493–513 (November) [151].

Maurer, D. 1940. *The Big Con.* Indianapolis: Bobbs-Merrill Company, Inc. [124].

———. 1964. *Whiz Mob.* New Haven: College and University Press [124].

Mayer, A. J. 1972. "Men working: Builders seek to end the ancient tradition of on-the-job larcenies." *The Wall Street Journal,* **86:**1, 12 (June 19) [143].

McArthur, C., et al. 1958. "The psychology of smoking." *Journal of Abnormal and Social Psychology,* **56:**267–276 (June) [151].

McClelland, D. C. 1953. *The Achievement Motive.* New York: Appleton-Century-Crofts, Inc. [268].

———. (ed.). 1955 *Studies in Motivation.* New York: Appleton-Century-Crofts, Inc. [268].

———. 1961. *The Achieving Society.* Princeton: D. Van Nostrand Company, Inc. [268].

McClintock, F. H. 1963. *Crimes of Violence.* London: Macmillan & Co., Ltd. [276].

McClosky, H., and J. H. Schaar. 1965. "Psychological dimensions of anomy." *American Sociological Review,* **30:**14–40 (February) [180].

McCord, H. 1951. "Discovering the 'confused' respondent: A possible projective method." *Public Opinion Quarterly,* **15:**363–366 (Summer) [132].

McCurdy, H. G. 1961. *The Personal World: An Introduction to the Study of Personality.* New York: Harcourt, Brace & World, Inc. [127].

McDonald, L. 1969. *Social Class and Delinquency.* London: Faber and Faber, Ltd. [142].

McDowell, E. 1973a. "Tending the spirit." *The Wall Street Journal,* **88:**1, 11 (March 26) [78].

———. 1973b. "An iconoclast looks at foreign aid." *The Wall Street Journal,* **89:**18 (June 21) [269].

McGlothlin, W. H., and L. J. West. 1968. "The marijuana problem: An overview." *American Journal of Psychiatry,* **125:**370–378 (September) [166].

McGuire, C. 1950. "Social stratification and mobility patterns." *American Sociological Review,* **15:**195–204 (April) [201].

McKissick, F. 1966. "A communication: Is integration necessary?" *The New Republic,* **155:**33–36 (December 3) [218].

McLuhan, M. 1964. *Understanding Media: The Extension of Man.* New York: McGraw-Hill Book Company [19n.].

McNemar, Q. 1964. "Lost: Our Intelligence? Why?" *American Psychologist,* **19:**870–882 (December) [203].

Mead, M. 1973. "On solving environmental problems." Public lecture, San Diego, Calif. (February 9) [27].

———. 1974. "World population: World responsibility." *Science,* **185:**1113 (September 27) [236].

Mechoulam, R. 1970. "Marihuana chemistry." *Science,* **168:**1159–1166 (June 5) [152].

Medvedev, Zh. 1971. *A Question of Madness.* New York: Knopf [70n.].

Meehl, P. E. 1962. "Schizotaxia, schizotypy, and schizophrenia." *American Psychologist,* **17:**827–838 (December) [73].

Meltzer, H. 1930. "The present status of experimental studies on the relationship of feeling to memory." *Psychological Review,* **37:**124–193 (January) [21].

Mencken, H. L., and G. J. Nathan. 1920. "Repetition generale." *Smart Set Magazine,* **63:**39–52 (December) [91].

Mercer, J. R. 1965. "Social system perspective and clinical perspective: Frames of reference for understanding career patterns of persons labelled as mentally retarded." *Social Problems,* **13:**18–34 (Summer) [66].

Merton, R. K. 1941. "Intermarriage and the social structure: Fact and theory." *Psychiatry,* **4:**361–374 (August) [103].

————. 1957. *Social Theory and Social Structure.* Glencoe, Ill.: The Free Press [141].

Meyer, J. K. 1964. "Attitudes toward mental illness in a Maryland community." *Public Health Reports,* **79:**769–772 [69].

Milgram, S. 1963. "Behavioral study of obedience." *Journal of Abnormal Psychology,* **67:**371–378 (September) [176].

Mill, J. S. 1859. *On Liberty.* Reprinted 1964. New York: E. P. Dutton & Co., Inc. [167–169].

Miller, N. E., et al. 1941. "The frustration-aggression hypothesis." *Psychological Review,* **48:**337–342 (July) [288].

Miller, O. L., Jr. 1973. "The visualization of genes in action." *Scientific American,* **228:**34–42 (March) [50].

Miller, R. L. 1973. *Economics Today.* San Francisco: Canfield Press [268].

Miller, S. M. 1960. "Comparative social mobility: A trend report and bibliography." *Current Sociology,* **9:**1–89 (No. 1) [200].

————, and E. G. Mishler. 1964. "Social class, mental illness, and American psychiatry: An expository review." In F. Riessman et al. (eds.), *Mental Health of the Poor.* Glencoe, Ill.: The Free Press [60].

Mills, C. W. 1956. *The Power Elite.* New York: Oxford University Press [201, 202].

Minogue, K. R. 1963. *The Liberal Mind.* London: Methuen & Co., Ltd. [16*n.*].

Mischel, W. 1969. "Continuity and change in personality." *American Psychologist,* **24:**1012–1018 (November) [38].

Mitchell, G. D. 1968. *A Dictionary of Sociology.* London: Routledge & Kegan Paul, Ltd. [4*n.*].

Monahan, T. P. 1970. "Are interracial marriages really less stable?" *Social Forces,* **48:**461–473 (June) [118].

Moore, B. 1954. *Terror and Progress in the USSR.* Cambridge, Mass.: Harvard University Press [142].

Moore, M. J. 1974. *Death of a Dogma? The American Catholic Clergy's Views of Contraception.* Chicago: Community and Family Study Center [225].

Morgenstern, O. 1963. *On the Accuracy of Economic Observations.* Princeton: Princeton University Press [262].

Morlan, G. K. 1949. "A note on the frustration-aggression theories of Dollard and his associates." *Psychological Review,* **56:**1–8 (January) [288].

Morris, A. 1955. *Homicide: An Approach to the Problem of Crime.* Boston: Boston University Press [276[.

Morrison, P. 1969. "The Condon report on unidentified flying objects, and other matters." *Scientific American,* **220:**139–140 (April) [130].

Morse, N. C., and R. S. Weiss. 1955. "The function and meaning of work and the job." *American Sociological Review,* **20:**191–198 (April) [176, 177, 178].

Mouledous, J. C., and E. C. Mouledous. 1964. "Criticisms of the concept of alienation." *American Journal of Sociology,* **70:**78–82 (July) [180].

Moulton, H. G. 1949. "The promise of the next 100 years." *Fortune,* **40:**84–94 (August) [261].

Mowrer, E. H. 1939. "A study of personal disorganization." *American Sociological Review,* **4:**475–487 (August) [57].

Mowrer, O. H. 1960. " 'Sin': The lesser of two evils." *American Psychologist,* **15:**301–304 (May) [80].

————. 1964. *The New Group Therapy.* Princeton: D. Van Nostrand Company, Inc. [37].

———— (ed.). 1967. *Morality and Mental Health.* Chicago: Rand McNally & Company [37].

Murray, H. A., et al. 1938. *Explorations in Personality.* New York: Oxford University Press [104*n.*].

Myrdal. G. 1969. *Asian Drama.* New York: Pantheon Books [268].

———. 1970. *The Challenge of World Poverty: A World Anti-Poverty Program in Outline, A Summary and a Continuation of Asian Drama.* New York: Pantheon Books [268].

Myrdal, J., and G. Kessle. 1971. *China: The Revolution Continued.* New York: Pantheon Books [255].

Nahas, G. G. 1973, *Marihuana: Deceptive Weed,* New York: Raven Press [156,157].

National Review. 1973. "The week." **25**:1280 (November 23) [273].

Neter, J. 1970. "Measurement errors in reports of consumer expenditures." *Journal of Marketing Research,* **7**:11–25 (February) [132].

Nettler, G. 1955. "The code of the salesman." Mimeographed. Edmonton, Canada: The University of Alberta, Department of Sociology [183].

———. 1957. "A measure of alienation." *American Sociological Review,* **22**:670–677 (December) [92, 180].

———. 1959. "Antisocial sentiment and criminality." *American Sociological Review,* **24**:202–218 (April) [132].

———. 1964. "Occupational interests of career police officials." Mimeographed. Edmonton, Canada: The University of Alberta, Department of Sociology [183].

———. 1965. "A further comment on 'anomy,'" *American Sociological Review,* **30**:762–763 (October) [204].

———. 1970. *Explanations.* New York: McGraw-Hill Book Company [39, 47*n.*].

———. 1972. "Knowing and doing." *The American Sociologist,* **7**:3–7 (February) [77*n.,* 94, 262].

———. 1973. "Wanting and knowing." *American Behavioral Scientist,* **17**:5–25 (September–October) [14*n.,* 49, 77*n.,* 94, 233, 245].

———. 1974a. *Explaining Crime.* New York: McGraw-Hill Book Company [39, 66, 71, 127, 128, 145, 208].

———. 1974b. "On the difference between believing and knowing." Seminar Paper No. 6. Edmonton, Canada: The University of Alberta, Department of Sociology [68*n.*].

———. 1974c. "On perceiving and conceiving." Seminar Paper No. 11. Edmonton, Canada: The University of Alberta, Department of Sociology [68*n.*].

———. 1974d. "The politics of reality: Two hypotheses." Seminar Paper No. 12. Edmonton, Canada: The University of Alberta, Department of Sociology [68*n.*].

———. 1974e. "On construing the relations between perceiving and conceiving." Seminar Paper No. 13. Edmonton, Canada: The University of Alberta, Department of Sociology [68*n.*].

———. 1974f. "More on the reality of 'reality.'" Seminar Paper No. 16. Edmonton, Canada: The University of Alberta, Department of Sociology [68*n.*].

———. 1974g. "On perceiving and the meaning of objectivity." Seminar Paper No. 18. Edmonton, Canada: The University of Alberta. Department of Sociology [68*n.*].

———. 1974h. "On 'the politics of reality' II." Seminar Paper No. 24. Edmonton, Canada: The University of Alberta, Department of Sociology [68*n.*].

———. 1974i. "On 'the politics of reality' III." Seminar Paper No. 25. Edmonton, Canada: The University of Alberta, Department of Sociology [68*n.*].

Newcomb, T. M. 1956. "The prediction of interpersonal attraction." *American Psychologist,* **11**:575–587 (November) [99].

Newcomer, M. 1955. *The Big Business Executive: The Factors That Made Him, 1900–1950.* New York: Columbia University Press [201–203].

Newsweek. 1973a. "Out of this world." **81**:64 (January 29) [24].

———. 1973b. "Voodoo U." **81**:91 (April 9) [24].

———. 1973c. "The light-fingered shopper." **82**:23 (November 26)[130].

———. 1974a. "Crime doesn't pay." **83**:59 (June 17) [138].

———. 1974b. "The population bomb ticks on." **84**:42 (September 2) [221, 226].

———. 1974c. "China's green revolution." **84**:65 (October 14) [256].

———. 1974d. "Nobel prizes: Surprise, surprise." **84**:49 (October 21) [298*n*.].

Nichols, R. C. 1966. "Schools and the disadvantaged." *Science,* **154**:1312–1314 (December 9) [211–212].

Nieburg, H. L. 1970. "Agonistics: Rituals of conflict." *The Annals of the American Academy of Political and Social Science.* **391**:56–73 (September) [290].

Nisbet, R. 1974. "The pursuit of equality." *The Public Interest,* **35**:103–120 (Spring) [7*n*.].

Nizer, L. 1944. *My Life in Court.* New York: Doubleday & Company, Inc. [183].

Noonan, J. T., Jr. 1965. *Contraception: A History of Its Treatment by the Catholic Theologians and Canonists.* Cambridge, Mass.: Harvard University Press [224].

Nott, K. 1964. "Exchange of letters with Professor H. J. Eysenck." *Encounter,* **23**:91 (November) [66].

Odiorne, G. 1963. "The trouble with sensitivity training." *Training and Development Journal,* **3**:9–20 (October) [86].

Ohmann, O. 1942. "The psychology of attraction." In H. M. Jordan (ed.), *You and Marriage.* New York: John Wiley & Sons, Inc. [104].

O'Neil, W. 1970. "Properly literate." *Harvard Educational Review,* **40**:260–263 (May) [215].

Oregon v. Mitchell. 1971. Attorney General 400 *U.S.* 112. Washington, D.C.: U.S. Government Printing Office [216].

Orlansky, H. 1949. "Infant care and personality." *Psychological Bulletin,* **46**:1–48 (January) [74].

Ortega y Gasset, J. 1946. *Concord and Liberty.* New York: W. W. Norton & Company, Inc. [4*n*.].

———. 1958. *Man and Crisis.* New York: W. W. Norton [98].

Orwell, G. 1933. *Down and Out in Paris and London.* New York: Harper & Brothers [183*n*.].

———. 1946. *Animal Farm.* New York: Harcourt, Brace & World, Inc. [195].

———. 1954. *A Collection of Essays.* Garden City, N.Y.: Doubleday & Company, Inc. [98].

Osgood, C. E., et al. 1957. *The Measurement of Meaning.* Urbana: University of Illinois Press [273].

O'Toole J., et al. 1972. *Work in America: Report of a Special Task Force.* Washington, D.C.: U.S. Government Printing Office [175, 189].

Overall, J. E., and J. H. Patrick. 1972. "Unitary alcoholism factor and its personality correlates." *Journal of Abnormal Psychology,* **79**:303–309 (June) [165*n*.].

Ozawa, R. 1955. "Conception control in Japan." In *Report of Proceedings of the Fifth International Conference on Planned Parenthood.* London: International Planned Parenthood Federation [236].

Pantaleone, M. 1966. *The Mafia and Politics.* London: Chatto & Windus [48].

Paranjape, W. 1970. *Some Aspects of Probation: An Exploration of Labelling Theory in Six Urban Junior High Schools.* Edmonton, Canada: The University of Alberta, Department of Sociology. M.A. thesis [210].

Parducci, A. 1968. "The relativism of absolute judgments." *Scientific American,* **219**:84–90 (December) [30].

Parry, H. J., and H. Crossley. 1950. "Validity of responses to survey questions." *Public Opinion Quarterly,* **14**:61–80 (Winter) [132–133].

Patterson, G. R., et al. 1965. "A behaviour modification technique for the hyperactive child." *Behaviour Research and Therapy,* **2**:217–226 (January) [83].

Paul VI, Pope 1968. *Humanae Vitae.* New York: Paulist-Newman Press [224].

Peach, C. 1974. "Homogamy, propinquity, and segregation: A re-evaluation." *American Sociological Review,* **39**:636–641 (October) [100].

Peaker, G. F. 1971 *The Plowden Children Four Years Later.* London: National Foundation for Educational Research [211].

Pearl, R. 1938. "Tobacco smoking and longevity." *Science,* **87**:216–217 (March 4) [149*n*., 155].

Pearlstine, N. 1974. "Tarnished image: Global trust in firms in Japan is damaged by a major collapse." *The Wall Street Journal,* **90**:1, 11 (June 19) [125].

Pelcovits, N. A. 1946. "World government now." *Harper's Magazine,* **193**:396–403 (November) [304–305].

Petersen, R. C., et al. 1972. *Marihuana and Health: Second Annual Report to Congress from the Secretary of Health, Education and Welfare.* Washington, D.C.: U.S. Government Printing Office [162, 163].

Petersen, W. 1969. *Population.* 2d ed. New York: Macmillan Company [225, 227, 234, 256*n*.].

Peterson, C. R., and L. R. Beach. 1967. "Man as an intuitive statistician." *Psychological Bulletin,* **68**:29–46 (July) [249*n*.].

Peterson, D. R., et al. 1959. "Personality and background factors in juvenile delinquency as inferred from questionnaire responses." *Journal of Consulting Psychology,* **23**:395–399 (October) [210].

Petrie, A. 1967. *Individuality in Pain and Suffering.* Chicago: The University of Chicago Press [104].

Petrov, A. I. 1968. "Distribution of the national income in the U.S.S.R." In J. Marchal and B. Ducros (eds.), *The Distribution of National Income: Proceedings of a Conference Held by the International Economic Association.* London: Macmillan Company [193, 257].

Pettigrew, T. J., et al. 1973. "Busing: A review of 'the evidence.'" *The Public Interest,* **30**:88–118 (Winter) [219].

Phares, E. 1968. "Differential utilization of information as a function of internal-external control." *Journal of Personality,* **36**:648–662 (December) [287].

Phillips, D. L. 1967. "Social participation and happiness." *American Journal of Sociology,* **72**:479–488 (March) [27].

Phillips, D. P. 1974. "The influence of suggestion on suicide: Substantive and theoretical implications of the Werther effect." *American Sociological Review,* **39**:340–354 (June) [290].

Pincus, G. 1965. *The Control of Fertility.* New York: Academic Press, Inc. [230].

Pipes, R. 1964. "Marx and 'alienation.'" *Encounter,* **23**:94 (August) [180].

Plath, S. 1971. *The Bell Jar.* New York: Harper & Row Publishers, Incorporated [28].

Platt, J. J., et al. 1970. "Importance of considering sex differences in relationship between locus of control and other personality variables." *Proceedings of the Annual Convention of the American Psychological Association,* **5**:463–464 (Part I) [287].

Plog, S. C., and R. B. Edgerton (ed.). 1969. *Changing Perspectives in Mental Illness.* New York: Holt, Rinehart and Winston, Inc. [66].

Podhoretz, N. 1967. *Making It.* New York: Random House, Inc. [192].

Pohlman, E. 1967. "Unwanted conceptions: Research on desirable consequences." *Eugenics Quarterly,* **14:**143–154 (June) [245].

Popenoe, P., and D. Wicks. 1937. "Marital happiness in two generations." *Mental Hygiene,* **21:**218–223 [112].

Popham, R. E., and W. Schmidt. 1958. *Statistics of Alcohol Use and Alcohol in Canada, 1871–1956.* Toronto: University of Toronto Press [159].

Popper, K. R. 1957. *The Poverty of Historicism.* London: Routledge & Kegan Paul Ltd. [270].

———. 1962. *Conjectures and Refutations.* New York: Basic Books Inc., Publishers [262].

Population Council. 1968. *Roman Catholic Fertility and Family Planning: A Comparative Review of the Research Literature.* New York: The Council [240].

Postan, M. M. 1968. "A plague of economists?" *Encounter,* **30:**42–47 [262].

Provine, W. B. 1973. "Genetics and the biology of race crossing." *Science,* **182:**790–796 (November 23) [49].

Queen, S. A. 1940. "The ecological studies of mental disorder." *American Sociological Review,* **5:**201–209 (April) [57].

Raddock, P. 1973. "Unhappy professionals." *The Wall Street Journal,* **88:**4 (February 2) [187].

Rader, D. 1973. An exchange with Arnold Beichman and William Buckley as cited in *Encounter,* **40:**50–52 (March) [277–278].

Rainwater, L. 1960. *And the Poor Get Children: Sex, Contraception, and Family Planning in the Working Class.* Chicago: Quadrangle Books, Inc. [230–231].

Rand, A. 1963. "The ethics of emergencies." *The Objectivist Newsletter,* **2:**5–6 (February) [98].

Rao, S. 1959. "Awakening rural India." *Journal of Family Welfare,* **6:**24–31 (No. 1) [236].

Ratliff, F. 1965. *Mach Bands: Quantitative Studies in Neural Networks in the Retina.* San Francisco: Holden-Day, Inc., Publishers [68*n.*].

Rauschning, H. 1939. *Hitler Speaks.* London: Thornton, Butterworth [278].

Rawls, J. 1971. *A Theory of Justice.* Cambridge, Mass.: Harvard University Press [7, 7*n.,* 8].

Regan, D. T., et al. 1974. "Liking and the attribution process." *Journal of Experimental Social Psychology,* **10:**385–397 (July) [39, 274, 275].

Reich, W. 1973. *The Function of the Orgasm: Sex-Economic Problems of Biological Energy.* New York: Farrar, Straus & Giroux, Inc. [79].

Reik, T. 1944. *A Psychologist Looks at Love.* New York: Farrar & Rinehart, Inc. [98].

Retherford, R. D. 1974. "Tobacco smoking and sex ratios in the United States." *Social Biology,* **21:**28–38 (Spring) [149*n.*].

Rettig, S., et al. 1958. "Status overestimation, objective status, and job satisfaction among professions." *American Sociological Review,* **23:**75–81 (February) [187–188].

Reuters News Agency. 1972. Release of August 18 [139].

———. 1974. "Economic growth seen overpopulation answer." August 24 [226].

Richards, J. M., Jr., et al. 1965. "An investigation of the criterion problem for one group of medical specialists." *Journal of Applied Psychology,* **49:**79–90 (April) [195].

Richardson, H. M. 1939. "Studies of mental resemblance between husbands and wives and between friends." *Psychological Bulletin,* **36:**104–120 (February) [100].

Richardson, L. F. 1960a. *Arms and Insecurity*. Chicago: Quadrangle Books, Inc. [294–295, 302].

———. 1960b. *Statistics of Deadly Quarrels*. Chicago: Quadrangle Books, Inc. [294–295, 298, 301].

Richman, B. M. 1969. *Industrial Society in Communist China*. New York: Random House, Inc. [255].

Riis, R. W. 1941a. "The repair man will gyp you if you don't watch out." *Reader's Digest*, **39**:1–6 (July) [131].

———. 1941b. "The radio repair man will gyp you if you don't watch out." *Reader's Digest*, **39**:6–13 (August) [131].

———. 1941c. "The watch repair man will gyp you if you don't watch out." *Reader's Digest*, **39**:10–12 (September) [131].

Riley, J. W., Jr., and C. F. Marden. 1947. "The social pattern of alcoholic drinking." *Quarterly Journal for the Study of Alcohol*, **8**:265–273 (September) [160].

Risdon, R. 1954. "A study of interracial marriages based on data for Los Angeles County." *Sociology and Social Research*, **39**:92–95 (November–December) [101].

Rivera, R. J., and J. F. Short, Jr. 1967. "Occupational goals: A comparative analysis." In M. W. Klein (ed.), *Juvenile Gangs in Context: Theory, Research, and Action*. Englewood Cliffs, N.J.: Prentice-Hall, Inc. [210].

Robinson, H. A. 1953. "Job satisfaction researches of 1952." *Personnel and Guidance Journal*, **32**:22–25 (September) [176].

———. 1957. "Job satisfaction researches of 1956." *Personnel and Guidance Journal*, **36**:34–37 (September) [176].

———. 1964. "Job satisfaction researches of 1963." *Personnel and Guidance Journal*, **43**:360–366 (December) [176].

———. 1966. "Job satisfaction researches of 1964–1965." *Personnel and Guidance Journal*, **45**:371–379 (December) [176].

Rodman, S. 1971. "What drives Latin Americans left?" *National Review*, **23**:1348–1350, 1369 (December 3) [267].

Roeder, K. D. 1967. *Nerve Cells and Insect Behavior*. Cambridge, Mass.: Harvard University Press [274].

Roe et al. v. Wade. 1973. 410 *U.S.* 113 [240].

Roff, M. 1961. "Childhood social interactions and young adult bad conduct." *Journal of Abnormal and Social Psychology*, **63**:333–337 (September) [38].

Rogoff, N. 1953. *Recent Trends in Occupational Mobility*. Glencoe, Ill.: The Free Press [200, 201].

Rosenhan, D. L. 1973. "On being sane in insane places." *Science*, **179**:250–258 (January 19) [67–69].

Rosenthal, D. 1971. *Genetics of Psychopathology*. New York: McGraw-Hill Book Company [51, 54].

——— et al. 1968. "Schizophrenics' offspring reared in adoptive homes." In D. Rosenthal and S. S. Kety (eds.), *The Transmission of Schizophrenia*. London: Pergamon Press [54].

Roth, G. M. 1951. *Tobacco and the Cardiovascular System: The Effects of Smoking and of Nicotine on Normal Persons*. Springfield, Ill.: Charles C Thomas Publisher [151].

——— et al. 1960. "Summary of recent reports on the biologic effects of cigarette smoking on the cardiovascular system." *Circulation*, **22**:161–163 (July) [151].

Rotter, J. B. 1966. "Generalized expectancies for internal versus external control of reinforcement." *Psychological Monographs*, **80**:1–28 (Whole No. 609) [286].

Rousseau, J. J. 1754. "Discourse on the origin of inequality." Reprinted 1910 in C. W.

Eliot (ed.), *The Harvard Classics, v.34: French and English Philosophers.* New York: P. F. Collier & Son Corporation [8].

Royal College of Physicians. 1962. *Smoking and Health.* London: Pitman Medical Publishing Company [156].

Rubin, J. 1970. Speech at Kent State University as reported in the *Akron Beacon Journal,* "Kill Parents, Burn Suburbs—Rubin." (April 11) [279].

Rubin, V., and L. Comitas. 1975. *Ganja in Jamaica: A Medical Anthropological Study of Chronic Marihuana Use.* The Hague: Mouton [165].

Rummel, R. J. 1969. "Dimensions of foreign and domestic conflict behavior: A review of empirical findings." In D. G. Pruitt and R. C. Snyder (eds.), *Theory and Research on the Causes of War.* Englewood Cliffs, N.J.: Prentice-Hall, Inc. [293].

Runciman, W. G. 1966. *Relative Deprivation and Social Justice: A Study of Attitudes to Social Inequality in Twentieth-Century England.* London: Routledge & Kegan Paul, Ltd. [188].

Ruppin, A. 1913. *The Jews of Today.* London: G. Bell & Sons, Ltd. [100–101],

Rush, C. H., Jr. 1953. "A factorial study of sales criteria." *Personnel Psychology,* 6:9–24 [195].

Rushing, W. A. 1972. *Class, Culture, and Alienation: A Study of Farmers and Farm Workers.* Lexington, Mass.: D. C. Heath and Company [182].

Rutstein, D. D. 1957. "An open letter to Dr. Clarence Cook Little." *The Atlantic Monthly,* 200:41–43 (October) [155].

Ryle, G. 1949. *Concept of Mind.* London: Hutchinson's University Library [292*n.*].

Sabin, A. B. 1973. Interview on Mike Wallace's program, "Sixty Minutes." CBS TV (May 6) [183].

Sales, S. M., et al. 1974. "Relationship between 'strength of the nervous system' and the need for stimulation." *Journal of Personality and Social Psychology,* 29:16–22 (January) [104].

Sampson, H., et al. 1963. *Schizophrenic Women: Studies in Marital Crisis.* New York: Atherton Press, Inc. [70].

Sanders, M. K. 1970. "The right not to be born." *Harper's Magazine,* 240:92–99 (April) [245].

Sarbin, T. R., and H. C. Anderson. 1942. "A preliminary study of the relation of measured interest patterns and occupational dissatisfaction." *Educational and Psychological Measurement,* 2:23–26 [185].

Sargant, W. 1964. "Psychiatric treatment: Here and there." *The Atlantic Monthly,* 214:88–95 (July) [80–81].

Sartre, J. P. 1973. Interview cited in *Encounter,* 40:96 (April) [278].

Scalapino, R. A. 1963. "Communist China: The first fourteen years." In W. Petersen (ed.), *The Realities of World Communism.* Englewood Cliffs, N.J.: Prentice-Hall, Inc. [255, 256*n.*].

Scheff, T. J. 1966. *Being Mentally Ill.* Chicago: Aldine Publishing Company [66].

Scheinfeld, A. 1943. *Women and Men.* New York: Harcourt, Brace & World, Inc. [128].

Schellenberg, J. A. 1960. "Homogamy in personal values and the 'field of eligibles.'" *Social Forces,* 39:157–162 (December) [100].

Schiffman, H., and R. Wynne. 1963. *Cause and Affect.* Princeton: Educational Testing Service, RM-63-7 (July) [275].

Schimek, J. G. 1968. "Cognitive style and defenses: A longitudinal study of intellectualization and field independence." *Journal of Abnormal Psychology,* 72:575–580 (December) [38].

Schlesinger, B., and A. Macrae. 1970. "Remarriages in Canada: Statistical trends." *Journal of Marriage and the Family,* **32**:300–303 (May) [108].

Schmidt, H. O., and C. P. Fonda. 1956. "The reliability of psychiatric diagnosis: A new look." *Journal of Abnormal and Social Psychology,* **52**:262–267 (March) [68].

Schmitt, R. C. 1965. "Demographic correlates of interracial marriage in Hawaii." *Demography,* **2**:463–473 [103].

Schoeck, H. 1966. *Envy: A Theory of Social Behavior.* New York: Harcourt, Brace & World, Inc. [250, 290].

Schoeffler, S. 1955. *The Failures of Economics.* Cambridge, Mass.: Harvard University Press [262].

Schooley, M. 1936. "Personality resemblances among married couples." *Journal of Abnormal and Social Psychology,* **31**:340–347 (October–December) [100].

Schroeder, C. W. 1942. "Mental disorders in cities." *American Journal of Sociology,* **47**:40–47 (July) [57].

Schumpeter, J. A. 1951. *Imperialism and Social Classes.* New York: Augustus M. Kelley Publishers [199].

Schur, E. M. 1965. *Crimes without Victims: Deviant Behavior and Public Policy.* Englewood Cliffs, N.J.: Prentice-Hall, Inc. [136].

Schwartz, C. 1957. "Perspectives on deviance: Wives' definitions of their husbands' mental illness." *Psychiatry,* **20**:275–291 (August) [70].

Schwarz, S. M. 1948. The living standard of the Soviet worker: 1928—1938— 1948." *Modern Review,* **2**:272–286 (June) [257].

Scott, J. P. 1966. Review of K. Lorenz, "On Aggression." *Science,* **154**:636–637 (November 4) [291].

Sears, R. R., et al. (eds.). 1957. *Patterns of Child Rearing.* Evanston, Ill.: Row, Peterson & Company [127].

Seeman, M. 1959. "On the meaning of alienation." *American Sociological Review,* **24**:783–791 (December) [180].

Segovia-Riquelme, N., et al. 1971. "Appetite for alcohol." In Y. Israel and J. Mardones (eds.), *Biological Basis of Alcoholism.* New York: John Wiley & Sons, Inc. [165n.].

Selling, L. S. 1940. "The role of alcohol in the commission of sex offenses." *Medical Record,* **151**:289–291 (April 17) [160].

Seltzer, C. C. 1963. "Morphologic constitution and smoking." *Journal of the American Medical Association,* **183**:639–645 (February 23) [165n.].

Selzer, M. L., and S. Weiss. 1965. "Alcoholism and fatal traffic accidents: A study in futility." *The Municipal Court Review,* **5**:15–20 [160].

Shafer, R. P., et al. 1972. *Marihuana: A Signal of Misunderstanding.* First Report of the National Commission on Marihuana and Drug Abuse. Washington, D.C.: U.S. Government Printing Office [147, 156].

Sheppard, H. L., and N. Q. Herrick. 1972. *Where Have All the Robots Gone?: Worker Dissatisfaction in the '70s.* New York: The Free Press [189].

Shils, E. 1972. *The Intellectuals and the Powers and Other Essays.* Chicago: University of Chicago Press [19n.].

Shoham, S. 1970. *The Mark of Cain: The Stigma Theory of Crime and Social Deviation.* Jerusalem: Israel Universities Press [39].

Shub, A. 1969. *The New Russian Tragedy.* New York: W. W. Norton & Company, Inc. [176, 258].

Shupe, L. M. 1954. "Alcohol and crime: A study of the urine alcohol concentration found in 882 persons arrested during or immediately after the commission of a felony." *Journal of Criminal Law and Criminology,* **44:**661–664 (December) [160].

Shuraydi, M. A. 1973. *The Mystification of the "Self" in Two Socio-Psychological Theories: Symbolic Interactionism and Humanistic Psychology.* Edmonton, Canada: The University of Alberta, Department of Sociology. Ph.D. dissertation [179].

Siassi, I., et al. 1974. "Loneliness and dissatisfaction in a blue collar population." *Archives of General Psychiatry,* **30:**261–265 (February) [181–182, 184].

Skinner, B. F. 1955–1956. "Freedom and the control of men." *The American Scholar,* **25:**47–65 (Winter) [84].

———. 1956. "Some issues concerning the control of human behavior." *Science,* **124:**1057–1066 (November) [84].

———. 1972. *Beyond Freedom and Dignity.* New York: Alfred A. Knopf, Inc. [84].

Sklar, J., and B. Berkov. 1974. "Teenage family formation in postwar America." Paper presented at the annual meeting of the Population Association of America. New York (April 18–20) [107].

Slater, E. 1953. *Psychotic and Neurotic Illnesses in Twins.* London: HMSO [51].

———. 1968. "A review of earlier evidence on genetic factors in schizophrenia." In D. Rosenthal, and S. S. Kety (eds.), *The Transmission of Schizophrenia.* London: Pergamon Press [53].

———, and V. Cowie. 1971. *The Genetics of Mental Disorders.* London: Oxford University Press [51–53].

Smigel, E. O. 1956. "Public attitudes toward stealing." *American Sociological Review,* **21:**320–327 (June) [124, 127].

———, and H. L. Ross (eds.). 1970. *Crimes against Bureacuracy.* New York: Van Nostrand Reinhold [124].

Smith, D. E. 1968. "Acute and chronic toxicity of marihuana." *Journal of Psychedelic Drugs,* **2:**37–47 [166].

Soares, L. M., and A. T. Soares. 1969. "Social learning and social violence." Proceedings, 77th annual convention of the American Psychological Association [290].

Sommer, G. R., et al. 1955. "An empirical investigation of therapeutic 'listening.'" *Journal of Clinical Psychology,* **11:**132–136 (April) [76].

Sommer, R. 1969. *Personal Space: The Behavioral Basis of Design.* Englewood Cliffs, N.J.: Prentice-Hall, Inc. [99].

Sontag, L. W. 1963. "Somatopsychics of personality and body function." *Vita Humana,* **6:**1–10 (Nos. 1–2) [38].

Sorensen, R. C. 1973. *Adolescent Sexuality in Contemporary America; Personal Values and Sexual Behavior Ages Thirteen to Nineteen.* New York: World Book Company [106, 115*n.*].

Sorokin, P. A. 1937–1941. *Social and Cultural Dynamics.* 4 vols. New York: American Book Company [245, 294–295].

———. 1944. "The conditions and prospects for a world without war." *American Journal of Sociology,* **49:**441–449 (March) [301].

———. 1959. *Social and Cultural Mobility.* Glencoe, Ill.: The Free Press [199].

Soueif, M. 1967. "Hashish consumption in Egypt with special reference to psychosocial aspects." *Bulletin of Narcotics,* **19:**1–12 [157, 165].

Sowell, T. 1974. "Black excellence: The case of Dunbar High School." *The Public Interest,* No. 35:3–21 (Spring) [211, 218].

Spain, D. M., and D. J. Nathan. 1961. "Smoking habits and coronary atherosclerotic heart disease." *American Medical Association Journal,* **177:**683–688 (September) [151].

Sports Illustrated. 1968. "Vanishing sport." **29:**9 (August 30) [300].

Srole, L. 1956. "Social integration and certain corollaries: An exploratory study." *American Sociological Review*, **21**:709–716 (December) [180].

———et al. 1962. *Mental Health in the Metropolis: The Midtown Manhattan Study.* New York: McGraw-Hill Book Company [25, 46, 61–62].

Stafford, J. 1973. "Touch and go." *The New York Review of Books*, **20**:30–33 (April 5) [86].

Statistics Canada. 1972. *Illegitimate Births, Canada and Provinces, 1936–1970. Table B.7.* Ottawa: Information Canada [107].

———. 1974. *Murder Statistics.* Ottawa: Information Canada [282].

Stern, P. J. 1972. *In Praise of Madness: Realness Therapy—The Self Reclaimed.* New York: W. W. Norton & Company [66, 79].

Stinchcombe, A. L. 1964. *Rebellion in a High School.* Chicago: Quadrangle Books, Inc. [142].

Stockwell, E. G. 1966. "Patterns of digit preference and avoidance in the age statistics of some recent national censuses." *Eugenics Quarterly*, **13**:205–208 (September) [132].

———., and J. W. Wicks. 1974. "Age heaping in recent national censuses." *Social Biology*, **21**:163–167 (Summer) [132].

Stolnitz, G. J. 1955. "A century of international mortality trends." *Population Studies*, **9**:24–55 (July) [227].

———. 1956. "A century of international mortality trends." *Population Studies*, **10**:17–42 (July) [227].

Stott, M. B. 1950. "What is occupational success?" *Occupational Psychology*, **24**:105–112 [197].

Stouffer, S. A., et al. 1949. *The American Soldier.* Princeton: Princeton University Press [30, 188].

Stycos, J. M. 1974. "Demographic chic at the UN." *Family Planning Perspectives*, **6**:160–164 (Summer) [236].

Sudnow, D. 1966. *Passing On.* Englewood Cliffs, N.J.: Prentice-Hall, Inc. [244].

Sumner, W. G. 1911. *War and Other Essays.* New Haven: Yale University Press [289].

Super, D. E. 1939. "Occupational level and job satisfaction." *Journal of Applied Psychology*, **23**:547–564 [177, 188].

Sutherland, E. H., and D. R. Cressey. 1970 *Criminology.* 8th ed. Philadelphia: J. B. Lippincott Company [144].

Szasz, T. S. 1957. "Commitment of the mentally ill: 'Treatment' or social restraint?" *Journal of Nervous and Mental Disease*, **125**:293 (April–June) [70n.].

———. 1958. "Politics and mental health: Some remarks apropos of the case of Mr. Ezra Pound." *American Journal of Psychiatry*, **115**:508 (December) [70n.].

———. 1961. *The Myth of Mental Illness.* New York: Paul B. Hoeber, Inc. [67, 76].

———. 1963. *Law, Liberty, and Psychiatry: An Inquiry into the Social Use of Mental Health Practices.* New York: Macmillan Company [70n.].

———. 1973. *The Second Sin.* Garden City, N.Y.: Doubleday & Company, Inc. [23].

———. 1974. "Our despotic laws destroy the right to self-control." *Psychology Today*, **8**:19–29, 127 (December) [169n.].

Szczepanski, J. 1970. *Polish Society.* New York: Random House, Inc. [176].

Talmon, Y. 1956. "The family in collective settlements." In *Transactions of the Third World Congress of Sociology, Vol.IV.* London: International Sociological Association [103].

———. 1972. *Family and Community in the Kibbutz.* Cambridge, Mass.: Harvard University Press [114n.].

Tannenbaum, F. 1938. *Crime and the Community.* Boston: Ginn and Company [66].

Tappan, P. W. 1947. "Who is the criminal?" *American Sociological Review*, **12**:96–102 (February) [135].

Tate, B. G., and G. S. Baroff. 1966. "Aversive control of self-injurious behavior in a psychotic boy." *Behaviour Research and Therapy*, **4**:281–287 [83].

Taylor, C. W., et al. 1964. "An investigation of the criterion problem for a medical school faculty." *Journal of Applied Psychology*, **48**:294–301 (October) [195].

Taylor, I., et al. 1973. *The New Criminology: For a Social Theory of Deviance*. London: Routledge & Kegan Paul, Ltd. [139].

Taylor, M. C. 1952. "Neo-Malthusianism in Puerto Rico." *Review of Social Economy*, **10**:42–54 (March) [224].

Taylor, N. 1966. "The pleasant assassin: The story of marihuana." In D. Solomon (ed.), *The Marihuana Papers*. New York: Signet Books [152].

Teele, J. E., et al. 1966. "Teacher ratings, sociometric status, and choice-reciprocity of anti-social and normal boys." *Group Psychotherapy*, **19**:183–197 (September–December) [210].

Tennant, F. S., and C. J. Groesbeck. 1972. "Psychiatric effects of hashish." *Archives of General Psychiatry*, **27**:133–136 (July) [166].

Terman, L. M. 1925. *Genetic Studies of Genius. Vol.I: Mental and Physical Traits of a Thousand Gifted Children*. Stanford: Stanford University Press [204].

———. 1938. *Psychological Factors in Marital Happiness*. New York: McGraw-Hill Book Company [106, 109, 112].

———, and M. H. Oden. 1947. *Genetic Studies of Genius. Vol.IV: The Gifted Child Grows Up: Twenty-five Years' Follow-Up of a Superior Group*. Stanford: Stanford University Press [204].

———. 1959. *Genetic Studies of Genius. Vol. V: The Gifted Group at Mid-Life: Thirty-Five Years' Follow-Up of the Superior Child*. Stanford: Stanford University Press [204].

———, and P. Wallin. 1949. "The validity of marriage prediction and marital adjustment tests." *American Sociological Review*, **14**:497–504 (August) [111].

Terrien, F. W. 1954. "Who thinks what about education?" *Public Opinion Quarterly*, **18**:157–168 (Summer) [208].

Thant, U. 1967. Cited in "Thirty governments review human rights appeal." *International Planned Parenthood News*, **168**:i–iv (February, 1968) [231].

Tharp, R. G. 1963. "Psychological patterning in marriage." *Psychological Bulletin*, **60**:97–117 (March) [110].

Thimmesch, N. 1973. "The abortion culture." *Newsweek*, **82**:7 (July 9) [244].

Thomas, A. E. 1972. "Community power and student rights." *Harvard Educational Review*, **42**:173–216 (May) [137].

Thomas, A., et al. 1970. "The origin of personality." *Scientific American*, **223**:102–109 (August) [38].

Thomas, C. B. 1960. "Characteristics of smokers compared with nonsmokers in a population of healthy young adults, including observations on family history, blood pressure, heart rate, body weight, cholesterol and certain psychologic traits." *Annals of Internal Medicine*, **53**:697–718 (October) [151, 165*n*.].

———. 1968. "On cigarette smoking, coronary heart disease, and the genetic hypothesis." *The Johns Hopkins Medical Journal*, **122**:69–76 (February) [151].

———, and G. H. Cohen. 1960. "Comparison of smokers and nonsmokers. I: A preliminary report on the ability to taste phenylthiourea (P.T.C.)." *Bulletin of the Hopkins Hospital*, **106**:205 [165*n*.].

————et al. 1964. "Precursors of hypertension and coronary disease among healthy medical students: Discriminant function analysis. I: Using smoking habits as the criterion." *Bulletin of Hopkins Hospital,* **115:**174 [165*n.*].

Thomas, H. 1971. *Cuba: Or the Pursuit of Freedom.* London: Eyre and Spottiswoode [259].

Thomas, J. L. 1951. "The factor of religion in the selection of marriage mates." *American Sociological Review,* **16:**487–491 (August) [102–103].

————. 1956. *The American Catholic Family.* Englewood Cliffs, N.J.: Prentice-Hall, Inc. [103].

Thomas, W. I. 1937. *Primitive Behavior.* New York: McGraw-Hill [273].

Thorndike, R. L. 1963. "The prediction of vocational success." *Vocational Guidance Quarterly,* **11:**179–187 (Spring) [197].

Tietze, C. 1973a. "Two years' experience with a liberal abortion law: Its impact on fertility trends in New York City." *Family Planning Perspectives,* **5:**36–41 (Winter) [240].

————. 1973b. "The international medical experience." In H. J. Osofsky & J. D. Osofsky (eds.), *Abortion Experience in the U.S.* New York: Harper & Row, Publishers, Incorporated [243].

————, and D. Dawson. 1973. *Induced Abortion: A Factbook.* New York: The Population Council [240].

Tietze, C., et al. 1973. "Mortality associated with legal abortion in New York City, 1970–1972: A preliminary report." *Journal of the American Medical Association,* **225:**507–509 (July 30) [242].

Time. 1970. "Protest season on campus." **91:**26 (May 11) [305*n.*].

Tinbergen, N. 1953. *Social Behavior in Animals.* London: Methuen & Co., Ltd. [289].

Tolor, A., et al. 1970. "Psychological distance, future time perspective, and internal-external expectancy." *Journal of Projective Techniques and Personality Assessment,* **34:**283–294 (August) [287].

Torrey, E. F. 1973. *The Mind Game.* New York: Emerson Hall [76].

Traina, P. J. 1974. "Catholic clergy on abortion: Preliminary findings of a New York state survey." *Family Planning Perspectives,* **6:**151–156 (Summer) [225].

Trost, J. 1973. Cited in E. D. Macklin (ed.), *Cohabitation Research Newsletter,* **2:**13–14 (April) [117].

Tuchman, B. W. 1972. *Notes from China.* New York: Collier Books [149].

Tyler, C. W., Jr. 1972. "Abortion: Need, impact, and problems." Paper presented at the annual meeting of the American Public Health Association. Atlantic City, N.J. (November 16) [243].

Underwood, W. J. 1965. "Evaluation of laboratory method training." *Training Directors' Journal,* **19:**34–40 (No. 5) [86].

Uniform Crime Reports for the United States, 1973. 1974. Washington, D.C.: U.S. Department of Justice [282].

United Nations. 1954. *Foetal, Infant, and Early Childhood Mortality. 1: The Statistics.* New York: Department of Social Affairs, Population Division [240].

————. 1970. Statistical Yearbook. New York: Department of Economic and Social Affairs [256*n.*].

United Press International. 1973a. "Contract bridge banished from socialist society." (January 27) [137].

————. 1973b. " 'Criminal' harsh, Reagan says." (May 2) [138].

————. 1973c. "Teachers face suits if pupils fail to learn." (July 2) [215].

U.S. Census of Population, 1960. *Marital Status.* Washington, D.C.: U.S. Government Printing Office [101].

———. 1970. *Marital Status.* Washington, D.C.: U.S. Government Printing Office [101].

U.S. Department of Health, Education and Welfare. 1971. *Stimulants: Some Questions and Answers.* Publication No. HSM-71-9026. Washington, D.C.: U.S. Government Printing Office [155].

U.S. News & World Report. 1970. "How Cuba has fared under its Red ruler." **69:**35–36 (September 21) [259].

———. 1971. "Stronger voice now for Russia in Cuba." **70:**26 (January 18) [259].

———. 1973. "Is the American family in danger?" **74:**71–76 (April 16) [116].

———. 1974a. "Why a rich region still wants U.S. aid." **76:**20–21 (June 17) [268].

———. 1974b. "How business grapples with problem of the drinking worker." **77:**75–76 (July 15) [159].

———. 1974c. "Castro's 'New Cuba.'" **77:**44–46 (October 28) [259].

———. 1974d. "As famine spreads—What's to be done?" **77:**87 (November 18) [226].

U.S. Surgeon General. 1964. *Smoking and Health.* Publication No. 1103 of the U.S. Department of Health, Education and Welfare. Washington, D.C.: U.S. Government Printing Office [156].

van den Haag, E. 1957. "Of happiness and of despair we have no measure." In B. Rosenberg, and D. M. White (eds.), *Mass Culture.* Glencoe, Ill.: The Free Press [16].

———. 1960. "Social science testimony in the desegregation cases: A reply to Professor Kenneth Clark." *Villanova Law Review,* **6:**69–79 (Fall) [216].

Vandivier, K. 1972. "The aircraft brake scandal." *Harper's Magazine,* **244:**45–52 (April) [142].

van Stolk, M. 1972. *The Battered Child in Canada.* Toronto: McClelland and Stewart [137].

Vernon. W., and R. Ulrich. 1966. "Classical conditioning of pain-elicited aggression." *Science,* **152:**668–669 (April 29) [290].

Vicker, R. 1974. "The food crisis." *The Wall Street Journal,* **91:**1, 16 (October 23) [226].

Vidich, A. J., and J. Bensman. 1958. *Small Town in Mass Society: Class, Power, and Religion in a Rural Community.* Princeton: Princeton University Press [63].

von Mises, L. 1944. *Bureaucracy.* New Haven: Yale University Press [265].

von Neumann, J., and O. Morgenstern. 1947. *Theory of Games and Economic Behavior.* Princeton: Princeton University Press [250].

Wahler, R. G., et al. 1965. "Mothers as behavior therapists for their own children." *Behaviour Research and Therapy,* **3:**113–114 (September) [83].

Wainwright, L. 1968. "The Kennedy's." *Life,* Special edition, p. 73 [260].

Waldfogel, S. 1948. "The frequency and affective character of childhood memories." *Psychological Monographs,* **62** (No. 4) [21].

Walker, R. L. 1955. *China Under Communism: The First Five Years.* New Haven: Yale University Press. [256*n.*].

Wall Street Journal, The. 1972. "And somebody stole our carpet and chairs." **86:**12 (June 19) [130–131].

Wallerstein, J. A., and C. J. Wyle. 1947. "Our law-abiding law-breakers." *Federal Probation,* **25:**107–112 (April) [131].

Wallis, D. I. 1965. "Division of labour in ant colonies." In P. E. Ellis (ed.), *Social Organization of Animal Communities.* New York: Academic Press, Inc. [289].

Walsh, R. P. 1961. "A generation of skeptics." *American Psychologist,* **16:**712–713 (November) [88].

Warriner, C. K. 1958. "The nature and functions of official morality." *American Journal of Sociology*, **64**:165–168 (September) [124, 171].

Wason, P. C., and P. N. Johnson-Laird. 1972. *The Psychology of Reasoning: Structure and Content*. Cambridge, Mass.: Harvard University Press [249*n*.].

Watts, W., and L. A. Free. 1973. *State of the Nation*. New York: University Books, Inc. [19].

Weaver, C. N., and C. L. Swanson. 1974. "Validity of reported date of birth, salary, and seniority." *Public Opinion Quarterly*, **38**:69–80 (Spring) [132].

Wechsler, J. A., et al. 1972. *In a Darkness*. New York: W. W. Norton & Company, Inc. [28, 40, 42].

Weil, S. 1946. "Words and war." *Politics*, **3**:69–73 (March) [260].

Weingold, H. P., et al. 1968. "Depression as a symptom of alcoholism: Search for a phenomenon." *Journal of Abnormal Psychology*, **73**:195–197 (June) [165*n*.].

Weinstock, N. 1970. Introduction to A. Leon, *The Jewish Question: A Marxist Interpretation*. New York: Pathfinder Press [101].

Weiss, D. J., and R. V. Davis. 1960. "An objective validation of factual interview data." *Journal of Applied Psychology*, **44**:381–385 (December) [132].

Weiss, J. H. 1963. "Effect of professional training and amount and accuracy of information on behavioral prediction." *Journal of Consulting Psychology*, **27**:257–262 (June) [48].

Weissman, S. 1971. "Foreword" to R. L. Meek (ed.), *Marx and Engels on the Population Bomb*. Berkeley: Ramparts Press [225].

Weitz, J. 1952. "A neglected concept in the study of job satisfaction." *Personnel Psychology*, **5**:201–205 (Autumn) [185].

Weldon, T. D. 1953. *The Vocabulary of Politics*. Baltimore: Penguin Books, Inc. [5].

Werry, J. S. 1972. "Organic factors in childhood psychopathology." In H. C. Quay, and J. S. Werry (eds.), *Psychopathological Disorders of Childhood*. New York: John Wiley & Sons, Inc. [35*n*.].

Wessman, A. E., and D. F. Ricks. 1959. "Temporal alternation of affective states in male and female subjects." Paper read at the annual meeting of the American Psychological Association. Cincinnati [16].

———. 1966. *Mood and Personality*. New York: Holt, Rinehart and Winston, Inc. [16].

Westoff, C. F., and N. B. Ryder. 1967. "United States: Methods of fertility control, 1955, 1960 and 1965." In W. T. Liu (ed.), *Family and Fertility*. South Bend, Ind.: University of Notre Dame Press [225].

———. 1969. "Recent trends in attitudes toward fertility control and in the practice of contraception in the United States." In S. J. Behrman et al. (eds.), *Fertility and Family Panning: A World View*. Ann Arbor: The University of Michigan Press [225].

———et al. 1961. *Family Growth in Metropolitan America*. Princeton: Princeton University Press [227].

———. 1963. *The Third Child: A Study in the Prediction of Fertility*. Princeton: Princeton University Press [227].

Wheeler, L., et al. 1966. "The contagion of aggression." *Journal of Experimental Social Psychology*, **2**:1–10 (January) [290].

Wheelis, A. 1958. *The Quest for Identity*. New York: W. W. Norton & Company, Inc. [88–89].

Whiting, J. M. V. 1944. "The frustration complex in Kwoma society." *Man*, **44**:140–144 (November–December) [288].

Whitworth, W. 1970. "Some questions about the war." *The New Yorker*, **46**:30–56 (July 4) [307].

Wickler, W. 1972. *The Sexual Code: The Social Behavior of Animals and Men.* Garden City, N.Y.: Doubleday & Company, Inc. [27].

Wildavsky, A. 1971. "Does planning work?" *The Public Interest*, **24**:95–104 (Summer) [261–262].

Wilensky, H. L. 1964a. "Mass society and mass culture: Interdependence or dependence?" *American Sociological Review*, **29**:173–197 (April) [199–200].

———. 1964b. "Varieties of work experience." In H. Borow (ed.), *Man in a World at Work.* Boston: Houghton Mifflin Company [178, 181].

Willams, E. P. 1972. "Behavioral ecology: The limp arm of the health sciences." Mimeographed. Houston: The University of Houston [57].

Williams, R. J. 1956. *Biochemical Individuality: The Basis for the Genetotrophic Concept.* New York: John Wiley & Sons, Inc. [28].

Williams, R. L. 1974. "Scientific racism and IQ: The silent mugging of the black community." *Psychology Today*, **7**:32–41, 101 (May) [136].

Williams, W. 1925. *Mainsprings of Men.* New York: Charles Scribner's Sons [183].

Willing, M. K. 1971. *Beyond Conception: Our Children's Children.* Boston: Gambit [136].

Willis, F. N., Jr.,et al. 1966. "Persistence of conditioned fighting in a hen pigeon." *Psychonomic Science*, **5**:323–324 [290].

Willoughby, R. R. 1936. "Neuroticism in marriage: IV. Homogamy. V. Summary and Conclusions." *Journal of Social Psychology*, **7**:19–48 (February) [100].

Wilson, J. Q. 1973. "On Pettigrew and Armor: An afterword." *The Public Interest*, **30**:132–134 (Winter) [219].

Wilson, W. 1967. "Correlates of avowed happiness." *Psychological Bulletin*, **67**:294–306 (April) [23, 27, 28].

Winch, R. F. 1958. *Mate-Selection: A Study of Complementary Needs.* New York: Harper & Row Publishers, Incorporated [104–105, 107].

———. 1963. *The Modern Family.* 2d ed. New York: Holt, Rinehart and Winston, Inc. [102].

Winston, E. 1934. "The alleged lack of mental diseases among primitive groups." *American Anthropologist*, **36**:234–238 (April–June) [65].

Winthrop, H. 1946. "Semantic factors in the measurement of personality integration." *Journal of Social Psychology*, **24**:149–175 (November) [241].

Withery, S. B. 1954. "Reliability of recall of income." *Public Opinion Quarterly*, **18**:197–204 (Summer) [132].

Witkin, H. A. 1973. *The Role of Cognitive Style in Academic Performance and in Teacher-Student Relations.* Princeton: Educational Testing Service [38].

———et al. 1962. *Psychological Differentiation.* New York: John Wiley & Sons, Inc. [128].

Wixen, B. N. 1973. *Children of the Rich.* New York: Crown Publishers, Inc. [22, 63].

Wolf, L. 1974. "Surrogate wives: A closer look at the new professionals." *Playgirl*, **1**:34–55, 136 (May) [79].

Wolfgang, M. E. 1958. *Patterns in Criminal Homicide.* Philadelphia: University of Pennsylvania Press [160, 276, 282].

———, and F. Ferracuti. 1967. *The Subculture of Violence: Towards an Integrated Theory in Criminology.* London: Tavistock [276, 281, 282, 284].

Wolpe, J. 1958. *Psychotherapy by Reciprocal Inhibition.* Stanford: Stanford University Press [82].

Woodley, R. 1974. "How to win the soap box derby." *Harper's Magazine,* **249:**62–69 (August) [142].

Woolf, V. 1921. "The new dress." In *A Haunted House and Other Short Stories.* New York: Harcourt, Brace and Company [29*n.*].

World Health Organization. 1951. *Expert Committee on Mental Health: Alcoholism Subcommittee. First Report.* Geneva: WHO Technical Report Series No. 42 [159].

———. 1952. *Expert Committee on Mental Health: Alcoholism Subcommittee. Second Report.* Geneva: WHO Technical Report Series No. 48 [159].

Wortis, J. 1950. *Soviet Psychiatry.* Baltimore: Williams & Wilkins Company [80].

Wright, Q. 1942. *A Study of War.* Two Volumes. Chicago: The University of Chicago Press [294–297].

Wrigley, C. F., et al. 1957. "Use of the square-root method to identify factors in the job performance of aircraft mechanics." *Psychological Monographs,* **71 (Whole No. 430)** [195].

Wyatt, R. J., et al. 1973. "Reduced monoamine oxidase activity in platelets: A possible genetic marker for vulnerability to schizophrenia." *Science,* **179:**916–918 (March 2) [50, 56].

Yarrow, M., et al. 1955. "The psychological meaning of mental illness in the family." *The Journal of Social Issues,* **11:**12–24 (No. 4) [70].

Zarnowitz, V. 1967. *An Appraisal of Short-Term Economic Forecasts.* New York: Columbia University Press [262].

Zax, M., et al. 1968. "Follow-up study of children identified early as emotionally disturbed." *Journal of Consulting and Clinical Psychology,* **32:**369–374 (August) [38].

Zeitlin, M. 1967. *Revolutionary Politics and the Cuban Working Class.* New York: Harper & Row Publishers, Incorporated [149].

Zelnik, M. 1964. "Errors in the 1960 census enumeration of native whites." *Journal of the American Statistical Association,* **59:**437–459 (June) [132].

———, and J. F. Kantner. 1972. "Sexuality, contraception, and pregnancy among young unwed females in the United States." In C. F. Westoff and R. Parke, Jr. (eds.), *Demographic and Social Aspects of Population Growth.* Volume I: Commission on Population Growth and the American Future. Washington, D.C.: U.S. Government Printing Office [228–229].

Zerbin-Rüden, E. 1967. "Hirnatrophische Prozesse." In P. E. Becker (ed.), *Humangenetik: Ein Kurzes Handbuch.* Volume Two. Stuttgart: G. Thieme [51].

Zigler, E., and L. Phillips. 1961. "Psychiatric diagnosis: A critique." *Journal of Abnormal and Social Psychology,* **63:**607–618 (November) [68].

Subject Index